THE FRONTAL LOBES
AND VOLUNTARY
ACTION

RICHARD PASSINGHAM

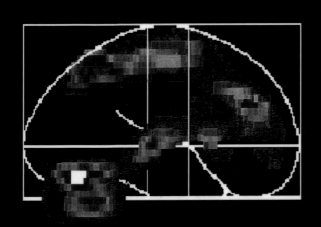

THE FRONTAL LOBES
AND VOLUNTARY ACTION

OXFORD PSYCHOLOGY SERIES

Editors

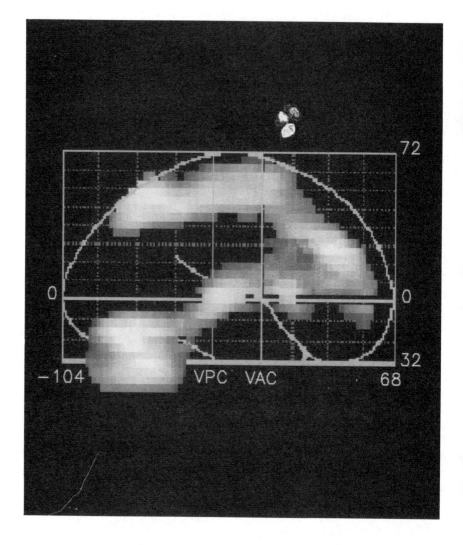

The motor system at work. Areas in which there is a significant increase in regional cerebral blood flow when subjects learn new motor sequences compared with a rest condition. The brain is shown as if it was transparent, showing the activity in both hemispheres and in subcortical as well as cortical structures. The figure shows activity in motor cortex, the premotor areas and prefrontal cortex, in the somatosensory cortex and parietal association areas which project to the frontal lobes, in the cerebellar cortex and cerebellar nuclei, in the basal ganglia, and in the ventral thalamic nuclei through which the cerebellum and basal ganglia influence the motor cortex. Figure from data from Jenkins *et al.* (1992b). Study from the MRC Cyclotron Unit, Hammersmith Hospital, London.

The Frontal Lobes and Voluntary Action

Richard Passingham

Department of Experimental Psychology
University of Oxford

OXFORD PSYCHOLOGY SERIES
NO. 21

OXFORD   NEW YORK   TOKYO
OXFORD UNIVERSITY PRESS

Oxford University Press, Great Clarendon Street, Oxford OX2 6DP

Oxford New York
Athens Auckland Bangkok Bogota Bombay Buenos Aires
Calcutta Cape Town Dar es Salaam Delhi Florence Hong Kong
Istanbul Karachi Kuala Lumpur Madras Madrid Melbourne
Mexico City Nairobi Paris Singapore Taipei Tokyo Toronto Warsaw
and associated companies in
Berlin Ibadan

Oxford is a trade mark of Oxford University Press

Published in the United States
by Oxford University Press Inc.

© Richard Passingham, 1993

First published 1993
First published in paperback 1995
Reprinted 1997

A catalogue record for this book is available from the British Library

Library of Congress Cataloging in Publication Data
Passingham, R. E., 1943–
The frontal lobes and voluntary action / R.E. Passingham.
(Oxford psychology series; no. 21)
Includes bibliographical references and index.
1. Frontal lobes. I. Title II. Series.
QP382.F7P38 1993   612.8'25 –dc20   93–10270
ISBN 0 19 852364 5 (Pbk)

Printed in Great Britain by
Bookcraft (Bath) Ltd
Midsomer Norton, North Somerset

To Clare, Tom, and Susannah

It has been remarked that life's aim is an act,
not a thought.

Sherrington

Preface

Functional anatomy

This book is an exercise in functional anatomy. The aim is to describe the functional organization of the frontal lobes. In the jargon of today the book deals with the 'systems level'. Like a diagram of a car engine, it provides an idea of how the system works without specifying the mechanism by which any of the components operate.

It is for this reason that the book says relatively little about the activity of single cells. The point of recording from single cells is not usually to reveal the function of an area, but rather to find out how the mechanism works. To determine the function of an area it is better to take measures of the whole population of cells rather than of the activity of single cells. At the moment we have four techniques.

1. The first is to record gross potentials. In animals we can record potentials across the depth of the cortex; but in human subjects the electrodes are usually placed on the skull, which means that it is difficult to localize the source of the potentials.

2. Another technique is to measure the uptake in a brain area of radioactively labelled 2-deoxyglucose. The method depends on the fact that when an area is active it increases its uptake of glucose.

3. One can use single photon emission computed tomography (SPECT) or positron emission tomography (PET) to measure the flow of blood in the human brain. In PET scanning either ^{15}O is injected or the subject breathes ^{15}O while the brain is scanned. The degree of activity of a local population of neurones is inferred from the increase in blood flow to that area. When there is an increase in synaptic activity, the metabolic demands go up, and there is an increase in the local flow of blood (Raichle 1987). Since the blood is labelled, this increase in flow can be measured by detectors placed outside the head. The detectors record the gamma rays resulting from the annihilation reaction that is produced when positrons meet electrons.

4. The final method is the oldest: this is to study the effects of brain lesions. In animals one can remove populations of cells and study the effects on behaviour. In humans there are patients who have undergone neurosurgery to relieve epilepsy or remove tumours, and patients with infarcts as the result of strokes.

This method is often misrepresented as crude and out of date. There are two misunderstandings. First, it is not an alternative to single unit recording; it has a different purpose. Second, the method is crude only if it is supposed that the impairments will be evident to casual inspection. In fact, sophisticated tests are required. In the right hands, the method has greatly advanced our understanding of the specialization of the different visual areas (Cowey 1982), the components of the memory system (Mishkin 1982), or the functions of the tissue in the principal sulcus of prefrontal cortex (Goldman-Rakic 1987).

For the moment this method remains a useful technique for the study of functional anatomy. It is the only technique that reveals the *essential* function of an area; that is, the function that no other areas can perform.

Style of the book

I confess that this book was written for myself. If one wants to know if one's views are coherent, there is no better way than to set them down on paper. It is easier to pick holes in an argument when it is read.

The book is a monograph, written to make sense of the data collected by myself and my colleagues over the past years. This explains two features. The first is that I have shown more generosity in citing my own papers than would be afforded by an unbiased authority. The second is that the text betrays a certain meanness of spirit: I have made little mention of other reviews, and have cited other authors mainly when they have something to add to the argument of this book.

I hope that the account given in these pages is at least coherent. Since it is now on paper, it should be possible for others to prove it coherent but wrong.

Stylistic devices

There is a danger that the text may become dull. There are not many ways of saying that the removal of a cortical area had a particular effect. I have allowed myself to use abbreviations, as in 'LPC lesion' for lateral premotor cortex lesion. I have, however, avoided the ugly 'LPC animal'.

I have frequently used the term 'monkey' without giving the genus and species. This is not because I am an ignorant psychologist, unaware that there are many species of monkeys. It is because in almost all cases I am referring to research carried out on macaques, either the rhesus monkey (*Macaca mulatta*) or the cynomolgus monkey (*Macaca fascicularis*).

The term 'response' has been used throughout in the lazy way in which psychologists use this word. It has been used even when the subject is not strictly responding to anything in the world, for example when human subjects are generating movements of their own accord. The term may not always be strictly accurate, but it is convenient. I have also often used the term 'movement' when a philosopher would be right to comment that I should have used the word 'action'.

However, I have not been lazy in using the term 'frontal lobes'. This is often used loosely by neuropsychologists when they mean 'prefrontal cortex'. The term 'frontal lobe' is always used here to refer to the whole frontal lobe.

The reader will detect that I have frequently numbered the sentences or paragraphs. This is on the principle that if you are unable to say something clearly, and you wish to conceal this fact from the reader, you should number your sentences; someone may be fooled.

Oxford   R.E.P.
June 1993

Acknowledgements

There is a temptation to believe that the views one holds arrived *de novo* in one's brain. The truth is one has often pinched something here and something there, and that it is now impossible to reconstruct the true history of the ideas. I am pleased to be able to record here the names of the people with whom I have worked and with whom the ideas have been formed.

I am grateful first to my research students and research associates. The experiments on monkeys that are cited in the text were designed in collaboration with John Aggleton, Ulrike Halsband, Tony Canavan, Chantal Stern, Pierre Burbaud, David Thaler, Julie Tucker, and Yuchu Chen; and they did the work.

I have been very lucky to have as my research assistants Margaret Jones, Vicky Lightfoot, and Phil Nixon. Research assistants deserve more credit than they usually get. Phil Nixon has been helping me run experiments for the past seven years.

The experiments were carried out in the Department of Experimental Psychology in Oxford. In this Department I have had support and encouragement throughout from Larry Weiskrantz and Alan Cowey, and have greatly benefited from discussions with Edmund Rolls and David Gaffan.

The experiments on PET scanning were designed in collaboration with Richard Frackowiak, David Brooks, Marie-Pierre Deiber, Jim Colebatch, Di Playford, and Harri Jenkins. These experiments were carried out at the MRC Cyclotron Unit at the Hammersmith Hospital in London.

Several people have been good enough to read drafts and to offer me critical comments. Chris Frith, John Stein, Madeline Eacott, and Matthew Rushworth have read all the chapters, and Giacomo Rizzolatti, Steve Wise, and Ray Kesner have read several of them. Some of the comments have forced me to make major revisions to the ideas proposed in earlier drafts.

I am grateful to Phil Nixon for preparing most of the histograms, to Joyce Bennett for preparing many of the diagrams, and to Jeremy Broad and Anita Butterworth for photographing them.

I have written one book before, and I did not expect to write another. It has given my family a hard time; so I dedicate it to them.

Figure acknowledgements

Fig. 2.3 Kuypers, H.G.J.M. (1981) in Handbook of Physiology, vol.2 (ed. Brooks, V.) p. 630, American Physiological Society; Fig. 2.5 Passingham, R.E., Perry, H. and Wilkinson, F. (1983) Brain, 106, 686, by permission of Oxford University Press; Figs 2.6, 2.8, 2.10 Passingham, R.E., Perry, H., and Wilkinson, F. (1983) Brain, 106, 683, by permission of Oxford University Press; Fig. 2.7 Lawrence, D.G. and Hopkins, D.A. (1976) Brain, 99, 236, by permission of Oxford University Press; Fig. 2.9 Passingham, R.E., Perry, H. and Wilkinson, F. (1983) Brain, 106, 690, by permission of Oxford University Press; Fig. 2.11 Passingham, R.E., Perrry, H. and Wilkinson, F. (1983) Brain, 106, 691, by permission of Oxford University Press; Fig. 2.12 Colebatch, J.G., Deiber, M-P., Passingham, R.E., Friston, K.J. and Frackowiack, R.S.J. (1991) J. Neurophysiol, 65, 1395.

Fig. 3.3 based on Matelli, M., Luppino, G. and Rizzolatti, G. (1991) J. Comp. Neurol., 311, 133, copyright 1991, reprinted by permission by Wiley-Liss; Fig. 3.4 based on Barbas, H. and Pandya, D.N. (1987) J.Comp.Neurol., 256, 213, copyright 1987, reprinted by permission of Wiley-Liss; Fig. 3.5 Dum, R.P. and Strick, P.L. (1991) J.Neurosci., 11, 674; Fig. 3.6 Deiber, M-P., Passingham, R.E., Colebatch, J.G., Friston, K.J., Nixon, P.D. and Frackowiak, R.S.J. (1991) 84, 395; Fig. 3.7 Passingham, R.E. (1985c) Beh.Brain Res., 99, 176; Fig. 3.11 data from Petrides (1987) in The Frontal Lobes Revisited (ed. Perecman, E), p. 105, IRBN Press; Fig. 3.12 based on Petrides, M. (1985) Neuropsychol., 23, 611; Fig. 3.13 Halsband, U. and Freund, H-J. (1990) Brain, 113, 219, by permission of Oxford University Press; Fig. 3.14 Kertesz, A. and Ferro, J.M. (1984) Brain, 107, 925, by permission of Oxford University Press; Fig. 3.17 Mitz, A.R., Godschalk, M. and Wise, S.P. (1991) J. Neurosci., 11, 1861; Fig. 3.18 Mitz, A.R., Godschalk, M. and Wise, S.P. (1991) J.Neurosci., 11, 1863.

Fig. 4.4 Luppino, G., Matelli, M., Camarada, R.M., Gallese, V. and Rizzolatti, G. (1991) J.Comp.Neurol., 311, 466, copyright 1991, reprinted by permission of Wiley-Liss; Fig. 4.13 Deiber, M-P., Passingham, R.E., Colebatch, J.G., Friston, K.J., Nixon, P.D. and Frackowiak, R.S.J. (1991) 84, 396; Fig. 4.14 Playford, E.D., Jenkins, I.H., Passingham, R.E., Nutt, J., Frackowiak, R.S.J. and Brooks, D.J. (1992) Annals Neurol., 32, 158; Fig. 4.15 Playford, E.D., Jenkins, I.H., Passingham, R.E., Nutt, J., Frackowiak, R.S.J. and Brooks, D.J. (1992) Annals Neurol., 32, 158; Fig. 4.16 Romo, R. and Schultz, W. (1987) Exper. Brain Res., 67, 661; Fig. 4.17 Okano, K. and Tanji, J. (1987) Exper. Brain Res., 66, 160; Fig. 4.18 Shima, K., Aya, K., Mushiake.

H., Inase, M., Aizawa, H. and Tanji, J. (1991) J.Neurophysiol., 65, 196; 4.20
Passingham, R.E., Thaler, D.E. and Chen, Y. (1989) in Neural Programming
(ed. Ito, M.) P. 16, Karger; 4.22 Mushiake, H., Inase, M. and Tanji, J. (1991)
J.Neurophysiol., 66, 710.

Figs 5.3, 5.4 Bruce, C.J. (1988) in Neurobiology of Neocortex (ed. Rakic,
P. and Singer, W.), p.299, Wiley; Fig. 5.11 Goldberg, M.E. and Bushnell,
M.C. (1981) J.Neurophysiol., 46, 777.

Fig. 6.3 Barbas, H. and Pandya, D.N. (1989) J.Comp.Neurol., 286, 356,
copyright 1989, reprinted by permission of Wiley-Liss; Figs 6.6, 6.7
Friedman, H.R. and Goldman-Rakic, P.S. (1988) J. Neurosci., 8, 4995; Fig.
6.9 Goldman-Rakic, P.S. (1987) in Handbook of Physiology, vol.5 (ed. Plum,
F., and Mountcastle, V.) p. 383, American Physiological Society; Fig. 6.11
Mishkin, M. and Manning, F.J. (1978) Brain Res., 143, 318; Fig. 6.13
Funahashi, S., Bruce, C.J. and Goldman-Rakic, P.S. (1989) J. Neurophysiol.,
61, 334; 6.15 Funahashi, S., Bruce, C.J. and Goldman-Rakic, P.S. (1989) J.
Neurophysiol., 61, 343; Fig. 6.18 Passingham, R.E. (1986) Beh. Neurosci.,
100, 696, copyright 1986 by the American Psychological Association,
reprinted by permission of the publisher; Fig. 6.20 Passingham (1985d)
Neuropsychol., 23, 456.

Fig. 8.9 Percheron, G., Yelnik, J. François, C. (1984) J.Comp.Neurol., 227,
22, copyright 1984, reprinted by permission of Wiley-Liss; Fig. 8.12
Hikosaka, O., Sakamoto, M. and Usui, S. (1989) J. Neurophysiol., 61, 784;
Fig. 8.13 Alexander, G.E. and Crutcher, M.D. (1990) J. Neurophysiol., 64,
135; Fig. 8.15 Glickstein, M., May, J.G. and Mercier, R.E. (1985)
J.Comp.Neurol., 235, 347, copyright 1985, reprinted by permission of Wiley-
Liss; Fig. 8.17 Ilinsky, I.A. and Kultas-Ilinksy, K. (1987) J.Comp.Neurol., 262,
335, copyright 1987, reprinted by permission of Wiley-Liss; Fig. 8.19 Friston,
K.J., Frith, C.D., Passingham, R.E., Liddle, P.F. and Frackowiak, R.S.J. (1992)
Proc.Roy.Soc.Lond.B 248, 226.

Fig. 9.4 Deiber, M-P., Passingham, R.E., Colebatch, J.G., Friston, K.J.,
Nixon, P.D. and Frackowiak, R.S.J. (1991) 84, 397.

Fig. 10.1 Milner, B. (1963) Archiv.Neurol., 9, 91, copyright 1963, American
Medical Association; Fig. 10.2 Owen, A.M., Roberts, A.C., Polkey, C.E.,
Sahakian, B.J. and Robbins, T.W. (1991). Neuropsychol., 29, 997; Fig. 10.3
Roland, P.E. (1985) Beh.Neurobiol., 4, 160; Figs 10.4, 10.5, 10.6 Roland, P.E.
and Friberg, L. (1985) J.Neurophysiol., 43, 9; Fig. 10.7 Shallice, T. (1982)
Phil. Trans. Roy. Soc. Lond. B. 298, 204; Fig. 10.8 Eslinger, P.J. and Damasio,
A.R. (1985) Neurol., 35, 1734.

Fig. 11.1 Penfield, W. and Roberts, L. (1959) Speech and Brain
Mechanisms, p. 127, Princeton University Press; Fig. 11.2 Ojemann, G.A.
(1983) Beh. Brain Sci., 2, 196; Fig. 11.3 Wise, R., Chollet, F., Hadar, U.,
Friston, K., Hoffner, E. and Frackowiak, R. (1991) Brain, 114, 1807, by
permission of Oxford University Press; Fig. 11.4a redrawn from von Bonin,
G. and Bailey, P. (1947) The Neocortex of Macaca Mulatta, frontispiece,

University of Illinois Press; Fig. 11.4b redrawn from Bailey, P., von Bonin, G. and McCullogh, F. (1950) The Isocortex of the Chimpanzee, frontispiece, University of Illinios Press; 11.7 Mesulam, M-M. (1990) Annals Neurol., 28, 605; Fig. 11.8 redrawn from Hast, M.H., Fischer, J.M., Wetzela, B. and Thompson, V.E. (1974) Brain Res., 73, 234; Fig. 11. 9 Frith, C.D., Friston, K., Liddle, P.F. and Frackowiak, R.S.J. (1991b) Proc. Roy.Soc. Lond. B 244, 243; Figs 11.10, 11.11 redrawn from plate by Raichle, M. with permission; Fig. 11.12 Penfield, W. and Roberts, L. (1959) Speech and Brain Mechanisms, p. 301, Princeton University Press; Fig. 11.13 Passingham, R.E. (1975a) Brain Beh. Evol., 11, 75; Fig. 11.14 Uylings, H.B.M. and van Eden, C.G. (1990) Progr. Brain Res., 85, 53.

Contents

Contents

1 Voluntary action

It has been common to believe that only human beings are capable of voluntary action. Philosophy used to teach that it was this capacity that set us apart from animals. Thus, Descartes argued that animals operate like automata, and that only people are free to choose their destiny.

For a philosopher, a voluntary act may be defined as one that is consciously intended by the actor. Evidence that someone has acted voluntarily can be gained by asking whether the person was attending to what he or she was doing, had considered the alternative approaches, and had compared their consequences.

But there are two problems with making use of such criteria here. First, it is implied that the subject must be conscious of intending the action. Yet there are many actions that people perform automatically and without conscious thought, such as tying a shoelace or riding a bicycle. But activities of this sort are not 'involuntary': they can be altered whenever the subject wishes

There is a second problem. If the criterion is one that makes reference to conscious awareness, then there will be no way of finding out whether animals can act voluntarily. A person can be asked to report on his or her intentions, but it is not clear how an animal is to be asked the same question. Yet, most of what we know about the anatomy and physiology of the brain comes from studies of animals. If it is denied that animals can act voluntarily, it follows that little can be discovered about the brain mechanisms that support voluntary action.

The difficulty is caused by the use of the word 'voluntary'. In English it has been employed to draw several distinctions that are quite different. Each of these distinctions is worth drawing; but it is confusing that the same word can be applied in each case.

The distinctions are set out in Fig. 1.1. They are presented in a hierarchy, from the most broad at the top to the most restrictive at the bottom. The figure starts by dividing actions broadly into those that are learned and those that are not (level A). An action can be said to be voluntary only if the subject could perform some other action. Although a person can inhibit a reflex such as the knee jerk, the reflex is directed by the wiring of the nervous system, and this is part of our inheritance.

Of the actions that are learned, some are performed in reaction to an external event, while others are not (level B). In the one case there is a

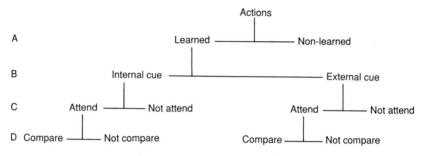

Fig. 1.1 Subdivision of actions. For the different levels A, B, C, and D, see text.

change in the external world, and in the other case there is no such change. We might say that in the first case the subject 'reacts', and that in the second the subject 'acts'. The dictionary allows the word 'voluntary' to be applied to actions that are not prompted or suggested by another.

Whether the action is a reaction or not, there is a further distinction (level C). Of the actions that we perform, we attend to some but not others. It is essential that this should be so: we are unable to attend to all things at the same time. There is a great advantage if we can learn some actions until they become second nature; they can be performed without directed attention, enabling us to think of other things. The penalty is that we will sometimes make errors, because we will perform actions automatically without noticing that the situation is altered and they are no longer appropriate. In such situations we may comment that we 'had not meant to do that'.

The most restrictive distinction is shown on the bottom line of Fig. 1.1 (level D). It requires, not only that the subject should attend to what is being done, but also that the subject compares the various alternative courses of action. Most of our actions are performed without such a conscious comparison. In many instances the choices have been made in the past, or the action is habitual. But when faced with new problems we are capable of sitting down, like Rodin's thinker, and considering the issue. It is not clear whether a chimpanzee can conceptualize the alternatives and make a rational choice; but it is clear that a human being can.

Learned actions

A voluntary act is one that can be withheld or altered. In this broad sense animals are also capable of voluntary action, since they can learn new actions and adapt their behaviour according to the consequences. Used in this way (Fig. 1.1, level A) the term 'voluntary action' refers to an action that is acquired by the process that psychologists term 'instrumental' or 'operant' learning (Mackintosh 1983). In this text the term 'response learning' is more frequently used.

Learned vocalizations

It is not as easy as it might be thought to establish whether an animal has the power to withhold or alter an action. Consider the question of whether a monkey has control over its calls. The question is not a trivial one. It has often been asserted that animals are unable to produce their calls at will, and thus that they must be unable to acquire human speech.

There is no disputing that animals have an unlearned repertoire of calls. If squirrel monkeys (*Saimiri sciureus*) are reared from birth with mute mothers, they still develop the normal range of vocalizations (Winter *et al.* 1974). Furthermore, in normal squirrel monkeys it is possible to evoke calls artificially by electrically stimulating a variety of non-neocortical regions; and all the calls in the repertoire can be evoked in this way (Jürgens and Ploog 1970). The same effect has been demonstrated by Robinson (1967) for the rhesus monkey (*Macaca mulatta*); and he concludes that monkeys lack the neocortical control of vocalization that is a necessary foundation for human speech.

But while it is true that monkeys have an unlearned repertoire of calls, it does not follow that they have no control over their calls. The issue can be settled by trying to teach the animal to call when presented with an arbitrary and neutral stimulus, and then rewarding it when it calls at the appropriate time. For example, Sutton *et al.* (1973) succeeded in teaching rhesus monkeys to coo every time a light came on.

However, this demonstration is not conclusive. The monkey has the opportunity to learn that it is fed only when the light is on and never fed when there is no light. So one explanation of the result could be that the monkey coos when it sees the light because it knows that food is currently available. The fact that the monkey calls does not prove that the monkey knows that the call *causes* the production of the food. In other words, the monkey may have learned about the sequence of events, not about the consequences of calling.

The problems of such experimental designs have been much discussed in the technical psychological literature (Mackintosh 1983). The example to which most attention has been paid is that of a pigeon pecking a key to obtain food. It had always been supposed that key pecking was an instrumental response, that is that the animal pecks because it has learned that its action had the effect of securing food. But Brown and Jenkins (1968) demonstrated that pigeons will peck a lit key even when the contingencies are altered so that, whenever the key was lit, food follows, irrespective of whether the pigeon has pecked the key or not.

This is the set-up for an experiment in classical conditioning (Mackintosh 1983). Yet, the pigeons still pecked the key. The explanation is presumably that, given information that food is in the offing, the pigeon pecks the key in search of the food. Pecking is the natural response of a pigeon when it expects food.

Evidence that this analysis may be correct comes from an experiment by Jenkins and Moore (1973). Some pigeons were taught that a light signalled food and others that a light signalled water. The pigeons taught to expect food pecked the key as if they were trying to eat it, and the pigeons taught to expect water pecked the key as if they were trying to drink it.

There is a neat way of escaping from the problem. This is to teach the monkey to produce not one call but two. For example, Sutton and his colleagues (Sutton *et al.* 1978) rewarded monkeys for producing a coo when a red light came on, and a bark when a green light came on. The beauty of the design is that both lights tell the animal that food is available, and thus whichever light is shown the animal has the same expectation. Yet, the monkeys could be trained to coo or bark as instructed by these arbitrary cues (Sutton *et al.* 1978; Sutton 1979). This must mean that the monkeys have some control over their calls.

Of course, it could still be that the degree of control is limited. It took special training procedures and many hundreds of trials to train the monkeys in these experiments. There is a way of measuring the degree of control, and that is to ask whether the animals find it much more difficult to learn when to call than when to make a limb movement. Sutton *et al.* (1981) made a direct comparison, training monkeys to coo on presentation of an amber light, and to press a lever on presentation of a blue light. On each trial the latency was measured between the onset of the light and the response. The monkeys were noticeably slower to produce a coo than to press the lever; the mean latency to make the call was 2.6 seconds, compared with only 0.8 seconds to press the lever. However, they were no more likely to coo when they saw the blue light than to press the lever when they saw the amber light. In other words, it was more difficult for them to produce the call, but none the less they could do so at will.

Learned movements of the limbs

The experimental design that has been described is that of a 'conditional' task. The logic of such a task is as follows:

If P, then make $R1$
If Q, then make $R2$
Where:
P and Q = contexts (e.g. amber or blue)
$R1$ and $R2$ = responses (e.g. coo or bark)

The coloured stimuli were deliberately chosen because they were arbitrary. Before the experiment begins, the colour blue does not provoke the monkey to any particular response, nor is it associated with any particular outcome.

The same design is equally suitable for studying control over other actions. For example, we have taught monkeys to operate a joystick (Canavan *et al.* 1989*a*). The instructions are given by the presentation of colours on a TV monitor. A blue light tells the monkey to pull the joystick, and a red light to move it to the right. The task is a conditional task because the animal's action must be guided by the conditions obtaining at the time. No one action will secure food: instead the animal must act in a flexible manner, now pulling the lever and now moving it to the right.

There are other experiments with the same formal design. For example, Petrides (1987) has taught monkeys to base their movements on the identity of an object presented in the background. On each trial an object appears in the background; if it is object A the monkey is rewarded for gripping a handle, and if object B for touching a button. Petrides (1987) finds it relatively easy to train monkeys to do this.

The logic of such tasks can be written as:¡

Given *A*, if *P*, then make *R*1
Given *A*, if *Q*, then make *R*2
Where:
A = the manipulandum (e.g. a joystick)
P and *Q* = the context (e.g. blue or red)
*R*1 and *R*2 = the responses (e.g. pull the joystick or move it to the right)

The logic differs from that of a response that is unlearned. There the logic is non-conditional. The animal makes a particular response given a particular stimulus, whatever the context. This can be written simply as:

Given *A*, make *R*1.

Animals other than primates

All the examples that have been quoted so far have come from primates. The reason for this bias is not that primates are unique in having control over their actions. It is simply that primates provide the best model we have of the neurological mechanisms that control voluntary action in people. There is no implication that primates can control their actions but that fish cannot.

Non-primate mammals and birds
Psychologists have devoted much attention to the learning abilities of the laboratory rat. It is a classical demonstration that a rat can easily be taught to press a lever to obtain food. It is not difficult to demonstrate that the rat can modify its actions according to the consequences that follow. For example, rats can be trained to push a lever up when the chamber is brightly lit and to press it down when the chamber is dimly lit (Passingham *et al.* 1988).

It has been more usual to make the same point by dividing the animals into two groups, and then training one group to perform action A and the other group to perform action B. The logic is the same as for the conditional task. Suppose that the aim is to train rats to press a lever to avoid shock. If the rats succeed, it can be objected that they have simply learned to predict the shocks and that they press on the lever because they are performing some unlearned startle response. This objection may not be plausible, but it must be answered. In an experiment described by Bolles (1978) this was done by training one group of rats to press the lever to avoid shock, and the other group to pull it. The fact that the training succeeds with both groups shows that a rat can learn either of two arbitrary actions according to the consequences that follow.

The same techniques can be used in the analysis of instrumental learning in birds. It was mentioned earlier in this chapter that there has been a dispute about whether pigeons learn to peck keys by instrumental learning. If a pigeon has control over pecking, it should prove possible to teach pigeons to withhold pecking by arranging that pecks will prevent the presentation of grain. Thus, one can try to teach some pigeons to increase their pecking, and others to decrease their pecking. The technique is described in the technical literature as 'bidirectional' learning.

One attempt was reported by Schwarz and Williams (1972). On some trials the pigeon was presented with a red key, and on these trials pecking prevented the presentation of food. On the other trials the pigeon was presented with a white key, and pecking the white key had no effect on the presentation of food. On trials with the white key, grain was deliberately given at the same rate as for trials with the red key, and thus the pigeon's expectation of grain was matched for the two types of trial. The pigeons pecked the white key at roughly twice the rate as they pecked the red key. This suggests that, while they found it difficult not to peck when food was in the offing, they had learned the consequence of pecking the red key.

It would seem that pigeons have control over pecking, but that it is limited. But it is not difficult to show that there are other actions over which their control is more complete. For example, Jenkins (1977) trained pigeons to wave their head to and fro in order to gain food. This is an arbitrary action that does not form part of the pigeons' repertoire when they are looking for food; yet they can learn to perform it.

Perhaps the most dramatic demonstration comes from a study of a parrot. Pepperberg (1981) describes an attempt to teach a parrot, Alex, to name objects. Like other parrots Alex can mimic some words from human speech. In order to train Alex to name an object, such as a triangle, one of the experimenters prompted Alex by first naming the object. If Alex copied correctly he was rewarded both with praise and with the chance to play with the object. On test trials Alex was encouraged to name the object without any prompting from the trainer. Thus, he had to say 'triangle' when shown a triangle, and 'square' when shown a square. Alex has learnt to name a large number of objects (Pepperberg 1987). It is clear that he can perform a vocal conditional task; that is he can say 'A' when shown object A and 'B' when shown object B. The parrot can retrieve the appropriate word from his vocabulary at will.

Fish
Psychologists have concentrated their attentions on birds and mammals; the abilities of fish, reptiles, and amphibians have been greatly neglected. A review of the available studies is provided by Macphail (1982). There have been several attempts to teach fish a simple instrumental response (Warren 1965). For example, Voronin (1962) taught fish to catch beads with their mouths to gain food.

But this is not an arbitrary response. A critical test was performed by Van Sommers (1962). He used a bidirectional design with goldfish (*Cassius auratus*). The fish were taught to interrupt a photobeam when a red light came on and to withhold their response when a green light came on. The experimenter controlled the oxygenation of the water, and the reward for a correct response was an increase in the level of oxygen. The animals were rewarded both when they correctly moved, and when they correctly withheld their response. The fish could learn this task. This demonstrates convincingly that they were sensitive to the relations between their actions and the consequences.

Involuntary action

In discussing animals so far, the criterion for voluntary action has been that the response be learned by instrumental learning. It has been argued that instrumental learning can be demonstrated in fish, birds, and mammals. But the reader may have the suspicion that the criterion is too lenient. Perhaps many responses that are conventionally regarded as involuntary could be modified if the animals were trained on the paradigms described above. It is necessary to validate the criterion by demonstrating that there are responses which cannot be modified by experimentally manipulating the consequences.

A series of experiments was carried out in Miller's laboratory to see if it is possible to teach rats to control directly their autonomic nervous system (Dworkin and Miller 1986). There has been much interest in whether people can voluntarily alter their heart rate or blood pressure; and it would be of importance to psychosomatic medicine if they could. However, there is a problem with experiments using human subjects. It is always possible that any effect is exerted indirectly by means of the skeletal musculature: for example, the subject can tense the skeletal muscles. The advantage of experimenting on animals such as rats is that the animals can be given curare to paralyse the skeletal musculature, and the animals can be artificially respirated during the experiments.'

The design of the experiments was exemplary. In one study by DiCara and Miller (1968) one group of rats was taught to avoid a shock by increasing their blood pressure, and another group to avoid the same shock by decreasing their blood pressure. Two control groups were included: each control animal was yoked to an animal in one of the experimental groups, so that it received exactly the same shocks, though it was unable to control them. The authors reported a clear-cut result: those experimental animals rewarded for increasing their blood pressure showed a greater increase than the yoked control animals; those animals rewarded for decreasing their blood pressure showed a greater decrease than the yoked control animals. In other words, the experiment appeared to show that rats had direct voluntary control over their blood pressure.

The design used in this experiment is the same design that has been recommended in this chapter as a satisfactory test for instrumental learning. The same design was also used in other studies on gastric motility, heart rate, and peripheral vasomotor functions; these studies are reviewed by Dworkin and Miller (1986). It is therefore embarrassing that there should be claims that rats can voluntarily control their viscera.

Fortunately, there is no further need to agonize about the data, since later attempts to replicate the findings have failed (Dworkin and Miller 1986). There is still no satisfactory account of why the earlier studies produced positive results and the later ones negative results. For the moment we can conclude, with relief, that there is no evidence that such visceral responses as heart rate or blood pressure are under voluntary control.

There are also skeletal responses that cannot be modified by instrumental learning. For example, Bolles (1978) arranged that for some rats freezing led to the avoidance of shocks, and that for other rats freezing led to the onset of shocks. If the animals can learn the effects of freezing, the animals in the second group should freeze less than those in the first. This is not what happened. When in danger rats tend to freeze, and they do so whatever the consequence.

There are other examples, such as scratching or yawning. It is very difficult to teach a rat to scratch to obtain food, and much easier if the rat is given a collar to provoke the scratches (Pearce *et al.* 1978). Similarly it is difficult to teach a dog to yawn to obtain food; the dogs tend to cheat by producing a pseudo-yawn, simply opening the mouth (Konorski 1967).

In both of these studies some improvement in performance was recorded. However, yawning and scratching are displacement activities that occur when an animal is in conflict; and animals might well be in conflict when they are uncertain whether they will get food. A convincing test would be to try to teach rats that given one cue they should scratch and given another cue they should yawn. It may well be that they will fail.

Instructions

The conditional task has been used to establish whether or not a response is under voluntary control. One way of describing the technique is to say that the experimenter uses external cues to *instruct* the animal which act to perform.

Now consider what happens in the clinic. In the examination for ideomotor apraxia, neuropsychologists require patients to perform simple acts such as sticking out the tongue, coughing, or saluting (De Renzi 1985). The patient is instructed in two ways, either by verbal command or by being required to copy the gestures made by the examiner.

The logic is the same whether the animal learns a conditional task or the patient obeys commands. Where the instructions are verbal we can write the logic as:

If {P}, then make R1
If {Q}, then make R2
Where:
{P} and {Q} = the verbal contexts (e.g. 'show your tongue', cough')
R1 and R2 = the nonverbal responses (e.g. show tongue, cough)'

Methods of instruction

There is, however, a clear difference between the way in which instructions are given to patients and animals. Two examples from the clinic will suffice.

A patient is asked, let us say, to show the examiner his or her left hand, and does so immediately. But the monkey must first be trained so that it acquires a conditional rule. Using a procedure devised by McGonigle and Flook (1978), we trained monkeys by trial and error to push a panel with one hand if it was illuminated red, and with the other hand if it was illuminated green (Passingham 1985*a*). The monkeys could put out their left or right hand at will, but they made between 200 and 400 errors in learning the task.

To take another example, a patient can be asked by the examiner to bite or put out the tongue, and again the response can be right first time. But monkeys must be taught by trial and error. Sutton *et al.* (1978) were able, with great patience, to train monkeys to bite or lick, depending on which of two colours was presented.

There are two basic differences between the ways in which monkeys and human subjects are typically instructed.

1. A monkey is unable to follow verbal instructions. It is, therefore, necessary to give arbitrary instructions, such as colours. The association between the colour and the response is not symbolic. Blue does not *mean* 'pull' in any language.

   However, this is not to say that *no* animal could obey instructions that are given in a language. Chimpanzees have been taught a simple symbolic system. and can look at the symbols and obey simple requests, such as to pick up particular foods or tools (Savage-Rumbaugh 1986).

2. The human subject need make no errors; the subject can make the correct response first time. Yet the animal is typically taught by trial and error over many trials.

   The difference is not, however, one between animals and human subjects. It is possible to instruct chimpanzees directly without requiring them to learn by trial and error. This can be done by demonstration. The chimpanzee Viki could imitate actions or facial expressions demonstrated by his foster-parents (Hayes and Hayes 1952); and the chimpanzee Nim, taught a gesture language of the deaf, frequently copied the signs that his teachers made (Terrace *et al.* 1979). It should prove possible to train chimpanzees so effectively that they could reliably copy new gestures first time.

It would be wrong to assume that the motor programmes, set up in the brain, differ fundamentally according to the method of instruction. It may not matter that the monkey learns by experience and the human subject obeys a verbal command. The way in which the programmes are represented in the brain may be identical.

We do not understand how verbal instructions can have the effect of setting up motor programmes. It is a mystery how verbal instructions can establish a set in the brain. Sperry (1955) provides the example of instructing a subject to lift the hand when a bell sounds. The subject quickly lifts the hand, even though there have been no trials in which the correct response was established. A preparatory set is temporarily set up in the relevant pathways. The instruction can only have this effect because the human subject already knows the meaning of the words used in the instruction, and can therefore know what to do without prior experience of the situation.

Another example is discussed by Evarts *et al.* (1984). If the experimenter gives the instruction 'add' and then provides the numbers five and three, the subject replies 'eight'. If the experimenter first gives the instruction 'subtract', and then provides the same numbers, the subject replies 'two'. The instruction establishes a preparatory set, and so influences the operation performed, but we do not know how it does this.

Plan of the book

It is the aim of this book to explore the contribution made to response learning by the frontal lobes. The message is naïve. It claims for the frontal lobes a function which is very basic, a function which they perform not only in the higher primates but also in the most lowly mammal.

Consider the prefrontal cortex alone. It can be identified even in an insectivore, such as a tree shrew (*Tupaia belangeri*) (Divac *et al.* 1978), or a monotreme, such as the echidna or spiny antèater *(Tachyglossus aculeatus)* (Divac *et al.* 1987). Furthermore, a region has been identified in the brain of the pigeon that is similar in its biochemistry (Divac and Mogenson 1985).

The claim is that the frontal lobes as a whole subserve the ability to learn what responses are appropriate given the environmental context. This is an ability that would confer selective advantage on any animal in evolution.

The monkey model

None the less, Chapters 2–9 rely mainly on data obtained with macaque monkeys. The reason is simple. The aim is to produce an account of the functional anatomy of the frontal lobes. This restricts the choice for the following reasons.

First, there is only limited information available on the cortico-cortical connections of the frontal lobes in rats. The rat has a smooth neocortex, and it is difficult to identify the borders of cytoarchitectonic areas at the time of injecting the tracers used for demontrating the connections.

Second, fortunately for the conservation of the species, there has been very little experimental work on the chimpanzee brain.

Finally, there is still no non-invasive method for charting anatomical connections. The result is that there are almost no data on the details of these connections in the human brain.

Thus the macaque brain is the nearest model that we have for which we can work out a flow chart. There is, of course, the possibility that human specializations have led to changes in organization. Chapters 10 and 11 mount a rearguard action in an attempt to play down this possibility.

Voluntary action

In the treatment of the monkey data, 'voluntary action' refers to actions that are learned (Fig. 1.1, level A). The tests include simple response learning, such as lever pressing, and conditional response learning, such as moving a joystick according to colour cues. It is important to appreciate that the term 'response learning' covers both these types of task. A conditional task is a neat way of demonstrating that a response is learned instrumentally; but that does not mean that a simple task such as lever pressing is not learned in the same way.

The distinctions illustrated in Fig. 1.1 are used throughout the text. The discussion includes responses that are prompted by external cues such as colours (Chapter 3), and also those that are self-initiated (Chapters 4 and 6) (Fig. 1.1, level B). The discussion is extended to deal with the situation in which the contextual cues are held in working memory (Chapter 6). This situation puts a premium on the ability to attend to one's actions (Fig. 1.1, level C).

Chapters 10 and 11 deal with voluntary action in the most restrictive sense (Fig. 1.1, level D). This refers to the ability that people have to decide what to do by consciously comparing alternative courses of action. It is this ability that is responsible for much of the success of the human species.

2 Motor cortex (area 4)

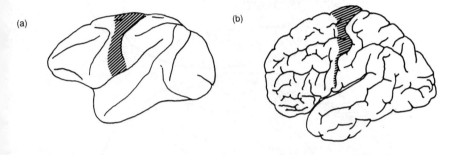

(a)

(b)

Fig. 2.1 Motor cortex in (a) the macaque monkey and (b) the human brain.

Response learning occurs by the selection of actions according to their consequences. If new responses are to be learned there must be a mechanism for directing the different movements. This chapter considers motor cortex (Fig. 2.1), part of the mechanism for executing movements of the limbs and face.

Divisions of the frontal lobe

The cortex of the frontal lobe divides into four strips. Figure 2.2 shows these on a drawing of the macaque brain. The strips will be referred to as motor cortex, premotor cortex, prefrontal cortex, and the anterior cingulate cortex. The first three strips are arranged vertically and they wrap round on to the medial surface; they include the upper bank of the cingulate sulcus. The last strip is arranged horizontally, and this includes the lower bank of the cingulate sulcus. The distinction between the strips is best drawn on the basis of differences between the areas in cytoarchitecture (Brodmann 1925).

1. The first strip, area 4, is characterized by the fact that there are few granule cells in layer IV, and that there is a high density of very large pyramidal cells (Betz cells) in layer V.

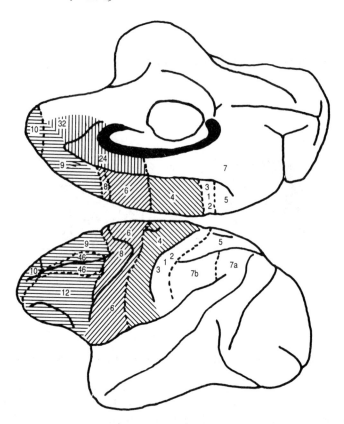

Fig. 2.2 Four functional divisions of the frontal lobe: motor cortex (4), premotor cortex (6 and 8), prefrontal cortex (9, 46, 12, 11, 13), cingulate cortex (24 and 32).

2. In front of it lies area 6, which is also agranular but has few Betz cells. The reader should be warned that I will use an unconventional terminology for this area: The term 'premotor cortex' will be used for the whole of area 6. I will then distinguish the lateral premotor cortex (LPC) and the medial premotor cortex (MPC). The medial premotor cortex has usually been termed the 'supplementary motor area' (SMA), because it is possible to evoke movements by electrical stimulation of this area (Woolsey *et al.* 1952). But we now know that is also possible to elicit movements by stimulation of the lateral premotor cortex (Kurata and Wise 1988). Thus, there is no reason to treat the medial premotor area as different in kind.

   In front of area 6 lies area 8. In a macaque the ventral part of area 8 was called area 45 by Walker (1940); he identified it with area 45 of the human brain (Brodmann 1925). In Fig. 2.2 area 8 is included with area 6 in the second strip.

3. The prefrontal cortex lies in front. It differs from area 6 in that there is a marked granular layer IV. In monkeys the prefrontal cortex includes areas 9 to 14 (Brodmann 1925).

4. Finally on the medial surface in and below the cingulate sulcus lies a strip of paralimbic cortex, areas 24, 25, and 32. *cingulate cortex*

The four broad divisions described above are agreed by all. Von Bonin and Bailey (1947) made the same distinctions, but they followed von Economo (1929) in attaching letters rather than numbers to the different regions. They divide the frontal cortex into FA (4), FB and FC (6), FD gamma (8), FD (9,10,11,12,13), and LA (24). The present account will use the numbering system.

Boundaries of motor cortex

Motor cortex includes all of area 4. However, it has been controversial whether it is confined to this area (Philips and Porter 1977). One problem is that the border between area 4 and area 6 is not sharp. In area 4 there is a high concentration of giant pyramidal cells in layer V, but there are also a few such cells in area 6. If histological cross-sections are taken within areas 4 and 6 the more anterior the section the fewer the giant pyramidal cells (Weinrich and Wise 1982).

One way of identifying motor cortex is by the effects of electrical stimulation. Weinrich and Wise (1982) used microelectrodes, and were able to elicit movements by stimulating the motor cortex with currents of less than 60 microamps. The zone delineated in this way roughly corresponds to the region with a high concentration of giant pyramidal cells (Weinrich and Wise 1982; Kurata and Wise 1988). However, there is a transitional zone, rostral to this area, where the effects of microstimulation with these currents are inconsistent, and it is not clear how this area should be classified (Weinrich et al. 1984). This may explain the apparent discrepancy between the results of the study by Weinrich and Wise (1982) and the earlier one by Kwan et al. (1978) who reported that the primary motor cortex as mapped by microstimulation included part of area 6.

Manipulative and orienting movements

Motor cortex is specialized for the control of the movements of the limbs and face. In this book the term 'manipulative' will be used to describe such movements. It is, of course, strictly a misnomer for movements of the face; but most of the studies to be quoted concern arm and finger movements.

These are distinguished from 'orienting' movements of the neck or eyes. The somatotopic map in area 4 includes all the parts of the body including the tongue, but the eyes have no place in the map (Woolsey *et al.* 1952). This is not because subjects are unable to produce voluntary eye movements; a person has no trouble in moving the eyes in the direction specified by the doctor during an examination.

One reason for the absence of an eye representation in area 4 is that orienting movements differ from manipulative movements in the way in which they are directed. The goal of an orienting movement is an external target in space, whereas the goal of a manipulative movement is the position of a limb relative to the body. It is with manipulative movements that motor cortex is concerned.

Unlearned movements

Physiologists have long believed that the ability to execute voluntary movements depends on the primary motor cortex (Philips and Porter 1977). Chapter 1 has distinguished several uses of the word 'voluntary'. Philips and Porter (1977) prefer the term 'least automatic' as suggested by Hughlings Jackson (reprinted 1931). This implies that the subject must attend to the action; this corresponds to the distinction in Fig. 1.1, level C. For the purposes of this chapter we will use 'voluntary' in the broad sense of learned as opposed to unlearned (Fig. 1.1, level A).

If motor cortex is specialized for the execution of learned movement, then some unlearned movements should be possible even after the removal of motor cortex. It is impressive that motor cortex can be removed in mammals without having a dramatic effect on the animal's ordinary life.

Rodents

Consider rats that have had either the whole of the frontal cortex removed (Kolb and Whishaw 1981) or the whole neocortex removed (Vanderwolf *et al.* 1978). These rats can walk, rear, climb, and swim. They can eat pellets, although they are poor at holding food in the paws; and they can drink from an open dish or spout.

They can also wash their face, and produce all the normal components of grooming, although the sequence may be disrupted (Kolb and Whishaw 1981). Male rats can still copulate, although they are poor at initiating the activity and at orienting themselves with respect to the female (Whishaw and Kolb 1985). Finally, female hamsters (*Mesocricetus auratus*) deprived of the neocortex at birth can still give birth, nurse young and rear them successfully (Murphy *et al.* 1981). While it is not claimed that the performance of the animals is unimpaired, it is remarkable that so much of the normal repertoire is preserved.

Some of the relevant behaviour patterns can even be directed without a contribution from the forebrain. Woods (1964) studied rats in which he had removed all the forebrain including the basal ganglia, while sparing the hypothalamus. The rats could still walk, lap water, bite food pellets, groom themselves, and attempt to defend themselves if pinched.

Furthermore, electrical stimulation in brainstem structures can induce eating, grooming, and attack (Bernston and Micco 1976). Electrical stimulation in the general region of the mesencephalic pedunculopontine nucleus causes rats and cats to walk when placed on a treadmill; this mesencephalic locomotor region is known to modulate oscillators for spinal locomotion (Garcia-Rill 1986).

Non-human primates

It is not just in rodents that motor lesions can spare many unlearned behaviour patterns. We have studied monkeys in which motor cortex had been removed from one hemisphere, either in infancy or in adulthood (Passingham *et al.* 1983). In three infant monkeys motor cortex (MI) was removed alone, but in four other infants and two adult monkeys the somatosensory cortex (SI) was removed together with MI.

All the animals were studied over a year and a half after surgery when we supposed that maximum recovery had occurred. The animals were observed while running around a large enclosure. All the monkeys could reach for food and pick it up. All could cling without difficulty to the mesh walls and support their own weight; all could climb, jump off and land safely. The monkeys walked on all fours and would stretch out the affected arm when climbing or leaping. This is not to say that their movements were as efficient as normal; indeed the animals tired easily. But it was impressive that they could make these movements at all.

It is obviously possible that bilateral lesions might have had a more disruptive effect. Unfortunately, descriptions in the literature of adult monkeys with bilateral lesions of motor cortex are available only for a few weeks after surgery (Kennard 1942; Travis 1955).

But we do know the effects of bilateral section of the pyramidal tract. This operation cuts the pyramidal output of motor cortex, while preserving the other cortico-subcortical outputs of the motor cortex; but it also cuts the pyramidal fibres that originate from the lateral and medial premotor cortex, as well as those that originate from somatosensory cortex (SI) and parietal area 5 (Murray and Coulter 1981; Dum and Strick 1991). Lawrence and Kuypers (1968*a*) describe the period of recovery for eight rhesus monkeys in which the section was reasonably confined to the pyramidal tract. The authors show photographs of animals standing on two legs, walking, climbing, and reaching for food.

There is a further line of evidence. If motor cortex is specialized for the execution of learned movements, the activity of the cells should be less closely related to movements in the animal's natural repertoire than to performance on learned tasks. Hoffman and Luschei (1980) recorded from the precentral face area in rhesus monkeys. They trained the monkeys to bite a bar with a particular specified force, feedback being provided by a visual display. Of the cells they recorded, 50 per cent responded while the animal applied force to the bite bar. Recordings were taken from 69 of these cells while the animals spontaneously chewed; and only 29 per cent of the cells responded during natural chewing. The authors point out that even decerebrate rats can still chew (Woods 1964).

Hoffman and Luschei (1980) argue that the mechanisms of motor cortex are required for learned non-rhythmical movements of the mouth and jaw. However, there is another interpretation. It may be that the learned and unlearned movements activate different muscles, and this is the reason why some cells respond during one type of movement but not during the other.

This objection is less forceful in the case of another study in which human subjects were used. Colebatch *et al.* (1991*a*) studied the control of breathing by scanning subjects with the PET scanner. In one condition the subjects breathed passively, and in the other the subjects were asked to control their inspiration voluntarily. There was greater activation of motor cortex when the breathing was under volitional control.

Patients

There is, however, a puzzle. Neurologists frequently see patients who suffer a long-lasting, or even permanent, hemiplegia or hemiparesis as a result of a stroke involving the middle cerebral artery. Furthermore, Laplane *et al.* (1977*a*) have published descriptions of the clinical outcome for two patients in whom the surgeon was forced to remove the whole sensorimotor strip (MI and SI) from one hemisphere. These patients were still very handicapped when they were reassessed nearly three years after the operation. The neurological examination showed that a variety of unlearned reflexes were still abnormal in the two patients. Furthermore, both patients had considerable difficulty walking more than a few yards, and neither could hop on either foot. The patients did not use the affected arm, which was paretic.

Long-term outcome

Why then do neurologists see patients who suffer a long-lasting hemiplegia? The truth is that nature is a poor surgeon, and the lesions are often not as restricted as those that can be made in animals. Large strokes involving the middle cerebral artery often compromise the basal ganglia as well as motor cortex. In the patients studied by Laplane *et al.* (1977*a*) the white matter was invaded, whereas in our study on monkeys with sensorimotor lesions only the cortical surface was removed (Passingham *et al.* 1983).

It is difficult to find human cases with discrete lesions lower in the pyramidal tract and proper documentation of the lesion. Bucy *et al.* (1964) describe a patient in whom the surgeon cut the pyramidal tract unilaterally in order to mitigate the severity of hemiballismus. By the 24th day the patient could get into and out of a chair without help, and on the 29th day he could walk unaided.

Unfortunately, this case does not decide the issue. While the histology showed that the lesion was confined to the pyramidal tract, it also showed that only 83 per cent of the fibres were cut. Like monkeys with incomplete section of the tract, the patient could make some discrete finger movements (Lawrence and Hopkins 1976; Chapman and Wiesendanger 1982). Thus, it is open to someone to argue that unlearned motor patterns might have been more disrupted had the lesion been complete.

Other cases in the literature have been reviewed by Ropper *et al.* (1979). They also report a case in which hemiplegia followed an infarct which was confined to the pyramid. The patient recovered to a considerable extent. However, though the right pyramid was small, the lesion was not complete.

There are, however, two major studies in which the degree of recovery could be related to the size and location of the lesion as assessed by computed tomographic (CT) scans.

Warabi et al. (1990) report that the degree of recovery in hemiparetic patients is related to the magnitude of the shrinkage of the cerebral peduncles. The patients were studied more than one year after the stroke. Recovery of arm and hand movements was incomplete if the cerebral peduncles were less than 60% of their normal size. However, this study does not examine the extent to which the lesions involved non-pyramidal as well as pyramidal pathways.

Fries *et al.* (1993) compared seven patients in which infarcts were confined to the internal capsule with four patients in which the infarcts extended beyond the internal capsule into the ventral thalamus. Recovery was less complete in those with the more extensive infarcts. These lesions not only disrupt the pyramidal tract but also disturb the influence of the basal ganglia and cerebellum on the frontal cortex.

Similarly, Bucy *et al.* (1964) report that their surgical patients with pyramidal section recovered better than patients with haemorrhagic lesions. Haemorrhagic lesions affecting the pyramidal tract at lower levels usually disrupt other non-pyramidal pathways. If the pyramidal tract is cut in monkeys, but the lesion extends into the reticular formation, the disability is much greater than if the lesion is confined to the pyramidal tract (Lawrence and Kuypers 1968*b*).

The outcome is much better if the lesions are confined to the pyramidal tract. Fries *et al.* (1993) have followed up seven patients with lesions in the posterior limb of the internal capsule. These patients all recovered good motor skills as assessed on a quantitative battery. The conclusion is that patients with lesions in the upper pyramidal tract recover slowly, but like monkeys with pyramidal section they recover to a remarkable degree.

Recovery in the short term

Although patients can recover to a remarkable degree, it is possible that there is a difference in the time course of recovery compared with monkeys. If areas 4 and lateral 6 are removed from one hemisphere in monkeys, the animals suffer a flaccid paresis which changes to a hypertonic paresis for a few weeks after surgery (Gilman *et al.* 1974). Although in some patients the spastic paresis can recover in the weeks after a haemorrhagic lesion in the internal capsule, there are other patients who show little recovery at all in the first two months (Twitchell 1951).

It is, of course, possible that the difference is due to a difference in the lesions; but we also have to explain why it is that motor lesions are initially more disabling for a monkey than they are for a cat or a rat. Section of one pyramidal tract causes longer lasting paresis in a monkey than in a cat (Liddell and Philips 1944) or rat (Barron 1934). The removal of motor cortex also causes a dissimilar effect: the initial flaccid paresis is less severe in a cat than in a macaque monkey, and is much more severe in a chimpanzee (Walker and Fulton 1938). These effects are probably not the result of differences in the size of the experimental lesions, or differences in the assessment of the symptoms. Some other agent may be responsible.

One such agent is the difference in development of direct connections from motor cortex to the motor neurones in the ventral horn of the spinal cord. Kuypers (1981) summarizes the relevant facts. The findings are as follows:

1. In rats, cats, and dogs almost all the corticospinal fibres terminate in the intermediate zone of the cord. Few synapse in the ventral horn of the cord, where the motor-neurones lie (Fig. 2.3).

2. In macaque monkeys and baboons (*Papio*) there is a substantial contribution that is directed to the lateral part of the motorneuronal pool (Fig. 2.3).

3. In the chimpanzee (*Pan*) and man there are dense terminations in the whole of the motor neuronal pool, and this includes the ventral part of the horn where the proximal musculature is represented (Fig. 2.3).

It seems that the greater the projection to the motorneurones, the more severe are the *generalized* effects of a lesion in the pyramidal system. It is not clear why this should be so. Perhaps there is a useful analogy with the effect known as 'spinal shock'. Even if the spinal cord is cut at a high level,

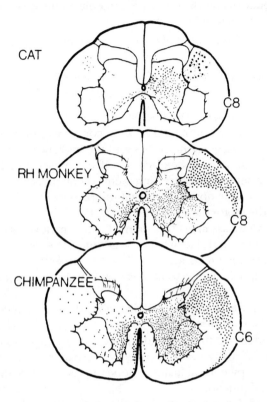

Fig. 2.3 Distribution of cortico-spinal fibres from left hemisphere to low cervical spinal grey matter in the cat, rhesus monkey, and chimpanzee. From Kuypers (1981).

patients initially lose all reflexes; and we believe this to be due to the loss of descending influences on the cord (Ruch 1965).

This suggests the following hypothesis. The interruption of the direct cortico-motor neuronal pathway may have a major effect on the excitability of the cells in the motor neurone pool. This change in excitability may interfere with the influence of the brain pathways directing unlearned movements, since these pathways must have their influence through the motor neurones, even though indirectly via cells in the intermediate layers. The interference could be more severe as the number of motor neurones that receive direct projections from the cortex increases.

Conclusion

If the data on rats, monkeys, and people are considered together, what have we learned about the domain of movements over which motor cortex exercises control? There are three findings.

1. For both monkeys and patients, the immediate effects of a motor lesion are paralysis and paresis.
2. Given time, rats and monkeys can recover much of their unlearned repertoire.
3. In patients recovery is sometimes less complete, but it can be remarkably complete if the lesions are confined to the pyramidal tract.

Now compare two views, the first naïve, and the second slightly less so. The naïve view is that motor cortex is concerned only with learned behaviour, but this view cannot withstand the evidence that motor cortex does play a role in some reflex activity. If the muscles of the hand are stretched while a subject is contracting them voluntarily, the reflex response has a long latency. It is now agreed that the pathway for this long latency reflex includes the motor cortex (Matthews 1991).

The second view assumes that normally the motor system works as an integrated whole, and that whenever an animal or person moves, cells in motor cortex change their activity. This view accepts that the immediate effects of motor lesions imply some contribution of the cortex to unlearned behaviour.

How then can we explain the remarkable degree of recovery that is possible after lesions in motor cortex or the pyramidal tract? The implication is that motor cortex and the pyramidal system do not play an *essential* role in the execution of many unlearned behaviour patterns. The normal brain does not work in a piecemeal fashion; none the less, if the brain is dissected the pieces can still function.

It is because of the profusion of parallel pathways in the motor system that movement is possible after cortical lesions. Figure 2.4 provides a simplified diagram of the motor system in primates. Even if the neocortex is removed, there are still many motor pathways that retain some inputs and have intact outputs. The basal ganglia still have inputs from the thalamus, and send projections to the area of the pedunculopontine nucleus in the hindbrain (Parent 1986). The red nucleus retains a large input from the cerebellum and the rubro-spinal tract is intact (Brodal 1981). The reticular formation can still be influenced by the cerebellum, and the reticulo-spinal tract remains. The disruption of one output leaves others intact and thus allows residual, though impoverished, function.

Discrete finger movements

The specialized contribution of motor cortex is determined by its outputs. The motor cortex sends connections to the red nucleus, reticular formation, basal ganglia, and cerebellum; but its *essential* contribution is made possible by the pattern of its connections to the spinal cord

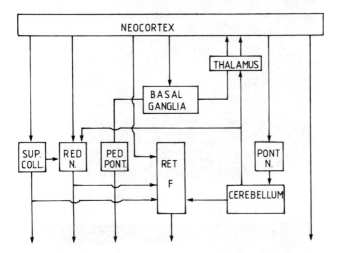

Fig. 2.4   Block diagram of some connections of the motor system. Sup. coll. = superior colliculus, Red n. = red nucleus, Ped. pont. = pedunculopontine nucleus, Ret. F. = reticular formation, Pont.n. = pontine nuclei.

This contribution will not necessarily be seen if one simply observes animals with motor lesions as they live out their lives in cages. The experimenter must devise special tests for the fingers, hand, wrist, and arm.

Pyramidal tract

Monkeys are unable to use their fingers independently if the pyramidal tract is cut. This was first noted by Tower (1940), who commented that the monkeys were incapable of modifying the shape of the hand to take food from between the experimenter's fingers.

A proper test was devised by Lawrence and Kuypers (1968*a*). They studied monkeys with complete section of both pyramidal tracts. The monkeys had to retrieve small pieces of food from holes in a board. The food could be picked out of the smaller holes only if the monkey could grip it with thumb and forefinger. Napier (1961) dubs this 'the precision grip' and distinguishes it from the 'power grip' in which objects are picked up in the whole hand.

After the pyramidal section, the monkeys could scoop the food out of the largest holes, but were quite unable to pick food out of the smaller ones. The photographs in the paper show that the monkeys could grip only with the whole hand, and were unable to make discrete movements of the thumb and forefinger.

Pyramidal section abolishes the ability to form the precision grip only if the lesion is complete. Chapman and Wiesendanger (1982) describe three

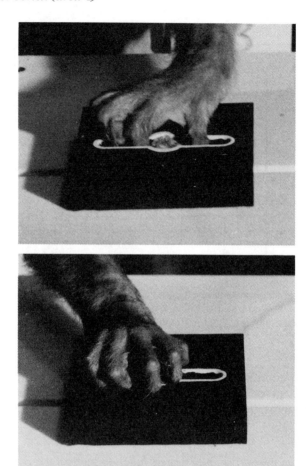

Fig. 2.5 Hands of monkeys reaching for food from a slot. (a) precision grip; (b) power grip. Lower figure (b) for monkey with lesion in sensorimotor cortex. From Passingham *et al.* (1983).

monkeys with unilateral pyramidal lesions. The monkeys improved after surgery until, after four to five weeks, they were as adept at removing food from small holes as they had been before surgery. But in the three animals the lesion only cut 66, 85, and 87 per cent of the fibres.

It has been argued that the animals can recover if given prolonged training. Hepp-Reymond and Wiesendanger (1972) trained monkeys extensively on a task in which they had to press a thin strain gauge. After unilateral section of the pyramidal tract, the monkeys were still able to press the strain gauge between their fingers. There are two reasons for doubting that this is a demonstration that monkeys can recover the precision grip after section of the pyramidal tract. First, the lesions were not complete

(Hepp-Reymond and Wiesendanger 1974). Second, there was no requirement that the monkeys press with thumb and forefinger while tucking the other fingers away; in other words the test did not require the animals to move the thumb and forefinger independently of the other fingers.

Motor cortex

Monkeys are also unable to grip with thumb and forefinger if motor cortex is removed. We tested two adult monkeys in which both motor cortex and somatosensory cortex (SI) had been removed unilaterally (Passingham *et al.* 1983). We tested the precision grip by using a variation of a test that was devised by Haaxma and Kuypers (1975). A pellet of food is presented in a slot; if the animal inserts its thumb and forefinger into the slot it can pick the food up from the central hole. Figure. 2.5(a) shows the hand of a normal monkey as it retrieves food from such a slot.

Neither operated monkey could pick the food up if the slot was oriented sideways. The monkeys simply closed all the fingers together (Fig. 2.5(b)). They were able to remove the food only if the slot was oriented towards them; this is because they cheated by clawing at the food until they dislodged it.

The problem is not that the monkeys are unable to grip, but that they are unable to move the fingers one at a time. This is shown by another test which was devised to require the animals to put out a single finger (Passingham *et al.* 1983). A peanut or currant was placed on a shelf behind a perspex screen, and the only way the monkey could obtain the food was to push the forefinger through a small hole and thus knock the food off the shelf (Fig. 2.6). The food then fell into a tray from which it could be picked up with the other hand. After the unilateral removal of motor and somatosensory cortex, the monkeys were totally unable to do this. Typically they just flattened their hand against the Perspex screen.

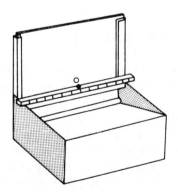

Fig. 2.6 Apparatus used for testing the ability to push a single finger through a hole. The monkey sat on the far side of the apparatus. The food is shown as a black ball. From Passingham *et al.* (1983).

It is only if the lesion is complete that it results in an inability to make independent movements of the fingers. In the same study there were three monkeys in which motor cortex alone was removed from one hemisphere when the animals were infants. Two of the monkeys failed the test, but the third one passed; in this animal a considerable proportion of the anterior bank of the central sulcus had been spared (Passingham *et al.* 1983).

The animals do not recover the ability to use their thumb and forefinger with time. The monkeys with lesions in motor cortex alone were not trained until over two years after the operation. There were also four monkeys in which both motor and somatosensory cortex were removed in infancy, and these also failed the test, though tested from 21–25 months after surgery.

Cortico-motor neuronal paths

Kuypers (1981) has suggested that the ability to move the fingers independently depends on the cortical fibres that form direct connections on to the motor neurones in the ventral cord. There are no such fibres from any subcortical motor area. In a macaque monkey these cortical fibres originate in the limb representation of motor cortex (Kuypers and Brinkman 1970; Kuypers 1981); and they terminate in the dorsal part of the ventral horn where the motor neurones for the distal musculature are situated (Kuypers 1981).

There are four reasons for implicating these fibres. The first two depend on correlational evidence, but the others draw on the results of experiments.

Development

The first reason comes from the developmental study by Lawrence and Hopkins (1976). Kuypers (1962) had shown that there are almost no direct connections from cortex to the motor neurones in a rhesus monkey at the age of four days (Fig. 2.7). The terminations are concentrated in the dorsal and lateral parts of the intermediate zone. The bulk of the direct connections are not established until well after birth, and the adult pattern is not reached until approximately eight months of age.

The crucial observation is that normal rhesus monkeys do not develop the ability to move the fingers independently until they are seven to eight months of age (Lawrence and Kuypers 1976). When the pyramidal tract was sectioned completely in four infant monkeys, the animals failed to develop the capacity for independent finger movements at the appropriate age.

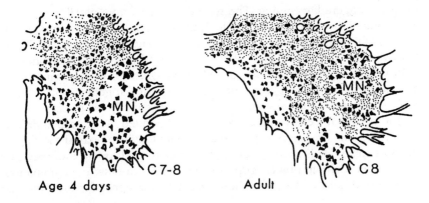

Fig. 2.7 Terminal distribution of cortocospinal fibres in lower cervical segments in infant and adult rhesus monkey. From Lawrence and Hopkins (1976).

Comparative studies

The second strand of the evidence comes from comparative studies (Philips 1971; Kuypers 1981). We can relate the capabilities of the animals to the site of termination of the pyramidal fibres.

1. Mammals with paws, such as rats or cats, lack the ability to move the digits independently. In such mammals there are few cortico-motor neuronal fibres.

2. Some mammals have hands, but hands that are only capable of a whole hand grip, not a precision grip. This is true for the prosimians and many New World monkeys (Napier 1961). In the bushbaby (*Galago*) and the squirrel monkey (*Saimiri*) there is only a very limited distribution of cortico-spinal fibres to the motorneurones of distal muscles.

3. Old World monkeys and apes have a well-developed precision grip with an opposable thumb (Napier 1961). In the macaque monkey (*Macaca*), baboon (*Papio*), and chimpanzee (Pan) there is a pronounced distribution of cortico-spinal fibres to the motorneuronal pool of the ventral horn.

4. It is of particular interest that one carnivore, the racoon (*Procyon*), has a very capable hand, but a foot that is no more specialized than that of other carnivores. There are a significant number of cortico-spinal fibres that terminate in the motor neuronal pool for the hand in the cervical cord; but no cortico-spinal fibres distribute to the motor neuronal pool for the foot in the lumbo-sacral cord.

Cell activity and grip

The last two clues come from electrophysiological studies carried out on monkeys. Cortico-motor neuronal cells can be identified by the technique of spike-triggered averaging. The record of spikes from a cell triggers the averaging of the activity of a muscle. If the firing of the cell is related to the activity of that muscle, the averaged muscle activity will be more significant than if there is no such relation. The measure' is of 'post-spike facilitation'.

Buys *et al.* (1986) recorded from cells in motor cortex in rhesus monkeys. The animals were taught to press two springs together with thumb and forefinger. Forty-seven cells were classified as direct cortico-motor neuronal cells, and all 47 cells responded when the monkeys performed this precision grip. The experiment also compared the degree of post-spike facilitation when the monkeys performed the precision grip rather than a power grip. Twenty-four cell-muscle combinations were tested, and in 18 cases there was a better signal for the precision grip.

Muscle field

There is a final reason for associating discrete movements with direct fibres from the cortex to the motor neurones. To produce discrete movements, a mechanism is needed for exciting one muscle while inhibiting other muscles. This may be difficult to achieve if the cortico-spinal fibres terminate in the intermediate layers, and the motor neurones receive a generalized influence from these layers. But discrete movements are possible if a single cortical cell innervates only a few muscles. Shinoda *et al.* (1981) have reported that a single cortico-motor neuronal cell may have collaterals such that it innervates up to four motor neuronal pools.

The power of such a device is shown by the elegant physiological studies carried out by Lemon and colleagues (Buys *et al.* 1986; Lemon 1988). Electrophysiological criteria were used to identify cortico-motor neuronal cells in the motor cortex of macaques. The experimenters selected for study cells that were related to movements of the finger and thumb muscles. Using spike-triggered averaging they plotted the 'muscle field' for each cell, that is the set of muscles to which the firing of the cell is related.

The muscle field usually consisted of only two or three out of ten finger muscles. Of the cells recorded, the activity of seven related to both the first dorsal interosseous muscle and the adductor pollicis. Both muscles are essential for performance of the precision grip.

Similar studies have been carried out for the forearm muscles by Fetz and Cheney (1987). They add one crucial finding. This is that cortico-motor neuronal cells can also influence the muscles that are the antagonists of their target muscles by collaterals that terminate on interneurones. In many cases these interneurones are thought to have inhibitory effects on the antagonist muscles. One study recorded the activity of cortico- motor

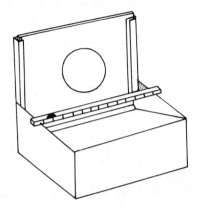

Fig. 2.8 Apparatus used for testing deviation of the wrist. The monkey sat on the far side of the apparatus and reached through the hole for food. The food is shown as a black ball. From Passingham *et al.* (1983).

neuronal cells that influenced extensor muscles, and found that the activity of 40 per cent of these cells also had indirect and reciprocal effects on the antagonists of their target muscles; for the flexor muscles the comparable figure was 18 per cent (Kasser and Cheney 1985).

Conclusion

Four reasons have been given for supposing that discrete finger movements depend on direct cortico-motor neuronal paths. The evidence supports the claim made by Kuypers (1981, p.647) that the cortico-spinal pathway is crucial for a 'high degree of fractionation of movements as exemplified by individual finger movements'. His further contention is also supported, that the direct cortico-motor neuronal fibres may provide the specialized apparatus for the production of discrete finger movements.

Discrete hand and arm movements

The claims above tempt one to look for other examples of discrete movement. It is important to note that Kuypers (1981, p. 647) took individual finger movements to be only *one* example of fractionation of movement.

Monkeys

Special tests are required to encourage animals to use the relevant joints. We devised two such tests to examine use of the wrist and forearm in two adult monkeys after the left motor cortex and somatosensory cortex (SI) had

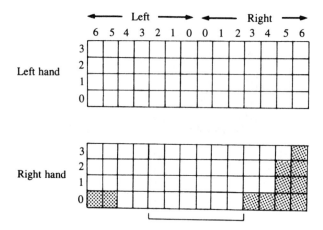

Fig. 2.9 Grid of positions in which food was placed to test the use of the wrist. The positions are seen from above. The figures on the left give four distances from the monkey, position 0 being the closest. The location of the hole through which the monkeys reached is shown at the bottom. If a square is empty the monkey could reach food at that position; if it is filled the monkey failed at that position. Data for the left and right hands of one monkey. From Passingham *et al.* (1983).

been removed from the left hemisphere (Passingham *et al.* 1983).

The first test required the monkeys to deviate the wrist in order to obtain a piece of food. The apparatus is shown in Fig. 2.8. The monkeys put their hand through a large hole in a wall of clear Perspex. The food was placed on a shelf behind the Perspex, and if the monkeys could knock the food off the shelf they could pick it up from the tray below with their other hand.

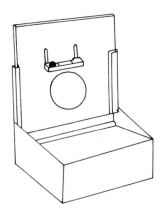

Fig. 2.10 Apparatus used for testing supination of the forearm. The monkey sat on the far side of the apparatus and reached through the hole for the food. The food is shown as a black ball. From Passingham *et al.* (1983).

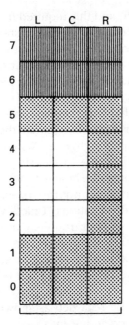

Fig. 2.11   Grid of positions in which food was placed to test the ability to supinate. The positions are seen from above. Data for the shelf in the high position. The figures to the left give distances from the monkey. R = right, C = centre, L = left. If a square is empty the monkey could reach food at that position; if it is stippled the monkey failed at that position. The monkey could not reach the far positions at all (marked with lines). Hole shown at bottom of figure. From Passingham *et al.* (1983).

The food was placed at one of 14 positions on the shelf from left to right, and the shelf was located at one of four distances behind the Perspex sheet. The 56 positions are shown in Fig. 2.9.

With the left hand the monkeys could knock the food from any position by turning the wrist. But with the right (affected) hand there were areas that the monkeys could no longer reach. These are shown by the filled squares in the figure. Neither monkey could deviate the wrist to the right to obtain food to the far right. Fig. 2.9 shows the data for one monkey which was also unable to reach the near positions to the far left. It was unfortunate that, because the hole in the Perspex was large, the monkeys could reach many of the more central positions without deviating the wrist; and because the right arm was naturally held at an angle, it was easier to reach the positions on the left without abducting the wrist.

The second test required the monkeys to supinate their forearm. The apparatus is shown in Fig. 2.10. Again the monkeys reached through a hole in Perspex. There were three positions for the food on the shelf, which was placed at one of two heights, and the apparatus was placed at one of seven distances from the monkey. The task for the monkey was as before, to knock the food off the shelf; and this required the monkey to supinate the forearm so as to bring the palm up towards the shelf.

Figure 2.11 shows the grid of positions. Both monkeys could reach all positions with the left hand. One animal was unable to reach any position with the right hand. The data for the shelf in the high position are shown for the other monkey in Fig. 2.11. There were positions that the monkey was unable to reach with the right hand; these are shown by the filled squares in the figure. Though the monkey could supinate the forearm to some degree it was not able to turn the hand right over. When the apparatus was close, the monkey was unable to help itself by raising the elbow, and it failed to supinate at all, reaching through the hole without rotating the arm.

It is clear that the monkeys had not recovered to the extent that might be supposed from casual observations. Unless they were restricted, the monkeys could reach food without trouble. Outside the formal tests there was no requirement that they bend their arm; they had only to move their bodies and use the arm as a straight rod. In contrast the formal tests required them to move one joint but not others, as in deviating the wrist.

Figures 2.9 and 2.11 can be regarded as showing a behavioural 'motor field'. The grid gives the positions in space which the animals could command by moving particular joints. It is clear that the removal of motor and somatosensory cortex restricts their command of space.

Patients

The clinical literature on recovery from hemiplegia in patients tells the same story. An account of the first 54 days after the stroke is given by Twitchell (1951). Even when the patients had greatly recovered, they were sometimes unable to move one finger at a time; if asked to move the index finger the patients tended to flex or extend the other fingers as well.

The same lack of discrete movement is apparent at the other joints. Early in recovery, patients are unable to flex the wrist or elbow without some contraction at the shoulder. Authors of the earlier literature were rightly intrigued by such 'synergistic' movements.

Colebatch and Gandevia (1989) required hemiparetic patients to contract particular groups of muscles. By using plates to restrict movement at other joints, the authors took care to ensure that the contractions were discrete, and not part of a whole arm movement. Ten patients were studied who were recovering from an acute weakness of the arm. Myometers were employed to measure strength at the shoulder, elbow, wrist, fingers, thumb, and forefinger. The degrees of impairment was measured by comparing the values for the affected and non-affected side; and measurements were taken of the relative degrees of impairment for the different muscle groups, by relating the impairment to the mean impairment for the arm as a whole.

In all but two patients the impairment for adduction or abduction of the shoulder was less than the mean impairment for the arm as a whole. But the pattern for the other muscle groups was very similar. In general, patients were impaired whether they were asked to flex or extend the elbow, wrist, or fingers. One test required the patients to abduct the index finger independently of the other fingers by means of the first dorsal interosseous muscle. The patients were no worse at this than they were at contracting other muscle groups.

The same conclusion follows from the studies of monkeys and patients. Motor cortex is specialized for the production of any discrete movements. This can be demonstrated by restricting the arm, and thus forcing the subject to attempt isolated movements.

PET scanning

It is easy to ask human subjects to make discrete voluntary movements. We measured the activity in motor cortex, using the PET scanner, while the subject carried out such movements (Colebatch *et al.* 1991*b*). There were two rest periods that served as a control: the subjects lay still resting quietly. Four periods were experimental: in each of these the subjects performed one of the movements repetitively. To ensure that the rate of movement was the same in all conditions, a tone was used to pace the movements.

The subjects were required to make one of four movements: to raise the arm by flexing the shoulder (shoulder), to open and close the hand (fist), to touch the forefinger to each of the other fingers in turn (opposition), and to abduct the index finger (index). In all cases care was taken to ensure that the subjects made isolated discrete movements and kept the other joints still.

The increase in blood flow was calculated by comparing the blood flows for each of the experimental conditions with the flows for rest. The increases in flow for motor cortex are shown in Fig. 2.12. There was a large increase in activity for the proximal movement (shoulder). The increase in activity was the same for the power grip (whole hand) as for the precison grip (finger touching).

One's first thought is that it is odd that motor cortex was activated as much by a whole hand movement as by the independent movements of the fingers. After all, monkeys with removal of motor cortex are still capable of grasping with the whole hand, but incapable of opposing thumb to forefinger (Passingham *et al.* 1983). But further thought brings three considerations to mind, and these resolve the apparent discrepancy.

Power grip in monkeys
The first consideration is that although the monkeys can pick up objects, this does not show that their power grip is normal. One has only to look at

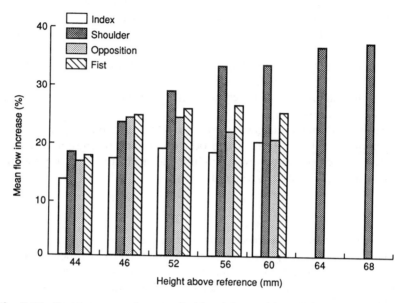

Fig. 2.12   Per cent mean increase in blood flow in the left sensorimotor cortex compared with the rest condition. The four movements are described in the text. The abscisson gives the height of the plane above the intercommissural plane. Figure from Colebatch *et al.* (1991*b*).

Fig.2.5(b) to see that it is not. There are three obvious defects. The hand is not shaped at all so as to be appropriate for the object that is to be picked up; the monkeys are clumsy; and the handgrip does not have its normal power. Black *et al.* (1975) removed the arm area unilaterally in rhesus monkeys and found that even after extensive retraining their grip was only 82 per cent of normal strength.

One tends to be impressed that the monkeys can pick things up at all and to ignore the inefficiency of their grip. It is clear that motor cortex makes a contribution to the direction of the power grip.

Learned versus unlearned movements
The second consideration is more fundamental. The monkeys were not asked to do the same thing as the human subjects. The people were asked to open and close their hand without moving the elbow or shoulder, and without being given an object to hold. The monkeys were simply given the opportunity to pick up a piece of food. They did so by reaching in a stereotyped way, at the same time clawing with the hand. In other words the human subjects were asked to open and close the hand at will, whereas the monkeys performed a whole arm movement from their unlearned repertoire. In the PET scanner,

motor cortex was activated because the subjects performed a learned act, whereas in the monkey experiment the action was unlearned.

Discrete movements of the arm
The final point is the most critical. Movements can be discrete whether performed with distal or proximal musculature. Consider the shoulder movement. The human subjects had to keep their elbow and hand unmoving while carrying out a precise movement at the shoulder. The movement differs from raising the index finger in the muscles involved; but it is alike in being a discrete voluntary movement.

There is support for this view from anatomy. Kuypers (1981) was careful not to claim that *the only* discrete movements that are directed by motor cortex are those of the distal extremities. He cited anatomical evidence that in the human brain there are cortico-motor neuronal connections to the part of the ventral horn in which there are motor neurones for the proximal musculature.

Confirmation of this comes from a study by Colebatch and Gandevia (1989) using electrophysiological techniques. They excited the human motor cortex either by magnetic stimulation or by means of scalp electrodes; and they recorded the discharge of motor units from the deltoid muscle of the shoulder. The latency of the movements that were evoked was consistent with a direct projection to the motor neurones. This finding should come as no surprise, given the skill with which the human shoulder can be used, as for example in throwing a ball.

Conclusion
The discussion started with the observation that, in the PET scanner, motor cortex is activated as much by a whole hand movement as by the independent movements of the fingers. It has taken some words to tease apart the issues but we can conclude, with relief, that the PET data are consistent with the monkey data. There is nothing to upset the conclusion that we reached earlier, that motor cortex is specialized for discrete movement.

Learned discriminative movements

Why is the primary motor area specialized for the control of discrete movements? An analogy with the primary visual area will be helpful. When striate cortex is compared with the superior colliculus, an important difference is that the striate cortex has a much higher spatial resolution. This makes possible the discrimination by visual association areas of numerous shapes or patterns. Thus if we consider monkeys, this can be shown by testing the animals on visual discriminations between pairs of stimuli shown on a TV monitor. The experimenter sets up the problems by arranging that, for each pair, one of the patterns is correct and the other incorrect. The animal wins food if it touches the correct pattern.

Now consider the primary motor cortex. Here it is the spatial resolution of movement that counts. A monkey has a wide variety of discrete movements in its repertoire. This makes possible the discrimination by motor association areas of numerous acts. Thus again, the experimenter can set a variety of discriminations. Consider three examples of monkeys making such motor discriminations.

1. We trained monkeys to deviate the wrist in the apparatus illustrated in Fig. 2.8. We used standard 'shaping' procedures. To persuade the animals to deviate the wrist to the right, we offered them food and rewarded them when they made the appropriate movement. The monkeys were first offered food on the shelf ahead of them; they could knock it off by simply reaching forwards with a straight arm. Later they were tempted to try pieces placed slightly to one side; they could still touch these by reaching with their arm at an angle. But finally, food was placed far to one side; and now the monkeys had to deviate their wrist. Thus the monkeys learned a motor discrimination: a whole arm movement did not work, and nor did bending the arm at the elbow; only deviating the wrist brought success.

2. Monkeys can also be taught to operate latches. They are faced with a box containing food. They can only open the box if they can work out how to operate the latches on the door. At first the animals try gross movements, pulling the latch or biting it, but slowly they discover the specific movement that works.

This learning is only possible if there is a mechanism that can produce a repertoire of specific movements as candidates to be tried. It is from such behavioural variants that the learning process selects.

3. Consider last the learning of very fine discriminations. Fetz and Finocchio (1975) undertook a labour of love by training monkeys to contract the flexors of the wrist, the flexors of the elbow, the extensors of the wrist, or the extensors of the elbow. Actual movement was prevented by placing the arm in a cast. The monkeys viewed records of the muscle activity and could use the feedback to control their performance.

With training, human subjects can learn to contract one of a pair of synergistic hand muscles (Gandevia and Rothwell 1987). The subjects' task was to prepare to contract the particular muscle. They viewed the record of muscular activity on an oscilloscope, and could thus ensure that no motor units were recruited in the other muscle of the pair. This is an impressive feat; but then, we can also learn to play the piano.

Summary

The motor cortex is specialized for the control of the movements of the limb and face ('manipulative movements'). It is not essential for the control of non-learned movements such as reaching and walking. Although motor cortex is active during the normal performance of such movements, subcortical mechanisms have some control over them even in the absence of motor cortex.

Motor cortex provides a mechanism for the execution of the fine behavioural variants which are selected in voluntary action. The ability to perform discrete movements depends on the direct connections from motor cortex to the motor neurones in the spinal cord.

3 Lateral premotor cortex (area 6)

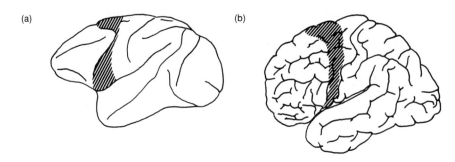

(a)   (b)

Fig. 3.1 Lateral premotor cortex in (a) the macaque monkey and (b) the human brain.

Two sorts of mechanism are required for movements to be learned. The first is the means for producing the alternatives, and this was discussed in the last chapter. The second is the means for selecting the movement that it is appropriate to execute. This is the topic of the present chapter.

Suppose we teach a monkey a conditional motor task. Given a blue patch on a TV monitor the monkey must pull the joystick, and given a red patch the monkey must move it to the right. The executive mechanisms of motor cortex must be able to direct the relevant flexion and extension movements of the wrist and forearm.

But how does motor cortex know which movements to make? Information about the context must be taken into account if the appropriate movement is to be made. It is the claim of this chapter, and the next, that it is through the premotor areas (Fig. 3.1) that motor cortex receives much of its instructions. This is not an original claim, but it is one that is proclaimed here with missionary zeal.

Inputs to motor cortex

Projections to motor cortex

If this claim is to be plausible, it must be shown that the premotor areas can influence the motor cortex. Figure 3.2 provides a summary diagram of the

Fig. 3.2 Projections to motor cortex from parietal and premotor cortex.

cortical areas that project to motor cortex. Details of these projections are summarized below.

Parietal cortex
The cortical projections to motor cortex have been described by Jones *et al.* (1978), Leichnetz (1986), and Ghosh *et al.* (1987). There are direct projections to motor cortex from areas 3a, 1, and 2 of the primary somatosensory area (SI), and also from the secondary somatosensory area (SII) (Fig. 3.2). There are also direct projections from areas 5 and 7b, the somatic association areas of the parietal lobe. There is no significant projection from area 3b of SI; this is significant because most cells in 3b respond to cutaneous sensation, whereas a large proportion of the cells in areas 2 and 5 respond to movement of the joints (Mountcastle and Powell 1959; Mountcastle *et al.* 1975).

Premotor cortex
The second contribution to motor cortex comes from the premotor areas (Fig. 3.2). This is best demonstrated by placing horseradish peroxidase in parts of the motor cortex. Muakkassa and Strick (1979) showed with this

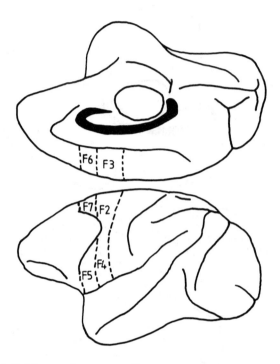

Fig. 3.3 Subdivisions of premotor cortex as suggested by staining with cytochrome oxidase. Based on Matelli *et al.* (1985) and Luppino *et al.* (1991).

method that there are heavy projections to motor cortex from the lateral premotor cortex (LPC) and medial premotor cortex (MPC), and that there is also an independent projection from another premotor area in the lower bank of the cingulate sulcus. The projections from the medial premotor areas have been confirmed by Dum and Strick (1991).

We also know that the connections from the lateral premotor area respect the mapping of the motor cortex. The projections from the the cortex under the bow of the arcuate sulcus terminate in the 'hand' area of MI as identified by microstimulation; and the projections from the lower convexity of the lateral premotor cortex terminate in the 'face' area (Godschalk *et al.* 1984; Strick 1985).

There are two areas that are traditionally included in the premotor cortex although they do not send direct connections to motor cortex (Pandya and Barnes 1987; Matelli *et al.* 1991; Luppino *et al.* 1991). They are shown in Figs 3.3 and 3.4. One is the anterior part of the medial premotor cortex, labelled F6 by Matelli *et al.* (1991); the other is the anterior part of the dorsal lateral premotor cortex, labelled 6DR by Barbas and Pandya (1987) and F7 by Matelli *et al.* (1991). However, these areas are interconnected with more posterior parts of area 6, and these in turn have direct connections with motor cortex (Pandya and Barnes 1987; Luppino *et al.* 1990).

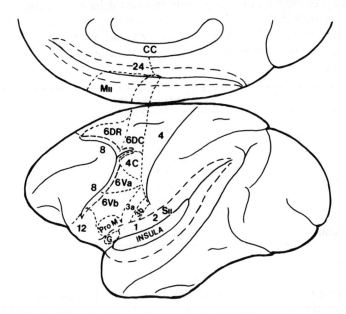

Fig. 3.4   Cytoarchitectural divisions of the lateral premotor cortex as suggested by Barbas and Pandya (1987).

Thalamus
The final contribution to motor cortex comes from the thalamus. The heaviest projection is from two groups of nuclei: the anterior group is labelled VA by Ilinksy and Kultas-Ilinsky (1987) and VA plus VLa by Jones (1985); the posterior group is labelled VL by Ilinsky and Kultas-Ilinsky (1987) and VLp by Jones (1985).

The significance of the distinction is that the basal ganglia project to the more anterior group and the cerebellar nuclei connect to the more posterior group (Jones 1985; Ilinsky and Kultas-Ilinsky 1987). Both groups of thalamic nuclei send direct connections to motor cortex (Asanuma *et al.* 1983; Matelli *et al.* 1989; Holsapple *et al.* 1991).

The contributions from parietal cortex, premotor cortex, and thalamus appear to be of similar weight. This is shown by an experiment by Ghosh *et al.* (1987) in which they injected horseradish peroxidase into much of the limb area of motor cortex in a macaque (animal M3). Table 3.1 gives the number of cells labelled in areas outside the motor cortex itself. As a rough guide, we may say that a third of the contribution is from parietal cortex (SI, SII, area 5), a third from the premotor areas (LPC, MPC, cingulate), and a third from the thalamus. Each of these relays could be important in providing a mechanism by which movements can be influenced by the context.

Table 3.1 Per centage of retrogradely labelled cells in a monkey with an injection of HRP in the hand area of motor cortex. LPC = lateral premotor cortex, MPC = medial premotor cortex, VA and VL = nucleus ventralis anterior and ventralis lateralis of Ilinsky and Kultas-Ilinsky (1987). Data from Ghosh *et al.* (1987).

Areas	Labelled cells (%)	
LPC	7.2	
MPC	17.1	26.9
24	2.6	
SI, SII	18.8	
5, 7b	18.1	36.9
VA	5.7	
VL	19.1	24.8
Other thalamus	11.1	11.1

Pyramidal outputs

The premotor areas can also directly influence movement via projections through the pyramidal tract to the spinal cord. The size of the contribution to the pyramidal tract has been demonstrated by Strick and his colleagues (Martino and Strick 1987; Hutchins *et al.* 1988; Dum and Strick 1991), who made injections of horseradish peroxidase (HRP) into the upper or lower cervical segments in macaques. Figure 3.5 shows the pattern of labelling in frontal cortex for an injection at the level of C2. The findings were as follows.

1. There were clusters of labelled cells in the lateral premotor cortex. These were found in the posterior bank of the lower limb of the arcuate sulcus and on the lateral surface in and around the superior precentral sulcus.

2. There was also a dense cluster of labelled cells on the convexity of the medial premotor cortex.

3. Finally there were separate clusters in the upper and lower bank of the cingulate sulcus (Hutchins *et al.* 1988; Dum and Strick 1991).

Size of premotor cortex

The premotor areas are large in a monkey, but it is of note that they are especially well developed in the human brain. Figures 3.1 and 4.1 show the extent of area 6 as charted by Brodmann (1925) for the human brain. Von Bonin (1944) compared the extent of areas 4 and 6 in a macaque and a human brain. He found that area 6 formed 51.2 per cent of the precentral tissue in the macaque and 85.8 per cent in the human brain. These figures

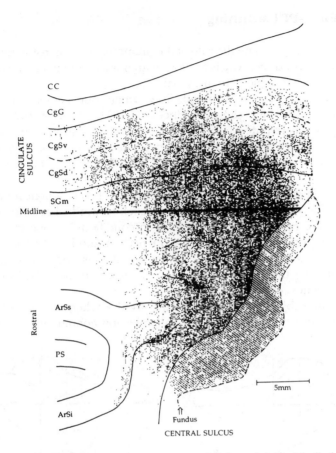

Fig. 3.5 Map of cortico-spinal neurones in the frontal lobe labelled by HRP injected into the contralateral dorsal funiculus at C2. Each labelled cell is shown by a dot. ArSi = inferior limb of arcuate sulcus, PS = sulcus principalis, ArSs = superior limb of arcuate sulcus, SGm = superior frontal gyrus, CgSd = cingulate sulcus, dorsal bank, CgSv = cingulate sulcus, ventral bank, CgG = cingulate gyrus, CC = corpus callosum. Figure from Dum and Strick (1991).

have proved reliable: Blinkov and Gleser (1968) give figures of 42.9 per cent for a baboon (*Papio*) and 88.2 per cent for the human brain.

It is unlikely that the development of area 6 in the human brain reflects a specialization for executive functions. It is true that there are pyramidal projections from area 6 as well as from area 4. But the total number of fibres in the pyramidal tract of the human brain is very close to the number predicted for a simian primate of our size (Passingham 1981). It will be argued in this chapter and the next that area 6 plays a role in the selection of movement. The development of area 6 in the human brain may therefore be related to the importance of learning.

Selection—PET scanning

If one wishes to examine the role of the premotor areas in instructing motor cortex, the most direct way is to work with human volunteers: it is quicker to instruct human subjects than animals.

We measured cerebral blood flow while our subjects performed movements in the PET scanner (Deiber *et al.* 1991). In the control condition the subject was required to make the same movement on every occasion. Whenever a tone sounded the subject pushed the joystick forwards. We called this the 'fixed' condition because the subject had to make repetitive movements.

In the 'selection' conditions the subject had a choice. Whenever the tone sounded the subjects could push the joystick forwards, backwards, to the left or to the right. There were four such conditions. In one the subjects moved the joystick in a random sequence; in another they followed a learned sequence; and in two other conditions their response was determined by the type of tone. The conditions are described in greater detail in the next chapter.

Thus, the subjects always moved the joystick when they heard a tone. The difference between the fixed and selection conditions is that in the

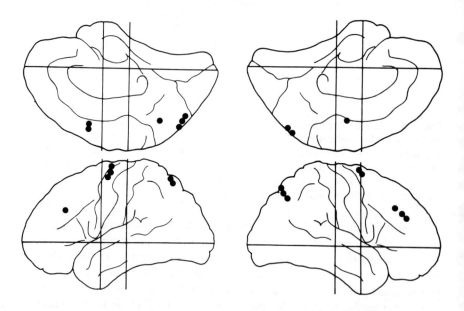

Fig. 3.6 Location of peaks of maximal significant change in regional cerebral blood flow between the four selection conditions taken together and the fixed conditions. Lateral view below, medial above; left hemisphere on left, right hemisphere on right. From Deiber *et al.* (1991).

fixed condition they had no choice, whereas in the selection conditions they made a choice each time.

The experiment allows a simple test of the view that the premotor areas play a role in the selection of learned movements. The regional blood flow to these areas can be derived, for each condition, from the PET scans. The relevant measure is of the flow to the premotor areas over and above any general increase in the global flow of blood to the brain. The critical comparison is of the flow to the premotor areas for the combined selection conditions compared with the flow for the fixed condition.

We found a significant effect of selection. For the selection conditions there was an additional increase in regional blood flow to the lateral and medial premotor areas, over and above the increase for the fixed condition. Figure 3.6 shows the localization of the peaks at which the increases were most statistically significant.

It is important to note that there was no significant increase in blood flow in motor cortex flow over and above the global flow. An inelegance in the study is that in the fixed condition only one movement is made, whereas in the selection conditions four different movements are made. None the less, the increase in motor cortex was the same in the two cases. This increases our confidence that the selection effect in the lateral and medial premotor cortex really represents the fact that selection occurs in one case and not in the other.

This experiment shows clearly that the lateral and medial premotor areas play a role in the selection of movements. This influence could be exerted via cortical or pyramidal projections.

Selection and premotor cortex in monkeys

Conditional tasks

We have also taught monkeys to select between limb movements. This can be done by training them on conditional motor tasks. The monkey has to move a handle in one of two ways depending on the context.

In our first experiment we presented a colour cue on a central panel which the monkey pushed aside to gain access to the handle (Halsband and Passingham 1985). In another experiment the background behind the lever could be lit red or blue (Passingham 1988). In both experiments one colour told the animal to pull the handle, and the other colour to rotate it.

In both experiments we removed the lateral premotor cortex from both hemispheres. A representative lesion is shown in Fig. 3.7, taken from the

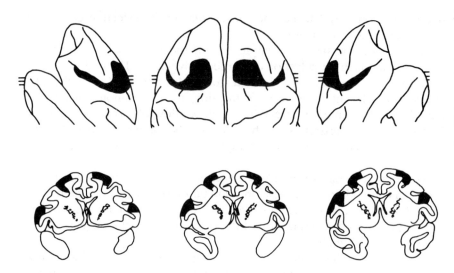

Fig. 3.7 Representative lesion in lateral premotor cortex. Upper figures show lateral and dorsal surface, lower figures show three coronal sectionns taken at the levels marked by the lines in the upper figures. Lesion shown in black. From Passingham (1985).

experiment by Halsband and Passingham (1982, 1985). The animals were retrained two weeks after surgery. All six animals were very impaired in their post-operative performance. Figure 3.8 gives the trials to relearn the task for the operated and unoperated animals in the first experiment.

I have described these experiments first for self-advertisement; they came from our laboratory. However, exactly the same result was obtained independently and at the same time by Petrides (1982). This bolsters one's confidence in the result.

Petrides (1982) taught his monkeys to grasp a handle if one object appeared in the background and to touch a button if another object appeared. In three monkeys the tissue was removed from the upper limb of the arcuate sulcus: the removal included both the posterior bank (area 6) and the anterior bank (area 8), and also the tissue on the dorsal convexity of area 8 anterior to the upper limb of the sulcus. This lesion is illustrated in Petrides (1985b). After surgery the monkeys with arcuate lesions failed to relearn the task in 1020 trials. The data are given in Fig. 3.9.

Using information from the cues

These results would be of little interest if the animals were poor at using information from the cues or at executing the movements required. But there is direct evidence that the animals can use information from the cues. This has been shown by both groups of experimenters.

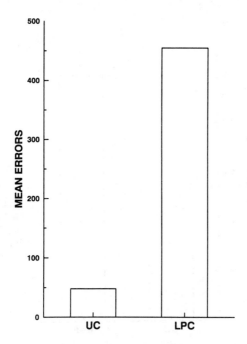

Fig. 3.8 Mean errors taken to relearn a visual conditional motor task in which the cues were colours and the monkeys responded by pulling or rotating a handle. UC = 3 unoperated control animals, LPC = 3 animals with lateral premotor lesions. Data from Halsband and Passingham (1985).

We trained monkeys on a visual conditional task on which they had to choose one object (a sphere) given one colour, and another object (a block) given another colour (Halsband and Passingham 1985). The task is illustrated in Fig. 5.7 (p. 110). Monkeys with bilateral LPC lesions learned this task at a normal rate (Fig. 3.10).

In a similar demonstration Petrides (1987) taught monkeys to choose one box (the lit one) given one object, and the other box (the unlit one) given another object. Monkeys with dorsal LPC lesions learned normally (Fig 3.11).

Clearly the monkeys in these two studies could not have learned had they not been able to use information from the instructing cues. The reason for the success of the animals on these tasks will be discussed in Chapter 5.

If further proof were needed, it is provided by an elegant experiment carried out by Petrides (1986). He compared two tasks which look very similar at first glance. In both the monkeys were trained to open a box when object A was presented in the background, and to refrain from opening it when object B was presented. In both versions the monkeys found food in the the box when shown object A. The difference between

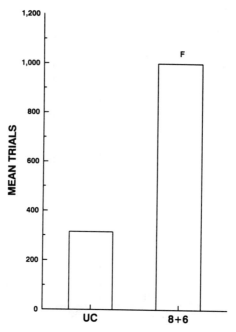

Fig. 3.9   Mean trials taken to learn a visual conditional motor task in which the cues were objects and the monkeys responded by gripping a handle or touching a button. UC = unoperated control animals, 8+6 = monkeys with lesions in area 8 and dorsal lateral premotor cortex. F = failed. Data plotted from Petrides (1982).

the versions is in the outcomes on trials when object B was presented: on the 'asymmetrical' version they were not rewarded for withholding a response, whereas on the 'symmetrical' version they were given food if they failed to respond. Thus, the animals could solve the 'asymmetrical' version by learning when food was or was not available; but on the 'asymmetrical' version they had to learn which response to make to gain the food

Monkeys with dorsal LPC lesions were given these 'go, no-go' tasks to learn. The monkeys had no trouble in learning the asymmetrical version, but they were very slow to learn the symmetrical version. Yet in both versions the animals had to attend to the objects that served as cues. The animals were clearly able to take in the information from the cues.

But there is an important experiment which might be taken to challenge this conclusion. Rizzolatti *et al.* (1983) made small unilateral lesions in the posterior bank of the arcuate sulcus (area 6) in monkeys. They tested the animals in the first two weeks after surgery and found that the monkeys failed to respond to stimuli in the contralateral half of space.

However, the neglect was much more severe in the first two weeks after operation than in succeeding weeks. By eight to ten weeks the only

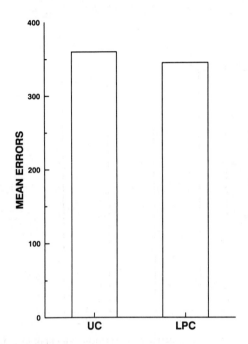

Fig. 3.10 Mean errors to learn a visual conditional task in which the cues are colours and the monkeys choose between objects. UC = 3 unoperated control animals, LPC = 3 animals with lateral premotor lesions. Data from Halsband and Passingham (1985).

indication was that, when presented with two pieces of food, the monkeys tended to react to food presented on the side ipsilateral to the lesion, in preference to food presented on the contralateral side.

In our experiments (Passingham (1985c, 1988) and those by Petrides (1987), the monkeys were not trained in the first two weeks after surgery. The monkeys never failed to respond to the cues. In the experiment by Petrides (1987) we know that the monkeys noticed the cues because they were not allowed to respond until the cues appeared.

Execution of the movements

There is no difficulty in demonstrating that the animals can make the required movements To take first the experiments carried out by Petrides (1982): he only required his monkeys to make very simple movements, gripping the handle or touching the button. Even monkeys with unilateral lesions in motor cortex can perform movements of this sort (Passingham *et al.* 1983).

In our experiments (Halsband and Passingham 1985; Passingham 1985c, 1988) the monkeys had to pull or rotate a handle. We have direct evidence

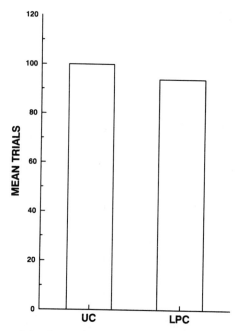

Fig. 3.11   Mean trials taken to learn a visual conditional task in which the cues are objects and the monkeys choose between a box that is lit and a box that is not lit. UC = unoperated control animals, LPC = monkeys with lesions in lateral premotor cortex. Data replotted from Petrides (1987).

that monkeys with LPC lesions can pull or rotate a handle without trouble. We have trained monkeys on a 'motor reversal' task. On each trial the monkey must choose whether to pull or rotate a handle. A simple rule specifies which movement is correct: on any day only one of the two movements is correct, but if on one day the animal reaches a criterion level of performance, the conditions reverse and on the next day the other movement is defined as correct. Thus the animal learns a series of reversals.

We found that monkeys with bilateral LPC lesions performed as well as unoperated animals in learning these reversals (Chen *et al.*, in preparation). They could not have done so had they had problems in executing the relevant movements.

This is not to claim that premotor lesions have no effects on the control of movement; only that animals with these lesions can execute the movements required for the learning tasks. There could, of course, be subtle changes in the control of movement that are not obvious when watching the animals. For example, if an observer simply watches a monkey with an MPC lesion as it picks up food, nothing untoward will come to notice. But by using film to analyse the performance in detail, Brinkman (1984) was able to show that the monkeys are in fact poor at shaping their hand when they pick up food from small holes.

Similarly, if a monkey with an LPC lesion is required to reach for a peanut the observer fails to detect any impairment. But in fact the monkey's reaching is not fully normal. This became apparent when we faced monkeys with a vertical screen with an array of 121 holes arranged in 12 rows (Passingham 1985*c*). On each trial there was a peanut in one hole which the monkey could obtain by using a finger to push it out of the hole and on to a tray below. Of the six monkeys with LPC lesions that we have tested, five made more errors than control animals in reaching out to push a peanut from a hole. The monkeys were slightly clumsy, sometimes hitting the Perspex wall between holes and occasionally pushing their finger into the neighbouring hole.

Immediately after surgery, animals with LPC lesions show clear motor impairments (Passingham 1985*c*). In the first week or two after surgery the animals tend to be clumsy in their movements, and some animals appear stiff and awkward as they walk about the cage. At first the monkeys grasp small objects such as peanuts with their whole hand rather than with finger and thumb, and they are clumsy when they pick up objects or take them from the experimenter. A similar pattern has been reported by Deuel (1977) and by Traverse and Latto (1986). However, within two weeks the animals are greatly improved.

To repeat, the issue is not whether premotor lesions have effects on movement but whether, at the time at which they were tested, the animals could make the movements required for the task. And the answer is that in the learning experiments cited above they could (Petrides 1982; Halsband and Passingham 1985; Passingham 1985*c*, 1988).

Selection and premotor cortex in patients

It is easier to work with human subjects. Petrides (1985*a*) devised a version of the conditional motor task that was suitable to give to patients in the neurological clinic. The task does not start until it has been established that the patients can discriminate the relevant cues and demonstrate the relevant movements.

The patients are required to learn six different postures of the hand. To give three examples of the postures: in one the forefinger is extended and the other fingers flexed; in another the fingers are flexed in a fist; and in a third the palm is up and the fingers are extended.

The task is more difficult than that used for animals, in that the subjects have to learn the meaning of six rather than two visual cues. Petrides used small coloured objects as cues. The subject must learn to make one posture given colour A, another posture given colour B, and so on. As in the

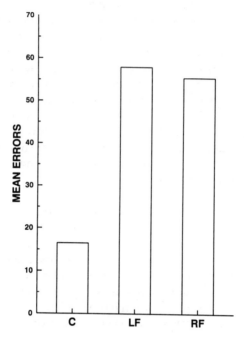

Fig. 3.12   Mean errors to learn a visual conditional motor task in which the cues are colours and the responses were gestures. C = control subjects, LF = patients with left frontal lesions, RF = patients with right frontal lesions. Replotted from Petrides (1985*a*).

experiments with animals, the subject learns by making a response and then finding out whether that response is correct or incorrect.

On each trial the tester pushes an object of one colour towards the subject, and requires the subject to produce the relevant posture of the hand. At first the subject can only guess and must wait to be told by the tester whether the guess is correct or incorrect; the trial continues until the subject produces the correct response. On the next trial a different colour is presented, and again the subject must find the correct response. The task continues until the subject has learned the correct response given each of the six colours.

Petrides (1985*a*) tested twenty patients with frontal lobectomies, and compared their performance with that of patients with temporal lobectomies and normal control subjects. None of the patients had trouble in executing the responses. But the patients with frontal excisions were very slow to learn the task, and this was true whether the excisions were on the left or right side. The results are shown in Fig. 3.12

While it is easier to interpret the results of tests carried out on people rather than animals, it is a problem that the lesions are less discrete in

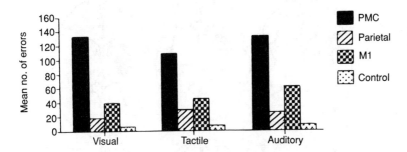

Fig. 3.13 Mean errors to learn a visual conditional motor task in which the cues were colours and the responses were gestures. From Halsband and Freund (1990).

patients. Petrides (1985*a*) provides drawings of the extent of the lesions made at the time of surgery. Many of the lobectomies are very large and clearly include not only prefrontal but also premotor cortex. Casual inspection, with a biased eye, suggests that the lateral premotor cortex is invaded in most of the patients who perform poorly on the conditional motor task. But the diagrams are only placed on outline drawings of the brain, and no comparison with a stereotaxic atlas of the human brain is possible.

We replicated the findings of this study, studying ten patients with frontal lobe lesions, of whom four had undergone unilateral lobectomies for intractable epilepsy (Canavan *et al.* 1989*b*). The cues were again colours, but the responses were chosen to be more similar to those required in the studies on monkeys. Instead of producing hand gestures the subjects were required to move a joystick in one of six different ways. Seven of the ten patients with frontal lesions were slow to learn. However, the information available on the lesions is again not adequate to allow a proper assessment of the extent to which the lateral premotor cortex was damaged in these patients.

Fortunately, Halsband and Freund (1990) have published data on patients with premotor lesions. In one respect the lesions are less easy to delineate; they are infarcts or tumours, not clean surgical excisions. But on the other hand the lesion diagrams are more precise; the authors have reconstructed the lesions on to the proportional grid system of the atlas by Talairach *et al.* (1967).

Ten patients had lesions that included parts of the lateral premotor cortex. In three of these the lesion extended into the motor cortex, and in two into the medial premotor cortex. There were a further two patients with lesions that mainly involved the medial premotor cortex.

All the patients were tested on a version of Petrides' (1985*a*) visual conditional motor task. The cues were coloured plaques and the responses were hand postures. All patients with premotor lesions (PMC) made many more errors in learning the task than control subjects. The two patients with

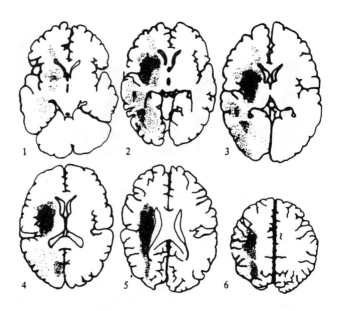

Fig. 3.14 Six transverse CT sections. The overlap between the lesions of the different patients is shown in black. From Kertesz and Ferro (1984).

lesions in motor cortex (M1) made many fewer errors. The data are shown in Fig. 3.13.

Selection and apraxia in patients

Patients with premotor lesions can also shows the symptoms of ideomotor apraxia. Faglioni and Basso (1985) present 16 cases from the literature in which the lesions appear to be restricted to premotor cortex. Basso *et al.* (1987) give the CT scans of a further six patients in which the lesion appears to involve premotor cortex, but not parietal cortex.

It is, of course, considered more usual for ideomotor apraxia to result from a parietal lesion. However, Kertesz and Ferro (1984) have made a careful study of CT scans, and they found that the critical factor was not the extent of the lesions across the cortex, but the extent in depth. Figure 3.14 shows standard transverse sections showing the area of overlap between the lesions of nine patients with small lesions and moderate to severe apraxia. There are two important findings. The first is that in seven of the nine patients the lesion extensively invaded the white matter. The second is that the area that was common to the lesions lay in the white matter of the frontal lobe. A lesion in this place will probably sever fibres running from parietal cortex to the premotor and prefrontal areas, and may also sever fibres running from parietal lobe to the basal ganglia and cerebellum.'

Analysis of ideomotor apraxia

In discussing conditional learning above, it was argued that it is essential to check that the instructing cues can be understood, and the relevant movements can be executed. The same demonstration is necessary when testing apraxic patients. Most patients with apraxia are also aphasic; and thus the observations would be of little interest if the patients failed to understand the verbal instructions. Similarly, a stroke that involves premotor cortex often extends into the motor areas; and thus the patients will tend to have a unilateral paralysis or paresis. Furthermore, premotor lesions may directly cause motor problems, such as a weakness of shoulder and hip muscles (Freund and Hummelsheim 1985).

Instructions
There are two reasons for rejecting the notion that apraxia is simply the result of aphasia.

1. There are cases of apraxia without aphasia. Kertesz *et al.* (1984) have described six severely aphasic patients who were not apraxic, and four cases in which there was mild aphasia but moderately severe apraxia. The reason for the usual association between aphasia and apraxia is that the lesion that causes one symptom also invades the tissue that causes the other.

That this can be so is well illustrated by the case of oral apraxia resulting from infarcts in the territory of the middle cerebral artery. Patients with oral apraxia are poor at putting out their tongue, blowing up their cheeks and so on when asked to do so. Tognala and Vignolo (1980) analysed the CT scans of 28 patients with oral apraxia; 27 of these patients were also aphasic. The results are illuminating. In many cases the lesions were very extensive: they included a large expanse of the lateral neocortex; and penetrated deep into subcortical structures. Typically the lesions included the depth of the insula, and disrupted the underlying fibres. Most involved the internal capsule and the basal ganglia. Looking at the reconstructions of the lesions it is not surprising that patients who are apraxic are usually aphasic. All the lesions, whether large or small, included both the face area of premotor cortex and Broca's area which lies adjacent in the operculum.

2. There is a second reason for thinking that apraxia is not simply a failure to understand the instructions: the patients can be given non-verbal instructions using one of.two simple methods (De Renzi 1985). The first is to ask the patient to copy gestures that are modelled by the tester; for example the tester salutes, and invites the patient to do the same. It is rarely

difficult to make the patient understand that the task is to copy. That the patient understands this is proved by the fact that the patient attempts movements, even if the copy is poor.

The second method is to show the patient a series of objects, and to require the patient to demonstrate in mime how the objects should be used. The patient is not allowed to grasp the object, but must perform the movements in mid-air. That the patient understands the nature of the task is shown by the attempts that the patient makes. If, when shown a pair of scissors, the patient makes the movements of cutting with a knife, it is clear that the patient has grasped the point of the exercise but is apraxic.

Execution

It is as important to be sure that the patient's errors do not result from a disorder of execution. If patients have a paralysis or paresis of the right arm, they can be tested by asking them to demonstrate the movements with their left arm.

In the most dramatic cases there can be convincing evidence that the patients are able to make the relevant movements, but fail to make the appropriate movement when required. This evidence can be provided by a dissociation between the performance of the subject when instructed in one way and when instructed in another. Consider the case of a patient who was asked to blow, and failed to do so even though he understood what was required; yet, when presented with a lit candle the patient blew it out. It is clear that the impairment was not one of blowing, but of blowing to command.

Similar dissociations are not that uncommon. In one study De Renzi *et al.* (1982) found that 85 per cent of the patients who were poor at copying gestures were also poor at using gestures to mime the use of an object; but there were also 15 patients who were poor at imitating but not at miming, and 13 patients who were poor at miming but were able to imitate. In a later study De Renzi and Lucchelli (1988) compared the scores that patients obtained on both tasks. The correlation was low, only 0.44; in other words there were many patients who could execute the required action given one instruction, but not given another.

The conclusion must be that the problem need not be simply one of execution. There are apraxic patients in which there is a problem of selecting the *appropriate* action given the context. This is not to claim that this is necessarily true for all patients with ideomotor apraxia or that it is the only problem. Apraxic patients often produce movements that are distorted or incomplete.

Ideomotor apraxia and selection

Ideomotor apraxia has been treated as analagous to failure on a conditional motor learning task. This is not a view that would be popular among clinical neurologists. They have traditionally regarded apraxia as the failure to perform movements to command. In one case the correct movement is specified by learning and in the other by verbal instructions.

But the task for the subjects is similar in both cases. They must 'recall' the appropriate movement. This is true however the motor programmes were set up in the brain. The task is similar to that posed by tests of human verbal memory in which the subject is required to produce a word from memory. The task of verbal recall differs from a recognition task in that no words are presented from which the subject must choose.

When a person tries to find a word some search must take place to locate the word in memory and retrieve it. The production of movements must involve a similar process. If movements are learned then some search must be made for the appropriate movement given the present context. Consider a visual conditional motor task: given the colour red the subject must access the movement that is associated with it. The same operation is carried out by a word processor when it searches for a document given the name that has been entered on the keyboard.

Thus, whether the subject is a monkey or a patient we may say that the effect of damage to the lateral premotor cortex is to impair the retrieval of the appropriate movement given the instruction. It does not matter whether the instruction is given by learning, by word of mouth, or by mime.

Apraxia and monkeys

It is not usual to describe monkeys as 'apraxic'. Indeed, neurologists have generally assumed that apraxia is a disorder that is unique to people. However, LPC lesions render both patients and monkeys incompetent at producing simple movements when required, even though they can execute the movements and understand the instructions.

The neurologist could point to the fact that the monkeys manipulate handles, whereas the patients perform gestures in mid-air, as in saluting. There are two reasons for not being concerned about the difference.

1. The first reason is that monkeys can also be taught to make gestures. Deuel has taught monkeys to reach up and touch the ear, not a perfect salute but good enough for our purposes (Deuel 1977; Deuel and Dunlop 1979). The instruction was provided by the colour of a plaque: if it was red the monkey was required to touch its ear, if white to do nothing. In two separate experiments the tissue was removed from dorsolateral area 6 and dorsal area 8. The effect was that the monkeys no longer made the correct movement when the red cue appeared; instead they reached forward to the plaque. They had to be retrained to reach up and touch their ear.

We have also taught monkeys to make gestures in mid-air (Thaler and Passingham 1989). The monkeys were required to raise their arm in order to win food. When their hand cut an infra-red beam a peanut was delivered to a food-well below. The animals were unable to see the beam. Thus, whenever they wanted food they raised their arm. This task will be described in greater detail in the next chapter.

2. There is a second reason for not being overly concerned over the differences in the way in which patients and monkeys are tested. Consider the conditional motor task used by Halsband and Passingham (1985). The monkeys are presented with a handle which can be pulled or rotated. It is true that the monkeys perform by using an object; but that is an irrelevance. The object is the same object on each trial, and it provides no information to assist retrieval of the appropriate movement. The situation is logically no different from requiring the monkey to make pulling or turning movements in mid-air; the handle supports the movement, but that is all.

Apraxia is an impairment in producing movements at will. The movements are voluntary because the instructions are arbitrary. It is as arbitrary that a red plaque should mean that the monkey should touch its ear as that the word 'salute' should mean that the person should salute. It is only convention that leads neurologists to test apraxia by giving commands or putting on demonstrations.

Cortical inputs to premotor cortex

We have argued that the lateral premotor cortex plays a role in the selection of movements. If this is true, we should be able to show two things. First, it should receive the information relevant to the selection of movements. Second, it should contain cells that change their firing when specific movements are performed, and when new movements are learned. The next section deals with the cortical inputs. There is also a massive subcortical input to the premotor areas from the thalamus, but the details of this will be described later (Chapter 8). The last three sections deal with the results of recording studies.

Anatomy

Area 6 can be divided broadly into three parts: ventrolateral, dorsolateral, and medial cortex. The divisions are demonstrated by the cytoarchitectonic studies of Barbas and Pandya (1987) and the cytochrome oxidase studies of Matelli *et al.* (1985, 1991). The maps are shown in Figs 3.3 and 3.4.

The inputs from parietal cortex respects the broad divisions of the premotor cortex. Figure. 3.15 shows these in diagram form, and the studies are summarized below.

1. Medial 6 receives a major input from medial parietal area 5 (Jones *et al.* 1978; Bowker and Coulter 1981; Dum and Strick 1991).

2) Dorsolateral 6 receives from the dorsal parietal area 5 (Petrides and Pandya 1984).

Fig. 3.15 Cortico-cortical inputs to premotor cortex from parietal association cortex. For references see text.

3) Ventrolateral 6 receives from the ventral parietal area 7b (Petrides and Pandya 1984; Godschalk *et al.* 1984; Cavada and Goldman-Rakic 1989)

Recording

We can try to identify the nature of these inputs by examining evidence as to the functions of parietal areas 5 and 7b. Both area 5 (Pearson and Powell 1985) and area 7b (Robinson and Burton 1980) have a full representation of the limbs and face.

These areas differ in their input from the somatosensory areas. Area 5 receives mainly from area 2 of the primary somatosensory cortex (S1) (Vogt and Pandya 1978; Pandya and Selzer 1982). Area 7b receives a large input from SII (Neal *et al.* 1987). It is controversial whether there is an input from SI: Vogt and Pandya (1978) and Andersen *et al.* (1990) claim evidence for such a projection, but Neal *et al.* (1987) were unable to demonstrate it.

Both in area 2 and in area 5 there is a large proportion of cells that are responsive to passive movements of the joints and tendons (Mountcastle and Powell 1959; Mountcastle *et al.* 1975). Both in SII (Whitsel *et al.* 1969) and in 7b (Robinson and Burton 1980; Hyvarinen 1981) many cells respond to touch to the body surface; but there has been no proper study of sensitivity to proprioceptive stimuli in area 7b.

Cells in area 5
Recordings have been taken in area 5 in awake monkeys while they actively maintained a limb position (Georgopoulos *et al.* 1984). The monkeys were trained to hold a manipulandum in one of nine positions over a working surface by moving the shoulder and elbow. Eighty-two per cent of the responsive cells in area 5 varied their discharge according to the position of the limb.

Recordings have also been taken while monkeys performed conditional motor tasks (Seal *et al.* 1983; Crammond and Kalaska 1989). The activity of many of the cells is related to a specific movement. Furthermore, if the animal is required to wait before responding, many directional cells are active during the delay (Crammond and Kalaska 1989).

These results suggest that the dorsolateral premotor cortex receives information about movement from area 5. Hummelsheim *et al.* (1988) have recorded in area 6 in monkeys while the elbow was passively flexed or extended. They report a proprioceptive input to both the dorsal and medial part of area 6. Twenty-seven per cent of the responsive cells reacted to the displacement of the joint.

Cells in area 7b
There are cells in 7b which are active in relation to movement. Hyvarinen (1981) reported cells that changed their activity when the monkeys actively moved their mouth or hand. Godschalk and Lemon (1989) recorded while monkeys performed a task on which they had been trained. The animals were required to wait for one second after seeing food in a particular location and before retrieving it. The authors found that many of the cells were active in relation to a specific movement, and continued to fire while the monkeys prepared to respond.

It is clear that parietal area 7b contributes a somatic input to ventrolateral 6, but the nature of the input is unclear. Rizzolatti *et al.* (1981) report that there are many cells in ventrolateral 6 that respond to tactile stimuli to the face or hand. However, the activity of the cells may be related, not to the nature of the tactile stimulus, but rather to the action that the animal takes in response

PET scanning
There is independent evidence from PET scanning that the parietal association cortex plays a role in movement. Figure 3.6 shows the areas that

are active in the human brain when subjects select movements with a joystick (Deiber *et al.* 1991). The comparison is with the fixed condition in which the subject always moves the joystick in the same direction. In the selection conditions there is activity in the superior and medial parietal association cortex.

The next chapter discusses this experiment in more detail; in particular it describes the results for each of the four selection tasks separately. On one of the tasks (random) the subject was asked to move the joystick at will, choosing the direction randomly. On this task there was also activation in the anterior part of the right inferior parietal cortex (Fig. 4.13). This area is designated PF in the human brain (Eidelberg and Galaburda 1984) and macaque brain (von Bonin and Bailey 1947). In the monkey it is probably equivalent to area 7b.

Conclusion

A major input to the lateral premotor cortex comes from the parietal association cortex. It is likely that this carries information about the position of the limbs and jaw, and the expression of the face. This information is coded in proprioceptive coordinates. It is of especial importance when the individual must select between movements.

Movement–related cells

If the lateral premotor cortex is involved in the selection of movements, there should be cells that respond differently 'according to the movement to be made. Physiological studies of cells in the lateral premotor cortex indicate that this requirement is fulfilled. There are cells that alter their activity before movement, cells that fail to respond if no movement is made, and cells that behave differently depending on the movement to be made. Each of these three claims will be documented in turn.

Movement–related cells

In a study of cells in the lateral premotor cortex, Weinrich and Wise (1982) classified cells as 'movement–related' if the change of activity was synchronized with and preceded the onset of movement. Using the same classification Weinrich *et al.* (1984) compared the proportions of movement–related cells in the lateral premotor and motor cortex. The monkeys were trained to flex or extend the elbow on a visual tracking task. Eighty-five per cent of the cells in motor cortex were related to movement, and in the lateral premotor cortex as many as 65 per cent of cells responded in relation to movement, though many of these cells also responded in relation to other aspects of the task.

Withholding a response

If the activity of a cell is related to movement it should not respond unless the animal moves. Weinrich *et al.* (1984) taught monkeys a 'go, no-go' task. The monkey's arm was in a brace which allowed flexion or extension of the elbow. The position of the arm was indicated by a 'position' light on a display panel. 'Go' trials started with the movement of a target light to a new position; a short delay followed; and when the target light dimmed the monkey was rewarded if it moved its arm to align the position light with the target light. On 'no-go' trials the light failed to move; again a short delay followed; and then the animal was rewarded if it made no movement.

An analysis was made of 'set-related' units, that is of cells that altered their activity during the delay and before the animal was able to respond. Of 77 such units in lateral premotor cortex, 65 per cent responded during the delay on 'go' trials and failed to respond during the delay on 'no-go' trials. Most of the remaining cells showed a greater change on 'go' trials.

Directional cells

The last expectation is that there should be cells that respond differentially depending on which movement is made. In the experiment described above, Weinrich *et al.* (1984) classified the cells as directional or bidirectional. The directional cells were those that responded only when the animal was moving or preparing to move in one direction. The authors report that 49 per cent of the movement-related cells and 52 per cent of the set-related cells fired in relation either to flexion or extension of the elbow. When Crammond and Kalaska (1989) used eight spatial positions, they found that over 90 per cent of the cells altered their activity in relation to the direction of movement.

If the cell responds for a specific movement, it should change its response if the animal is required to change its movement. This prediction was tested by Wise and Mauritz (1985). The task was modified. The monkey looked at a display panel; if the target light appeared on a the left, the monkey had to press a key on the left, and, if on the right, the monkey had to press a key on the right. As in the previous experiment a short delay occurred before the animal was allowed to respond. On one third of the trials the target changed from one side to the other during the delay.

Recordings were taken from 70 set-related cells that responded during the delay and responded differentially, depending on the movement to be made. An analysis was made of the activity of 17 of these cells as a sample, comparing activity before and after the change. The mean number of impulses per second was 30 before the change, and it fell to two after the target light had moved to the other position. This decrease was not shown by 24 bidirectional cells.

In parallel experiments, Godschalk *et al.* (1985) recorded from cells around the bow of the arcuate sulcus. The authors taught monkeys to retrieve food with their hand after a delay in which they could see the position of the food but were unable to reach it. Of the 306 cells recorded with activity that was related to the task, 56 per cent changed their activity just before or during the movement, though only 25 per cent responded exclusively in relation to the movement.

In the experiments described so far, the monkeys have been taught to carry out standard tasks in which there is considerable control over the movements made. Rizzolatti and colleagues have explored a wider range of movements, by presenting monkeys with pieces of food and correlating the discharge of cells in the lateral premotor cortex with the sorts of movement that the animal makes (Rizzolatti *et al.* 1988). They have recorded in the inferior convexity of the lateral premotor cortex, including the posterior bank of the lower limb of the arcuate sulcus. They label this region F5 on the basis of cytoarchitectural studies using cytochrome oxidase (Matelli *et al.* 1985) (Fig. 3.3).

They report that in this region there are cells that respond to one specific movement but not to another. For example, 42 per cent of their cells only responded when the monkey grasped food with the hand, and a further 24 per cent when the food was grasped whether by hand or mouth. Of the cells related to the hand grasp, seven per cent were active when the monkey used a whole hand grasp, and 38 per cent when the food was held in the fingers. It is difficult, in a clinical situation, to pinpoint the aspect of the monkey's performance that is critical, but it is clear that the activity of cells in the lateral premotor cortex often relates to the type of movement that the monkey makes.

Set-related cells

Once the subject has retrieved the correct response, there will be occasions on which it is appropriate to act immediately; but there are other occasions on which the correct response is known before the subject has the chance to act. As an animal approaches an object the sight of it tells it how to react. Information from the distance receptors gives advanced notice of the necessary action.

Delayed conditional motor task

In the laboratory we can set up a simple version of this situation. The basic task is a conditional motor task, but a trigger stimulus is added:

Given *A*, if cue *P*, make *R*1 when trigger *T*
Given *A*, if cue *Q*, make *R*2 when trigger *T*
Where:
A = the manipulandum
P and Q = the cues
R = responses
T = trigger stimulus

The cues P and Q are the instructional stimuli. After their presentation there is a delay before the animal is allowed to respond. It is the function of the trigger stimulus to tell the animal when it can respond.

This situation is discussed in detail in the monograph by Evarts *et al.*, (1984). It has been been much used by Wise and colleagues in their electrophysiological studies of the lateral premotor cortex, showing that many of the cells are active while a monkey waits. They have demonstrated such set-related activity when a monkey waits for a few seconds before a light dims to allow the animal to reach for a target (Wise and Mauritz 1985), or to flex or extend its forearm (Weinrich *et al.* 1984). More is occuring than simply an increase in general excitation before impending movement. As mentioned earlier, 52 per cent of these set cells respond differentially according to the movement the animal is waiting to make; and the proportion of such cells is much higher in the lateral premotor cortex than in motor cortex (Weinrich *et al.* 1984).

Similar experiments have been performed by Godschalk *et al.* (1985). As described earlier, the monkeys were shown the location of food in one of three locations, but were then required to wait for one second before being allowed to retrieve it. A buzzer served as the trigger stimulus. Seventy-five per cent of the cells changed their firing during the waiting period while the target remained visible.

There is no need for the instructional stimulus to stay on during the delay. Wise and Mauritz (1985) removed the instructional stimulus during the delay on some trials. The activity of set related cells that were directionally selective was the same whether the instructional stimulus was present or absent during the delay period.

Preparation for movement

One interpretation of this finding is that the set-related cells in the lateral premotor cortex could form the neural substrate for holding a response in working memory while the monkey prepares to act. We tried to test this interpretation (Passingham 1988). We reasoned that if the primary role of the lateral premotor cortex is to prepare for future action, the monkeys should be able to perform a conditional motor task when there is no delay, but fail when they have to wait.

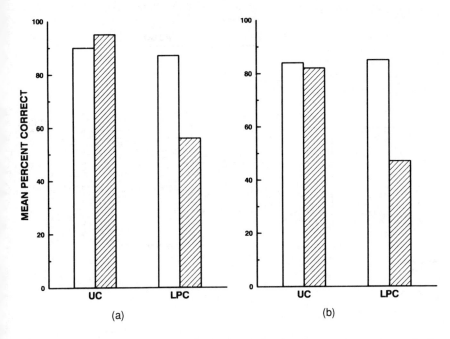

Fig. 3.16 Per cent correct performance on visual conditional motor task on which the cues were colours and the monkeys responded by pulling or rotating a handle. Unshaded = pre-operative, shaded = post-operative, (a) = no delay, (b) = delay, UC = 3 unoperated control monkeys, LPC = 3 monkeys with lesions in lateral premotor cortex. Data from Passingham (1988).

Monkeys were trained to pull a handle if a cue was red, and to turn it if the cue was blue. The cues were presented by lighting a panel in the background behind a handle. There were two versions of the task. In one version (no delay) the cue light was still on when the animal was allowed to respond; in the other version (delay) the cue was extinguished and the animal had to wait for 3 seconds before being allowed to respond.

The data are shown in Fig. 3.16 which compares performance on the 500 trials just before surgery and two weeks after surgery. The monkeys with bilateral LPC lesions made errors whether there was a delay or not, although one monkey performed more poorly on the delayed than the non-delayed condition.

This result does not disprove the notion that the lateral premotor cortex can hold movements in memory. The experiment shows only that the role of the lateral premotor cortex is not *restricted* to that task. The suggestion is that the primary role is that of selecting responses. Once selected, the response can be held in memory until the appropriate time

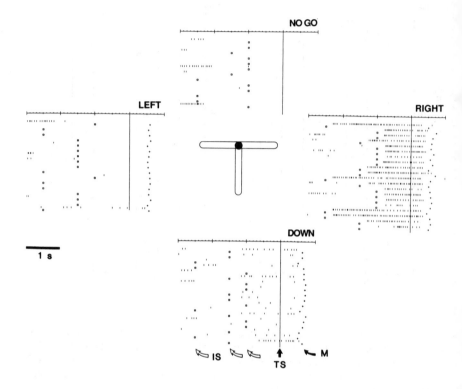

Fig. 3.17 Activity of cell during the presentation of four familiar stimuli. Each raster indicates the times of neuronal discharge during one trial aligned on the time at which the trigger stimulus (TS) was presented. Open square denotes time at which the instructional stimulus (IS) was presented. The time of the movement (M) is shown by the plus sign. A drawing of the handle is shown. Time scale major divisions = 1 second, minor divisions = 100 milliseconds. Figure from Mitz *et al.* (1991).

Cells and learning
Gross potentials

The contribution of an area to learning can be assessed by recording gross electrical potentials; these reflect the activity of the population of cells. Sasaki and Gemba (1982) have recorded field potentials with electrodes implanted in the cortex in macaques. They measure a surface-positive depth-negative potential in the dorsal lateral premotor cortex as monkeys learn to lift a lever on presentation of a light. The potential increases in size as the monkey learns.

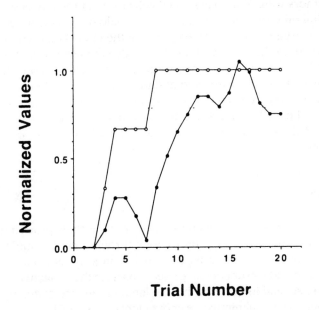

Fig. 3.18 Activity of cell (open circles) and performance of animal (solid circles) on a visual conditional motor task. Adapted from Mitz *et al.* (1991).

Single cells

Studies of cells in the lateral premotor cortex have not usually laid any emphasis on learning (Wise 1985*a*, *b*). A typical recording study starts by teaching the animals a task; only when the animals perform reliably are recordings then taken. This contrasts with a typical lesion study, in which the lesion is made and its effects on learning or relearning are then examined

To study the activity of cells during learning, it is necessary to record at a time when the animal is still learning. Mitz *et al.*(1991) have performed an elegant experiment. They first taught macaques a visual conditional motor task. On each trial one of four coloured text characters appeared on a monitor, and the monkey learned which of four responses was associated with each cue. The responses were to move the joystick to the left, to the right, to move it down, or to withhold a response.

In the next stage new cues were presented, and the monkey had to learn the appropriate movement for each novel cue. The two monkeys had been trained so well that they could learn the appropriate response in just a few trials

Recordings were taken from cells in the lateral premotor cortex while the monkeys learned these new associations. Many cells were found to discharge differentially according to the movement to be made. Figure 3.17 shows such a cell.

The authors were able to assess 69 cells to see if their activity related to the learning process. A significant relation could be demonstrated in 63 per cent of the instances tested. An example of the effect is shown in Fig. 3.18. This shows both the activity of a cell and also the level of performance of the animal. When the cue is novel the cell is inactive, even though the monkey is making responses and attending to the cues. But as the animal learns to select the movement that is appropriate given the new cue, so the activity of the cell increases. This supports the claim that the lateral premotor cortex plays a role in the learned selection of voluntary movements.

Summary

The premotor areas can influence movement via their projections to the motor cortex and subcortical projections through the pyramidal tract. In turn the premotor areas are influenced by projections from the parietal areas 5 and 7b and by subcortical projections from the thalamus.

There are several indications that the lateral premotor cortex plays a role in the selection of manipulative movements. First, PET scans show that there is greater activation in this area when subjects must select between movements rather than simply repeat the same movement.

Second, LPC lesions in monkeys and patients impair the learning and relearning of conditional tasks on which the subject must learn to select between movements on the basis of external cues. Conditional motor tasks of this sort are all 'recall' tasks in the sense that the subject must retrieve the movement that is appropriate to the context.

Finally, there are many cells in the lateral premotor area that increase their activity when a monkey is preparing to move, and this increase is selective depending on the movement to be made. Many of the cells also show a selective increase in their activity during the time in which monkeys learn visual conditional motor tasks.

4 Medial premotor cortex (SMA) (area 6)

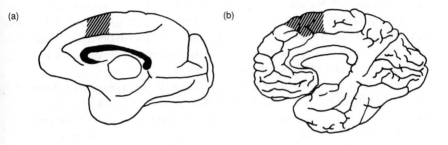

(a)

(b)

Fig. 4.1 Medial premotor cortex in (a) the macaque monkey and (b) the human brain.

The previous chapter considered voluntary movements made in response to some prompt. The monkey pulls the lever when the red light appears; the patient salutes when the examiner commands. In both cases the act that is appropriate depends on the context, and the context is some event in the world. We may say that the individual 'reacts'.

But there also occasions when animals and people act even though no event has occurred. Consider a dog lying on the floor. It comes when its master calls; but there are other occasions on which it gets up and comes of its own accord. In the first case there is a change in the environment: it hears the call. In the second case there is no change in the environment: instead there is a change in the animal itself. In one instance the animal reacts to an external event, and in the other its action is self-initiated. We may say that the individual 'acts'.

The dictionary allows the use of the word 'voluntary' for those actions that are taken without external prompting. The use of 'voluntary' in this sense is given in Fig. 1.1, level B. It has to be said that it is an odd use, since it implies that when the dog answers its master's call its behaviour is involuntary.

We should not suppose that there is no context for self-initiated movements. The difference is only that there is no *external* context; that is, no event in the outside world. Many of the movements that we make are appropriate in the context of our previous behaviour. They fit a 'motor' context. Thus for an animal experiment the logic might be:

Given A, if P, then make $R1$
Given A, if Q, then make $R2$
Where:
A = a manipulandum
P and Q = motor contexts
$R1$ and $R2$ are two limb movements

An example is provided by the motor reversal task described in the previous chapter. We have taught monkeys to operate a handle which can be either pulled or turned to the left (Thaler and Passingham 1989). On any day only one of the two actions will be correct, but if on one day the animal reaches a criterion level of performance the conditions reverse; on the next day the other movement is defined as correct.

The apparatus looks identical from trial to trial, and there is no change in the environment to remind the animal how to win the food. In other words, there is no external sensory prompt or instruction. To master the task the animal must base its present movement on the success or otherwise of past movements. It is the animal's past behaviour that must guide its decisions.

The term 'internal' context is sometimes used, but it is vague. It could cover several quite different situations. For example:

1. The context is past behaviour.

2. The context is current behaviour.

3. The context is an external instruction that is now stored in memory.

4. The individual makes an arbitrary decision.

What all these situations have in common is that there is no external instruction at the time that the subject acts.

Repetitive movements in monkeys

Arm raise task

Consider first an instrumental learning task on which there are no external sensory cues. We have taught monkeys to perform a simple gesture (Thaler and Passingham 1989). To win a peanut they have only to raise their arm. An infra-red beam is set above shoulder height, and when the monkey's arm interrupts the beam a peanut is delivered. The animals are unable to see the beam, and thus they have to learn the height to which to raise their arm. The monkeys work at their own pace, raising their arm, picking up a peanut, and then raising their arm again. In the first experiment the animals performed in total darkness, because we wished to ensure that there would be no visual cues.

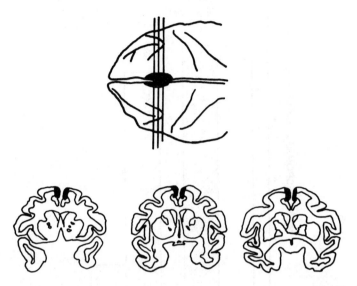

Fig. 4.2   Lesion in medial premotor cortex. The lesion is shown in black. The lines give the locations of the three representative coronal sections. From Thaler (1988).

This is not a conditional task, since the same movement is correct on all trials; but it is a voluntary task in the sense that it is learned. Conditional tasks are a convenient test of whether a movement is learned, but they are not the only test. Consider an experiment by Jenkins (1977) that was mentioned in Chapter 1. He taught pigeons to wave their heads in order to win grain. We can be sure that they learned this, because in the wild waving the head has no such effect. Pigeons do not naturally wave their heads to obtain food, and monkeys do not raise their arms. It is crucial for our argument only that the movement be learned; it matters not how it is established that this is the case.

Removal of the medial premotor cortex

The arm raise task was initially devised for a study on the functions of the medial premotor cortex (MPC)—more usually called the SMA (Fig. 4.1). There had been several proposals in the literature that the medial premotor cortex played a crucial role in voluntary behaviour, in the sense of self-initiated behaviour (Eccles 1982). In an extensive review Goldberg (1985) concludes that the medial premotor cortex is concerned with the processes by which internal context influences action.

If the medial premotor cortex plays a crucial role in self-initiated movement, it follows that removal of this area should interfere with the production of such movements. In three monkeys we removed the medial premotor cortex bilaterally (Thaler and Passingham 1989) (Fig. 4.2).

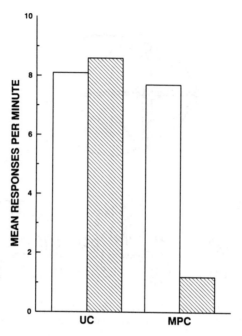

Fig. 4.3 Mean responses per minute on the arm raise task. The unshaded histograms show the data before surgery and the shaded histograms the data after surgery. UC= 3 unoperated control monkeys, MPC = 3 monkeys with lesions in medial premotor cortex. Data from Passingham (1987).

The monkeys were trained on the arm raise task before surgery, and were then retrained two weeks after surgery. Figure 4.3 compares the performance of monkeys with MPC lesions with that of unoperated control animals. The operated animals made few successful attempts on the first four days on which they were retrained.

Removal of cingulate premotor area

Figure 4.2 shows that the MPC lesion included the medial convexity cortex (area 6) and the upper bank of the cingulate sulcus. The tissue in the lower bank of this sulcus forms a separate premotor area; Matelli *et al.* (1991) and Luppino *et al.* (1991) identify an area which they term 24d with a somatotopic representation of the limbs (Fig. 4.4). This is probably the area which sends a projection to motor cortex (Strick 1985; Dum and Strick 1991), and also contributes fibres to the pyramidal tract (Hutchins *et al.* 1988; Dum and Strick 1991).

In two animals we have removed the lower bank of the cingulate sulcus (area 24) together with the rest of the anterior cingulate cortex including area 32 (Stern 1987). The monkeys with cingulate lesions were trained in a separate experiment. To compare their scores with those of the MPC

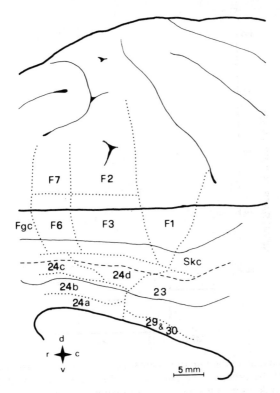

Fig. 4.4 Distribution of cytoarchitectonic areas in motor, premotor, and anterior cingulate cortex according to Matelli *et al.* (1991). Divisions are based on staining with cytochrome oxidase. The medial surface is unfolded below to show the areas buried in the cingulate sulcus. Figure from Luppino *et al.* (1991).

animals, Fig. 4.5 plots the scores as a percentage of the preoperative scores. It can be seen that the monkeys with cingulate lesions were as severely impaired as those with MPC removals.

Behavioural analysis

There could be many explanations of the results shown in Fig. 4.3. Perhaps the monkeys are unable to move, slow or poorly motivated. The data are only interesting if trivial explanations have been ruled out. These three possibilities can be quickly discarded.

1. The animals can move. In a further session we tested the monkeys with MPC lesions in the light. On each trial in this session, we placed a peanut just behind the infra-red beam, so that if the monkey reached up for the peanut its hand would break the beam. It was remarkable that the monkeys with MPC lesions now reached up to for the peanut at the same

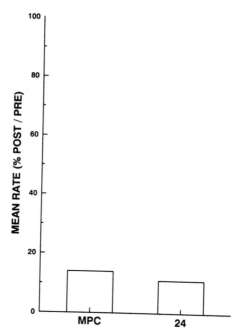

Fig. 4.5   Mean change in the rate of responses on the arm raise task, calculated as the percentage of the preoperative rate. MPC = 3 monkeys with medial premotor lesions, 24 = 2 monkeys with lesions in anterior cingulate cortex (areas 24 and 32). Data from Thaler (1988) and Stern (1987).

rate as the control animals (Thaler and Passingham 1989). The data are shown in Fig. 4.6.

2. The monkeys can make quick movements. Before surgery we also taught the monkeys a reaction time task. The animal had to hold a lever until a light went out, and then release this lever so as to press another one. Removal of the MPC affected neither the reaction time nor movement time (Passingham 1987).

3. The monkeys are motivated, and will work on learning tasks for food. We also trained them on a timing task. They had to press a button, wait for a period of five to eight seconds and then operate a joystick. The monkeys with MPC lesions relearned the task as easily as the control animals (Thaler and Passingham 1989).

The results are consistent with the hypothesis that the medial premotor cortex is concerned with self-initiated behaviour. But if so, there is a further prediction. We should be able to show that the animals can raise their arm normally if they are provided with an external cue.

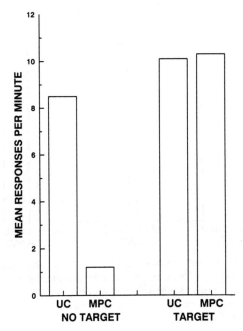

Fig. 4.6 Mean responses per minute on the arm raise task. The histograms on the left refer to the task when there were no external cues, the histograms on the right to the task in which the monkeys reached for peanuts placed above them. UC = 3 unoperated monkeys, MPC = 3 monkeys with medial premotor lesion. Data from Passingham (1987).

Externally cued arm raise task

We therefore taught three more monkeys to raise their arm (Passingham *et al.*, 1989). The difference was that tones were presented to tell them when to do so. A peanut could only be obtained if the animal raised its arm within 2 seconds after a tone sounded. The monkeys were trained in the light. We compared the performance of these animals with that of three other monkeys which had previously been trained on the self-paced version of the task in the light (Thaler and Passingham 1989).

Figure 4.7 shows that there was a dramatic difference in the effects of MPC lesions on the two tasks. On the self-initiated version the monkeys made few correct movements; but on the version with the tones the monkeys worked at a reasonable pace (Passingham *et al.* 1989).

The analysis of the film was also revealing. We noted the number of attempts that the animals made, and also the success of their attempts, that is, the percentage of attempts in which the arm broke the beam. On the self-initiated task the animals made few attempts, and many of the attempts were inaccurate (Fig. 4.7). On the auditory version of the task, the animals made many more attempts and were more accurate.

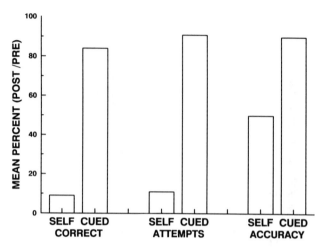

Fig. 4.7 Mean change in performance on the arm raise task, calculated as the percentage of the preoperative level. Self = task with no external cues (3 monkeys), cued = task with auditory cues (3 monkeys), attempts = rate of responses whether successful or unsuccessful, accuracy = percentage of successful responses. Data from Passingham *et al.* (1989).

These results show that the monkeys can make the relevant movements and have the required motivation. They also show that the explanation is not that the monkeys are unable to locate the target zone on the basis of proprioceptive input.The evidence supports the view that they are poor at motor learning when there is no external prompt.

Role of the tone
Why does the tone help? It has three functions: it tells the animal when to act; it reminds the animal that food is available, and so motivates; and it reminds the animal of what to do. We can call these the role of the stimulus as trigger, predictor, and instruction.

Consider the dog again. The owner says 'sit' and the dog sits obediently at the kerb. The word 'sit' tells the dog when to sit (trigger); it leads the animal to expect either praise or a titbit (predictor); but it also reminds the dog of what it should do (instruction).At first the owner prompts the animal by touching its back; then later the command alone is sufficient. The command acts as an instruction. If the owner had said 'lie down' the dog would not have sat.

On the self-initiated version of the arm raise task there is no external stimulus to fulfil any of these functions. But which of the functions is crucial? We tried to find out by devising an experiment in which there was an external stimulus to act as trigger and predictor, but no external instruction.

The task was the motor reversal task described earlier. At the start of a trial, a screen is raised to give the animal access to the handle. The raising of

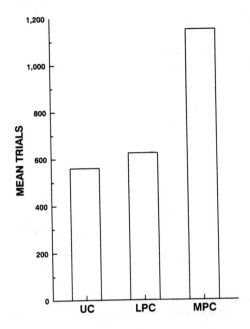

Fig. 4.8   Mean trials to learn a series of reversals on a task in which the monkeys had to pull or rotate a handle. UC = 3 unoperated control monkeys, LPC = 3 monkeys with lesions in lateral premotor cortex, MPC = 3 monkeys with lesions in medial premotor cortex. Data from Thaler (1988) and Chen *et al.* (in preparation).

the screen tells the animal when to act, and also serves to tell the animal that food is available. The animal must pull or turn the handle, but the sight of the handle gives no information as to which movement to perform. In other words there is no sensory instruction telling the animal what to do; the animal must act according to the success of its previous actions.

We taught this task to three monkeys with MPC lesions and three control monkeys (Thaler and Passingham 1989). Two of the three operated monkeys learned very slowly, though the third was much less impaired (Fig. 4.8). This suggests that one crucial factor is the type of instruction. Monkeys with MPC lesions are impaired if they must depend on motor cues to tell them what to do. One reason why monkeys with MPC lesions are helped by a sound is that it reminds them of what to do.

Sequences in monkeys

Sequences

There are other tasks on which the correct response is not specified by

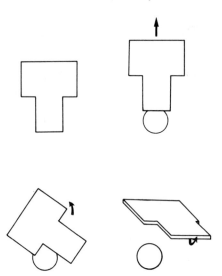

Fig. 4.9 T-shaped manipulandum. Arrows indicate the direction in which the manipulandum can be moved. The circle shows the food-well.

external cues. One such is a motor sequence. Take a sequence of three limb movements: *R2* must be performed in the context of having just performed *R1*, and *R3* in the context of *R2*.

This is not to say that all sequences must be learned in this way. Some sequences can be programmed as a whole, as if they were a single movement. This point is well illustrated by an experiment by Benecke *et al.* (1986). They asked human subjects to perform sequences such as squeezing the hand and then flexing the elbow. On four of the sequences they used, there was no correlation between the times taken to complete the two components of the sequence. The authors suggest that these sequences are programmed as two separate acts. But they also looked at a fifth task, in which the subject flexed and then extended the elbow. Here the times for flexing and extending did correlate, and this was taken as evidence that a single programme was in operation.

Presumably, it is more difficult to develop a single programme the more different are the movements required, and the longer the interval between movements. We taught a difficult sequence to monkeys: they were presented with a T-shaped piece of plastic, and to win food they had to first push it up, then twist it, and finally lift it up (Halsband 1987) (Fig. 4.9). After each movement the apparatus was withdrawn and then presented again. Thus, there was a delay between the movements, and it would have been difficult to programme them as a single unit.

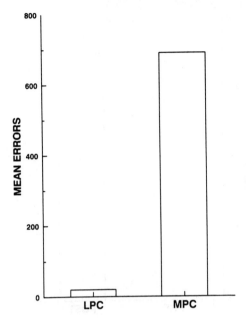

Fig. 4.10 Mean errors for post-operative relearning of a motor sequence with 3 movements. LPC = 3 monkeys with lesions in lateral premotor cortex, MPC = 3 monkeys with lesions in medial premotor cortex. Data from Passingham (1987).

The forwards movement of the apparatus served as a trigger to tell the animal when to act. But there was no visual or auditory cue to tell the animal which movement to make. Each time the apparatus was presented the T-piece was in its original orientation; so the sight of it was uninformative. The correct movement depended on what the animal had just done.

The task was taught preoperatively, and then operations were performed on four monkeys. In two animals much of the medial premotor cortex was removed from each hemisphere. In a further two animals some of the medial prefrontal cortex was removed, but in one of these animals the lesion also included the anterior part of the medial premotor cortex. Figure 4.10 plots the data for the three animals with lesions that included the medial premotor cortex. All three failed to relearn the sequence at all in 1000 trials.

More recently we have taught a simpler sequence (Chen *et al.*, in preparation). The monkeys had only to make two movements on a joystick. First the animals pushed the joystick to the left; then a delay was enforced; finally they were required to push the joystick forwards. After the task had been retaught before surgery we removed the medial premotor cortex bilaterally in three animals. Figure 4.11 shows that after surgery they were slow to relearn. This confirms the results of the earlier study.

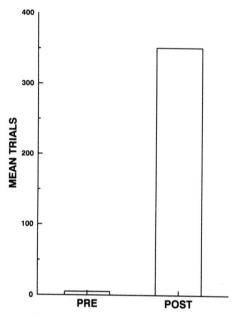

Fig. 4.11   Mean trials to relearn a motor sequence with 2 movements. Pre = preoperative, post = post-operative. Data for 3 monkeys. Data from Chen *et al.* (in preparation).

These experiments have measured the number of errors made by animals in relearning a motor sequence. An alternative approach is to measure the time taken to initiate a second movement on completion of the first. Rea *et al.* (1987) taught monkeys to move a handle to one of three targets in turn. They then removed the medial premotor cortex together with the dorsal part of the lateral premotor cortex. After surgery they found that, having reached one target, the monkeys took longer to initiate the next movement away from that target.

A similar finding is reported by Smith *et al.* (1981). They taught monkeys to press a strain gauge with the thumb and forefinger. When the monkeys had pressed it for one second, they had to release it for one second and then press it again. After removal of the medial premotor cortex contralateral to the hand, once the monkeys had squeezed the strain gauge they were slow to open the hand so as to initiate the next trial.

Bimanual simultaneous movements

There is another situation which requires the animal to use information from its own actions. The ability to make simultaneous movements with the two hands requires coordination. The movement of one hand provides the context for the other; one hand must know what the other is doing.

Brinkman (1984) performed a delightful experiment. She offered rhesus monkeys a currant in a hole in a horizontal plate. To retrieve the currant the monkey had to poke it through with one hand and catch it from below with the other. Monkeys with unilateral MPC lesions tended to carry out the same movements with each hand; for example, they tried to poke the currant out both from above and below at the same time.

One explanation is that the intact medial premotor cortex had an influence over the movements of both hands, and had difficulty in directing different movements. The left medial premotor cortex can direct movements of the right hand directly via its connections to the left motor cortex, and movements of the left hand indirectly via its callosal connections with the right lateral premotor cortex. Brinkman (1984) reasoned that, if this was the cause of the problem, then cutting the corpus callosum should solve it. She found that, as predicted, after section of the callosum the monkeys made fewer mirror movements.

Conclusion

Monkeys with MPC lesions are poor at sequence tasks, but this fact alone does not specify the role of the medial premotor cortex. The monkeys are also poor at repeating the same movement (on the arm raise task), and at changing between two repetitive movements (on the motor reversal task). What is common to all these tasks is that the animal must learn the correct movement without the aid of external cues. The basic effect of MPC lesions is to impair retrieval of the appropriate movement in the absence of external prompts.

The medial premotor cortex in human subjects

Lesions

There is independent evidence from studies of patients. Dick *et al.* (1986) studied a patient with an infarct that affected the right medial premotor cortex. The patient was required to perform sequential movements, with no external cue present at the time of the performance.

The patient could still flex the elbow or squeeze the hand. But using the right limb, he was slow to flex the elbow after squeezing the hand; and using the left limb, he could not perform this simple sequence at all. He also found it difficult to squeeze the right hand and then flex the left elbow: there was a prolonged pause between movements.

The patient also had difficulty in directing two movements simultaneously. Thus, he was slow to flex the left elbow while squeezing the right hand at the same time, or to flex the right elbow while squeezing the left hand. In other words he had an impairment in coordinating two movements, whether they were simultaneous or successive.

Unfortunately, the report does not say whether this patient could make repetitive movements at the normal rate. This could have been tested by asking the patient to repeatedly open and close the hand. Patients with Parkinson's disease make increasingly small amplitude movements on this task; and we know that a lesion affecting the medial premotor cortex can cause some of the symptoms of Parkinson's disease (Straub and Sigel 1988).

Potentials

A comparison of sequential and repetitive movements has been attempted in studies in which evoked potentials are recorded. Lang *et al.* (1989) instructed their subjects to make movements of the hand. In the condition for repetitive movements the subjects simply flexed and extended the fingers. In the condition for sequential movements, they flexed a finger, then extended the wrist, then extended the finger and finally flexed the wrist.

Potentials were recorded from several sites. Those recorded over the central midline (Cz) were presumed to originate from the medial premotor cortex. At this location the amplitude of the potentials recorded during performance was larger for the sequence than for the repetitive movements.

There is an inelegance in this study. For the condition with repetitive movements the subjects only moved the fingers; whereas for the condition with sequential movements the subjects moved the hand as well as the fingers. A study by Lang *et al.* (1988) used a better control. They recorded gross cortical potentials while subjects performed either sequential movements or simultaneous movements with the fingers of each hand. In the simultaneous condition the subjects flexed and extended the forefinger of each hand through three positions. In the sequential condition the finger of one hand moved to the first position, then the finger of the other hand, and so on, the two fingers alternating their movements.

In the control condition the subjects moved both fingers, but not in a coordinated manner. Thus, the same movements were made in all conditions. Again the potentials for the central midline (Cz) were larger in amplitude for the sequential than the control task. These potentials were also larger than those recorded during the simultaneous task.

PET scanning in normal subjects

However, studies of potentials recorded from the scalp cannot be taken as conclusive. In the studies just described it has not been rigorously demonstrated that the potentials at Cz represent the activity of the medial premotor cortex. Furthermore, there is no way of distinguishing between the contribution of the medial premotor and the cingulate premotor cortex. Fortunately, PET scanning can achieve the required accuracy of localization.

Repetitive movements
Several authors have examined regional cerebral blood flow in the medial premotor cortex while subjects perform the same movement repetitively. Roland *et al.* (1980) used the [133]Xenon method and two-dimensional imaging to visualize blood flow. They required subjects to flex the index finger repeatedly against a spring. They reported that there was no significant increase in blood flow to the medial premotor cortex while subjects performed this simple task.

However, more recent studies using the PET scanner have produced different results. Fox *et al.* (1985) asked their subjects to open and close the hand repeatedly; a tone paced the task. In this case there was a significant increase in activity in the medial premotor cortex—over and above any increase in global flow.

We also find the same result. An experiment by Colebatch *et al.* (1991*b*) has already been described in Chapter 3. The experiment compared different movements, paced by tones. One was a finger movement: the subjects raised and lowered the index finger. In another condition the subjects opposed the thumb to the fingers in turn. In another the subject opened and closed the hand as in the study by Fox *et al.* (1985). In the last condition the subjects were to raise and lower their arm. In all four conditions there was a significant increase of blood flow to the medial cortex; the mean increase was 13.7 per cent. The peak of activity was in the posterior part of the medial premotor cortex.

Sequences
Now compare the performance of sequences. In their pioneering study using the [133]Xenon method and two dimensional imaging, Roland *et al.* (1980) contrasted repetition of a finger movement with performance of a complex sequence. The sequence was a series of 16 movements; the subject had to oppose the thumb to the different fingers in an order which was taught before the scans. The task was difficult and the subjects were allowed to practise for 80 minutes. No tone was given to pace the task.

After correcting for the general increase in blood flow, there was a 28 per cent increase in flow to the medial premotor cortex opposite the hand being used. There was also an increase of a similar size in the ipsilateral medial premotor cortex. This result was confirmed by Roland *et al.* (1982) using the PET scanner. They report an increase of 22 per cent in the contralateral medial premotor cortex and of 18.0 per cent in the ipsilateral medial premotor cortex.

These findings could be taken to suggest that the medial premotor cortex has a special role in the direction of motor sequences. But there was an inelegance in the original comparison between repetitive movements

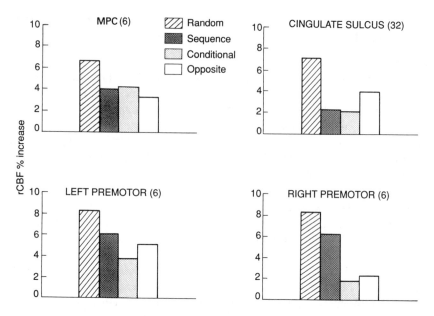

Fig. 4.12   Regional blood flow (ml/100 ml/minute) for four tasks compared with the Fixed condition. MPC = medial premotor cortex, premotor = lateral premotor cortex, cingulate sulcus = area 32. Data from Deiser *et al* (1991).

and sequential movements. As Fox *et al.* (1985) pointed out, the rate at which the sequential movements were made was much faster than the rate at which the repetitive movements were made. We therefore repeated the comparison between single movements and sequential movements with a tone to pace the tasks (Deiber *et al.* 1991). The study has already been mentioned in Chapter 3.

The subjects moved a joystick each time they heard a tone. In one condition, the subjects repeated the same movement, pushing a joystick forwards; we may call this the 'fixed' or 'repetitive' condition. In another condition ('sequence'), the subjects followed a learned sequence eight moves long; each time a tone sounded the subject made the next movement in the sequence, starting again at the end of sequence. In a third condition, the subjects decided their own sequence; they were given a free choice on each trial as to which movement to make, that is they generated their own movements. This condition was called the 'random' condition, though we now prefer the term 'free selection'.

We calculated the increase in blood flow to the medial premotor cortex for the two sequence conditions over and above the increase in flow for the repetitive condition. Figure 4.12 compares the increase for the learned sequence and free selection conditions. Both in the medial premotor and anterior cingulate cortex, the increase was significant for the random sequence but not for the learned sequence.

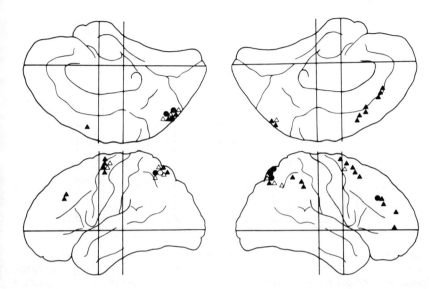

Fig. 4.13 Location of peaks of maximal significant change in regional cerebral blood flow for the comparison between the four selection conditions taken separately and the fixed condition. ▲ = random, △ = sequence, O = conditional, ● = opposite. Lateral view below, medial above, left hemisphere on left, right hemisphere on right. From Deiber *et al.* (1991).

For the free selection condition, Fig. 4.13 shows the location of the peaks of the activity in the premotor areas. It can be seen that the peaks lie in the anterior part in the medial premotor cortex. The activity also extends forwards into the most anterior part of the cingulate sulcus, probably in area 32.

There are three possible explanations of the fact that Roland *et al.* (1982) found significant activation of the medial premotor cortex when subjects performed a learned sequence whereas Deiber *et al.* (1991) did not.

1. Roland *et al.* (1982) compared the sequence with a rest condition whereas Deiber *et al.* (1991) compared it with a condition in which the subjects made repetitive movements. We have found significant activation of the medial premotor cortex when subjects perform repetitive movements (Colebatch *et al.* 1991*b*).
2. The sequence task used by Roland *et al.* (1982) was much more difficult than the one we taught.
3. In the experiment by Roland *et al.* (1982) the task was self-paced, whereas we paced the task with tones. There is significant activation of the medial premotor cortex when subjects perform self-paced repetitive movements (Zeffiro *et al.* 1991; Jahanshahi *et al.* in preparation).

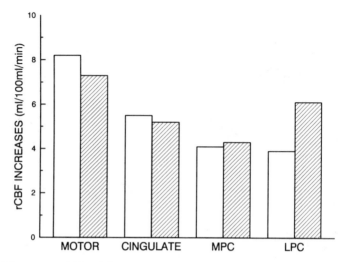

Fig. 4.14   Regional blood flow (ml/100 ml/minute) for the repetitive (fixed) task compared with the rest condition. Unshaded histogram = 6 control subjects, shaded histogram = 6 patients with Parkinson's disease. Motor = motor cortex, cingulate = anterior congulate cortex, MPC = medial premotor cortex, LPC = lateral premotor cortex. Data from Playford *et al.* (1992).

PET scanning in patients

Parkinson's disease

There is a further test of the belief that the medial cortex plays a role in self-initiated movement. If this is the case, then the medial frontal areas should be less active in patients who are poor at producing such movements.

Patients with Parkinson's disease are not fluent in their movements; at their worst they simply freeze. We studied six such patients who were moderately affected. They lay in the PET scanner and moved the joystick at a pace determined by tones (Playford *et al.* 1992). There were just two experimental conditions, 'repetitive' and 'free selection', but we also included a 'rest' condition in which the subject rested quietly. The comparisons were made with this rest condition.

The patients completed both tasks successfully; they were only 0.1 second slower than the control subjects in moving the joystick after the tone. For the repetitive condition the medial premotor cortex was activated relatively normally in the patients with Parkinson's disease (Fig. 4.14). This condition is equivalent to the arm raise task with a pacing tone. But for the free selection task the medial premotor cortex was significantly less activated in the patients (Fig. 4.15). In other words, when self-generated movements are required the medial premotor cortex is insufficiently activated in Parkinson's disease.

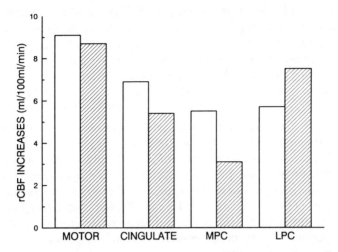

Fig. 4.15 Regional blood flow (ml/100 ml/minute) for the free selection task (random) compared wiht the rest condition. Unshaded histogram = 6 control subjects, shaded histogram = 6 patients with Parkinson's disease. Motor = motor cortex, cingulate = anterior cingulate cortex, MPC = medial premotor cortex, LPC = lateral premotor cortex. Data from Playford *et al.* (1992).

On and off states

There is another way of tackling the issue. Patients with Parkinson's disease often suffer from variation in their motor status; sometimes they are 'on' and sometimes 'off'. It is when they are 'off' that they find particular difficulty in generating movement. If the medial premotor cortex is concerned with self-generated movement, its activity should vary between the two states.

Jenkins *et al.* (1992*b*) tested this prediction by scanning patients while they were 'off', then giving them apomorphine to induce an 'on' state, and then scanning the patients again. The patients performed the same tasks as in the previous study by Playford *et al.* (1992). When a comparison was made between the activity of brain areas in the two states, the activity in the medial premotor cortex increased significantly when the state turned from 'off' to 'on'.

Conclusions

Combining the data from animals and human subjects, we can draw the following conclusions.

1. First, the medial premotor cortex plays a role in the selection of movements when there is no external cue to tell the subject when to move or what to do.

These situations have been described in the literature as involving 'self-initiated' movements or movements that are determined by 'internal' cues.

The term 'self-initiated' is too restrictive. 'Self-initiated' can suggest that the role of the cues are simply to determine when movements are to be made. The use of the term 'internal' cues is avoided here. It is better simply to state that there are no external ones at the time that the subject acts.

It is tempting to redescribe the critical condition by saying that it is crucial that there be a motor context. But this too is not a complete description. When subjects generate movements at will there is no motor context.

2. The role of the medial premotor cortex is not confined to the direction of motor sequences. The medial premotor cortex is also active when subjects perform repetitive movements. It is true that the peak of the activation is in the posterior part of the medial premotor cortex (Colebatch *et al.* 1991*b*) whereas when subjects generate sequences there is also activation of the anterior part of the medial premotor cortex (Deiber *et al.* 1991). But we have found that the anterior part is also activated when subjects perform self-paced repetitive movements (Jahanshahi *et al.* in preparation).

It is true, of course, that repetitive movements are sequential. It is an unfortunate restriction of PET scanning that subjects must repeat their assignment many times if enough counts are to be collected to provide a reliable image. But monkeys with lesions in medial premotor cortex are impaired on the arm raise task, and they are slow even to make the first movement in a session.

There is another reason for being cautious about saying that the medial premotor cortex is specialized for the direction of sequences. This is that the only sequences that have been investigated are sequences in which there is no external guide as to which movement to perform. But suppose we teach a monkey to press colours in a particular order, for example red, green, blue. Here the context for the next movement is a colour. It is quite possible that performance of such a sequence would be disrupted by LPC but not MPC lesions.

3. The medial premotor cortex is not specialized only for movements that are determined by the subject. Monkeys with MPC lesions are severely impaired in relearning a sequence of three movements that are determined by the experimenter (Halsband 1987; Passingham 1987).

Recording studies

The hypothesis is that the medial premotor cortex is particularly concerned with tasks in which movements are performed without any external prompt. If this is correct we can predict that cells in the medial premotor cortex should have the following properties: there should be cells with activity that is specifically related to particular movements; there should be cells that are active while the subject makes the decision; and there should be cells that are more active before a self-initiated movement than before one which is externally cued.

Cells related to specific movements

The first expectation is that there should be cellular activity that is related to specific movements. Alexander and Crutcher (1990*b*) taught monkeys to flex or extend the forearm; the task was a delayed response task (Fig. 8.13, p.188). The instruction was given by the movement of a target to the left or right, and the monkey moved its arm in the same direction. There was then a delay of 1.5 to 3 seconds. After the delay the animal had to move its arm in that same direction without any external prompt.

Recordings were taken from cells in the medial premotor cortex. Of the task related cells, 55 per cent showed changes in activity during the delay while the animal prepared to act. Of these cells, 86 per cent were activated selectively according to the direction in which the animal was preparing to move.

Mushiake *et al.* (1990) recorded during a sequence task. The monkeys were required to press three out of four touch pads in order. There were two conditions. In the visually cued condition the pads lit up in order, and the animal followed the lights. In the non-visual or 'remembered' condition the animal had to learn a particular order and press the pads without external guidance.

The authors recorded from 208 movement related cells in the medial premotor cortex. Eight per cent changed activity only for the remembered sequence, and 41 per cent showed a greater change for the remembered than the visual sequence. Of these cells there were some that were active for particular sequences, for example 'top–down–right' but not for others.

Preparation to move

There are two ways of detecting cellular activity while a subject prepares to act without external prompting. The first is to record gross potentials, the second to record from single cells.

Potentials

Suppose a person is asked to make repeated finger movements, and to do so at his or her own pace. In such circumstances it is possible to detect a *Bereitschaftspotential* (BP) in the 1000 milliseconds or so before the movements (Kornhuber and Deecke 1965). The BP is maximal in amplitude over the vertex (Cz). It is important to distinguish between the early phase of the BP (roughly 1000 to 500 milliseconds before movement) and the late phase, (roughly 500 msec to 0 milliseconds (Tamas and Shibasaki 1985). Deecke (1987) has argued that it is the early component that has it origin in the medial premotor cortex.

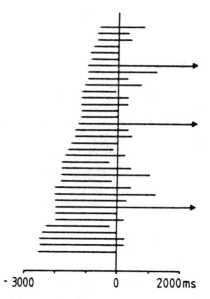

Fig. 4.16 Bar graph showing increased activity in cells in the medial premotor cortex in advance of self-initiated movements. Onset of movement (key release) occurs at time 0. Lines are rank ordered for increased leads for premovement times. Arrows mark activity lasting beyond the time of data collection after movement onset. Figure from Romo and Schultz. (1987).

He put forward an indirect argument on the basis of a study in which subjects made movements of the fingers or toes (Boschert *et al.* 1983). Over the central midline the BP was twice as large for toe movements as for finger movements. This could be explained if there was a contribution from the medial premotor cortex; the representations of the toe in motor cortex and medial premotor cortex are near together, whereas the representation of the fingers in the two areas are far apart.

The issue can be settled directly by taking recordings from the medial premotor cortex. Neshige *et al.* (1988) placed an electrode array over the lateral convexity cortex in patients undergoing surgery for epilepsy. These authors claim that for finger movements the origin of the early component of the BP is the hand area of both the left and right motor cortex.

However, Ikeda *et al.* (1992) were able to record with subdural electrodes over the medial premotor cortex in patients. They were able to record BP's from the medial premotor cortex of both hemispheres before subjects made movements of the fingers.

Single cells
There is no such problem of localization in studies in which recordings are taken from single cells. Romo and Schultz (1987) recorded from the medial

premotor cortex while monkeys prepared to make spontaneous movements. The monkeys were presented with a box containing food, and they were allowed to reach into it whenever they wanted.

On this task 25 per cent of the cells in the medial premotor cortex fired well in advance of the movement. It can be seen from Fig. 4.16 that some of these cells changed their activity more than two seconds before the movement.

Self-initiated and externally initiated tasks

Single cells
The final prediction was that there should be cells that are more active on self-initiated than on externally initiated tasks. Okano and Tanji (1987) taught monkeys to press a button. On some trials a red light came on 2.5 to 4.0 seconds after the beginning of the trial; this light told the animal when to press. On other trials the light failed to come on, and the monkey could respond whenever it wanted, as long as five seconds had elapsed since the beginning of the trial.

The cells were divided into 'short lead' cells that respond less than 480 milliseconds before movement, and 'long lead' cells that respond more than 480 milliseconds before movement. In the medial premotor cortex there was a clear difference between the proportion of long and short lead cells for the two tasks. Figure 4.17 shows the percentages of short and long lead cells that were active on the triggered (T) and self-paced (S) tasks. If a cell was active on both, this is shown as TS; if it was more active on one than the other, the smaller letter (T or S) is used for the task on which it was less active. Figure 4.17 shows clearly that there was a much higher percentage of cells that fired early on the self-initiated task.

It could be argued that there was a trigger even on the self-initiated task. The monkeys were waiting for the light; they decided to act when they detected that it was absent. This possibility could be minimized if the two tasks were given in separate blocks. We taught monkeys in alternating blocks of 17 or more trials (Thaler *et al.* 1988). During the block of self-initiated trials the animals knew that no signal would be given, and thus were not waiting to detect a signal. In other respects the conditions were much as in the study by Okano and Tanji (1987), except that a tone was used instead of a light, and the monkeys lifted their wrist instead of pressing a button.

Recordings were taken from 30 cells during performance of both tasks. On the triggered task 18 per cent of the cells fired before the earliest EMG, whereas on the self-initiated task 30 per cent of the cells did so. It has to be admitted that the sample of cells was small and the determination of the time at which a cell changed its firing was not very precise. But the results provide confirmation for the more robust findings of Okano and Tanji (1987).

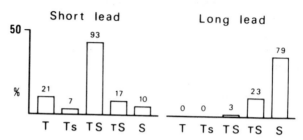

Fig. 4.17 Histograms showing percentage of cells classified according to the degree to which they were active in association with the visually triggered task (T) or the self-paced task (S). T = exclusively related to T, Ts = related more to T than to S, TS = equally related to both T and S, τS = related more to S than τ, S = exclusively related to S. Short lead = cells firing within 480 milliseconds before the movement, long lead = cells firing early than 480 milliseconds. The numbers above the histograms give the number of cells. Figure from Okano and Tanji (1987).

Recordings have also been made from cells in the upper and lower bank of the cingulate sulcus (Shima *et al.* 1991). The animals were given cues to tell them whether the trial was externally initiated or self-initiated. The cells were divided into those in the more anterior region (anterior to the genu of the arcuate sulcus) and those that lay more posteriorly. Figure 4.18 shows the times at which the more anterior cells changed their activity on the two tasks. On the self-initiated task 36.5 per cent of these cells changed their activity more than 500 milliseconds before the onset of the EMG. This compares with the much lower value of 8.8 per cent for the externally-initiated task.

PET scans

The same experiment can be carried out in the PET scanner. Zeffiro *et al.* (1991) required subjects to flex a finger when they decided or when a light told them to do so. They report that the medial premotor cortex, corresponding to the SMA, was significantly more activated during the self-paced than the visually triggered task.

Conclusion

There are cells in the medial premotor cortex that are active in relation to specific movements, and cells that are active before self-initiated movements. This activity is reminiscent of the set related activity recorded in the lateral premotor cortex (Weinrich and Wise 1982). In both cases the cells are active while the animal prepares to act. The difference is that on a self-initiated task no external cues are given to specify what is to be done or when.

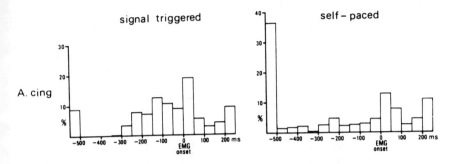

Fig. 4.18 Histograms of times of onset of movement-related cell activity in the anterior cingulate cortex (area 24), giving the time in milliseconds before or after the onset of EMG activity and the relative frequency of occurrence of cells as a percentage. Figure from Shima *et al.* (1991).

Medial and lateral lesions

There has been a symmetry between the treatment of the lateral premotor cortex (Chapter 3) and medial premotor cortex (this chapter). It has been proposed that both areas play a role in the selection of the movements that are appropriate to the context. The suggestion is that the difference lies in the context.

It is time to compare these two areas systematically and to consider how they might differ. Table 4.1 lists five tasks. On three of them performance is guided by motor cues, and on two by external cues. The table summarizes the effects of removing the medial or lateral premotor cortex. The details are given below.

Motor cues

This chapter has described three tasks on which monkeys with bilateral MPC lesions perform poorly. These are the arm raise task, the motor

Table 4.1 Five tasks on which the performance of monkeys with medial premotor lesions (MPC) and lateral premotor lesions (LPC) has been assessed. +++ = very impaired, ++ = moderately impaired, + = slightly impaired, 0 = not impaired , – = not assessed. For details see text.

	MPC	LPC
Arm raise	+++	+
Motor reversal	++	0
Motor sequence	+++	0
Auditory arm raise	+	–
Visual conditional	0	+++

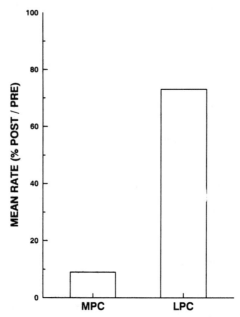

Fig. 4.19 Mean change in the rate of responses on the arm raise task, calculated as the percentage of the preoperative rate. MPC = 3 monkeys with medial premotor lesions, LPC = 2 monkeys with lateral premotor lesions. Data from Passingham *et al.* (1989).

reversal task and the motor sequence tasks. Monkeys with LPC lesions are either not impaired or only slightly impaired on these tasks.

Arm raise task

We have tested two monkeys with LPC lesions on the arm raise task. They were taught before surgery in the light, and under self-paced conditions (Passingham *et al.* 1989). The lateral premotor cortex was then removed, sparing the cortex medial to the superior precentral sulcus so as to avoid any possible damage to the medial premotor cortex. Figure 4.19 compares their post-operative performance with that of three monkeys with bilateral MPC lesions.

The two groups were taught in separate experiments, and their post-operative performance is therefore given as a percentage of their preoperative rate. In the first four days of post-operative testing, the two monkeys with LPC lesions raised their arm at a slower rate than before surgery; but their performance was still greatly superior to that of the monkeys with MPC lesions.

Analysis of the video tape of the sessions is revealing. We noted the attempts the animals made, that is the occasions on which the monkeys reached out of the cage, and we also noted the success of the attempts,

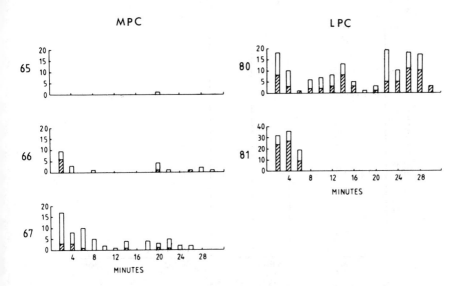

Fig. 4.20 Attempts and accuracy of attempts for the first post-operative session on the self-initiated arm raise task. The attempts are shown by the unshaded histograms, and the successful attempts by the shaded section of the histograms. The number of each animal is given to the left of each row. The sessions lasted up to 30 minutes. MPC = 3 monkeys with medial premotor lesions, LPC = 2 monkeys with lateral premotor lesions. From Passingham (1987).

that is the occasions on which the animals interrupted the beam. Compared with the animals with MPC lesions the monkeys with LPC lesions made many more attempts, and were more accurate in their attempts (Fig. 4.20).

Motor reversal task
Monkeys with LPC lesions have also been trained on the motor reversal task. The data for the monkeys with MPC lesions have already been given in Fig. 4.8 on p. 77. This same figure shows that the monkeys with LPC lesions learned the task as quickly as the three control animals.

Motor sequences
Finally, removal of the LPC bilaterally has no effect on the ability to relearn a sequence of three movements. Figure 4.10 (p.79) compares the performance of monkeys with MPC or LPC lesions (Halsband 1987; Passingham 1987). Before surgery the monkeys were taught to operate a catch by first pushing it up, then twisting it, and finally lifting it up. After surgery the three monkeys with bilateral LPC removal relearned the task immediately.

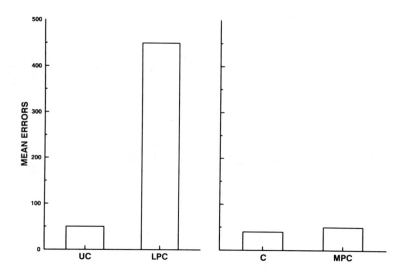

Fig. 4.21   Mean errors for post-operative relearning of a visual conditional motor task. UC = 3 unoperated monkeys, LPC = 3 monkeys with lateral premotor lesions, lateral premotor lesions, MPC = 3 monkeys with medial premotor lesions. Data from Passingham (1987).

External cues

Auditory arm raise task

Now consider how monkeys with MPC lesions make out on tasks on which there is an external cue to remind the animal of the appropriate act. Fig. 4.7 (p. 76) compared the performance of monkeys with MPC lesions on two versions of the arm raise task. The animals performed very much worse on the self-initiated version; when a tone reminded them of what to do they performed at a much higher rate. However, it has to be admitted that even on the externally cued version they failed to match their preoperative rate on the first four days of post-operative testing.

Visual conditional motor task

The last comparison is for the visual conditional motor task described in Chapter 3. A colour cue tells the animal which of two movements to make with a handle. We trained six monkeys on an automated version of this task, in which they moved a joystick, either by pulling it or by moving it to the side. When the monkeys had learned the task, we removed the MPC bilaterally in three animals, and then retrained all the animals. The monkeys with MPC lesions relearned the task with as few errors as the three control animals (Fig. 4.21). For comparison this figure also shows the data from an earlier experiment on the effects of removing the lateral premotor cortex.

This comparison is marred by the fact that the earlier experiment used a handle rather than a joystick. We have not yet checked that monkeys with LPC lesions perform badly on the automated version of the task; but it would be surprising if they did not.

Medial and lateral activity

The evidence from the effects of lesions suggests a double dissociation: on externally cued tasks LPC lesions disrupt performance, but MPC lesions much less so; and on tasks with motor cues MPC lesions disrupt performance, but LPC lesions much less so. The expectation is that the PET scanner will reveal similar dissociations.

PET scanning during performance

We have compared the activation when subjects perform a motor sequence or make movements that are directed by external cues (Deiber *et al.* 1991). The tasks have been briefly described before, but it will be helpful to give a fuller account here. There were four experimental conditions, and there was a control condition. The conditions were given in the following order:

1. Fixed (or repetitive): the subject moves the joystick forwards on each trial.
2. Learned sequence: the subject moves the joystick in the sequence F, L, L, R, B, R, B, F (where F = forwards, B = back, L = left, R = right). Each time a tone sounds the subject makes the next movement in the sequence. On finishing the sequence of 8 movements the subject starts at the beginning again.
3. Random (or free selection): the subject decides on each trial which of the four movements to make.
4. Auditory conditional: the subject is taught before the scan that sound A means forwards, sound B back, sound C left, and sound D right.
5. Opposite: the subject is told to make the movement opposite to that which had been correct on the previous condition. Thus if sound A is played the subject must move the joystick backwards, and so on.
6. Fixed: the subject moves the joystick forwards on each trial.

For all the conditions one of four tones is played on each trial. For conditions 1,2,3, and 6 the tone tells the subject when to move the joystick, but it tells the subject nothing about which movement to make. For conditions 4 and 5 the tone serves both as a trigger and as an instruction. Thus, the experiment is so designed that the same tones are played in all conditions and the same movements are made. The difference between the experimental conditions lies in the nature of the instructions.

The results for the premotor areas are shown in Fig. 4.12 (p. 84). The histograms show the increase in flow for the experimental conditions over and above the flow for the fixed condition.

Half of the experiment failed. The conditional and opposite tasks failed to activate the premotor areas at an acceptable level of statistical significance. The data fail to provide a test of the hypothesis. A better test might have been to teach the subjects the conditional task *while* they were being scanned, that is to take measurements during learning rather than retention.

The other half of the experiment worked, but the results were not as predicted from the animal data. For the sequence task there was little difference in the increase in blood flow between the medial and lateral premotor cortex. Indeed, if anything the results go in the opposite direction to that expected: the increase in the lateral premotor cortex was statistically significant, whereas it was not so for the medial premotor cortex.

It could be argued that the data for the sequence test are not reliable, because the increases over and above the fixed condition were small. But there are three reasons for dismissing this as an explanation.

1. The random task caused considerable activation; yet this task also excited the lateral as much as the medial premotor cortex.

2. In a later experiment we tested six normal subjects on the Random task, and compared the increase in blood flow with a rest condition (Playford *et al.* 1992). We replicated the finding that the Random task activates both the lateral and medial premotor cortex.

3. Seitz *et al.* (1990) taught subjects a much more complicated sequence. The experiment differed from that of Deiber *et al.* (1991) in two further important respects. First, the movements were unpaced. Second, scans were taken both early in learning and late, when the task was heavily overtrained. The authors report activation of both the medial and lateral premotor cortex, irrespective of whether the scans were taken early or late. The change in blood flow was of a similar magnitude in the two areas (Roland *et al.* 1991).

Degree of specialization

Why did the experiment by Deiber *et al.* (1991) fail to reveal a specialization between the lateral and medial premotor cortex? One answer is that, while there may be some specialization between the two areas, the difference in cellular activity may not be great. This point is made by several studies.

Recording
1. Kurata and Wise (1988) report the proportions of set-related and movement-related cells to be almost equal in the lateral and medial premotor cortex.
2. Okano and Tanji (1987) found more long lead cells in the medial than the lateral premotor cortex, but there were still 12.5 per cent of cells in the lateral premotor cortex and 14.2 per cent in motor cortex that responded early.
3. Romo and Schultz (1987) also compared performance on a trigger and a self-initiated task. Twenty-five per cent of the cells in the medial premotor cortex responded early on the self-initiated task, and 32 per cent of the cells in the lateral premotor cortex.
4. Kurata and Wise (1988) taught monkeys two tasks: in one (external cue) the monkeys pressed the left or right key as indicated by a light; in the other (internal cue) they reversed between left and right in blocks of 20 trials. There was only a minor difference between the activity of the cells in the medial and lateral premotor cortex: 13 per cent of the cells in the medial premotor cortex were more responsive in the internally instructed task, compared with a figure of 7 per cent for the lateral premotor cortex.

Lesions
If the differences in subpopulations are small, why do lesions of the two areas produce different effects? It would be difficult to understand this if the effects of the lesions were permanent; but they are not.

After removal of the lateral premotor cortex monkeys are slow to relearn a visual conditional motor task; but they can relearn it if given enough training (Passingham 1988). In other words the lateral premotor cortex is not *essential* for this task. Tanji *et al.* (1980) have shown that there are many cells in the medial premotor cortex that respond when a monkey performs such a task. The monkeys were trained to push or pull a handle as instructed by colour cues, and out of 201 cells 94 responded differentially during the delay according to the movement to be performed.

There is a similar outcome for the arm raise task. After removal of the medial premotor cortex monkeys are poor at raising their arm for food when there is no external cue to direct their performance (Passingham *et al.* 1989), but with training the monkeys improve (Thaler 1988). Again we should not be surprised that they can relearn, since there are cells in the lateral premotor cortex that respond on self-initiated tasks without external instruction (Romo and Schultz 1987; Kurata and Wise 1988).

The lesion gives a sensitive measure of the difference between cell populations. But the fact that a lesion has a differential effect does not imply that only one of the two areas is active on that task.

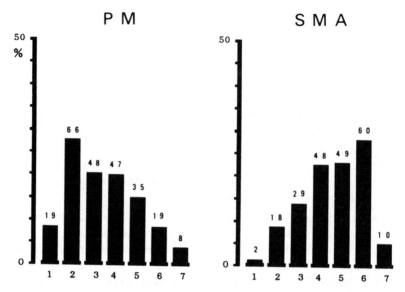

Fig. 4.22   Distribution of cells in lateral premotor cortex (PM), medial premotor cortex (SMA), and motor cortex (MI), classified according to the degree to which they were active in association with the visually guided sequence (VS) or the sequence performed from memory (MS). 1 = exclusively related to VS, 2 = much more related to VS, 3 = more related to VS, 4 = related equally to both VS and MS. 5 = more related to MS, 6 = much more related to MS, 7 = exclusively related to MS. The ordinate shows the percentage of cells, and the numbers above the histograms show the number of cells. Figure from Mushiake *et al.* (1991).

PET scanning during learning

There is another explanation of why the PET study by Deiber *et al.* (1991) failed to reveal the differences in specialization of the lateral and medial premotor areas. The conditional and sequence tasks had been taught before scanning, and thus it was not difficult to perform them during the scans. The assumption is that it is only if the tasks are very taxing that one can detect the specialized contribution of each area.

There is justification for this assumption. Mushiake *et al.* (1991) were able to show striking differences in the specialization of single units in the lateral and medial premotor cortex; they did this by comparing the activity of cells when monkeys either learned new motor sequences with the aid of visual prompts, or performed them automatically from memory.

They taught monkeys two sequences of three moves each. On the visual sequence a light told the animal which button to press; on the remembered sequence the monkey performed from memory without any external prompts. The activity of the cells was rated on a seven point scale according to the degree to which it was related to the visual sequence at one end (rating of 1) and the remembered sequence at the other end (rating of 7).

Figure 4.22 shows the specialization in the activity of cells in the lateral and medial premotor cortex. It is is true that in both areas there were many cells that were active in both types of sequence. But there is also a notable difference: in the medial premotor cortex there was a tendency for the activity to be greater on the remembered sequence, and in the lateral premotor cortex on the visual sequence.

We have therefore scanned human subjects in very similar conditions (Jenkins *et al.* 1992*b*). During two of the scans the subjects learned new motor sequences by trial and error; during two other scans they performed from memory a sequence on which they had been trained before scanning for over one hour until the task had become automatic.

The sequences were sequences of movements with the four fingers of the right hand. They were eight moves long. Every three seconds a tone sounded and the subject had to move one of the fingers. After each movement one of two sounds told the subject whether that movement was correct or incorrect. Thus, the subjects learned the sequences in the same way in which subjects learned conditional tasks in the experiments by Petrides (1985*a*).

The results were clear cut (Fig. 4.23). The medial premotor cortex was significantly activated when subjects performed the overlearned sequence and was more significantly activated than the lateral premotor cortex; by contrast the lateral premotor cortex was more significantly activated than the medial premotor cortex when subjects learned new sequences. Although external feedback was still given during automatic performance, the subjects no longer needed to pay attention to the sounds because the task was now automatic.

This result is consistent with the earlier finding of Mushiake *et al.* (1991) in which they related the activity of cells in the two areas to the nature of task. The lateral premotor cortex is especially active when the subject must use external cues to direct the appropriate movement, but the medial premotor cortex is more active when the task can be performed from memory without relying on external cues.

Summary

Like the lateral premotor cortex, the medial premotor cortex plays a role in the selection of movement; but the two areas differ in their specialization. The lateral premotor cortex makes the greater contribution when the subject uses external cues to direct the movements, and the medial premotor cortex when no such cues are available. However, the specialization is a matter of degree; it is by no means total.

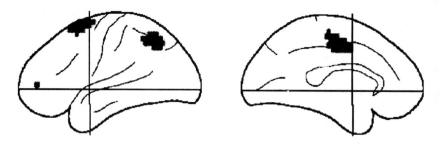

Fig. 4.23 Areas in which there was a significant increase in blood flow. The figure on the left shows the activation in the lateral premotor cortex when subjects learn new sequences compared with performing a pre-learned sequence. The figure on the right shows the activation in the medial cortex premotor cortex when subjects perform a pre-learned sequence compared with learning new sequences. Data from Jenkins *et al.* (1992*b*).

The evidence comes from the analysis of the effects of lesions, from PET scanning and from unit recording. Considering first tasks with no external cues, monkeys with MPC but not LPC lesions are severely impaired at performing self-paced arm movements, and at relearning motor sequences. This contrasts with the pattern of results for tasks on which performance is directed by external cues. Monkeys with LPC but not MPC lesions are impaired at relearning a visual conditional motor task, and monkeys with MPC lesions are only slightly impaired at making arm movements cued by an external signal.

In PET scanning experiments the medial premotor cortex is activated when subjects perform a well rehearsed sequence from memory, but there is more activation in the lateral premotor cortex when subjects must rely on external feedback to learn new sequences.

Recordings from single cells in monkeys show the same pattern. More cells are active in the medial premotor cortex when repetitive movements are self-paced, and in the lateral premotor cortex when these movements are externally triggered. Similarly, more cells are active in the medial premotor cortex when the animals perform motor sequences from memory, and in the lateral premotor cortex when they learn new sequences as directed by visual cues.

5 Premotor area 8

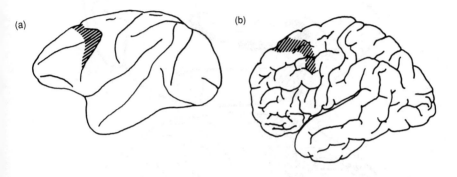

Fig. 5.1 Area 8 in (a) the macaque monkey and (b) the human brain.

The discussion has been limited so far to movements of the limbs. This chapter extends the argument to area 8 (Fig. 5.1) and the selection of eye movements.

It has not been clear whether area 8 should be treated as a premotor or a prefrontal area. Von Bonin and Bailey (1947) regarded it as transitional between area 6 (FC) and the dorsal prefrontal cortex (FD). For the macaque brain, Pandya and Yeterian (1985) include area 8 in a central strip of arcuate cortex, and use the term 'premotor' to include both areas 8 and 6 (Fig. 5.2).

This classification is supported by the functional evidence reviewed in this chapter. The argument is that, like area 6, area 8 plays a crucial role in the selection of movements. The difference lies in the nature of the movements.

Location

In a macaque brain, Brodmann (1925) identified area 8 as the tissue in the anterior bank of the arcuate sulcus, and on the convexity between the upper and lower limbs of the sulcus. Area 8 is very extensive in the human brain (Fig. 5.1).

Fig. 5.2   Premotor areas 6 and 8.

The 'frontal eye field' lies in the anterior bank of the arcuate sulcus. Stimulation of this area with microelectrodes evokes movements of the eyes (Bruce *et al.* 1985). The exact region is shown in Fig. 5.3. Much of it lies within the area identified by Walker (1940) as granular 8A (Fig. 5.4). However, Fries (1984) has identified an agranular region halfway down this sulcus, and demonstrated a projection from this region to the superior colliculus. Studies with the PET scanner suggest that in the human brain the frontal eye field occupies the ventral and caudal part of area 8 (Fox *et al.* 1985).

There is also a 'supplementary eye field'. This lies on the dorsal convexity above the frontal eye field and adjacent to the midline (Schlag and Schlag-Rey 1985, 1987). It lies within area 6 as outlined by Brodmann (1925). Camarda *et al.* (1991) locate it in the anterior part of dorsomedial F7 (Fig. 3.3, p.40) and the dorsomedial part of 8B as identified by Walker (1940) (Fig. 5.4).

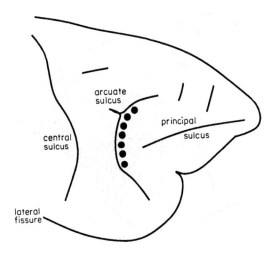

Fig. 5.3 The frontal eye fields as mapped by microstimulation in macaque brain; area shown by large dots. From Bruce (1988).

Anatomy

Outputs

Areas 8 and the dorsomedial eye field differ radically from area 6 in both inputs and outputs. They do not connect directly to any of the areas that are concerned with the execution of limb movements. Unlike area 6 they sends no projections to the forelimb area of MI (Strick 1985; Leichnetz 1986; Ghosh *et al.* 1987; Huerta and Kaas 1990) or to the spinal cord (Dum and Strick 1991).

There are descending outputs from these areas, but they are to areas specialized for eye movements. These are summarized below. A distinction is drawn between area 8 and the frontal eye field in particular.

Reticular formation
There are projections to the paramedian reticular formation and the adjacent pontine raphé from the frontal eye field (Stanton *et al.* 1988), the rest of area 8 (Leichnetz *et al.* 1984*a*), and the dorsomedial eye field (Shook *et al.* 1990). There are preoculomotor cells in this region that connect to the brainstem oculomotor nuclei in the dorsomedial pontine tegmentum (Fuchs *et al.* 1985).

Other preoculomotor areas
The dorsomedial field projects to the preoculomotor cells in the interstitial nucleus of Cajal and the rostral interstitial nucleus of the medial longitudinal

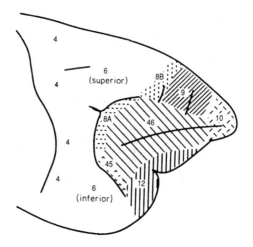

Fig. 5.4   Areas 8A, 45, and 8B as distinguished by Walker (1940). From Bruce (1988).

fasciculus (Huerta and Kaas 1990; Shook *et al.* 1990). There has been disagreement about whether the frontal eye field sends projections to these nuclei. Stanton *et al.* (1988) restricted their injections to the frontal eye field, and found no evidence for such projections. However, Huerta *et al.* (1986) claimed projections from the frontal eye field to these nuclei; and Leichnetz *et al.* (1984*b*) made less restricted injections in area 8, and they also report positive findings.

Superior colliculi
The dorsomedial eye field, the frontal eye field and the rest of area 8 influence head and eye movements via heavy projections to the deep layers of the superior colliculi (Catsman-Berrevoets *et al.* 1979; Stanton *et al.* 1988; Heurta and Kaas 1990; Shook *et al.* 1990). The superior colliculi project to the parabducens region near the oculomotor nuclei, and also to the cervical cord at a level at which the musculature of the neck is represented (Kuypers 1981).

Paraoculomotor nuclei
The dorsomedial eye field, area 8, and the frontal eye field project to the dorsomedial and dorsolateral part of the parvocellular red nucleus (Leichnetz *et al.* 1984*b*; Stanton *et al.* 1988; Shook *et al.* 1990). These areas connect to the inferior olive.

Inputs

Area 8 and the dorsomedial eye field also differ fundamentally from area 6 in their inputs. This can be appreciated from Figs 5(a) and 5(b). The details are as follows.

(a)

(b)

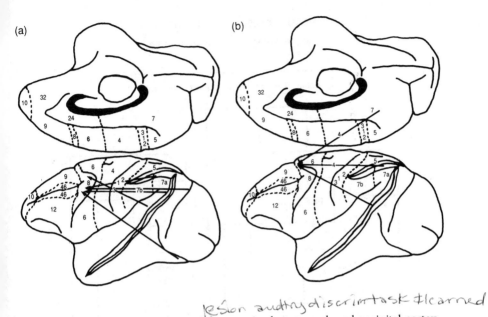

lesion auditory discrim task +learned

Fig. 5.5(a) Inputs to lateral area 8 from parietal,. temporal, and occipital cortex. For references see text. (b), Inputs to the dorsomedial eye fields from parietal and temporal cortex. For references see text.

Parietal cortex

Parietal areas 5 and 7b project heavily to the premotor area 6; but area 8 receives no input from areas 5 (Petrides and Pandya 1984) or 7b (Cavada and Goldman-Rakic 1989).

Parietal areas 7a and Lip (in the lower bank of the intraparietal sulcus) send no projection to area 6 (Petrides and Pandya 1984; Cavada and Goldman-Rakic 1989); yet both project to area 8, although the connection from the sulcus is the more substantial (Cavada and Goldman-Rakic 1989; Andersen *et al.* 1990). The dorsomedial eye field also receives a projection from the ventral bank of the intraparietal sulcus (Huerta and Kaas 1990).

Temporal cortex

There is no projection described from the infero-temporal cortex to area 6; but there is a projection to area 8 from the posterior infero-temporal cortex (Barbas and Mesulam 1981) and also from the ventral bank of the superior temporal sulcus (Seltzer and Pandya 1989). It is also impressive that lateral area 8 receives a heavy visual input from all the earlier visual areas—except striate cortex - that is, V2, V3, V4, V5 (MT), and V5a (MST) (Barbas 1988). Heurta and Kaas (1990) report that the dorsomedial eye field receives a projection from area V5a (MST) but none from areas V2, V3, V4, or V5.

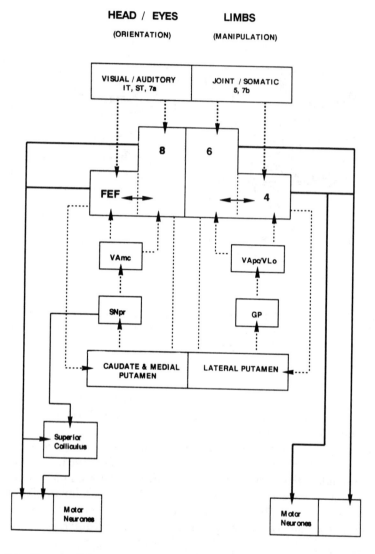

Fig. 5.6 Two parallel systems for manipulation and orientation. IT = infero-temporal cortex, ST = superior temporal cortex, 7a = parietal area 7a, 5 = parietal area 5, 7b = parietal area 7b, FEF = frontal eye field, 8 = Brodmann area 8, 6 = premotor cortex, 4 = motor cortex, VAmc = nucleus ventralis anterior, pars magnocellularis, VApc = nucleus ventralis anterior, pars parvocellularis, VLo = nucleus ventralis lateralis, pars oralis (terminology of ventral nuclei from Olszewski—1952), SNpr = substantia nigra, pars reticulata, GP = globus pallidus.

The superior temporal cortex does project to the rostral part of dorsal area 6 (Chavis and Pandya 1976); but this projection may well be destined for the dorsomedial eye field. Area 8 receives a heavy auditory input from the superior temporal association cortex (Petrides and Pandya 1988). There is also a projection to area 8 and the dorsomedial eye field from the upper bank of the superior temporal sulcus (Seltzer and Pandya 1989; Huerta and Kaas 1990).

The auditory inputs terminate in dorsal area 8, and the visual inputs in ventral 8 (Barbas and Mesulam 1981). This is confirmed by studies in the activity of single cells recorded while sounds or lights were presented; these studies are reviewed by Bruce (1988).

Functional significance

Area 8 is quite unlike area 6 in its connections. It appears not to receive any information directly about the joints—instead it receives sensory information about the outside world.

This can be best illustrated by considering vision. Area 8 receives from most of the earlier stages of visual processing. This includes areas in both the dorsal and the ventral visual systems outlined by Mishkin *et al.* (1983). The ventral pathway leads, through area V4, to the infero-temporal cortex, and the dorsal pathway to inferior parietal cortex (Desimone and Ungerleider 1989). Mishkin *et al.* (1983) argue that the ventral pathway analyses information about the identity of an object, based on colour and shape; whereas the dorsal pathway analyses information about the location of an object. Thus, area 8 receives inputs from areas which analyse the identity of an object, its location, and its movements.

Two systems

Areas 6 and 8 appear to be part of two different but parallel systems. These are summarized in Fig. 5.6. The figure is organized so as to suggest two systems, one for manipulative movements of the limbs, and the other for orienting movements of the eyes. That the systems are organized in this way is a hypothesis, not proven fact.

The systems are alike in that they are both motor systems, with projections to cells that directly influence the motor neurones, but they differ in their inputs. The manipulative system acts on information about the joints, and the orienting system on information about objects and locations in the outside world.

The systems also differ in their outputs. The manipulative system projects to levels of the cord controlling the face and limbs. The orienting system projects both directly and indirectly (via the basal ganglia and superior colliculi) to cells that are premotor for the oculomotor neurones.

Both systems have a motor and a premotor area. In the manipulative system these are areas 4 and 6. In the orienting system it is suggested that these are the frontal eye field and the rest of area 8. The frontal eye field

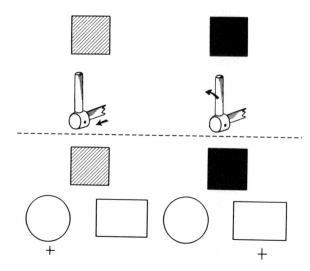

Fig. 5.7 Two conditional tasks. In the task illustrated at the top the monkey pulls or rotates a handle depending on the colour of the cue; in the task illustrated at the bottom the monkey chooses a sphere or a block depending on the colour of the cue.

only forms a small part of area 8, and the inputs from parietal and temporal cortex often terminate outside the frontal eye field itself (Cavada and Goldman-Rakic 1989; Seltzer and Pandya 1989).

The critic might object that it is invalid to regard the frontal eye field as an executive area comparable with motor cortex. In a primate some of the fibres from MI terminate on the motor neurones, but the fibres from the frontal eye field do not synapse directly on the oculomotor nuclei in the brain stem.

But this argument is not convincing, and for two reasons. The first is that there are no direct projections to the motor neurones from motor cortex in the rat or cat (Kuypers 1981). This has not led to the reclassification of motor cortex in these species.

The second reason is that we should not expect the cortical control of the eyes to require direct connections to the motor neurones. It was argued in Chapter 2 that direct connections were required for the production of discrete movements. But the eye is not a jointed structure; unlike a limb or the digits, it moves as a whole.

The notion that area 8 contains a premotor area is not novel. Pandya and Yeterian (1985) regard the whole of the arcuate cortex (areas 6 and 8) in a monkey as premotor cortex. What is novel in Fig. 5.6 is the brazen clarity with which two motor and premotor systems are identified.

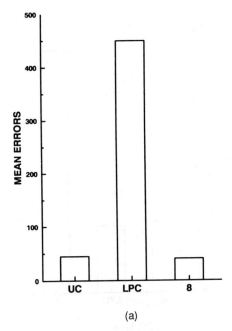

(a)

Fig. 5.8   Errors for post-operative relearning of a visual motor conditional task in which the cues are colours and the monkeys respond by pulling or rotating a handle.

Orienting and manipulation

There are two sorts of choice that animals make. The first is to choose between objects and locations. The second is to choose what action to perform with an object. When you go to your tool box, you first choose the hammer rather than the screwdriver, and you do this by looking for it (orienting). You then choose whether to bang the hammer or to screw it; that is, you decide how to use it (manipulating).

Objects

We set up an experiment to compare selection of these two types of response (Halsband and Passingham 1985). There were two tasks, illustrated in Fig. 5.7.

The first is the visual conditional motor task described in Chapter 3. We taught monkeys to pull or turn a handle according to the colour of the instruction cues.

The second task is also illustrated in Fig. 5.7; it is further shown in diagram form as task **a** in Fig. 5.10. The choice is between two objects which differ in colour and shape, a brown block and a white sphere. The monkey pushes one of them and finds a peanut under the lid if the choice is correct. The

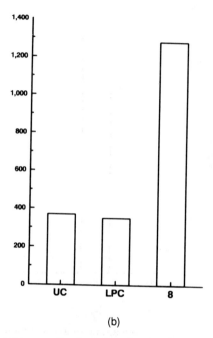

(b)

Fig. 5.9   Errors for post-operative learning of a visual conditional task in which the cues are colours and the choice is between two objects. UC = 3 unoperated control monkeys, LPC = 3 monkeys with lesions in lateral premotor cortex, 8 = 2 monkeys with lesions in Brodmann area 8.

position of the two objects is varied randomly; on half the trials the sphere is on the left, and on half the trials on the right.

The cue or instruction is given by the central panel. The monkey starts the trial by pushing this panel. If the panel is orange, the monkey is rewarded for pushing the brown block; if the panel is green, for pushing the sphere.

Eight monkeys were taught these two tasks. In two animals area 8 was then removed bilaterally, and in three animals the lateral premotor cortex (area 6). Three monkeys served as unoperated controls.

There is a double dissociation. Consider first the selection between limb movements: the monkeys with LPC lesions were slow to relearn, whereas monkeys with area 8 lesions relearned at the normal rate (Fig. 5.8). Now consider the selection between objects: the monkeys with LPC lesions learned as quickly as the control animals, but the monkeys with area 8 lesions failed to learn the task at all in 3500 trials (Fig 5.9).

This impairment has been confirmed by an experiment carried out independently by Petrides (1985*b*). The task is illustrated as task **b** in Fig. 5.10. The choice was between two boxes that differed in that one of them

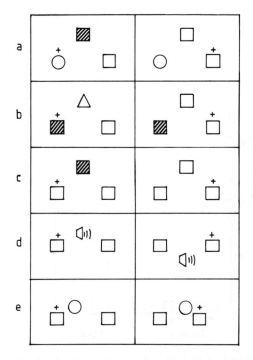

Fig. 5.10 Conditional tasks on which monkeys are impaired after removal of Brodmann area 8. For each task the set-up is shown for two trials, one on the left and the other on the right. + = rewarded.

was lit and the other was not. On half the trials the lit box was on the left and in half it was on the right. The cue or instruction was given by an object, and the rule was if object A was presented the monkey should push the lit box, and if object B the box that was not lit. Three monkeys with bilateral lesions including area 8 failed to learn this task in 1020 trials.

Locations

Visual or auditory cues
Two other studies complete the picture by providing a choice between locations rather than objects. The tasks are **c** and **d** in Fig. 5.10. On both tasks the monkeys had to select the left or the right. In the experiment by Lawler and Cowey (1987) the instruction was given by a central plaque: if this was black the monkeys should choose the plaque on the left, and if white the plaque on the right. In the experiment by Goldman *et al.* (1970) the cue was given by sounds: if the sound came from above the monkey was rewarded for choosing one location (for example the left), and if from below for choosing the other location (for example the right).

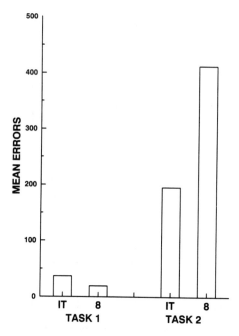

Fig. 5.11   Mean errors to learn two tasks. The tasks are described in the text. IT = monkeys with infero-temporal lesions, 8 = monkeys with lesions in Brodmann area 8. Data plotted from Lawler and Cowey (1987).

In the study by Lawler and Cowey (1987) animals with area 8 lesions were severely impaired (Fig. 5.11, task 2). Two of the animals failed to learn the task at all in 1200 trials. This confirms a similar finding reported previously by Milner *et al.* (1978).

In the study by Goldman and Rosvold (1970) the cortex was removed bilaterally from both banks of the arcuate sulcus; this includes much of areas 8 and 6. The animals were slow to relearn. Monkeys with lesions in area 6 alone (LPC) were only slightly impaired, if at all.

Spatial cue

There is one last demonstration: the task differs in that the cue is a spatial one, rather than a colour or shape. The task is shown in diagram form as task **e** in Fig. 5.10. Latto (1986) trained monkeys on a 'landmark' task developed by Pohl (1973). In this version the monkey selected between two squares, one on the left and one on the right. On any trial the correct square was indicated by the position of the circle above. If the circle was nearer to the square on the left, the monkey was required to push that square; and if it was nearer to the square on the right, the monkey was required to respond to the right. After the removal of area 8 on both sides the monkeys made errors, and especially so as the distance between the circle and the correct square was increased.

Orienting to stimuli

Why are the animals with lesions in area 8 impaired? We need to know whether they are able to look at or attend to the critical stimuli.

Gaze

Monkeys with area 8 lesions do not have paralysis of gaze. In this respect the frontal eye field in area 8 is not like motor cortex, since the removal of motor cortex can cause paralysis immediately after surgery.

The reason for the difference lies in the pattern of the descending projections. There is a projection to the deep layers of the superior colliculi from the lower bank of the intraparietal sulcus (Lynch *et al.* 1985), the frontal eye field (area 8), and the dorsomedial eye field (Huerta and Kaas 1990). Removal of area 8 alone has only a small effect on spontaneous eye movements; the colliculi can still be influenced by cortex. But removal of area 8 and the superior colliculi does cause paralysis of gaze (Schiller *et al.* 1979). It would be interesting to see whether the removal of both the frontal eye field and the dorsomedial eye field had the same effect.

Foveation

Monkeys with area 8 lesions can still foveate normally. Deng *et al.* (1986) taught monkeys to fixate a central point; a spot of light then appeared in the periphery of the visual field; and the monkeys were rewarded if they moved their eyes to foveate that spot. After the unilateral removal of area 8 the monkeys could still do this normally. This result has been obtained independently by Schiller *et al.* (1987).

Reporting stimuli

Monkeys do, however, show a unilateral neglect immediately after removal of area 8 from one hemisphere.In a classic paper Latto and Cowey (1971) measured the visual fields of monkeys after removal of the frontal eye field either unilaterally or bilaterally. In the weeks after surgery monkeys with unilateral removal of the frontal-eye field failed to report seeing test flashes in the contralateral visual field. A monkey with a bilateral removal of the frontal eye fields was less likely to report flashes in either visual field.

But the monkeys recover. Latto and Cowey (1971) give data for two monkeys with unilateral lesions; both monkeys had near to normal visual fields two weeks after surgery. Latto and Cowey (1971) also give data for one monkey with a bilateral lesion; this animal was much recovered in 39 days.

Orienting to stimuli

Van der Steen *et al.* (1986) studied the head and eye movements of monkeys before and after removing area 8 unilaterally. Immediately after surgery, the animals tended to direct their gaze to the side ipsilateral to the lesion, and failed to track targets with their eyes alone if the targets moved into the contralateral field. However, when targets were presented one week after surgery, the latency for initiating movements of the head and eyes had returned to normal.

Scanning stimuli

Monkeys with area 8 lesions can look for natural rewards. This has been shown under two conditions.

1. The monkey must find all the pieces of food that are presented. Schiller *et al.* (1987) presented monkeys with a board in which there were either 9 or 17 slots, each containing a piece of apple. One to three weeks after surgery, the animals scanned the board efficiently and removed all the pieces of apple.
2. The monkey must find a single piece of food amongst distractor items. Collin *et al.* (1982) showed that monkeys with bilateral lesions could still find a peanut among 24 inedible items presented in a 5 by 5 matrix; but it must be admitted that they were slightly slower than control animals in finding them.

Monkeys with area 8 lesions can also scan for targets that are associated with reward as the result of learning. Latto (1978) reported that a bilateral lesion in area 8 had only a slight effect on the ability to search for a circle among 39 other geometric shapes. Schiller *et al.* (1987) measured eye movements and required monkeys to locate with the eyes the letter A among other letter stimuli; bilateral removal of area 8 did not impair the ability to locate the target quickly.

Conclusion

Monkeys with area 8 lesions are not impaired on conditional learning tasks because they are unable to look at the relevant stimuli or fail to notice them. There is also direct evidence that they can attend to cues presented on learning tasks whether in the centre or the periphery. First, they can pull or turn a handle on the basis of the colour of a central cue (Halsband and

Passingham 1985). Figure 5.8 shows that they relearn this task as quickly as unoperated control animals. Clearly removal of area 8 does not prevent the detection and identification of a central colour cue.

Second, monkeys with area 8 lesions can also make choices between stimuli that are presented in the periphery. Lawler and Cowey (1987) taught monkeys to choose between two plaques in the periphery, one on the left and the other on the right. If both were black the monkey were required to choose the one on the left, and if both were white they were required to choose the one on the right. Monkeys with lesions in area 8 could learn this task at a normal rate (Fig. 5.11, task 1); this study confirms an earlier finding reported by Stamm (1973).

Yet lesions in area 8 greatly impair the ability of monkeys to choose between peripheral stimuli on the basis of a central cue (Lawler and Cowey 1987), and this is true even though they must start the trial by pushing the central cue (Fig. 5.11, task 2). We cannot argue that they fail because they do not notice the relevant stimuli.

Learning to orient

To understand this finding we must draw a distinction between orienting to stimuli and *learning* to orient on the basis of stimuli. It has been shown in the previous section that monkeys with area 8 lesions can orient to stimuli, and that this is true of stimuli which are associated with reward by learning. Monkeys with lesions in area 8 can learn visual discriminations without trouble (Goldman and Rosvold 1970). On such problems they learn which cue is associated with food; when they notice the cue they can orient to it. They do not have to learn what eye movements to make.

Conditional learning

Now contrast this with a conditional learning task. The monkeys must use the visual cue in the centre to tell them which stimulus to look for. There is a response rule: given one colour, the animal looks for object X, and given another for object Y.

An informative example is provided by the delayed response task. The animal is required to select a spatial location on the basis of a conditional cue that is held in memory. Deng *et al.* (1986) taught monkeys to fixate a central point. While they were fixating, a spot of light was flashed on for 300 milliseconds. However, the monkeys were not allowed to respond until later when the fixation spot had disappeared. Thus, they had to make a saccade into empty space. After the removal of area 8 on one side the monkeys made saccades that were both slow and inaccurate.

The same result has been reported by Funahashi *et al.* (1986). The spot of light was presented in one of eight locations, but the monkey was not allowed to move its eyes until a delay of 0.5, 1.5, 3, or 6 seconds after the spot had disappeared. Area 8 was removed unilaterally together with the posterior portion of the principal sulcus. After surgery, the monkeys made errors, that is they looked to the wrong locations. Patients with lesions in areas 8 and 46 also make errors when they must make saccades to the location in which targets have recently been presented (Pierrot-Deseilligny *et al.* 1991*a*). However, the patients either show no increase in latency or only a small increase in latency when making reflexive saccades to targets that are visible at the time (Pierrot-Deseilligny *et al.* 1991*b*).

The PET scanner reveals the same dissociation. Kertzman *et al.* (1992) compared the activation when subjects perform saccades to remembered targets with the activation when they made the same eye movements as visually guided saccades. There was more activation in area 8 and in the dorsomedial eye field when the subjects performed saccades to remembered targets.

It is usual to conclude that area 8 is specialized for the production not of reflexive eye movements but of eye movements to targets in memory. But this formulation is too restrictive. In the case of animals the crucial factor may be that the eye movements are learned. This hypothesis could be tested. After removal of area 8, monkeys should be poor at learning to move their eyes to the left given one colour cue and to the right given another.

A subtle variation would be to present the animals with two stimuli, and require that they look to the one on the left if the stimuli are the same and to the one on the right if the stimuli are different. Monkeys with lesions in area 8 should be impaired at learning to do this. Such a result would demonstrate two points. The first is that the crucial factor is that the eye movements are learned. The second is that there may be no need for the contextual cue to be presented in the centre.

Sequences

Removal of area 8 and the dorsomedial eye field also impairs the ability to orient to different locations in sequence. We have taught monkeys to respond to three manipulanda in order (Passingham 1985*d*). The monkeys had to press a button in the centre, pull a handle to the right, and then depress a lever to the left (Fig 6.20, p.148). The task was based on a sequence introduced by Deuel (1977). In her version the monkeys had to operate three latches in turn, removing a pin, turning a crank, and pressing a knob.

We trained three animals after removing areas 8, 8B and dorsal lateral 6, and the animals failed to learn the sequence in 2000 trials (Passingham 1985). This confirms the earlier findings of Deuel (1977) and Deuel and

Dunlop (1979); they reported a severe impairment on the latch sequence in monkeys with a similar lesion.

We have also trained two monkeys with lesions that were restricted to area 8; and both animals also failed to learn within the limits of testing (Halsband 1982). They also failed in 750 trials to learn to press two identical levers in the order left and then right (Halsband 1982). They were unable to learn to orient to two locations in order.

The next step would be to deliberately teach monkeys a sequence of eye movements. Barone and Joseph (1989) presented monkeys with three target spots. The spots lit up in turn, and the animals had then to move their eyes from one location to another in the sequence that had been presented. There were cells in area 8 that fired differentially according to the particular sequence that the animals were reproducing. It would be worth teaching the task to other monkeys and determining whether, as expected, a lesion in area 8 or 8B interferes with the learning of such sequences.

Detour reaching

There is one other piece of evidence that lesions in area 8 impair the ability to learn to make eye movements. Moll and Kuypers (1977) required monkeys to reach for food stuck on the bottom of a transparent plate. There was a hole in the plate to allow the monkeys to reach through the Perspex and then under it for the food. To solve the task the monkey had to learn to look away from the food and search for the hole.

Moll and Kuypers (1977) removed areas 6 and 8. They reported that the monkeys tended to try to reach for the food straight through the Perspex where it could be seen. The effect was not due to the removal of area 6. Diamond (1988) left area 6 intact and removed area 8 together with the prefrontal areas 46 and 9 from both hemispheres. Food was placed in a three-sided Perspex box. On the critical test the box was placed so that one Perspex wall was at the front, and the animals had to reach for the food through the opening at the side. The monkeys with lesions persisted in trying to retrieve the food by scrabbling at the front wall through which the food was visible. Further experiments are needed to compare the effects of removing either area 8 or area 46 alone.

Antisaccade task

On the detour reaching task the monkey must learn to look away from the food so as to notice the hole in the Perspex. Human subjects can be asked to look to the right if a light appears on the left, and to the left if the light appears on the right. This is the 'antisaccade' task.

Guitton *et al.* (1985) reported that patients failed to inhibit reflex saccades to the light if area 8 was damaged, but in this study the excisions were large and included other areas as well. Pierrot-Deseilligny *et al.* (1991*b*) claim that patients with infarcts in lateral area 8 are not impaired, but that patients with infarcts in dorsal prefrontal cortex make errors on this task. However, all such claims must be tentative given the inaccuracy involved in the reconstruction of the lesions on to a standard atlas.

The issue can be tackled with the PET scanner. Kertzman *et al.* (1992) compared the activation when subjects performed the antisaccade task with the activation when they made the same eye movements but as visually guided saccades. There was more activation during the antisaccade task in lateral area 8 and the dorsomedial eye field. The same was also true in the dorsal prefrontal cortex.

Recording from cells

If the argument is correct we should expect to find cells that are active before eye movements, and that are directionally specific. It should also be possible to find activity that relates to learning.

Specificity
Bruce and Goldberg (1985) recorded from the frontal eye fields. Fifty-four per cent of the cells discharged before visually guided saccades. All of these cells were selective in that their activity was tuned to an optimum direction. The cells differed in the fineness of their tuning.

Learning and memory
Recordings were also taken on two tasks in which the correct location was specified by learning (Bruce and Goldberg 1985). On the memory task, the target was only flashed for 50 milliseconds, but the animal was not allowed to make the saccade until over a second later. On the learning task, repeated trials were given in which the target appeared at the same location; on test trials the animal was given the opportunity to make a saccade to that location even though the target had not yet been presented. On the memory task there were cells that discharged during the delay. On the learning task there were cells that discharged before eye movements, even though the animals performed in the dark; these cells were either not active or less active before spontaneous eye movements made in the dark.

Enhancement
The mechanism of selection is suggested by the phenomenon of 'enhancement'. In an experiment by Goldberg and Bushnell (1981) monkeys fixated a central point, and a spot of light was then presented within the receptive field of the cell from the which the recording was being taken. In one condition the monkey was required to continue to fixate the central point; in the other the animal was allowed to make a saccade to the stimulus.

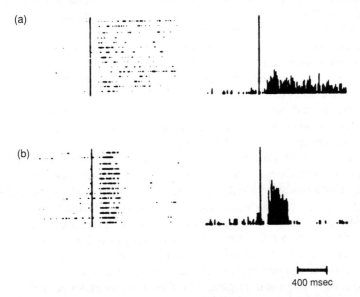

Fig. 5.12   Activity of a cell in lateral area 8 while a monkey performs two tasks. In (a) the monkey fixates a central spot while a peripheral target is shown. In (b) the monkey makes a saccade to the peripheral target. The activity is synchronized on the onset of the peripheral target. From Goldberg and Bushnell (1981).

The term 'saccadic enhancement' refers to the situation in which a cell shows greater activity when the monkey is allowed to make a saccade than when it is not. In the study by Goldberg and Bushnell (1981) 50 per cent of the cells in area 8 with visual responses showed significant enhancement. An example is given in Fig. 5.12.

There is an elegant twist to this experiment. On some trials two stimuli were presented, one in the receptive field and one outside it. Saccadic enhancement only occurred when the monkey made a saccade to the stimulus within the receptive field. Enhancement provides a mechanism for the selection of targets for saccadic eye movements.

Area 8 and dorsomedial eye field

This chapter has concentrated on lateral area 8. Less is known of the dorsomedial eye field. Lateral area 8 forms part of the lateral premotor cortex and the dorsomedial eye field part of the medial (supplementary) premotor cortex.

Chapter 4 argued that the lateral premotor cortex plays a role in the selection of movements when there are external cues and the medial premotor cortex plays a role in the selection of movements when there are no such cues. We may speculate that lateral area 8 and the dorsomedial eye field may be specialized in similar ways.

There are differences in anatomy. Lateral area 8 receives an input from all visual areas except for striate cortex (Barbas 1988). But there are no projections to the dorsomedial eye field from areas V2, V3, V4, and V5 (Huerta and Kaas 1990).

There are also differences in cellular activity. There are a significant number of cells in the dorsomedial eye field that discharge before spontaneous saccades (Schlag and Schlag-Rey 1985, 1987), but there appear to be fewer such cells in the frontal eye field (Bizzi 1968; Bizzi and Schiller 1970). Most of the cells in the frontal eye field discharge before saccades made to visual targets (Bruce and Goldberg 1985); many cells in the dorsomedial eye field do the same, but they tend to discharge less briskly and with a longer latency (Schall 1991).

One interpretation is that the dorsomedial eye field is specialized for eye movements that are not determined by visual targets and that the frontal eye field is specialized for eye movements made when visual targets have been presented. In human subjects the frontal eye field is activated when subjects make saccades to visual targets, but the dorsomedial eye field is not (Jenkins *et al.* 1992*c*; Kertzman *et al.* 1992).

It is necessary to clarify the proposal in two ways. First, the distinction is not between situations in which the subject can or cannot see stimuli. When a subject scans a picture there is a visual stimulus; but the subject generates the eye movements. Second, it is not a complete description to contrast eye movements in response to targets and eye movements that are self-generated in the sense that the subject decides where to look. If a subject is taught a sequence of eye movements, that sequence is not self-generated in that sense. Yet by analogy with the medial premotor cortex (Chapter 4), one might expect such a sequence to be disrupted by damage to the dorsomedial eye field. The hypothesis could be tested by comparing the effects of lesions in monkeys.

Summary

Motor cortex governs movements of the limbs and face, and the frontal eye fields the movements of the eyes. Just as the selection of limb and face movements depends on the premotor mechanisms of area 6, so the selection of eye movements depends on the premotor mechanisms of the rest of area 8. Both monkeys and patients with lesions in lateral area 8 are poor at directing their eyes on the basis of a learned context.

The selection of eye movements is to be described in terms of the objects of the search, the things or locations that we look for. Whereas area 6 selects our limb movements, area 8 selects things in the outside world. It is for this reason that area 6 receives proprioceptive information, and area 8 information from the external senses.

Area 8 forms part of the lateral premotor cortex and the dorsomedial eye field part of the medial (supplementary) motor cortex. It is proposed that area 8 is specialized for the selection of eye movements made when targets have been presented and the dorsomedial eye field for the selection of eye movements that are not determined by visual targets.

6 Dorsal prefrontal cortex (areas 46 and 9)

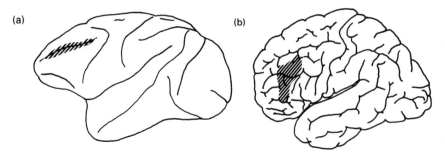

Fig. 6.1 Area 46 in (a) the macaque monkey and (b) the human brain.

This book has been written from the outwards in. It starts with the movements themselves (Chapter 2). It progresses to the selection of the movements, whether of the limbs (Chapters 3 and 4) or the eyes (Chapter 5). It now comes to the cognitive processes by which the individual knows what it is appropriate to do. This brings us to the prefrontal cortex proper.

Prefrontal areas

Figure 6.3 shows the subareas as identified by Barbas and Pandya (1989) in the macaque brain. Preuss and Goldman-Rakic (1991) present a similar scheme, though they differ in identifying more subareas. Areas 9 and 46 were first distinguished by Walker (1940); they are shown separately in Figs 6.1 and 6.2.

It will be convenient to use the term 'dorsal prefrontal cortex' for areas 9 and 46 combined, and the term 'dorsal prefrontal convexity' for area 9 alone. Areas 11, 12, 13, and 14 lie on the inferior convexity and orbital surface; these will be termed the 'ventral prefrontal cortex'.

It is unfortunate that most of the functional studies of the dorsal prefrontal cortex have concentrated on area 46. There are only a few studies in which area 9 has been removed without also removing area 46. The result is that we know much more about the contribution made by area 46 than of that made by area 9.

Anatomy

Areas 9 and 46 are closely interconnected (Kunzle 1978; Barbas 1988; Barbas and Pandya 1989). They also share many common inputs and outputs.

(a)

(b)

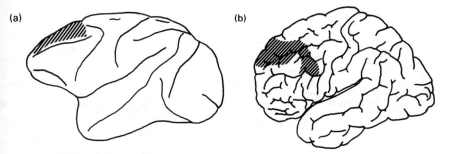

Fig. 6.2 Area 9 in (a) the macaque monkey and (b) the human brain.

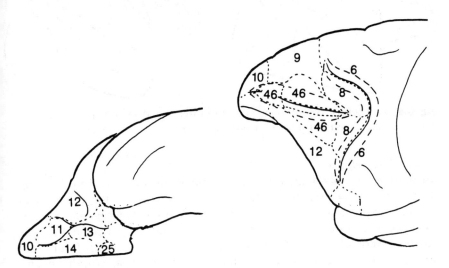

Fig. 6.3 Cytoarchitectural divisions of prefrontal cortex. From Barbas and Pandya (1989).

Outputs

Premotor areas

There are no projections from prefrontal cortex to motor cortex (Leichnetz 1986). The cortico-cortical projections from areas 9 and 46 are directed to the premotor areas 8 and 6. (Figs 6.4(a) and 6.4(b). Areas 9 and 46 are reciprocally connected with area 8 (Barbas 1988; Barbas and Pandya 1989) and the dorsomedial eye field (Huerta and Kaas 1990). They are also reciprocally connected with the lateral premotor cortex (area 6) (Kunzle 1978; Barbas and Pandya 1987, 1989) and the medial premotor cortex (area 6) (Wiesendanger and Wiesendanger 1984; Selemon and Goldman-Rakic 1988; Luppino *et al.* 1990).

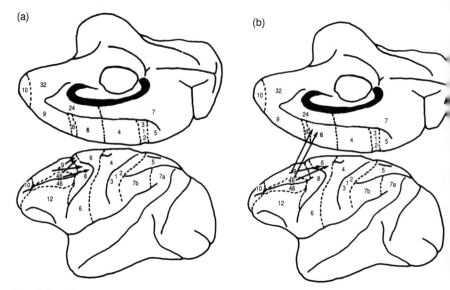

Fig. 6.4 (a) Cortico-cortical connections from areas 9 and 46 to area 8. (b) Cortico-cortical connections from areas 9 and 46 to area 6. For references see text.

Descending outputs

Areas 9 and 46 follow area 8 and the dorsomedial eye field in directing outputs to the oculomotor system. Area 46 projects to the paramedian pontine tegmentum (Leichnetz *et al.* 1984*a*). Anterograde studies are needed to establish whether the fibres terminate on premotor cells for the oculomotor system. There is also a heavy projection from areas 46 and 9 to the deep layers of the superior colliculi (Goldman and Nauta 1976; Catsman-Berrevoets *et al.* 1979; Fries 1984). Both areas can also influence the superior colliculi via a relay through the basal ganglia (Fig. 5.6, p.108). The details of this relay will be given in Chapter 8.

Cortical inputs

Parietal cortex

The main inputs to the dorsal prefrontal cortex come from the parietal cortex (Fig. 6.5). Area 7a projects to areas 46 and 9; there is a particularly heavy projection to the depths of the middle part of sulcus principalis (area 46) (Cavada and Goldman-Rakic 1989; Andersen *et al.* 1990). Area 7b projects to the ventral bank of sulcus principalis (Cavada and Goldman-Rakic 1989; Neal *et al.* 1990). The medial parietal area 7 sends an input to the posterior part of the dorsal prefrontal convexity and medial area 9, as well as to the dorsal bank of sulcus principalis (Petrides and Pandya 1984; Cavada and

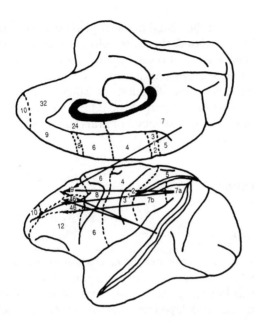

Fig. 6.5 Some cortico-cortical inputs to areas 9 and 46 from parietal and temporal cortex. For references see text.

Goldman-Rakic 1989). The posterior part of the dorsal prefrontal convexity sends return connections back to medial area 7 (Kunzle 1978).

Temporal cortex
There is also a projection to the dorsal prefrontal cortex from the upper bank of the superior temporal sulcus (Seltzer and Pandya 1989). The upper bank of this sulcus is interconnected with inferior parietal cortex (Seltzer and Pandya 1984).

The caudal part of sulcus principalis receives an input from the infero-temporal cortex (Barbas and Mesulam 1985; Barbas 1988) and from V5 (MT) and V5a (MST) (Seltzer and Pandya 1989). The cortex of the superior temporal convexity (area 22) sends a projection to areas 9 and 46 (Jacobsen and Trojanowsi 1977; Petrides and Pandya 1988).

Functional significance

The dorsal prefrontal cortex acts mainly on information from the parietal association cortex. Parietal areas 5 and 7b process information about the animal itself (Sakata and Iwamura 1978; Robinson and Burton 1980). Parietal area 7a processes information about the direction of gaze and the spatial position of objects in the world (Andersen 1987).

It is of particular signifance that area 46 receives a heavy input from parietal area 7a and area 8. First, there are many cells in areas 7a and 8 with visual receptive fields (Bushnell *et al.* 1981; Bruce and Goldberg 1985), though in parietal cortex the visual fields are larger in 7a than in area Lip (Andersen *et al.* 1990). Second, there are cells with 'gaze fields' in parietal areas 7a and Lip. The activity of these cells relates to the direction of gaze (Andersen and Mountcastle 1983; Andersen *et al.* 1990).

These properties allow the location of stimuli. This requires that information be available on the part of the retina that is stimulated and on the direction of gaze. The next section confirms that area 46 plays a role in the specification of spatial location.

Selecting locations

Delayed response task

We have known for over fifty years that the mechanisms of prefrontal cortex are necessary for normal performance of delayed response tasks (Jacobsen 1935). It has taken an embarrassingly long time to make sense of this observation.

Consider first the classic 'delayed response test'(DR). The standard way of teaching this to monkeys has been to train the monkey in a Wisconsin General Testing Apparatus; the experimenter works the apparatus by hand. More recently sophistication has set in, and a computer is used to run the display and time the intervals.

In the standard version of the task the monkey watches while the experimenter puts a peanut in one of two food-wells (Fig. 6.6). The food-wells are then covered with identical plaques. A screen is lowered so that the animal can no longer see the location of the food-wells. Some seconds later the screen is raised, and the animal is allowed to choose the food-well it supposes to contain the peanut. The next trial follows five seconds later, the position of the peanut being randomized from trial to trial.

The logic of the DR task is conditional. If the animal saw the peanut being placed on the left the animal should choose the food-well on the left; if the peanut was placed on the right it should choose the food-well on the right. The correct choice is determined by the cue provided by the baiting. When the animal responds there is nothing in the set-up that tells it what to do; the monkey just sees two identical covers. The monkey must depend on a cue in memory. We can write this as:

Given A, if (P), make $R1$ when trigger T
Given A, if (Q), make $R2$ when trigger T
Where:
A = general context (2 food-wells)
(P) and (Q) are cues in working memory (location of food)
$R1$ and $R2$ = responses
T = trigger stimulus (raising of screen)

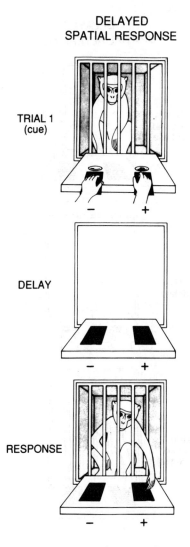

**DELAYED
SPATIAL RESPONSE**

TRIAL 1
(cue)

DELAY

RESPONSE

Fig. 6.6 Delayed response task. Figure from Friedman *et al.* (1988).

Delayed alternation

There are other versions of the delayed response task. One is termed delayed alternation (DA). In the standard version, the monkey is allowed to find a peanut in the food-well on the left or right (Fig. 6.7). The screen comes down so that the animal can no longer see the food wells. After a delay of 5 seconds, the screen is raised again for the next trial, and the animal can make its next choice. The rule is that, if the peanut was on the left on one trial, it will be on the right on the next trial; the correct side alternates from trial to trial.

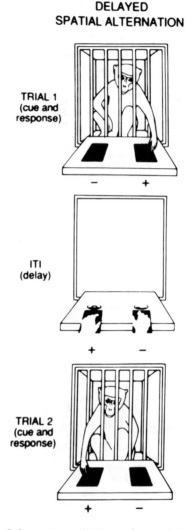

Fig. 6.7   Delayed alternation task. Figure from Friedman *et al.* (1988).

When the monkey responds it sees only two identical covers as on DR. The correct choice is specified by a conditional rule. The difference between the tasks is that on DR the animal chooses the food-well it has just seen baited, whereas on DA the animal avoids the food-well which it last found to be baited.

Spatial search task

The same logic applies to a search task devised by Collin *et al.* (1982). The monkey faces an array of 25 food-wells, arranged in 5 rows of five (Fig. 6.8).

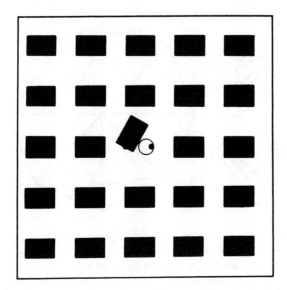

Fig. 6.8   Testing board for search task. A door is shown open revealing a food well behind.

Each foodwell is covered by a small opaque plastic door. Each trial starts with a peanut behind each door. The monkey is given the chance to collect the peanuts. However, when the monkey takes a peanut from one food-well, the door closes and the monkey has to depend on its memory to tell it where the remaining peanuts are located. It is fruitless for the monkey to return to a door it has already opened, since the peanut will have gone. In other words, if the monkey has just taken a peanut from one door, it should avoid that door for the rest of that trial.

As on DR and DA, the display gives no clues. On DR and DA the monkey must make a decision while facing two covered food-wells. On the search task it must decide between twenty-five doors that look alike.

All three tasks require the animal to choose a location, and to guide their choice by information stored in working memory. They are discouraged from cheating on DR and DA by interposing the screen, so as to prevent them from keeping their eye on the correct location throughout the delay. On the search task there are too many doors for the animals to keep their eye on all of them at the same time.

Delayed response for eye movements

When testing the animals on these tasks it has not been the practice to monitor their eye movements. But Funahashi *et al.* (1989) have devised a version of the DR task in which the animal is specifically taught to choose between eight locations by turning the eyes. The monkey is taught to fixate

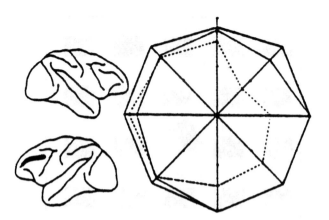

Fig. 6.9 Plot of performance on oculomotor delayed response task for a monkey with removal of sulcus principalis (area 46) on the left. The percentage correct for each target is shown along the axes drawn through the central fixation point. Thick line = performance at shortest delay (usually 0.5–1.5 seconds), thin line = percentage correct at 3 seconds delay, dashed line = percentage correct at 6 seconds delay. Figure from Goldman-Rakic (1987).

a central spot throughout the delay; this prevents the animal from peeking. The task is automated: a target light briefly appears in one of eight positions, a delay follows, and when the fixation light disappears the animal is allowed to make its choice. It does this by looking at the location at which the target light appeared. At the time of choice the animal faces eight locations, and nothing in the display tells the animal what to do.

Area 46

Delayed response tasks

Normal performance of delayed response tasks depends crucially on the tissue that lies in sulcus principalis (SP) (area 46). This is a deep sulcus that extends down 10 mm or more at the centre. If both banks are removed the monkeys fail to master the task the DR task and are at or near chance after 1000 trials (Goldman *et al.* 1971). This is an astonishing result: all the animal has to do is pick the food well where it saw the food being placed. Monkeys with area 8 lesions are only slightly impaired on DR (Goldman *et al.* 1971),

Bilateral lesions in area 46 also impair performance on other versions of the delayed response task. After surgery monkeys fail to learn DA in 1000 trials, and their performance on the last 100 trials is at or near chance level (Goldman and Rosvold 1970).

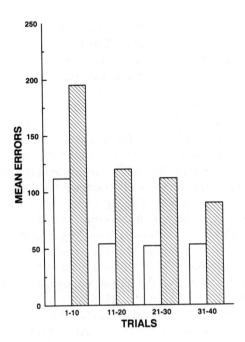

Fig. 6.10   Mean errors on trials 1–40 of the visual search task. Unshaded histogram = 3 unoperated control monkeys, shaded histogram = 3 monkeys with lesions in sulcus principalis (area 46). Data from Passingham (1985*b*).

Similar results are found using the oculomotor version of the delayed response task. After the unilateral removal of area 46, monkeys make errors on this task, and they make more errors as the delay increases (Funahashi *et al.* 1986) (Fig. 6.9). They are impaired when the targets are contralateral to the lesion, but not when they are ipsilateral. If area 46 is removed from both hemispheres, the animals are impaired irrespective of the side of the target.

Finally, monkeys with area 46 lesions also make errors on the search task (Passingham 1985*b*) (Fig. 6.10). On this task it pays the animal not to return to doors that it has already opened on the current trial. The operated animals are much more likely to return than are control animals.

Owen *et al.* (1990) have devised a version of the search task for human subjects. The subject is presented with boxes on a computer monitor, and must search for the blue token by touching the boxes until one of them reveals the token. It will not pay to open the same box on any one trial, since if the box was empty it remains empty. Patients with partial prefrontal lobectomies are significantly more likely than control subjects to open the same box more than once (Owen *et al.* 1990).

Metabolic studies

There is another way of demonstrating that area 46 plays a role in the performance of delayed response tasks. This is to measure the uptake of radioactively labelled 2-deoxyglucose while animals work on these tasks. Friedman *et al.* (1991) compared DR and DA which tax working memory with a visual simultaneous discrimination which does not. They found an enhancement of local cerebral glucose utilization in area 46 while the monkeys performed the delayed response tasks but not while they performed the visual discrimination. There was a similar enhancement in parietal area 7a and in Lip in the inferior bank of the intraparietal sulcus.

Friedman and Goldman-Rakic (1988) also measured glucose utilization in the hippocampus. Area 46 is reciprocally connected with the hippocampus and parahippocampal gyrus both directly (Selemon and Goldman-Rakic 1988) and indirectly via the cingulate cortex (areas 24 and 23) and retrosplenial cortex (Mufson and Pandya 1984; Vogt and Pandya 1987). It is also directly connected with the entorhinal cortex which projects into the hippocampus (Goldman-Rakic *et al.* 1984; Insausti *et al.* 1987). There is evidence from lesion studies that the hippocampus plays a specific role in the memory of locations (Parkinson *et al.* 1988).

When monkeys perform the DR and DA tasks there is a selective increase of uptake of labelled 2-deoxyglucose in the CA1 and CA3 fields and in the dentate gyrus (Friedman and Goldman-Rakic 1988). This increase is specific for the hippocampus; it does not occur in the amygdaloid nuclei.

Spatial responses

There are three respects in which all versions of the delayed response tasks are alike.

1. The animal has to learn to select between spatial targets.
2. The tasks are tasks which cannot be solved by learning that a particular location is associated with reward. Sometimes one location is correct, sometimes another. The animal has to learn to choose location A given one cue and location B given another.
3. The cue is not visible at the time of choice. It is held in working memory

Monkeys with area 46 lesions fail such tasks. But would they also be impaired on tasks which did not have these features? It was a classic paper by Mishkin (1964) that provided the first indication that the dorsal prefrontal cortex was involved in selecting between spatial locations. Later research tried to establish whether it was critical that the responses be spatial. This has been done by testing monkeys on non-spatial versions of DR and DA.

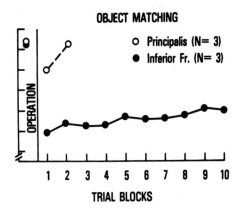

OBJECT MATCHING

○ Principalis (N= 3)
● Inferior Fr. (N= 3)

OPERATION

TRIAL BLOCKS

Fig. 6.11 Trials to relearn an object matching task. Scores before the operation are for 200 trials of retention testing. Scores after the operation are for 100 trial blocks. N = number of animals, open circles = monkeys with lesions in sulcus principalis (area 46), filled circles = monkeys with lesions in the inferior prefrontal convexity (area 12). Figures from Mishkin and Manning (1978).

Visual matching

A parallel task to DR is delayed matching, either for colours or objects. The monkey is shown a sample stimulus: on some trials it is A and on others B. After a delay the animal must pick the same stimulus it has just been shown from the pair A and B. On some trials A appears to the left of B and on some trials to the right. Thus the monkey must choose A or B irrespective of their spatial location.

After the removal of area 46, monkeys are only slightly impaired on relearning this task (Mishkin and Manning 1978) (Fig. 6.11). After the removal of area 46 together with lateral 9, the animals can still perform the task with delays of 14 to 19 seconds (Passingham 1975*b*).

Object alternation

A parallel task to DA is object alternation. The monkey faces two objects A and B, each object appearing sometimes on the left and sometimes on the right. The peanut is placed under A on one trial, B on the next, A on the next, and so on in alternation. Thus the monkeys must pick the correct object irrespective of its spatial location.

If areas 8, 46, and lateral 9 are removed together, the animals relearn the task slowly and only reach a level of 80 per cent correct after 1000 trials (Mishkin *et al.* 1969). But if the lesion is restricted to area 46 the animals reach their preoperative level in 400 trials or so (Mishkin and Manning 1978).

Table 6.1 Effects of lesions in area 46 (sulcus principalis) on 6 tasks. +++ = severely impaired, ++ = moderately impaired, + = slightly impaired. For details see text.

Task	Effect of area 46 lesion
Delayed response	+++
Oculomotor delayed response	+++
Delayed alternation	+++
Search task (25 doors)	++
Visual matching	+
Object alternation	+

The effects of cooling

When they were performed these lesion experiments were taken to suggest a specialization for the tissue in area 46 lying in sulcus principalis. The results are summarized in Table 6.1.

The results were challenged by an experiment by Bauer and Fuster (1976) in which they found an impairment on colour matching when they cooled the tissue in and around sulcus principalis, but these results could be accounted for in one of two ways. First, Bauer and Fuster may have inadvertently cooled area 12 on the ventral surface. Second, cooling produces acute effects, whereas after removal of the tissue animals can compensate for the acute effects of the lesions. Monkeys with lesions in area 46 are impaired at first both on object matching and object alternation (Mishkin and Manning 1978), although they can relearn these tasks fairly rapidly. Thus it could be argued that area 46 is not *essential* for the selection of objects on the basis of object cues.

Lesions in areas 9 and 46

The belief that area 46 is specialized for spatial responses was given further support by the fact that removal of lateral area 9 has no effect on the performance of spatial delayed response tasks. The monkeys have no trouble in learning DR (Goldman *et al.* 1971) or DA (Mishkin 1957). Furthermore, these animals do not make significantly more errors than normal animals on the spatial search task (Passingham 1985*b*).

However, the issue has now been reopened by a study reported by Petrides (1991*a*). He found monkeys with lesions in area 46 and lateral area 9 to be very severely impaired on a task in which the animals made choices between objects. On a presentation trial the monkeys were faced with three new objects, each covering a food-well containing a peanut. The monkeys were allowed to push any one of the objects and retrieve the peanut. A test trial then followed on which the monkeys were presented with the object they had picked and one of the ones that they had not picked. The correct response was to choose the object that had not been chosen before. After removal of areas 46 and 9 the monkeys failed to perform above chance level.

Yet Petrides (1991*a*) also showed that the same monkeys could perform as well as control animals on a version of the object matching task. In this version the monkeys were again shown three new objects on each presentation trial, and allowed to choose one of the objects. The difference is that on the test trial they were presented with the object they had chosen together with a new object they had not seen before. The correct response was to choose the new object.

The crucial difference between the two tasks is that the second task can be solved on the basis of recognition memory alone. The monkey has only to recognize the object that it has not seen before. On the first task the monkey has just seen both the objects presented on the test trial, and cannot choose between them on the basis of familiarity. Instead it must remember which object it had picked on the presentation trial and then avoid it on the test trial.

These experiments challenge the belief that area 46 is specialized for spatial responses. However, the issue is not yet settled. One obvious possibility is that the impairment on the first task is due to damage in area 9. The prediction is that if only area 46 was removed the animals would be able to succeed on the first task.

This prediction has not yet been tested, and no firm conclusion can therefore be reached. This is disappointing considering the number of years during which the issue has been under debate. We will return to the same issue in a later section which describes other experiments in which monkeys have been required to make manipulative responses that differ in respects other than their spatial direction.

Delay

Delayed response tasks are also alike in that the animal must act on the basis of information in working memory. It is usually assumed that the delay is crucial, but we need to consider the evidence in detail.

A non-delayed version of DR poses no problems for any animal. If the monkey is allowed to take the food immediately after watching it being loaded, it can start reaching to the correct foodwell when the food is still in sight. On the oculomotor version of DR, if there is no delay the animal has only to look at the target. In such situations, the animals do not have to learn anything about what responses to make.

Visual–spatial tasks
Non-delayed tasks that require the monkeys to learn can be devised by making up conditional tasks in which the cues differ in spatial location from

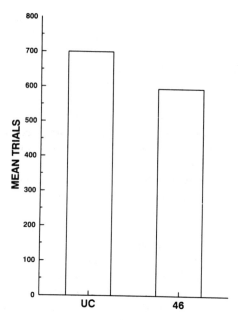

Fig. 6.12 Mean trials to relearn a spatial conditional task with no delay. UC = 3 unoperated control monkeys, 46 = 3 monkeys with lesions in sulcus principalis (area 46). Data from Passingham (1985*b*).

the food-wells to which the animal responds. In two experiments the monkey was taught to respond to one side given one colour cue, and the other side given the other colour. In one experiment all four monkeys with lesions in area 46 were impaired: they relearned the task in a mean of 50 trials whereas the control animals relearned immediately (Soper 1979). In the other experiment one of three animals with lesions in area 46 was impaired (Milner *et al.* 1978).

Gaffan and Harrison (1989) taught monkeys two types of task. On one (visual–spatial) the monkeys chose the left given objects A and B, and the right given object C and D. On the other task (spatial–visual) the monkeys chose A if the objects A and B were on the left, and B if they were on the right. In each case there were four problems, each with new objects. The monkeys with area 46 lesions were impaired. On the first set of tasks they made a mean of 78 errors compared with 45 for the controls, and on the second a mean of 134 errors compared with 71.

Spatial–spatial tasks

These impairments are mild. It could be argued that area 46 would be more greatly taxed by tasks in which both the cues and the responses are spatial, but the prediction is not borne out. Goldman and Rosvold (1970) taught monkeys to choose one side if a sound was played above them, and the other side if the sound was played from below. Monkeys with lesions in area 46 relearned the task without trouble.

In two other studies monkeys were taught with visuospatial cues. The cues were provided by two panels in the centre, one above the other; the monkeys were taught that if the upper panel was lit, they should respond to one side, and if the lower panel to the other. Again lesions in area 46 had no effect (Soper 1979; Passingham 1985*b*) (Fig. 6.12).

In all these studies all the tissue was removed from sulcus principalis. It may be that the results would have been more consistent had the lesions avoided the posterior quarter or so of the sulcus. The posterior part lies within the bow of the arcuate sulcus, and is often removed in studies of area 8. Von Bonin and Bailey (1947) treated it as transitional cortex, labelling it (FDΔ), and it is possible that it is functionally distinct from the anterior three quarters of the sulcus.

Delayed response in children

Studies of children provide another line of evidence, though the evidence is very indirect. Diamond has shown that young children also make errors on the DR task (Diamond 1988), and that the pattern of errors is similar in these children and in monkeys with dorsal prefrontal lesions (Diamond and Goldman-Rakic 1989). In both cases errors are made when the subject is required to respond to side B when side A was correct on the previous trial. It seems likely that the children make this error because their prefrontal cortex is immature (Diamond 1988; Diamond and Goldman-Rakic 1989).

In the literature on children the error has come to be known as the 'A, not B' error. Children can be induced to make the error even if the toy is visible through a transparent screen in container B at the time as the child makes its choice (Butterworth 1977; Harris 1989). However, the best way of causing young children to make the error is to require the child to choose on the basis of information in memory, and to lengthen the delay since the toy was last seen in container B (Diamond 1988).

Cell recording

Delay

During the DR task, there are cells in area 46 that change their activity during the delay while the animal waits before responding, and some of these cells continue to modify their firing even if the delay is extended for as long as 60 seconds (Fuster and Alexander 1971; Fuster 1973). Niki (1974) reports that 17.6 per cent of task related cells modify their activity during the delay, and Kojima and Goldman-Rakic (1982) give a figure of 15.8 per cent as a proportion of all cells from which recordings were taken. Of the task related cells, the proportions showing selective changes during the delay are given as 6 per cent by Niki (1974) and 19 per cent by Niki and Watanabe (1976).

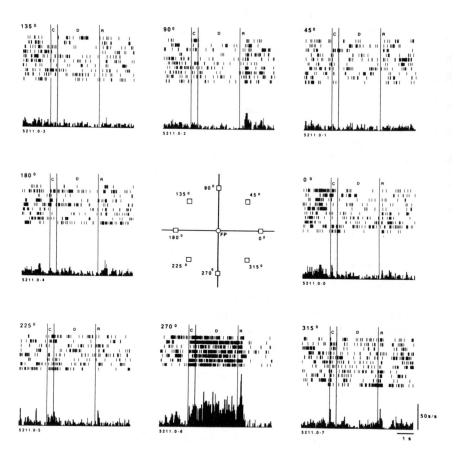

Fig. 6.13 Directional delay period activity of a cell in sulcus principalis (area 46) during the oculomotor DR task. The centre diagram shows position of visual cues. The cue period is shown between first two vertical lines, the delay period of 3 seconds is shown between the second and third vertical lines, the response period is shown after third vertical line. Figure from Funahashi *et al.* (1989).

However, the proportion of such cells has been found to be much higher in two other studies. In one the monkeys waited before rotating a handle to the left or right: Kubota and Funahashi (1982) found that of task related cells 51 percent changed their activity during the delay, and 29.4 percent selectively depending on the movement to be made. In the other study the monkeys waited before making saccades: Funahashi *et al.* (1989) report that of task related cells 51 per cent changed their activity during the delay, and 40.6 per cent changed their activity selectively during the delay. An example of a directional cell is given in Fig. 6.13, although not all the cells are as specific in their tuning.

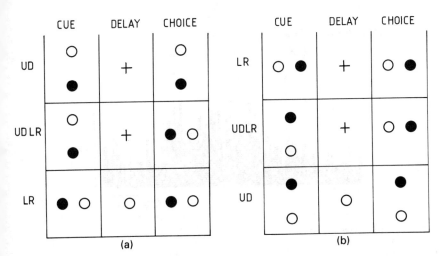

Fig. 6.14 (a) Activity of a cell in dorsal prefrontal cortex during the delay while a monkey performs three spatial conditional tasks. The cell codes the position of the cue. (b) activity of a cell in dorsal prefrontal cortex during the delay while a monkey performs three spatial conditional tasks. The cell codes the location of the stimulus that the monkey will respond to. + = cell responds during the delay, 0 means cell does not respond during the delay. In the cue period a black circle means lit, an open circle means unlit. In the choice period a black circle means the rewarded stimulus, an open circle means the non-rewarded stimulus. UD = 'up/down', LR = left/right', UDLR = 'up/down, left/right'.

Cue and response

Two interpretations of this activity are possible. It could relate to the location of the cue or to the location to which the animal is going to respond. In an elegant experiment Niki and Watanabe (1976) distinguished between these two possibilites by comparing the standard version of DR with a spatial conditional task in which the cues were presented above or below but the animal was required to respond to the left or right (UDLR). The logic of the experiment is illustrated in Fig. 6.14. Figure 6.14(a) shows the pattern for activity related to the cue (down); Fig 6.14(b) shows the pattern for activity related to the response (right). The authors found cells of both types, some that fired according to the position of the cue and others that fired according to the direction of the response. This result has been confirmed by Quintana *et al.* (1988)

Thus, area 46 contains the mechanisms necessary for computing the correct location given the cue. There is no implication that it determines the form of the movement required to reach for that location. The solution to delayed response tasks is a location, not a specific limb movement. The monkey could choose correctly by turning upside-down and using one arm or by pushing the cover to the food well with one foot. Prefrontal cortex computes the goal, not the means of achieving it.

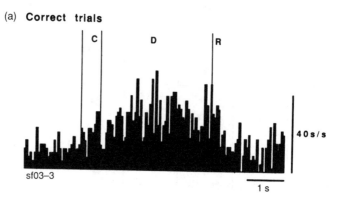

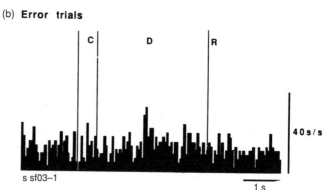

Fig. 6.15   Average discharge for nine cells during correct trials (a) and nine cells during trials in which the animal made an error (b). C = cue period, D = delay period, R = response period. From Funahashi *et al.* (1989).

Activity of cells and performance

It can be shown that the activity of the cells is related to the performance by the animal. Funahashi *et al.* (1989) compared nine correct and nine incorrect trials, and report that the activity of the cells was significantly greater on the correct trials (Fig. 6.15). They illustrate the pattern of firing for two cells: one cell ceases firing half way through the delay on an error trial; the other fails to discharge at all during the delay on the error trial.

Stamm and Rosen (1972) also recorded cortical steady potentials while monkeys were trained on DR. At the beginning of the delay the authors could record a surface negative potential shift over the dorsal prefrontal cortex. In four monkeys the correlation between the size of this potential and the level of performance varied between 0.74 to 0.90.

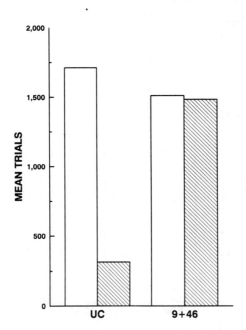

Fig. 6.16 Means trials for preoperative learning and post-operative relearning of the counting task. Unshaded histogram = pre-operative, shaded histogram = post-operative. UC = 3 unoperated control monkeys, 9 + 46 = 3 monkeys with lesions in lateral area 9 and area 46. Data from Passingham (1978).

Manipulative responses

On DR the monkeys must choose between spatial locations. One can devise tasks that are formally similar but which differ in that the response is non-spatial. In one such experiment we faced monkeys with two keys (Passingham 1978). At the start of the trial the key on the right was lit, and the monkeys pressed it repeatedly until the light went off. On some trials the light was extinguished by one press, and on others by five presses. The key on the left then lit up, either immediately (0 seconds) or after a delay (1-5 seconds). To gain a peanut the monkey had to repeat the same number of presses on the second key. We allowed the animals to respond by pressing one or two times or five or more times, since they were not accurate at counting.

We taught this task to monkeys, and then removed areas 9 and 46 in three animals. Totalling the data for all delays, it took these animals a mean of 1483 trials to relearn the task after the removal of area 9 and 46. This compares with only 314 trials for unoperated animals (Fig. 6.16).

There are two issues that require attention. The first is the question of whether areas 9 and 46 differ in their specialization. To answer this, we retrained the control animals to the level of 5 seconds delay, and then

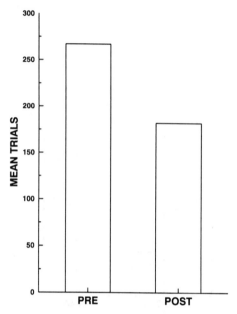

Fig. 6.17 Mean trials for preoperative learning and post-operative relearning of the counting task. Data for 3 monkeys with lesions in sulcus principalis (area 46). Data from Passingham (1978).

removed the tissue in sulcus principalis (area 46) alone. The monkeys relearned quickly (Fig. 6.17), but unfortunately no control group was included so as to allow comparison of the scores. However, one animal was clearly not impaired: it relearned in 0 trials, that is it performed at the criterion level in the first 100 trials.

The second question is whether the delay is crucial. The animals with lesions in areas 9 and 46 were slow to relearn even when the second key became available at once (0 seconds) (Passingham 1978). No experiment has been carried out in which the animal could respond while the cue was still available. This could be done by requiring simultaneous performance with the two hands.

We later repeated this experiment but with two changes (Passingham 1986). The first is that we compared the contribution of lesions in areas 9 and 46 on their own; we removed the areas separately. The second change is that the animals were only required to make single movements; the animals were not required to generate a series of movements (Passingham 1986).

The task was as follows. The monkey was presented with two levers; the choice was between squeezing them together or rotating the whole assembly (Fig. 6.18). At the beginning of each trial a lock was put on so that only one of the two movements could be made. The monkey grasped the levers and made the only movement that was possible. In this way the animal was forced either to squeeze the hand or rotate the wrist. A delay

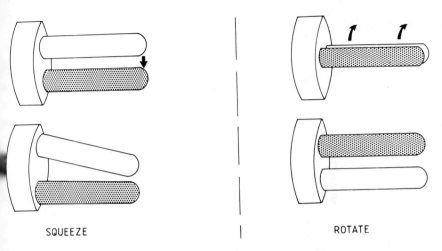

SQUEEZE | ROTATE

Fig. 6.18 Apparatus for the task on which the monkeys had to squeeze or rotate a handle. The handle is shown as it appeared when rotated (right) or squeezed (left). The figures on the left show the handle as it would appear from above; the figures on the right show the handle as it would appear from the front. The direction of movement is shown by the arrows. For purposes of illustration the rod nearest the monkey is shaded; in actual fact the two rods were identical. From Passingham (1986).

ensued, and the animal then had a free choice. The correct response was to repeat the same movement that it had made before the delay. The task proved difficult to learn. Yet animals with lesions in area 46 or area 9 relearned with very few errors (Fig. 6.19).

It is not clear why the results differ so dramatically from those we obtained with the counting task (Passingham 1978). It is possible that an impairment would be found if the lesion included the whole of the dorsal prefrontal cortex (areas 9 and 46). But one might have expected some slight impairment in the animals with areas 9 or 46 removed alone. It is more likely that the important difference is that in this experiment the animals were not required to generate a series of actions.

Cell recording

If the dorsal prefrontal convexity plays a role in generating movements, it should be possible to find cells in the region that fire in relation to such movements.

Ono *et al.* (1984) required monkeys to press a bar a pre-determined number of times in order to gain access to food. The number could be from 5 to 99. Thus, the monkeys had to generate a repetitive series, as on the counting task described above. Of 57 cells tested in area 9, 37 per cent changed their activity while the monkeys pressed the bar.

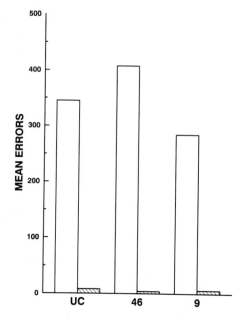

Fig. 6.19 Mean errors for preoperative learning and post-operative relearning of the task on which the monkeys had to squeeze or rotate a handle. Unshaded histogram = preoperative, shaded histogram = post-operative. UC = 3 unoperated control monkeys, 46 = 3 monkeys with lesions in sulcus principalis (area 46), 9 = 3 monkeys with lesions in lateral area 9. Data from Passingham (1986).

Manipulative cues

The last section described experiments in which the subject has to repeat a series of limb movements. This section describes experiments in which the subject must act on the basis of a non-spatial context. For example, the context can be the frequency or extent of limb movements.

Frequency

In an experiment by Manning (1978) monkeys reported the number of lever presses in one of two ways. One group was given a choice between identical keys on the left and right, and the other group between a red and a white key. For one group the rule was that after 64 presses the animals should press the left key, and after 32 the right key; and for the other group the rule was that after 64 presses the animals should press the white key, and after 32 the red key.

The monkeys took a long time to relearn the task after the removal of areas 9, 8, and 46. Two of the animals failed to relearn at all in 3000 trials.

In this experiment the animals could respond as soon as they had completed the count. This is equivalent to the condition called '0 seconds' in the parallel experiment by Passingham (1978).

Extent

Another parameter of movement is its extent. Both monkeys and patients have been taught to report the distance that a lever has moved on a semicircular track. Mishkin *et al.* (1977) taught two monkeys to move a lever with their hand. The animals had to report whether the displacement was long or short. They did this by opening the food-well if the distance was long, and refraining if the distance was short. There was no delay between completion of the movement and the opportunity to decide whether to open the food-well or not.

After the removal of the areas 9, 46, and dorsal 8 the animals were impaired. It took them a mean of 245 trials to relearn the task compared with 40 trials on the retention test before surgery.

Leonard and Milner (1991) repeated the experiment with human subjects. They required the subjects to move the lever until it stopped, and then to report the extent by moving it through the same distance without a cue. Patients with right frontal excisions were inaccurate.

It has to be said, however, that the lesions in this study were not confined to areas 9 and 46. Furthermore, inspection of the brain diagrams suggests that in many of these patients the lobectomy invaded the premotor areas.

Action cues and other cues

In all the experiments described above the context was given by an action. The monkey or human subject reported what they had done. But patients with frontal lesions are also poor at reproducing a series of gestures as demonstrated to them by the tester. Patients with unilateral frontal excisions make many errors in reproducing sequences of hand postures (Kolb and Milner 1981; Jason 1985).

The impairment is one of recalling a series of gestures. Patients with anterior lesions can reproduce single gestures without difficulty (Kimura 1982; De Renzi *et al.* 1983). Jason (1985) has also shown that patients with frontal excisions are impaired even if they are allowed to recall a series of gestures in any order.

Of course, it is not clear from these studies on patients where the critical damage lay. The excisions included large areas of the prefrontal cortex, and many of them also probably invaded area 6. However, it is clear from a PET study that dorsal prefrontal cortex is activated when subject respond on the basis of cues other than actions. Pardo *et al.* (1991) scanned subjects while they counted, but the stimuli were somaesthetic rather than kinaesthetic. The tester repeatedly touched the toe of the subject with a von Frey hair.

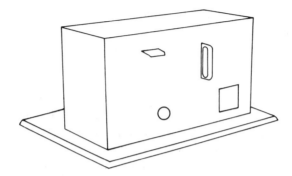

Fig. 6.20   Apparatus used for testing learning of an externally ordered sequence. The positions of the key, handle, lever, and door to the food well are shown. Figure from Passingham (1985*d*).

The task was to count the number of pauses in the stimulation. There was significant activation of the right prefrontal area 9, irrespective of whether it was the left or right toe that was stimulated.

Self-generated sequences

On DA the animal must learn a sequence that has been specified by the experimenter; that is the animal must always avoid the side to which it has just gone. An important variation is to allow the animal to determine the order in which it responds to a series of objects.

One version of the DR task is the search task devised by Collin *et al.* (1982). The monkey must remember which doors it has opened, but it has the choice of the order in which to open them. The task is analagous to the 'subject-ordered task' introduced by Petrides and Milner (1982) for testing patients with surgical excisions in the frontal lobe. On this task the subject is presented with up to 12 items, and must point to them in any order but without pointing twice to the same item. The difference is that on the latter the subject has to remember not spatial locations but words or pictures.

Petrides *et al.* (1993*a*) have PET scanned subjects while they perform the subject-ordered task. They report bilateral activation of the mid and dorsal prefrontal cortex. This probably corresponds to areas 9 and 46.

Monkeys

Petrides (1988, 1989) devised a version of the subject-ordered task for monkeys. The monkey faces several boxes which differ in colour and shape: it chooses one, and the screen is lowered; when the screen is raised the monkey makes a second choice, and so on. The rule is that the

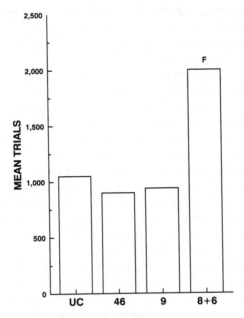

Fig. 6.21 Mean trials to learn an externally ordered fixed sequence. UC = 3 unoperated control monkeys, 46 = 3 monkeys with lesions in sulcus principalis (area 46), 9 = 3 monkeys with lesions in lateral area 9, 8 + 6 = 3 monkeys with lesions in Brodmann area 8 and the dorsal part of the lateral premotor cortex (area 6). F = fail. Data from Passingham (1985*d*).

monkey must not select the same box twice on the same trial. The relative position of the boxes is changed between choices, to ensure that the monkey chooses on the basis of the appearance of the box and not its location.

Brody and Pribram (1978) and Pinto-Hamuy and Linck (1965) had previously trained monkeys on a similar task: the animals had to press three colours—or patterns—in any order, so long as they did not press any particular one twice. In these experiments the whole lateral surface (areas 8, 46, 9, and 12) was removed. Petrides (1988) made more selective lesions, removing only areas 9 and 46. After surgery, the monkeys made significantly more errors than controls on the self-ordered task.

Yet monkeys with dorsal prefrontal lesions can learn a fixed sequence in which the order is determined by the experimenter. We trained monkeys on the apparatus shown in Fig. 6.20. They had to press the button in the centre, pull the handle to the right, and then depress the lever to the left. Our animals were trained after surgery. In some monkeys we removed area 46 (sulcus principalis) and in others the tissue on the lateral superior convexity (area 9). The animals in both groups learned the task as quickly as unoperated animals (Fig. 6.21).

But it is not clear why the monkeys are impaired on the subject-ordered task but unimpaired on the fixed sequence. The tasks varied in several respects. For example, on the fixed sequence task the sequence was continuous; no delay was interposed between responses. Thus the subject-ordered task differed both in requiring the subject to generate the sequence and in taxing working memory.

It is clear that varying order is one important factor. Petrides (1991*b*) has tested monkeys for their ability to remember the order in which objects are presented. The monkeys were shown up to five objects in sequence, and on the test trial they were presented with two of the objects. They were rewarded if they chose the object that had occurred earlier in the sequence.

After removal of areas 46 and 9 the monkeys were never able to reach the criterion level when faced with the objects that were second and third, or second and fourth or third and fourth in the sequence. Yet it is clear that the monkeys understood what it was they were supposed to do because they had no trouble in distinguishing a pair presented further apart in the sequence, for example the second from the fifth.

This elegant study stresses the importance of order. But it also poses a new challenge. It cannot be assumed that if a monkey with a dorsal prefrontal lesion is poor at choosing between items in whatever order it decides, the animal is impaired because it is poor at generating orders. The study by Petrides (1991*b*) shows that monkeys with this lesion are unable to distinguish the order of items which were presented to them. In this experiment the monkeys did not generate the order themselves.

This point is also made by another study by Petrides (1991*a*) that was mentioned earlier. In this study the monkeys were presented with three objects and allowed to choose whichever one they wanted. In the test trial they were presented with the chosen object and one of the other two. The object that was correct was the object that the monkey had not chosen on the presentation trial. Monkeys with lesions in areas 9 and 46 never performed above a chance level.

Yet, on the test trial the correct response was determined by the experimenter, not by the monkey. We are forced to conclude that the fact that monkeys with lesions in areas 9 and 46 are impaired on the self-ordered task is not independent evidence that the problem is only one of generation.

PET scanning

The issue is whether the dorsal prefrontal cortex plays a role in memory of previous responses, in the process of generating responses, or both. In producing varying orders the subject must remember which items have already been chosen, and thus the task also taxes working memory.

The same issue is raised by a study we have carried out in which we required human subjects to learn new sequences of finger movements while they lay in the PET scanner (Jenkins *et al.* 1992*b*). The study has already been described in Chapter 4. Every time a tone sounded the subject had to move a finger, and the computer told them whether the response was or was not correct. In this way the subjects learned finger sequences eight moves long.

There was very extensive activation of the dorsal prefrontal cortex while subjects learned two new sequences, and the percentage change in regional blood flow was marked (Fig. 9.5, p.210). But in learning these sequences the subjects had two tasks. The first was to generate possible orders so as to discover by trial and error which were correct. The second was to keep the sequences in mind as they learned them by rehearsing them in working memory.

It should be possible to dissociate these two requirments by asking normal subjects to generate random sequences. In the study by Deiber *et al.* (1991) we asked subjects to generate joystick movements at will, and we found significant activation of both the left and right dorsal prefrontal cortex (areas 9 and 46) (Fig. 4.13,p85). But unfortunately we also asked the subjects not to repeat the same movement twice. This means that it is not clear whether on the self-generated task the activation represents the operation of working memory or the generation of movements.

However, in a parallel study, Frith *et al.* (1991*b*) required subjects to generate a sequence of movements without instructing them not to repeat movements. In principle the subjects could generate a random order by making an independent decision on each trial. There were two conditions. In both conditions the subject had to move either the forefinger or the second finger, and in both the cue to do so was a touch to one or other finger. In one condition the subject had to move the finger that had been touched. In the other condition the subject had a free choice; a finger was chosen at will.

The analysis compared the activation in the two conditions. There was significant activation in the dorsal prefrontal cortex when the subject freely selected which finger to move (Fig. 11.10, p.250).

It could still be objected that, when the subjects made up their mind on any one trial, they kept in mind their previous moves, even though there was no requirement that they should do so. In principle the issue could be resolved.

The logic of a self-generated movement is that given the identical context A the subject performs movement X, Y, or Z at will. As on conditional tasks the subject performs now this movement, and now that. The difference is that the movement can be independent of the context.

There is no logical requirement that the subject performs the movements in series. The subject could generate a movement every day, and in such a case each movement would be independent. It is only the practical requirement of present-day PET scanners that the subject acts repeatedly for a minute or two. Under such conditions the context for each movement will necessarily vary. However, the experiment could be performed in principle using functional imaging with the MRI scanner with short acquisition times and scanning on successive days.

There is another way of deciding the issue. If it is crucial that the subject determines the response, one would predict that the dorsal prefrontal cortex would be less activated in patients who spontaneously produce few responses. PET scans have been taken in the resting state for schizophrenic and depressed patients (Liddle *et al.* 1990; Bench *et al.* 1993). Some of the schizophrenic patients suffered from psychomotor poverty and some of the depressed patients had a retarded depression. In both these states the patients are retarded and inert, generating little activity unless prompted.

In both the schizophrenic and depressed patients there was a relation between decreased regional cerebral blood flow in the dorsal prefrontal cortex (areas 9 and 46) and psychomotor retardation. It is clear that the dorsal prefrontal cortex plays an important role in the spontaneous generation of movements.

It is an independent question whether the dorsal prefrontal cortex is also activated when subjects generate actions on the basis of information in working memory. Petrides *et al.* (1993*b*) have tackled this question by scanning subjects while they performed one of two tasks. In the first they generated the numbers from one to ten at random. In the second they heard nine of the numbers in random order and had then to generate the remaining number. The finding was that areas 9 and 46 were activated when subjects performed either of these tasks, and that the degree of activation was the same in both conditions.

Conclusions

We are still not clear about the exact role played by the dorsal prefrontal cortex. But we do know what the critical questions are, and one can devise experiments that would answer them.

This chapter has argued that the dorsal prefrontal cortex plays some role in the selection and generation of responses. It is not intended to imply that it is involved in deciding the details of the movements themselves.

The data are not complete enough to permit us to decide for certain whether areas 9 and 46 are specialized for different functions. Removal of area 46 alone severely disrupts spatial responses (Goldman and Rosvold 1970; Goldman *et al.* 1971) whereas removal of area 9 has no such effect (Mishkin 1957; Goldman *et al.* 1971). Removal of areas 46 and 9 together severely disrupts non-spatial responses (Passingham 1978; Petrides 1988, 1991*a*), but there has been no adequate study of the effects of removing areas 46 or 9 separately.

The dorsal prefrontal cortex appears to play a crucial role in the generation of actions. Actions must be generated when there is no external cue. On delayed response tasks actions must be generated on the basis of information in working memory. But there are also situations in which actions can be generated by the subject, and these can be generated without reference to working memory. Human subjects can make arbitrary decisions. They make these on the basis of 'inner representations' (Goldman-Rakic 1987, 1990), but not necessarily on the basis of their memory of events.

Frith (1991) uses the term 'willed action' when the decision as to what to do is made by the subject. If the dorsal prefrontal cortex is specialized for generating actions at will, this would explain why lesions in area 46 have only a mild effect on the ability to respond on the basis of cues that are available at the time of response. If there are no such cues available, the subject must generate an action.

There is, however, a danger in using the term 'willed action'. The action could be voluntary in one of two senses. The first requires that there be no external cue (Fig. 1.1, level B). The second requires that it be the person that decides and that the person could have taken a different decision (Fig. 1.1, level D). The evidence is that prefrontal cortex is involved in generating actions both when the action is specified by a cue in working memory and when the action is determined by arbitrary decision.

Summary

Areas 9 and 46 receive their main input from the parietal lobe which processes information about the animal itself and about the space in which it moves and manipulates things.

Monkeys with lesions in area 46 fail to learn delayed response tasks. These are conditional tasks on which the animal must choose between locations on the basis of information in working memory. The same impairment can be demonstrated on an oculomotor version of the DR task on which monkeys must direct their eye movements on the basis of the locations in which they recently saw a spot of light. During the delay on this task many cells in area 46 change their activity selectively according to the location of the target.

Monkeys with lesions in area 9 and 46 are impaired at selecting between objects on the basis of their past responses, and also at generating a series of actions. In PET scanning experiments with human subjects, the dorsal prefrontal cortex is activated when the subjects generate a series of actions at will. In patients there is also a relation between psychomotor retardation and a decrease in regional cerebral blood flow in the dorsal prefrontal cortex. This suggests a role for the dorsal prefrontal cortex in generating actions.

7 Ventral prefrontal cortex (areas 11, 12, 13, and 14)

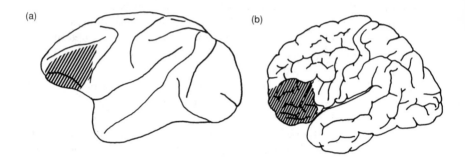

Fig. 7.1 Ventral prefrontal cortex in (a) the macaque monkey and (b) the human brain.

This book places naïve faith in anatomy. If the key to the dorsal prefrontal cortex is the superior colliculus and the parietal lobe, the key to the ventral prefrontal cortex (Fig. 7.1) is the amygdala and the temporal lobe.

Amygdala and hypothalamus

There are few if any connections to the superior colliculi from the ventral convexity and orbital surface (Catsman-Berrevoets *et al.* 1979; Fries 1984). The ventral cortex connects instead to the amygdala and hypothalamus. Electrical stimulation of the postero-medial orbital cortex (areas 13 and 14) (Fig. 6.3, p.125) produces a variety of autonomic responses in monkeys (Kaada 1960). These include changes in blood pressure, decreased gastric motility, pupillary dilatation, piloerection, and alterations in respiration.

We now know that there are descending pathways through which the orbital frontal cortex can indirectly influence the brainstem nuclei of the autonomic nervous system. These pathways run via the amygdala and hypothalamus. They are illustrated in Fig. 7.2.

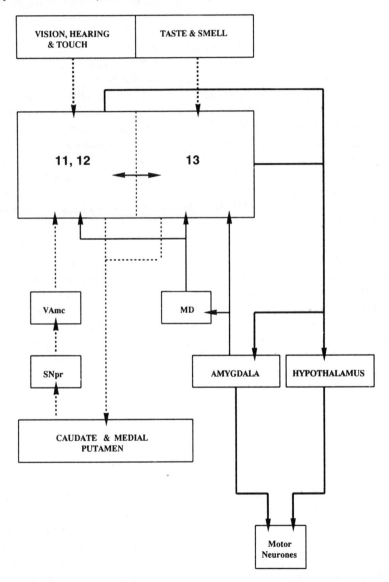

Fig. 7.2 Connections between areas 11, 12, 13, and the amygdala and hypothalamus. MD = mediodorsal nucleus of the thalamus, VAmc = ventral anterior nucleus, pars magnocellularis of the thalamus (Olszewski 1952), SNpr = substantia nigra, pars reticulata.

Amygdala

Outputs

There are direct projections from the orbital surface to the amygdala. We injected HRP into the different nuclear groups of the amygdala (Aggleton *et al.* 1980). With injections into the lateral or accessory basal nuclei, we found labelled cells in the postero-medial sector, areas 13 and 14. With injections centred on the medial nucleus, we also found cells in the more anterior area 11; but in this case the interpretation is not clear cut because the injection involved a small area of the basal forebrain.

The amygdala sends a direct projection to the brainstem (Hopkins *et al.* 1981). The central nucleus sends fibres to the solitary nucleus and the dorsal motor nucleus of the vagus. Though it does not terminate in the nuclei of the trigeminal, facial, or glossopharyngeal nuclei, it does contribute a heavy projection to the adjacent lateral tegmental regions which do project to these nuclei.

Although we know that the orbital cortex projects to the amygdala, we do not know if it sends fibres directly to the central nucleus of the amygdala. The issue should be examined by injecting anterograde tracers into the orbital cortex.

Inputs

The amygdala influences the ventral prefrontal cortex in two ways. First, it projects directly to the orbital areas 12, 13, and 14 (Porrino *et al.* 1981; Amaral and Price 1984; Barbas and de Olmos 1990). Second, it influences prefrontal cortex via the thalamus. The amygdala sends a heavy connection to the rostral third of the magnocellular division of the mediodorsal nucleus (MD); and in turn this sector projects to the orbital frontal cortex (Russchen *et al.* 1987; Giguere and Goldman-Rakic 1988; Barbas and Pandya 1991).

Hypothalamus

Outputs

There appear to be direct projections from the orbital frontal cortex to the lateral hypothalamus. Unfortunately this claim depends on a study using the older anatomical method of tracing anterograde degeneration using the silver method; there has been no more recent study using transport methods. Johnson *et al.* (1968) report that the postero-medial area 13 sends a projection to the lateral hypothalamus, and that this projection is heavier than that from the medial sector 14. They also claim that the lateral hypothalamus receives a projection from the more anterior and lateral orbital cortex. The exact origin of this projection is unclear, since in the relevant case Johnson *et al.* (1968) removed the whole of the inferior convexity cortex, including areas 11 and 12.

The hypothalamus sends direct connections to the nucleus of the solitary tract and the dorsal motor nucleus of the vagus (Saper *et al.* 1976). Thus it has a direct influence over autonomic responses. At the same time it influences the endocrine system via its relations with the pituitary.

Inputs
We know less about the ways in which the hypothalamus can influence prefrontal cortex. It has been shown in the cat that the lateral and dorsal hypothalamic areas project to the MD nucleus (Velayos and Reinoso-Suarez 1985). But there has been no such demonstration yet for the macaque brain.

Dorsal and medial cortex

The dorsal prefrontal cortex (areas 9 and 46) does not interconnect with the amygdala and hypothalamus directly. It sends only a few fibres to the amygdala (Johnson *et al.* 1968; Aggleton *et al.* 1980) or the hypothalamus (Johnson *et al.* 1968). Furthermore, it receives few fibres from the amygdala (Porrino *et al.* 1981; Amaral and Price 1984; Barbas and de Olmos 1990), and receives no input from the magnocellular division of the MD nucleus (Tobias 1975; Giguere and Goldman-Rakic 1988).

However, the dorsal prefrontal areas 46 and 9 are interconnected with areas 32 and 24 (Barbas and Pandya 1989; Vogt *et al.* 1987); and areas 32 and 24 are reciprocally connected with the amygdala (Baleydier and Maugiere 1980; Amaral and Price 1984; Mufson and Pandya 1984; Vogt *et al.* 1987; Barbas and de Olmos 1990). Electrical stimulation of the anterior cingulate cortex evokes autonomic changes in monkeys (Kaada 1960). The contribution of the medial cortex to the visceral system is discussed in more detail by Reep (1984). Though dorsal prefrontal cortex does not interconnect with the limbic system directly, it has indirect access via medial cortex.

Connections with the temporal lobe

The inputs to the dorsal prefrontal cortex come mainly from the parietal lobe; parietal 7a also sends a moderate projection to the lateral orbital frontal cortex (Cavada and Goldman-Rakic 1989). However, the bulk of the inputs to the ventral prefrontal cortex come from the temporal lobe (Fig. 7.3). The fibres travel in the uncinate fascicle (Ungerleider *et al.* 1989).

The ventral prefrontal cortex receives information from all the external senses. Visual information is conveyed from the infero-temporal cortex. The lateral area 12 receives a heavy projection from the temporal areas TE (21) and TEm (Barbas 1988; Seltzer and Pandya 1989), that is the convexity cortex and the ventral bank of the superior temporal sulcus.

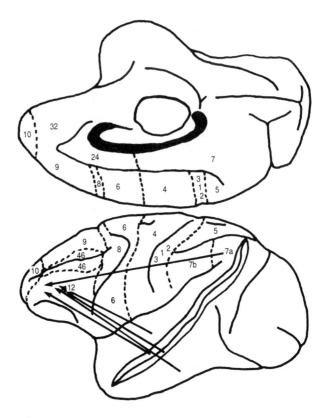

Fig. 7.3 Cortico-cortical projections from temporal and parietal cortex to the ventral prefrontal cortex. For references see text.

Auditory information is conveyed from the superior-temporal cortex. The lateral area 12 receives a heavy input from the temporal areas TA (22) and TAa (Barbas 1988; Seltzer and Pandya 1989), that is the convexity cortex and the dorsal bank of the superior temporal sulcus.

Information about the body surface is conveyed from area SII (Barbas 1988). The role of this area in the processing of tactile information is discussed by Mishkin (1979). Area SII projects both to the lateral area 12 and also to ventral 46.

The posterior orbital frontal cortex receives information about taste and smell. The primary cortical region for taste is located in the insula and opercular cortex (Mesulam and Mufson 1985). There is a direct projection from this region to the posterior orbital frontal cortex, area 13 (Wiggins *et al.* 1987).

The primary region for smell is located in the pyriform cortex. If this region is stimulated, electrically evoked potentials can be recorded in the posterior orbital frontal cortex (Tanabe *et al.* 1974). Furthermore, some cells in the caudolateral orbital frontal cortex respond when the monkey is presented with olfactory stimuli (Rolls and Wiggins 1989). The olfactory input probably comes via two routes, from pyriform cortex via entorhinal cortex, and from pyriform cortex via the mediodorsal nucleus of the thalamus (Potter and Nauta 1979).

Conclusion

The ventral prefrontal cortex can be regarded as the prefrontal area for the temporal lobe. The temporal lobe receives information from the near receptors (taste and touch) and distance receptors (smell, hearing and vision). This information about the outside world is passed on in turn to the ventral prefrontal cortex.

The temporal lobe and ventral prefrontal cortex are also alike in that they have access to interoceptive information. In the temporal lobe this is processed in the amygdala, insula and temporal pole (Mesulam and Mufson 1985). It is of particular significance that there are reciprocal projections between the amygdala and ventral prefrontal cortex, just as there are between the amygdala and the temporal lobe (Turner *et al.*1980; Amaral and Price 1984).

Area 12

Area 12 is a critical area, since it receives multimodal inputs from temporal association cortex (Barbas 1988), and also has a heavy input from the amygdala (Amaral and Price 1984). Table 7.1 (p. 162) lists experiments in which area 12 has been removed, either alone or together with rest of the orbital surface.

Sensory context

Area 12 receives visual, auditory and tactile inputs from the temporal lobe. It is not surprising that monkeys with removal of area 12 are impaired on learning tasks irrespective of the nature of the sensory cues.

Vision

These monkeys are poor at visual matching, whether for colours (Passingham 1975*b*) or objects (Mishkin and Manning 1978; Kowalska *et al.* in press); they also fail to learn the object alternation task (Mishkin and Manning 1978); and they are poor at object reversal (Butter 1969). They are also impaired on tasks with visuospatial cues, such as delayed response (Goldman 1971), delayed alternation (Mishkin *et al.* 1969; Goldman 1972), and spatial reversal (Butter 1969).

Hearing

The impairments are not confined to tasks with visual cues. Iversen and Mishkin (1970) taught monkeys to discriminate between auditory cues differing in frequency. Given one sound the animal had to respond ('go') and given another to refrain from responding ('no-go'). The animals were impaired after the removal of the inferior convexity, including area 12, but were not impaired after the removal of the more medial areas 11 and 13.

Touch

We have trained monkeys to discriminate between objects by touch (Passingham and Ettlinger 1972). The animals were trained on four pairs of objects in the dark; the monkey felt one or both of the objects in a pair, and were rewarded for choosing a particular object. After the removal of areas 12, 11, and 13 the monkeys were slow to learn the tactile tasks. However, we concluded that the animals made mistakes because they failed to feel the objects with enough care. They were not impaired if they were encouraged to feel the objects properly.

Cross-modal learning

The ventral prefrontal cortex receives both auditory and visual inputs. Gaffan and Harrison (1991) have shown that if these cortico-cortical inputs are cut monkeys are no longer able to learn a cross-modal conditional task. There were six sounds and six coloured shapes. Each sound served as an instruction as to which shape to choose; given any particular sound the animals had to pick a specific shape.

The left prefrontal and right superior temporal cortex were removed and the forebrain commissures were sectioned. This procedure isolates the right prefrontal cortex from cortico-cortical input from the temporal cortex. Under these conditions the animals performed virtually at chance level, even though the animal made its choice as soon as the sounds were presented.

Conclusion

Lesions of area 12 impair learning irrespective of the nature of the sensory context. It does not matter whether the cues are colours, locations, tones, or objects to be felt.

Delay

There is evidence suggesting that monkeys with area 12 lesions are impaired irrespective of whether there is or is not a delay between the presentation of the cue and the opportunity to respond. For example, they are impaired on an auditory 'go, no-go' task, even though they can respond on positive trials as soon as they see the cue (Iversen and Mishkin 1970). Similarly, after removal of areas 11, 12, and 13, monkeys are slow to relearn a task on which they have to respond to the right given one auditory cue and to the left given another (Lawicka *et al.* 1975). On this task no delay is imposed after presentation of the cue.

We have compared visual matching with and without a delay. We taught monkeys to match colours (Passingham 1975*b*). If red appeared on the sample key the monkey had to press the response key that was lit red, and if green appeared on the sample key the monkey had to press the response key that was lit green. The task was taught before surgery. For each monkey a delay was introduced after presentation of the sample cue, and the delay was increased in stages to determine the longest delay at which the animal could still perform reliably.

After preoperative training, area 12 was removed in three monkeys. After surgery the monkeys failed to relearn the task in 1000 trials even at the minimum delay, when the choice keys were lit as soon as the sample cue was extinguished. These animals were then retested on the simultaneous condition on which the sample cue remained on when the response keys were illuminated. One animal needed 500 trials to relearn this task, one needed 1700 trials, and the third failed in 2500 trials.

However, the evidence presented above is not fully convincing. There are two problems. The first is that in some of the studies the lesions were not confined to area 12. In the studies by Iversen and Mishkin (1970) and Lawicka *et al.* (1975) the lesions also involved area 8, and we already know that lesions in area 8 impair performance on non-delayed conditional tasks (Chapter 5). However, in our study of matching the lesions did not invade area 8 extensively (Passingham 1975*b*).

The second problem is that in this study the animals were only tested with no delays after they had already failed matching with delays. The animals might have developed a failure set. This objection does not apply however to a study by Voytko (1985) who reported that cooling the lateral orbital surface alone leads to a significant decline in performance of simultaneous matching.

For the moment we must admit that we cannot be entirely certain whether animals with area 12 lesions are impaired under conditions of no delay. The issue could easily be settled by testing monkeys with lesions that are restricted to area 12 lesions on either visual matching with no delay or visual conditional learning with no delay.

Responses

Monkeys with ventral prefrontal lesions are impaired irrespective of the type of the response to be made. Some tasks require them to choose between the left and right: this is true, for example, of DA, and lesions of area 12 impair performance on DA (Iversen and Mishkin 1970). Other tasks require the animals to choose between colours or objects: removal of area 12 leads to poor performance on colour matching (Passingham

Table 7.1 Tasks on which monkeys are impaired after removal of either area 12, the whole ventral and orbital surface (areas 12, 11, 13), or the postero-medial orbital surface (area 13). + = impaired, 0 = not impaired. For details see text.

Tasks	Area		
	12	12,11,13	13
Delayed response		+	
Delayed alternation	+		
Visual matching	+	+	
Object alternation		+	
Spatial reversal	+		0
Visual reversal	+	+	0
Go, no-go reversal		+	
Auditory, go, no-go	+	+	
Auditory, left–right		+	

1975*b*) and object matching (Mishkin and Manning 1978). Finally there are tasks on which the animal makes its choice by responding on some trials and not on others: on an auditory 'go, no-go' task monkeys perform poorly whether area 12 is removed alone (Iversen and Mishkin 1970) or in combination with areas 11 and 13 (Lawicka *et al.* 1975)

There is only indirect evidence concerning manipulative responses. Eacott and Gaffan (1992) have trained monkeys on manipulative tasks, and then cut the uncinate fascicle. This carries the fibres from the temporal lobe to the ventral prefrontal cortex (Ungerleider *et al.* 1989).

The tasks presented patterned stimuli on a screen: given one pattern the monkey was required to tap the screen eight times, and given another pattern to hold the finger on the screen for 1 second. A series of such tasks was taught both before and after surgery, each task presenting a different pair of patterns. After section of the uncinate fascicle the animals made significantly more errors than before surgery. It is important that this experiment be repeated with animals with ventral prefrontal lesions.

Response learning

Conditional tasks

The key to area 12 does not lie in the nature of the stimulus or response. What is common between the tasks listed in Table 7.1 is that they are all conditional response tasks.

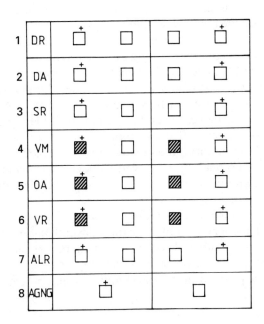

Fig. 7.4 Tasks on which monkeys with ventral prefrontal lesions are impaired. Two trials are shown for each task, one on the left and one on the right. The figure shows the stimuli as the monkeys sees them at the time of responding. On each task at the time of response the stimuli are identical on all trials. DR = delayed response, DA = delayed alternation, SR = spatial reversal, VM = visual matching, OA = object alternation, VR = visual reversal, ALR = auditory conditional task with responses to the left or right, AGNG = auditory go, no-go task, + = rewarded stimulus.

This is obviously true of delayed response tasks and visual matching. But it is also true of auditory 'go, no-go' tasks. The animal has to learn to respond to the cover of the food-well on some trials but not others. The sounds serve as the instructional cues.

It can be argued that reversal tasks are also conditional tasks. Take spatial reversal: the monkey is rewarded for responding to the left until it reaches a criterion level of performance; on the next day the monkey is rewarded for responding to the right until it again meets the criterion; then responses to the left are again rewarded, and so on through successive reversals. So, the animal must sometimes respond to the left and sometimes to the right, the correct location being conditional on the temporal context.

Goal

The use of the term 'conditional response learning' could be misleading. It could be taken to imply the learning of the movements that the animal makes when responding. So it is important to stress that the removal of area 12 has no effect on the movements themselves.

Consider object matching as one example. Before the experiment begins, all the animals are taught that pushing the objects uncovers the food-wells. The lesion has no effect on the ability to perform this simple task. Furthermore, it does not matter in what manner the animal pushes the objects, which hand it uses, or how it grasps the objects. Any movement will do, as long as it achieves the end of pushing the object out of the way.

It is the *goal* of the action that the animals learn, that object A, let us say, is correct. They learn to direct their interest towards object A. Of course, on a conditional task no one object is always attractive. The animal learns the *current* goal for any particular trial—or more strictly the current subgoal that leads to the ultimate goal of food.

In the clinic there is no temptation to suppose that it is the movements with which the patient has trouble. It is the answer that the subject attempts to find. On the subject ordered task patients with prefrontal lesions can still point to the pictures. Their problem is that they treat particular pictures as goals, when these pictures are no longer appropriate.

Sensory learning

It is an essential feature of conditional response tasks that they are not solved simply by associating sensory cues with reward. On all the tasks listed in Table 7.1 the monkey is faced with the same objects or patterns on each trial. This is shown in Fig. 7.4. On all these tasks the objects to which the animal responds give no clue as to the correct choice. Both objects are equally attractive, since overall they are associated with reward on the same number of occasions.

The animal's response must be determined by the context. The context is provided by sounds that are audible at the time of response (tasks 7 and 8), by an object or pattern that is visible at the time of response (task 5), by objects or patterns in memory (tasks 4 and 7), or by visuospatial cues in memory (1, 2, and 3).

Concurrent discrimination learning

If the essential feature is that the monkey must learn a response, we must predict that damage to ventral prefrontal cortex should not effect the learning of tasks on which the correct answer can be judged from the objects or pictures alone. A simultaneous visual discrimination is one such task; in principle it can be learned simply by associating the positive object or pattern with reward.

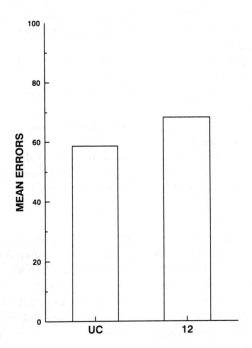

Fig. 7.5 Mean errors to learn three sets of visual stimuli with concurrent presentation of the stimuli within each stimulus set. UC = unoperated control monkeys, 12 = monkeys with lesions in area 12. Data plotted for sets A, B, and C from Kowalkska *et al.* (1991).

A rigorous test is provided by concurrent discrimination learning, in which the animal is given one trial of each of 20 discriminations on each day. Kowalska *et al.* (1991) trained monkeys on one such set of 20 discriminations, and then gave two further sets. In one group of monkeys area 12 was then removed, and in another group the orbital and medial cortex (areas 11, 13, 14, 25 and 24). Figure 7.5 shows the mean errors totalled over the three sets of problems. There was no significant difference between the scores for the either of the operated groups and the control monkeys.

Discrimination learning set
There have been two studies which have assessed the improvement in performance over a series of discriminations. Eacott and Gaffan (1992) cut the uncinate fascicle which provides temporal lobe inputs to the inferior prefrontal convexity and orbital surface. After surgery the monkeys were able to learn a series of new discriminations at a normal rate. Yet other monkeys with the same lesion failed in 4000 trials to relearn a conditional task on which the animals had to choose pattern X given pattern A, and pattern Y given pattern B.

However, Gaffan and Murray (1990) have reported that monkeys are slow to improve their performance on a series of new discriminations after the removal of the whole of the ventromedial cortex. The lesion included not only areas 12, 11 and 13 on the orbital surface but also areas 14 and 25, which lie on the medial surface.

It is not clear why the two studies gave different results. But whatever the explanation, Gaffan and Murray (1990) found an impairment on a non-conditional task. It could be argued in defence that when animals acquire learning sets, they learn a response rule over successive problems. The rule is that if the animal wins food it should make the same choice on future trials, and that it is fails to win food it should shift (Levine 1965). On concurrent discrimination learning no such response rule is acquired. On any one day only one trial is given for each discrimination, and the animals can solve the problems simply by associating the stimuli with reward.

Single discriminations
But this reply does not settle the issue. Monkeys have been found to be impaired at relearning *single* visual discriminations after the removal of either the inferior prefrontal convexity (Passingham 1975*b*) or the whole of the ventral and orbital cortex (Passingham 1972*b*). Baylis and Gaffan (1991) also presented monkeys with two objects which they could suck; one of the objects supplied them with fruit juice and the other did not. Two of the three animals with ventromedial lesions were slow to learn the discrimination. Finally, Voytko (1985) reported that cooling the orbital frontal surface impaired the learning of simultaneous discriminations. Two monkeys were tested on four easy tasks. They were slow to learn, though they retained the tasks well once learned.

In mitigation it can be pointed out that the impairment can be very mild. Goldman *et al.* (1970) removed the *whole* of the prefrontal cortex and trained the monkeys to discriminate a plus sign from a square. The operated animals learned the task in a mean of 200 trials; of the unoperated control animals three learned in a mean of 70 trials, although one animal was slow to learn and took 220 trials.

However mild the impairment, some explanation is needed. One defence would be to claim that when monkeys learn single discriminations, they normally learn about both the stimuli and their own responses. The animals choose one of the stimuli and find the peanut; the action is rewarded. It is, of course, embarrassing to claim this for no other reason than that otherwise the data fail to fit the theory. But there is one piece of evidence that points to a response bias in the performance of monkeys with ventral prefrontal lesions. Passingham (1972*b*) reported that their performance was disrupted by a tendency to make impulsive choices. The animals responded significantly more quickly than unoperated animals or animals with infero-temporal lesions.

PET scanning

The claim is that the ventral prefrontal cortex plays a role in the learning of responses. It has been argued that when monkeys learn a set of visual concurrent discriminations, they can solve the problems by learning about associations between the stimuli and reward; and that monkeys with ventral prefrontal lesions can solve such problems at a normal rate.

Fortunately, there is another way of testing the claim that prefrontal cortex need not play a role in the discrimination of stimuli. This is to scan human subjects while they carry out such discriminations. Haxby *et al.* (in press) required subjects to compare photographs of faces and judge if they were the same or not. The subjects had only to make perceptual judgements; during the scans they did not have to learn any new responses. There was significant activation in the temporal lobe, but no significant activation in prefrontal cortex.

Responses and rewards (orbital cortex)

The section on area 12 was based on the fact that it receives afferents from temporal cortex. This section treats the connections with the amygdala. The division between area 12 and the rest of the orbital surface may be arbitrary; both area 12 and the rest of the orbital surface are closely linked with the amygdala (Fig. 7.2). But it is necessary to try to impose some order on the data, and the discussion of reward deserves a separate section.

In response learning the animal learns about the consequences of its actions rather than the associations between a stimulus and reward. The previous sections have used conditional learning as a test for response learning. But there are other measures of instrumental learning, such as bar pressing. Bar pressing is an arbitrary action for monkeys, but they can be induced to press a bar in order to obtain a reward. The term 'reward' refers to the unlearned goals that an animal seeks.

Orbital cortex and reward

Self stimulation

There is direct evidence that the orbital prefrontal cortex is associated with the mechanisms of reward. Normal monkeys will learn to press a bar repeatedly to deliver brief electrical impulses to the orbital cortex (Mora *et al.* 1979; Rolls *et al.* 1980). The effective sites for self-stimulation lie within the posteror orbital frontal cortex, including area 13, and not in the more anterior orbital surface (Mora *et al.* 1980). Self-stimulation can also be induced when stimulation is applied to the amygdala or ventral striatum (Rolls *et al.* 1980).

The dorsomedial areas 32 and 24 are also reciprocally connected with the amygdala (Baleydier and Maugiere 1980; Amaral and Price 1984; Mufson and Pandya 1984). There have been no attempts to see if monkeys will self-stimulate if electrodes are implanted at these sites. However, we do know that rats will self-stimulate if electrodes are placed in the medial frontal cortex, at sites that probably include both areas 24 and 32 (Vives *et al.* 1983; Mora and Cobo 1990).

Self-administration of drugs
There have been several reports that rats will press a lever to obtain an injection of a rewarding drug into a specific brain site, for example the ventral striatum (Koob and Goeders 1989; Wise and Rompre 1989). Philips *et al.* (1981) taught monkeys to touch a bar in order to administer amphetamine to the orbital frontal surface. The animals worked to administer the drug in this way.

Incentive
It is a feature of a reward that its value depends on the motivational state of the animal; the attraction of food depends on the degree to which the animal is currently deprived. Thus satiating an animal makes foods less rewarding. Mora *et al.* (1979) compared the rates of self-stimulation of orbital frontal cortex in monkeys when they were more or less hungry. The animals were fed blackcurrant juice and glucose. There was a systematic effect: the animals worked at much lower rates when satiated.

Lesions
Monkeys with orbital lesions work less hard to obtain food or prevent shock. Butter (1969) trained monkeys on a variable interval schedule to press a lever to obtain food. After removal of area 13 the animals tended to press at a lower rate than that of normal animals.

Butter and Snyder (1972) also cite an unpublished experiment in which monkeys were taught to press a lever on a Sidman schedule to delay shocks. After removal of the orbital surface (areas 11,13 and medial 12) the monkeys were able to learn to avoid shock, but again they pressed the lever at a very slow rate.

Recording
There are cells in the posterior orbital cortex, area 13, that respond to reward. Thorpe *et al.* (1983) report that, of the cells that reacted to visual stimuli, 16 per cent responded when the monkey was presented with foods and 10 per cent when the monkey saw aversive stimuli. Sawaguchi (1987) recorded on the lateral surface during a reaction time task. He found that 23 per cent of task-related neurones changed their activity after the animal was rewarded with juice; of these, 26 per cent were located on the inferior convexity.

There are also cells on the orbital surface that respond to tastes (Rolls *et al.* 1990). It is an important observation that the activity of some of these cells depends on the motivational state of the animal. Rolls *et al.* (1989) presented monkeys with a particular fruit juice until the animals were satiated; as a consequence the monkeys showed more interest in other juices. There were also cells that behaved in the same way; that is they decreased their response to the original juice, while still responding to other juices.

Association of response and reward

There is one experiment which suggests that prefrontal cortex plays a role in the learning of associations between the response and reward. If an animal is poor at forming associations between response and rewards, it should be especially impaired if a delay is introduced between the time when the animal chooses and the time when the reward arrives. Mishkin and Weiskrantz (1958) taught monkeys visual discriminations with immediate presentation of the reward. When the animals had learned a problem, they were then tested with a delay imposed after the response before the reward was delivered.

Before training the whole of the lateral prefrontal cortex was removed, including the lateral part of area 12. If a delay of 8 seconds was imposed immediately after the task was learned with no delay, the monkeys with frontal lesions performed very poorly indeed. Combining the data for two experiments, the four frontal animals achieved a mean of only 59.9 per cent correct performance after 10 days at 8 seconds' delay. Two normal monkeys achieved a level of 72.5 per cent. There were also four animals with infero-temporal lesions, and they achieved a level of 76.9 per cent.

Thus, altering the association in time between the choice and the reward retards the learning of the animals with frontal but not temporal lesions. This is consistent with the hypothesis that the prefrontal cortex plays a role in the process by which responses are associated with reward. It is important that this experiment be repeated with selective lesions of the ventral convexity cortex (area 12).

Recording

It ought to be possible to find cells that fire in relation to such associations. Cells of two types have been found.

Stimulus-reward

There are cells in the orbital frontal cortex that respond to stimuli associated with reward by learning. Thorpe *et al.* (1983) found that, of the 463 cells tested, 8.6 per cent responded differently according to whether the monkey was presented with a positive (S+) or negative (S–) stimulus.

The stimuli were coloured syringes that either contained fruit juice (S+) or saline (S–).

Similar cells can be found in the inferior convexity cortex. Watanabe (1990) showed monkeys patterns. On any task, one pattern—for example a circle—predicted juice, and another—for example two vertical lines—predicted no juice. After presentation of the cue the animal had to release a lever to continue the trial, but releasing the lever had no effect on the outcome of the trial.

Recordings were made in areas 6, 8 and 46 and the posterior part of the inferior convexity. It is not clear from the figure in the paper how many of the cells were in area 12. Of 313 cells that responded to the cue, the activity of 38 per cent was related to the meaning of the cue, that is to the outcome of the trial.

It is, of course, possible that in both experiments the firing of the cells was related to movements of the mouth such as sucking. When the animal sees the cue it prepares to drink. Further experiments are needed to resolve this issue.

Response-reward
Funahashi (1983) recorded in posterior sulcus principalis and in the posterior part of the inferior convexity. He taught two monkeys to flex or extend the wrist as instructed by lights. The animals worked either to obtain water or to obtain self-stimulation in the basal forebrain. Of 66 task related cells, 39 per cent increased their activity after the monkey responded and before the reward was available. Of these cells, 88 per cent projected to the basal forebrain, as demonstrated by the fact that they could be driven antidromically from this site.

Conclusion

Both temporal cortex and orbital prefrontal cortex are linked with the amygdala. The amygdala is involved in the process by which stimuli are associated with reward (Mishkin and Aggleton 1981). If the connections between the temporal cortex and the amygdala are cut, the animals are poor at learning associations between stimuli and reward, even when they are only given the opportunity to passively observe these associations (Gaffan and Harrison 1988). This chapter has argued that the selection of responses involves the connections between the amygdala and the ventral prefrontal cortex.

Summary

The ventral prefrontal cortex receives a multimodal input from the temporal lobe. Monkeys are impaired at learning what response to make, irrespective of the modality of the cue. There is also evidence suggesting that it may not be essential that there is a delay between the presentation of the cue and the opportunity to respond; however this evidence is not conclusive. It is argued that the ventral prefrontal cortex selects the goal—for example an object—given the current context.

When monkeys learn visual concurrent discriminations they can solve the problems by learning only about the associations between the stimuli and reward. Monkeys with ventral prefrontal lesions can learn such problems at a normal rate. Furthermore, when human subjects make perceptual judgements there is no activation in the prefrontal cortex.

The ventral prefrontal cortex is heavily interconnected with the amygdala. Monkeys will learn to deliver rewarding stimulation to the orbital cortex or to deliver rewarding drugs. It is argued that the connections between the ventral prefrontal cortex and the amygdala are involved in the process by which responses are selected on the basis of their success.

8 Basal ganglia

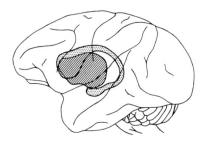

Fig. 8.1 The basal ganglia in the macaque monkey brain.

The last two chapters have argued that prefrontal cortex is involved in the process by which responses are selected as the result of learning. But how does prefrontal cortex influence the movements that the animal makes?

Orienting movements

The answer to this question depends on the task that the animal is performing. Suppose that the animal is learning delayed response tasks. The solution on any particular trial is to choose a spatial location.

It might be thought that if the animal is to make the correct choice, the prefrontal cortex must access the limb mechanisms of motor cortex. If that was so, we might expect lesions of the motor cortex itself to impair performance on these tasks, but we know that they do not. Pribram *et al.* (1955) studied two monkeys with radical bilateral ablations of motor cortex. The monkeys were not trained until they were much recovered. They learned the DR task in 210 and 270 trials; the mean for 35 unoperated monkeys that had been tested in the same laboratory was 375 trials.

The same point can be made for tasks on which the animal must choose between objects or patterns. Monkeys can still learn visual discriminations at a normal rate after removal of either the lateral premotor cortex (Goldman and Rosvold 1970) or the motor cortex (Pribram *et al.* 1955).

The implication is that the solution to these tasks is the choice of a location or object, not a particular limb movement. It does not matter how the choice is made: the monkey could choose the food-well on the left by using its leg, or by turning upside-down and using one arm. Lesions in prefrontal cortex impair performance because the monkeys no longer know the correct goal or target.

Once the animal has chosen the correct location or object by fixating it, there is no problem in directing the reaching movements. The animal has only to reach to the point to which its head and eyes are turned.

The point is that though the animal reaches, it is not the reaching that it *learns* during these tasks. Of course, there must be mechanisms for reaching; Glickstein and May (1982) have argued that these include the parietal and cerebellar cortex. But a detailed survey of these mechanisms is outside the scope of this book.

Thus, for tasks such as delayed response or object matching the issue is not how the information about goals influences the limb motor system. Instead the issue is how this information influences the mechanisms controlling the eyes. There are at least four routes.

1. The prefrontal areas 9 and 46 project directly to the superior colliculus (Goldman and Nauta 1976; Fries 1984) (Fig. 5.6, p.108).

2. Prefrontal areas 9 and 46 project across the cortex to area 8 and the dorsomedial eye fields (Barbas and Pandya 1989; Huerta and Kaas 1990) (Fig. 6.4(a), p.126).

3. The prefrontal cortex also projects to the striatum (Fig. 8.1) which sends efferents to the substantia nigra, pars reticulata (SNpr): in turn the SNpr influences the superior colliculus directly (Fig. 5.6).

4. The SNpr also projects indirectly back to frontal area 8 via the ventral thalamus (Ilinsky *et al.* 1985) (Fig. 5.6). More will be said about the SNpr in a later section.

Manipulative movements

Now consider a visual conditional task of the sort described in Chapter 3. If the monkey is shown one colour, it must pull the handle, and if another it must turn it. Here the answer is not an object but a particular limb movement. How, in such cases, does the prefrontal cortex influence the movement that the monkey makes with its arm?

There are two routes. First, there are projections across the cortex from pre-frontal cortex to the lateral and medial premotor cortex (area 6) (Barbas and Pandya 1987; Selemon and Goldman-Rakic 1988; Luppino *et al.* 1991). Second, there are massive projections from the prefrontal cortex to the basal ganglia (Percheron *et al.* 1984; Selemon and Goldman-Rakic 1985), and the

Fig. 8.2   Cortico-cortical connections from areas 9 and 46 to area 6. For references see text.

basal ganglia can in turn influence the premotor areas and motor cortex itself via the ventral thalamus.

Cortico-cortical paths

We will consider visual conditional motor tasks as a worked example, but the same argument applies to tasks in which the context is given in some other way. Information about the visual properties of things is relayed from infero-temporal cortex to the ventral prefrontal cortex, areas 11, 12 and ventral 46 (Ungerleider *et al.* 1989) (Chapter 7). Eacott and Gaffan (1992) have shown that monkeys are impaired at a visual–manipulative task after section of the fibres from temporal to the ventral prefrontal cortex.

The prefrontal cortex can influence the premotor cortex (area 6) via cortico-cortical connections (Fig. 8.2). There are interconnections between the lateral premotor cortex and dorsal prefrontal areas 9 and 46 and ventral

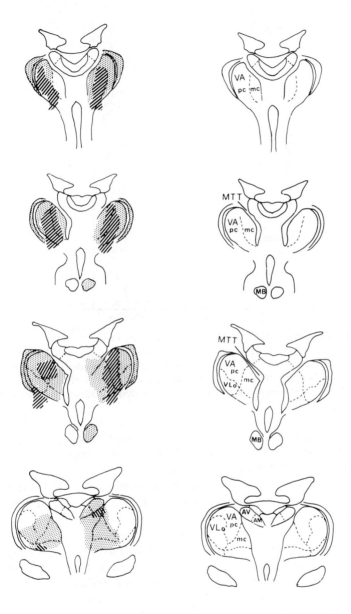

Fig. 8.3 Lesion in ventral thalamus in one monkey. The section at the top is the most anterior, and the section at the bottom the most posterior. Stripes = lesions, dots = gliosis. The thalamic nuclei are outlined in the figures on the right. MTT = mammillothalmic tract, VAmc = nucleus ventralis anterior, pars magnocellularis, VApc = nucleus ventral anterior, pars parvocellularis, VLo = ventrolateral nucleus, pars oralis, AV = nucleus anterior ventralis, AM = nucleus anterior medialis (terminology from Olszewski 1952). From Canavan *et al.* (1989*a*).

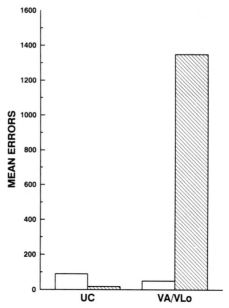

Fig. 8.4   Mean errors for post-operative relearning of a visual motor conditional task in which the cues were colours and the monkeys responded by pulling or rotating a handle. Unshaded histogram = preoperative, shaded histogram - post-operative. UC = unoperated control monkeys, VA/VLo = 3 monkeys with lesions in the VA and VLo nuclei (terminology from Olszewski 1952). Data from Canavan *et al.* (1989*a*).

area 12 (Barbas and Pandya 1987; Matelli *et al.* 1986). Area 46 is also connected with the anterior part of the medial premotor cortex (Selemon and Goldman-Rakic 1988; Luppino *et al.* 1990).

   If the monkey is performing a conditional motor task with a sensory cue, we can rule out the dorsal routes. Petrides (1982) reports that, after removal of area 46, monkeys are only slightly slower than normal monkeys at learning such a task. The mean trials to criterion was 470 for the operated animals and 320 for the controls. We have also described two monkeys with dorsal prefrontal lesions who were unimpaired at pulling or turning a handle on the basis of visual cues (Passingham 1987*a*). In both of these animals area 9 was removed on the lateral and medial surface, and in one of the animals area 46 was also removed bilaterally.

   This leaves the connections between ventral prefrontal cortex area 12 and the ventral part of the lateral premotor cortex (Matelli *et al.* 1986; Barbas and Pandya 1987). The function of this route remains to be examined. However, there is a problem. Suppose we find that, as we expect, monkeys with ventral prefrontal lesions are poor at learning a visual conditional motor task; this finding alone would say nothing about the information transmitted to the ventral premotor cortex. The lesion would disrupt both cortico-cortical and cortico-subcortical routes.

It is tempting to suppose that we could cut the cortico-cortical route without disrupting the cortico-subcortical route by using the 'cross-lesion' technique. The idea would be to remove, let us say, the left prefrontal cortex and the right premotor cortex, and then to examine the effects on learning of cutting at a later stage the commissures connecting the left and right neocortex. The argument would be that, if cutting these commissures disrupted learning, then this would demonstrate the importance of cortico-cortical fibres connecting the prefrontal to the premotor cortex. Unfortunately the experiment would not work: the bulk of the subcortical projections from the intact right prefrontal are to the basal ganglia on the right, and these would have no ready access to the intact left premotor area. Thus the commissural section would disrupt both cortico-cortical and cortico-subcortical pathways.

Basal ganglia

We can, however, study the cortico-subcortical pathways independently of the cortico-cortical paths. A lesion in the basal ganglia leaves the cortical pathways from prefrontal to premotor cortex intact. We have studied the effect of interfering with the output of the basal ganglia by placing lesions in the ventral thalamus. The globus pallidus and SNpr project to the thalamic nuclei VApc, VAmc, and VLo in Olszewski's (1952) terminology. These form the VA of Ilinsky and Kultas-Ilinsky (1987) and the VA and VLa of Jones (1985).

We taught monkeys to pull a joystick given one colour and to turn it given another, and then placed lesions in these ventral thalamic nuclei (Canavan *et al.* 1989*a*). Four animals had significant damage in these nuclei (Fig. 8.3, p.175). Figure 8.4 gives the data for three of these animals: two animals failed to relearn at all in 3000 trials, and the third regained criterion only after 1557 trials. The training of the fourth animal was discontinued when it had failed to perform above chance in 1000 trials.

This result would not be of interest if the animals were unable to make the appropriate movements. Two of the animals suffered bouts of akinesia in the first three weeks after surgery, and the other two were slow and unsteady during the first week after surgery. However, all the animals had recovered normal levels of activity by the time they were retested on the conditional manipulative task. All were able to pull or turn the handle.

The experiment demonstrates that the basal ganglia are critically involved in some stage of the process by which an animal learns to make the limb movements that are appropriate given the visual context. The next sections consider in more detail the way in which the outputs from the prefrontal cortex could influence the premotor cortex via the basal ganglia.

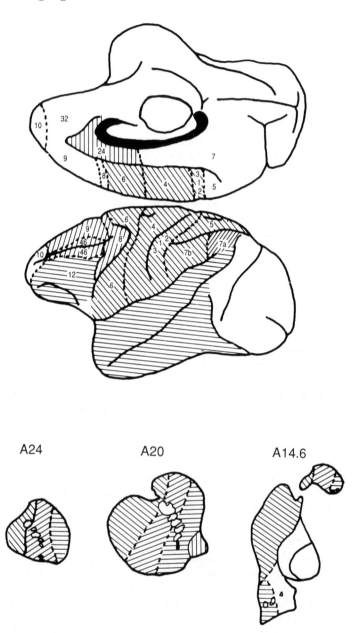

Fig. 8.5 Three sectors in striatum at 24 mm, 20 mm, and 14.6 mm anterior to the level of the ear bars. The shading shows the areas of cortex which project to these sectors. The diagram is a simplification; it fails to show the overlap between the projection areas. The projection to the tail of the ventral putamen is from inferotemporal cortex and not from superior temporal cortex as well, as implied by the shading. For references see text.

Striatum

Cortico-striatal projections
In the anterior striatum, the division between the caudate and putamen is arbitrary. It depends on the course of the fibres of the internal capsule that divide caudate from putamen. Selemon and Goldman-Rakic (1985) have clearly demonstrated that the cortical projections to the striatum do not respect this division. In the present account the interest is not in the connections of the caudate or putamen, but rather in the sectors of the striatum that receive an input from the prefrontal and premotor areas.

Figure 8.5 provides a rough guide to the sectors of the striatum in which the different cortical projections terminate (Percheron *et al.* 1984; Selemon 1990; Parent 1990). There are four main sectors in the striatum.

1. The medial sector receives an input from the temporal lobe (Van Hoesen *et al.* 1981; Selemon and Goldman-Rakic 1985), and from the inferior prefrontal area 12 with which the temporal lobe is connected (Selemon and Goldman-Rakic 1985).

2. The central sector receives an input from parietal area 7a and from the prefrontal areas 8 and 46 with which they are connected (Selemon and Goldman-Rakic 1985; Yeterian and Pandya 1991).

3. The lateral sector receives an input from three main areas: these are the motor cortex and somatosensory cortex (Kunzle 1975, 1977; Percheron *et al.* 1984), parietal areas 5 and 7b (Weber and Yin 1984), and the premotor areas with which they are connected (Kunzle 1977; Selemon and Goldman-Rakic 1985).

4. The ventral striatum receives an input from the anterior cingulate cortex (area 24) (Baleydier and Maugiere 1980).

Overlap between sectors
There is a general principle that where cortical areas are connected by cortico-cortical fibres there is overlap between the corresponding sectors in the striatum (Yeterian and van Hoesen 1978). For example, there is convergence in the caudate nucleus between the projections of the frontal eye-field and dorsomedial eye-field (Parthasarathy *et al.* 1992). Selemon and Goldman-Rakic (1985) argue that this principle does not always hold. One could point to the fact that the overlap between the sectors for the dorsolateral and orbital prefrontal cortex is not extensive (Selemon and Goldman-Rakic 1985; Yeterian and Pandya 1991). But this is not decisive: although the dorsolateral and orbital prefrontal cortex are themselves connected, the cortical interconnections are not heavy (Barbas and Pandya 1989).

If we consider a visual conditional motor task, the crucial question is whether there is overlap between the sectors for the ventral prefrontal and premotor areas. There are projections to the lateral putamen and lateral

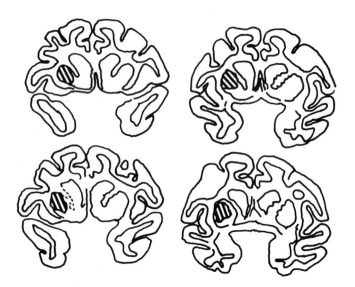

Fig. 8.6 Four sections through the brain of a monkey with a lesion in the left putamen. Shaded area = lesion. The order of sections from anterior to posterior is top left (anterior), bottom left, top right, bottom right (posterior).

caudate both from the dorsal lateral premotor cortex (Selemon and Goldman-Rakic 1985; Shook *et al.* 1991) and medial premotor cortex (Kunzle 1978; Selemon and Goldman-Rakic 1985). Unfortunately no-one has placed anterograde tracers in the ventral part of the lateral premotor cortex.

There is overlap at anterior levels between the projection areas of the dorsomedial premotor cortex and the ventral prefrontal cortex (Selemon and Goldman-Rakic 1985). There is also overlap at anterior levels between the projections areas of the dorsomedial and lateral premotor cortex and dorsal prefrontal cortex (Selemon and Goldman-Rakic 1985).

This is not to say that these cortical areas project to the same cells in the striatum. Selemon and Goldman-Rakic (1985) have shown that where there is overlap in the striatum, there is interdigitation of the terminal patches from the different projection areas.

Behavioural tasks

Lesions in a sector of the striatum produce the same effects as lesions in the cortical areas which project to that sector. Consider first the lateral caudate. This receives projections from area 46. Large lesions in the caudate nucleus impair the learning of the DR and DA tasks (Goldman and Rosvold 1972).

Lesions in the medial premotor cortex cause impairments on the arm raise task (Chapter 4); and the medial premotor cortex projects to the lateral putamen. We have trained three monkeys on this task, and then made large bilateral lesions in the anterior putamen ahead of the globus pallidus (Nixon

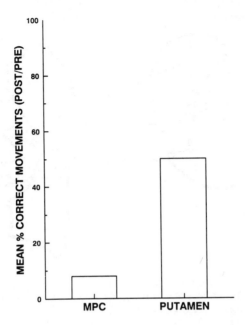

Fig. 8.7 Mean successful responses per minute as a percentage of preoperative levels on the arm raise task. MPC = 3 monkeys with lesions in medial premotor cortex, putamen = 3 monkeys with lesions in the putamen. Data from Thaler (1988) and Nixon et al. (1992).

et al. 1992) (Fig. 8.6). Two weeks after surgery the animals were retested for 200 trials. They were impaired, though not as severely as monkeys with MPC lesions (Fig. 8.7). It is possible that the impairment would have been greater if the lesion had not been confined to the anterior part of the putamen.

Globus pallidus

Overlap
There is another way in which the ventral prefrontal cortex could influence the premotor cortex via their projections through the basal ganglia. This could be achieved by arranging that the relevant striatal sectors project to overlapping regions of the globus pallidus. There are two possibilities.

The first involves the outputs of the lateral and medial putamen. Both the lateral and medial putamen project to the ventral GP (DeVito *et al.* 1980; Selemon 1990; Selemon and Goldman-Rakic 1990; Hedreen and DeLong 1991) (Fig. 8.8).

The second way involves the outputs of the caudate. The caudate receives inputs not only from the temporal, parietal, and prefrontal association areas (Selemon and Goldman-Rakic 1985), but also from

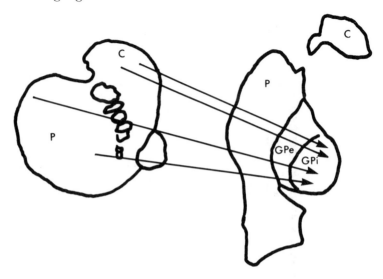

Fig. 8.8 Projections from the caudate and putamen to the globus pallidus, pars interna (GPi). (The projections to the globus pallidus, pars externa (GPe) are not shown.) For references see text.

the premotor areas (Kunzle 1978; Selemon and Goldman-Rakic 1985; Shook *et al*. 1991). There is a projection from both lateral and medial caudate to the dorsal GP (Smith and Parent 1986; Selemon and Goldman-Rakic 1990; Hedreen and DeLong 1991) (Fig. 8.8).

Overlap within the dorsal or ventral GPi
It is one thing to show that different sectors project to the same general region in a nucleus; it is another to show that there is overlap between the two projections. Percheron *et al.* (1984) have argued that the pallidum is built so as to allow cells to receive inputs from separate pathways. They have used the Golgi stain to allow measurements of the neurones in the globus pallidus (Yelnik *et al.* 1984). They point to the existence of large pallidal neurones in the shape of discs which are arranged perpendicular to the striatal axons (Fig. 8.9). The average size of the discs is 1500μ x 1000μ x 250μ.

The projections from the putamen form multiple bands covering a broad segment of the GPe and GPi (Hedreen and DeLong 1991). It appears that neighbouring regions of the lateral putamen may have overlapping territories in the GP. Unfortunately, Hedreen and DeLong (1991) did not place injections in the medial putamen, and there is therefore no proof that there is overlap between the projections of the lateral and medial putamen.

Nobody disputes that the cells in the GPi can collect from different striatal outputs. The issue is the extent to which they can collect from different

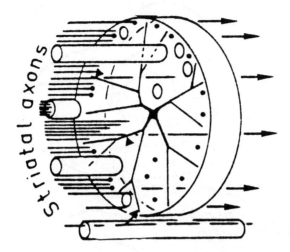

Fig. 8.9 Illustration of the orientation of the striatal–pallidal axons with respect to the pallidal discs. Adapted from Percheron *et al.* (1984).

striatal sectors, and this issue is not settled (Percheron and Filion 1991; Alexander and Crutcher 1991; Selemon and Goldman-Rakic 1991).

Outputs of the dorsal and ventral GPi
The dorsomedial and ventrolateral parts of the GPi differ in the areas of cortex that they influence (Fig. 8.10). The ventrolateral part of the GPi projects to the VLo nucleus (Kim *et al.* 1976; DeVito and Anderson 1982; Ilinsky and Kultas-Ilinsky 1987). In turn VLo sends a heavy projection to the medial premotor cortex (Schell and Strick 1984). Hedreen *et al.* (1988) placed a retrograde tracer in the medial premotor cortex and an anterograde tracer in the GPi. They found overlap of the labelling in the VLo.

The dorsomedial part of the GPi projects to the VApc nucleus of the thalamus (Kim *et al.* 1976; DeVito and Anderson 1982; Ilinsky and Kultas-Ilinsky 1987). In turn the VApc projects to parts of the lateral premotor cortex (Kievit and Kuypers 1975; Miyata and Sasaki 1983; Matelli *et al.* 1989; Shook *et al.* 1991). This linkage requires confirmation by studies that place retrograde tracers in the lateral premotor cortex and anterograde tracers in the dorsomedial GPi.

Hedreen and DeLong (1991) report that the more lateral and ventral part of the striatum (lateral putamen) projects more laterally and ventrally in the GPi, and the more dorsal and medial part of the striatum (caudate) projects more dorsally and medially in the GPi. The overall pattern of projections suggests that the medial premotor cortex may be influenced mainly by the lateral putamen and the lateral premotor cortex by the caudate.

One can also discern a topographical pattern in the organization of the thalamo-cortical relay. The VA nucleus extends more anteriorly than the

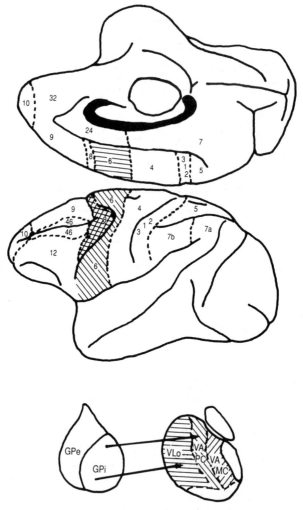

Fig. 8.10 Projections from the globus pallidus, pars interna (GPi) to the ventral thalamus, and from ventral thalamus to premotor cortex. Vlo = nucleus ventrolateralis, pars oralis, VApc = nucleus ventralis anterior, pars parvocellularis, VAmc = nucleus ventralis anterior, pars magnocellularis (terminology of Olszewski 1952). The projections from the ventral thalamus to the premotor cortex are shown by the shadings. Both VApc and VAmc project to Brodmann area 8. The projections from ventral thalamus to prefrontal cortex are not shown. For references see text.

VLo nucleus does. The VLo projects posteriorly to the medial premotor cortex and motor cortex, and the VA projects to cortex that lies more anteriorly. The VApc nucleus projects to the anterior lateral premotor cortex (Kievit and Kuypers 1977; Miyata and Sasaki 1983; Matelli *et al.* 1989; Shook *et al.* 1991), and both the VApc and VAmc nuclei send projections to area 8

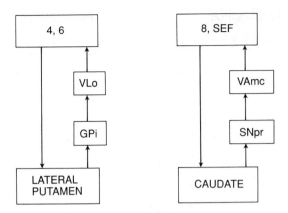

Fig. 8.11 Cortico-subcortical loops. 4 = motor cortex, 6 = premotor cortex, 8 = Brodmann area 8, SEF = supplementary eye field, VLo = nucleus ventrolateralis, pars oralis, VAmc = nucleus ventralis anterior, pars magnocellularis (terminology of Olszewski 1952), GPi = globus pallidus, pars interna, SNpr = substantia nigra, pars reticulata.

and the supplementary eye field (Shook *et al.* 1991). Both the VAmc and the VApc also send projections to the prefrontal cortex, though they are light compared with the heavy input from the MD nucleus (Ilinsky *et al.* 1985; Barbas *et al.* 1991).

There is also a functional distinction. The VLo nucleus projects to those motor areas which are least influenced by direct sensory input. The VA nucleus projects to those areas that are more readily influenced by external sensory inputs, that is the lateral premotor cortex, the frontal eye fields, and prefrontal cortex.

Substantia nigra

The above account has not considered the SNpr; yet both the caudate and putamen send projections to this nucleus (Smith and Parent 1986; Selemon and Goldman-Rakic 1990), and there is overlap between these projections (Hedreen and DeLong 1991). The loops through the GPi and SNpr are concerned with quite different motor performances. Movements of the limbs are controlled through the GPi and movements of the eyes through the SNpr.

As in the putamen, many cells in the GPi are responsive during active movements of the leg, arm, and axial musculature (Crutcher and DeLong 1984. Cells related to limb movements are rare in the SNpr (DeLong *et al.* 1983).

On the other hand, both in the caudate (Fig. 8.12) and in the SNpr a high proportion of cells respond when a monkey performs eye movement tasks (Hikosaka and Wurtz 1983; Hikosaka *et al.* 1989). Cells related to licking and chewing movements have also been reported both in the lateral SNpr and ventrocaudal GPi (DeLong *et al.* 1983). These neighbouring areas are

Sagittal   ## Horizontal

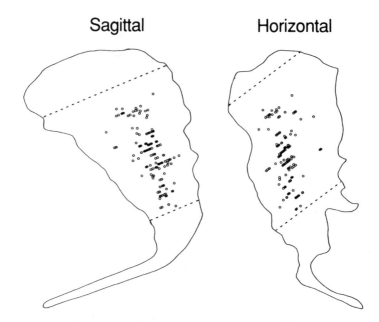

Fig. 8.12 Locations of all cells in the caudate showing saccade related activity. Right figure shows caudate in horizontal (transverse) section, left figure shows caudate in sagittal section. Area between dashed lines = area from which recordings were taken. Anterior = top, posterior = bottom. Figure from Hikosaka *et al.* (1989).

divided by the internal capsule and it could be argued that, as in the anterior striatum, the course of the fibres is arbitrary.

The GPi is concerned primarily with manipulative movements, and the SNpr with orienting movements. The role of the SNpr in orienting is further suggested by the fact that it sends an output to the deep layers of the superior colliculus. Using pharmacological techniques, Hikosaka and Wurtz (1985) have demonstrated that activity in the SNpr has a controlling influence over the activity of cells in the superior colliculus.

This distinction is maintained in the projections of the GPi and SNpr to ventral thalamus and thence to the frontal cortex (Fig. 8.11). The SNpr projects to the thalamic nucleus VAmc as well as to subdivisions of the mediodorsal nucleus (MDmf, MDp, and MDdc). The VAmc projects in turn to areas 8 and the dorsomedial eye field (Shook *et al.* 1991). Just as the frontal eye field is kept separate from the rest of the motor map, so orienting movements are separated from manipulative movements in the output nuclei of the basal ganglia. Alexander *et al.* (1991) make the same point by contrasting a 'motor' loop and an 'oculomotor' loop.

The contribution of the paths that pass through the SNpr and VAmc of the thalamus can be assessed by behavioural tests. Cianci (1962) used electrical stimulation to interfere with the normal activity of cells in this region. He found that this disturbed the performance of monkeys on the DR task on which they had to choose between spatial locations.

Conclusion

The prefrontal and premotor areas are connected by cortico-cortical fibres, and there is also overlap between their terminal zones in the anterior striatum. On a visual conditional motor task, the ventral prefrontal cortex must influence the lateral premotor cortex. It can do this via cortico-cortical projections and it seems likely that it can also do so by an overlap in projections of the ventral prefrontal and lateral premotor cortex as they course through the basal ganglia.

It is important, however, to distinguish two claims. The first is that each of the frontal regions is represented in the striatum and globus pallidus, but that there is *overlap* between the projections where the cortical areas are themselves interconnected. The second claim is that there is a *convergence* of the projections, such that there is complete overlap between the projection zones within the outputs of the basal ganglia. Though the first claim is still controversial, there is agreement that the second is incorrect and that the projections zones do not merge.

Cell recording

Set-related cells

If the basal ganglia play a role in the selection of responses, we should expect to find cells that change their activity before movement, and do so in relation to specific movements. There are many cells that fire well in advance of movement. Alexander and Crutcher (1990*a*) have reported that many cells in the putamen discharge while the animal waits to act on a delayed response task. Schultz and Romo (1988) have recorded while monkeys make self-initiated movements; the animals reached into a covered food box whenever they wanted. Eighteen per cent of cells in the caudate and 23 per cent of cells in the putamen increased their activity 700–3000 milliseconds before the movement; the earliest EMG activity started 350-400 milleseconds before the movement. These cells behave similarly to cells recorded in the medial premotor cortex (Romo and Schultz 1987).

Hikosaka *et al.* (1989) have recorded from 266 cells in the caudate while monkeys made saccadic eye movements (Fig. 8.12). Ten per cent of the cells showed sustained activity starting well in advance of eye movements.

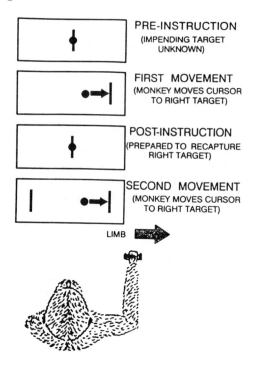

Fig. 8.13 Visuomotor delayed response task. The rectangles show the screen in front of the monkey at four different times within a single trial. Vertical bars = targets, closed circle = cursor. Figure from Alexander and Crutcher (1990*b*).

A further 68 per cent discharged before eye movements when a target spot was shown but extinguished before the animal was allowed to move its eyes. The change in activity occurred up to 300 milliseconds before the saccade.

Goal-related cells

Many cells in the caudate fire differently according to the location of the target (Hikosaka *et al.* 1989). It is likely that these cells code for the goal or target rather than the specific eye movements required to move the eyes to that target. The caudate influences the deep layers of the superior colliculus via the SNpr. One possibility is that the colliculus specifies the change in the desired position of the eyes (Sparks 1989).

In the putamen, the activity of many cells is also related to the spatial goal rather than to the particular movements that the animal makes in achieving it. Alexander and Crutcher (1990*b*) taught monkeys a motor version of the DR task. The procedure is illustated in Fig. 8.13. The monkey operates a handle so as to move the cursor to the left by flexing the wrist or to the right by extending it. At the beginning of each trial the cue is given by the movement of a light to the left or right, and the monkey follows this by moving the cursor to the position that is indicated. The cue light is extinguished and a delay of 1.5–3 seconds follows. After the delay, the monkey must move the cursor back to the same position.

The trick is to dissociate the goal from the movements that achieve it. This was done by setting up two conditions. In the first, flexion of the limb moved the cursor to the left, and extension to the right. In the other condition, flexion moved the cursor to the right, and extension to the left.

In the putamen there were cells that fired during the delay (set-related or preparatory cells) and others that fired in relation to the movement. The analysis that follows is for the set-related cells; these fire after the goal has been established but before the movement has been made. Thirty-three per cent of the cells responded during the delay. Of these, 38 per cent were active in related to the spatial target, and only 9 per cent in relation to the direction of the movement required to achieve it.

Movement-related cells

The evidence that there are set-related cells in the striatum supports the belief that the basal ganglia play some role in the selection of responses. But several physiologists have claimed that it is unlikely that the basal ganglia play such a role; the argument depends on the fact that movement related cells tend to discharge after the beginning of the first EMG and after the discharge of cells in motor cortex.

Aldridge *et al.* (1980) trained monkeys on a step-tracking task and found that the majority of cells in the caudate and globus pallidus were activated after the onset of muscle activity. More recently, Crutcher and Alexander (1990) studied movement-related activity in the putamen and motor cortex. On average, the cells in the putamen discharged 33 milliseconds later than those in motor cortex, though there was extensive overlap in the distribution of the times.

Georgopoulos *et al.* (1983) recorded cells in the globus pallidus while monkeys performed a visual step-tracking task, and they also report that most of the changes in neuronal discharge began after the first alteration in the EMG. Overall, the changes in cell activity occurred a little later than those in motor cortex.

Anderson and Horak (1985) trained monkeys to make a simple movement: the animals reached for a button when it lit up. Recordings were taken from various muscles in the back, shoulder, elbow, and wrist. The cells in the globus pallidus tended to discharge at or after the initial muscle activation and during the build-up of EMG activity.

Finally, Mink and Thach (1991*b*) trained monkeys on visual tracking. The target moved in steps on one task and in a ramp on the other. A comparison was made between the time at which cells became active in the globus pallidus and in the dentate and interpositus nuclei of the cerebellum. On the first task the cells in the cerebellum tended to start discharging earlier than those in the globus pallidus. But on neither task was there any difference between the globus pallidus and cerebellar nuclei in the time of the peak change in activity.

The issue is not as simple as some have taken it to be. Consider the history of studies of the timing of the change in activity of cells in the frontal eye fields. The earliest studies measured activity in this area while the monkeys moved their eyes spontaneously. It was found that the cells tended to discharge after saccades and not before (Bizzi 1968; Bizzi and Schiller 1970). This appeared to argue against the common assumption held by many that the frontal eye fields played some command role in the direction of saccades. It turned out that it was the task that was wrong: the majority of cells in the frontal eye fields discharge before eye movements if they are made to a visual target (Bruce and Goldberg 1985).

All the experiments listed above measured the timing of cells in the striatum or globus pallidus when the monkeys made movements to visual cues. If we do not know what the basal ganglia do, there must be a serious possibility that the tasks used in these studies are not those which best tax the basal ganglia.

We already know that there are many cells in the striatum that fire when monkeys prepare to make movements that are either self-generated (Schultz and Romo 1988) or specified by information in memory (Alexander and Crutcher 1990*a*). Mink and Thach (1991*a*) trained their monkeys on five tracking tasks: in three of them the monkeys tracked visual targets, and in the other two the monkeys generated the track. It is quite possible that Mink and Thach (1991*b*) would have found quite different results for the globus pallidus and cerebellar nuclei had they compared the timing of activity related to self-generated movements.

There is a further complication. It does not follow that if cells fire during or after movement they can play no role in the selection of movements. It follows only that on any particular trial the cell activity is not determining *that* movement; it could still be true that the activity affects future movements.

There are two possibilities. The first is that the cell is involved in the registration of the motor context. If an animal performs a motor sequence the cue for the next movement in the sequence is the movement that the animal has just performed.

The second possibility is more intriguing. This is that some of these cells are involved in the process by which movements are reinforced. If a monkey wins a peanut by pulling a handle, there must be a mechanism that registers what movement has been made and associates it with the consequence that follows. This possibility will be discussed further in the next chapter.

Premotor areas and the cerebellum

It has been argued that the frontal cortex–basal ganglia system plays a role in the selection of responses. This system has information about the sensory and motor context, and can thus determine what response is appropriate.

But we have said nothing about how the relevant movements are stored and retrieved. This section proposes that the storage and retrieval of the detailed motor programmes involve the circuitry linking the premotor areas and the cerebellum.

Conditional learning

It has been common to regard the cerebellum as if its main concerns are with balance and accurate reaching. If this were the case we would not expect cerebellar lesions to impair the learning of a visual conditional motor task. It is true that we would expect some loss of finesse in the movements themselves; but we would not expect the subjects to perform movements that were inappropriate given the context.

Patients with cerebellar lesions

In fact, lesions in the cerebellum severely impair such learning. This was first shown by Bracke-Tolkmitt *et al.* (1989). They studied five patients with circumscribed cerebellar pathology. The patients were required to learn by trial and error the association between six colours and six words. The patients pointed to the items, and were told when they were correct. The mean number of errors made by the patients in learning was 88 compared with 40 for the control subjects.

We repeated this study with a different version of the task. We compared nine patients with cerebellar pathology, eight patients in the early stages of Huntington's chorea, and eight patients with Parkinson's disease (Tucker *et al.* in preparation). The patients were matched with control subjects for age and IQ.

The task was to learn the association between six patterns and six buttons arrayed from left to right. The procedure was as for the visual–spatial associative task devised by Petrides (1985*a*). The patients learned the associations by trial and error using feedback from the tester. The results clearly confirm the earlier finding by Bracke-Tolkmitt *et al.* (1989): of the nine patients with cerebellar pathology, seven failed to learn the task at all within the limits of testing (Fig. 8.14). These patients were as impaired at learning as those in the early stage of Huntington's chorea. Their mean errors were 134, compared with 139 for the group with Huntington's chorea. Yet only one of the patients with Parkinson's disease failed to learn the task.

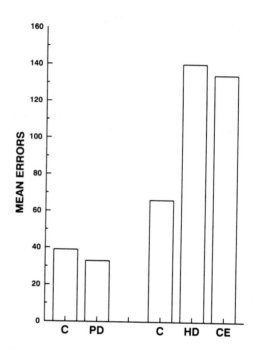

Fig. 8.14   Mean errors for subjects to learn a visual conditional task in which the cues were patterns and the subjects responded by pressing one of six buttons. C = control subjects, PD = patients with Parkinson's disease, HD = patients with Huntington's chorea, CE = patients with cerebellar pathology. Data from Tucker *et al.* (in preparation).

Localization

Both studies are, of course, open to the objection that the pathology might not be confined to the cerebellum. There are two answers to this objection. First, Fiez *et al.* (1992) have published data for a single patient with an infarct in the right posterior inferior cerebellar artery. MRI and CT scans revealed no pathology outside the cerebellum in this patient. The patient had an IQ of 131; yet he was very poor indeed at retrieving words on the basis of their associations with other words. One of the tests, for example, required him to generate verbs that were appropriate for the nouns that were presented. Thus 'scratch' would be an appropriate response to 'foot'; the patient's response of 'ten' was not appropriate.

The second answer is yet more convincing. Petersen *et al.* (1988) gave this same associative task to normal subjects while they were in the PET scanner. The activation was compared with a condition in which no associative process was required: the subject simply repeated the

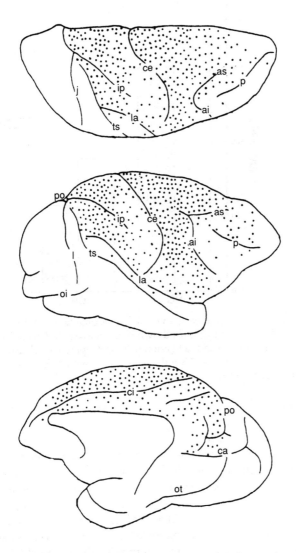

Fig. 8.15 Dorsal (top) lateral, (middle) and midsagittal (bottom) views of the brain showing the relative density of labelled cells in the cortex after injection of HRP into the pons. Figure from Glickstein *et al.* (1985).

nouns. In the associative task there was a significant reduction in the activity of the right lateral cerebellar hemisphere (Raichle 1991). This cannot reflect changes in the motor production of the words, because in the control condition the subjects repeated the words that were presented.

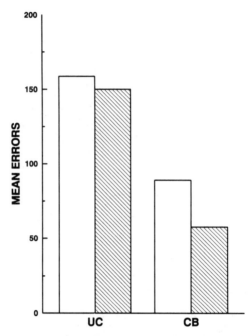

Fig. 8.16 Mean errors to relearn a visual conditional task in which the cues were colours and the monkeys responded by moving a joystick. Unshaded Histogram = pre-operative relearning, shaded histogram = post-operative relearning. UC = three unoperated control monkeys, CB = three monkeys with cerebellar cortical lesions. Data from Tucker *et al.* (in preparation).

Connections

Sensory association cortex

How can information about the context and goals influence the cerebellum? One's first thought is that the relevant information could be relayed from sensory association cortex. The cerebellum receives a relay via the pons from prestriate cortex, V5 (MT) and V5a (MST) and parietal area 7a (Glickstein *et al.* 1980; Ungerleider *et al.* 1984). But these areas analyse the spatial aspects of vision including movement, not information about colours or pattern. The pathways linking them with the cerebellum are probably involved in the control of reaching and tracking movements.

There is also a projection to the pontine nuclei from the auditory area AII and the upper bank of the superior temporal sulcus in front of V5 (MT) and V5a (MST) (Schmahmann and Pandya 1991). But retrograde studies suggest that these projections are not heavy (Glickstein *et al.* 1980, 1985) (Fig. 8.15, p.193).

We have direct evidence that these are not the relevant pathways. We have trained six monkeys on a visual conditional manipulative task

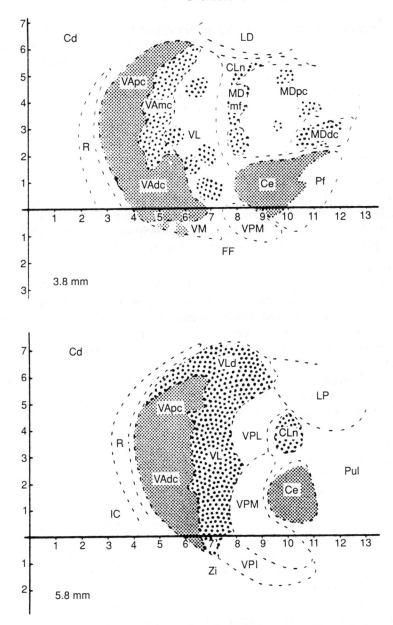

Fig. 8.17 Sagittal sections at 3.8 mm lateral and 5.8 mm lateral through the ventral thalamus of a macaque monkey. Horizontal line gives distance (mm) posterior to the anterior commissure, and the vertical line gives distance (mm) dorsal and ventral to the anterior commissure. ▨ = basal ganglia territory, ▨ = cerebellar territory. VApc = nucleus ventralis anterior, pars parvocellularis, VAdc - nucleus anterior, pars densocellularis, VL = nucleus ventrolateralis, VLd = nucleus ventrolateralis, pars dorsalis. From Ilinsky and Kultas-Ilinsky (1987).

(Tucker *et al.*, in preparation). The monkeys had to move a joystick to the left given one colour and to the right given another. After they had relearned the task before surgery we removed the dorsal paraflocculus bilaterally; this receives much of the cortical visual input that is relayed via the pons. We then retrained the animals on the task.

It will be seen from Fig. 8.16 that the lesion had no significant effect on retention of this task. Indeed, one animal was at the criterion level in the first post-operative session. This is consistent with the belief that the cerebellum does not receive any direct information from the neocortex about colours.

Frontal association cortex

There is also a sparse projection to the pontine nuclei from areas 8, 9, and 46 (Glickstein *et al.* 1980) (Fig. 8.15, p.194). The functional role of these projections has not been tested, but it is a plausible assumption that they are concerned with the control of eye movements in space.

Premotor areas

This leaves a final possibility. The premotor areas are heavily inter-connected with the cerebellum, and they are also interconnected with the prefrontal cortex and basal ganglia. This means that activity in the premotor areas can be influenced by information about the context and goals, and the premotor areas can also influence the cerebellar circuitry.

It is well established that there is a heavy projection from the premotor areas to the pontine nuclei (Brodal 1978; Glickstein *et al.* 1985). The cerebellum projects back to the premotor areas via a relay through the ventral thalamus. There is integration between the basal ganglia and cerebellar pathways at the level of the premotor areas.

The details of the relay through the basal ganglia have already been described. The details of the cerebellar relay are as follows. The dentate and interpositus nuclei are output nuclei of the cerebellum. These project to the VPLo, VPLc, VLc, and nucleus X of the thalamus in Olszewski's (1952) terminology (Asanuma *et al.* 1983). These nuclei are grouped together as VL by Ilinsky and Kultas-Ilinsky (1987) and as VLp by Jones (1985). It is generally agreed that at the level of the thalamus there is little overlap between the basal ganglia and cerebellar territory (Asanuma *et al.* 1983; Ilinsky and Kultas-Ilinsky 1987) (Fig. 8.17, p.195).

There are projections to the frontal cortex from the cerebellar territory of the ventral thalamus. The evidence is listed below.

1. Motor cortex receives a heavy input from VPLo (Schell and Strick 1984; Matelli *et al.* 1989; Shook *et al.* 1991).

2. The medial premotor cortex receives an input from nucleus X and VLc (Wiesendanger and Wiesendanger 1985*a*). Given long survival times, horseradish peroxidase injected into the medial premotor cortex is

carried transneuronally by retrograde transport through the thalamus to the cerebellar nuclei (Wiesendanger and Wiesendanger 1985*b*).

3. The lateral premotor cortex receives a projection from nucleus X and VLc (Schell and Strick 1984; Matelli *et al.* 1989).

4. It has been claimed that the cerebellum can influence caudal area 9 via the ventral thalamus (Sasaki *et al.* 1979). Leiner *et al.* (1991) argue that this link may be important. But they do not consider the alternative possibility, that these thalamic projections are directed at least in part to the dorsomedial eye field. This lies adjacent to caudal area 9 and has an input from the thalamus nucleus VLc (Shook *et al.* 1991).

Overlap in projection areas

It is a crucial observation that there is overlap at the cortical level between the relays through the basal ganglia and cerebellar nuclei. That there might be overlap first became obvious from the studies of Wiesendanger and Wiesendanger (1985*a*) and Matelli *et al.* (1989).

Wiesendanger and Wiesendanger (1985*a*) reported that both the VApc (basal ganglia relay) and nucleus X (cerebellar relay) project to the rostral third of the medial premotor cortex. But the injection of horseradish peroxidase was large and may have included parts of the medial premotor cortex, area 9, and the dorsomedial eye field.

Matelli *et al.* (1989) placed retrograde tracers in the more caudal part of the lateral premotor cortex—part of the area F4 of Matelli *et al.* (1991). They claimed that it received an input both from VLo (basal ganglia relay) and the nuclei X, VPLo, and VLc (cerebellar relay) (Matelli *et al.* (1989).

More recently, Shook *et al.* (1991) made small cortical injections of a retrograde tracer. They report that the dorsal lateral premotor cortex receives an input from the VApc and VLo (basal ganglia relay), and also from the VPLo, VLc, and the lateral part of nucleus X (cerebellar relay).

The issue of overlap has now been resolved by the systematic investigation of Darian-Smith *et al.* (1990). They used multiple retrograde fluorescent tracers, and made small cortical injections in motor cortex and the lateral and medial premotor areas. They report extensive convergence of the input from the two thalamic relays in all three areas and even to cortical regions as small as 0.5 mm. They found projections to motor cortex from VLo as well as VPLo; to the dorsal and anterior part of the lateral premotor cortex from VA as well as VPLo and X; and to the posterior part of the medial premotor cortex from VLo as well as nucleus X.

There has been controversy about whether both thalamic relays project to the area just inferior to the spur of the arcuate sulcus; this is called the 'arcuate premotor area' by Strick (1985) and forms the dorsal part of area F5 of Matelli *et al.* (1985). Schell and Strick (1984) and Matelli *et al.*

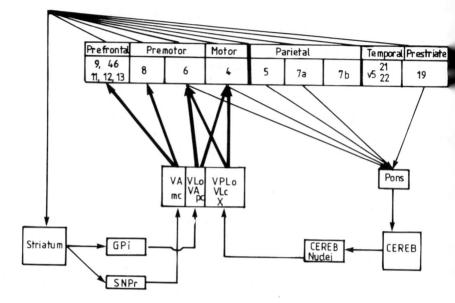

Fig. 8.18   The connections of the basal ganglia and cerebellum. The strip at the top gives various cytoarchitectural areas of the neocortex. VAmc = nucleus ventralis anterior, pars magnocellularis, VApc = nucleus ventralis anterior, pars parvocellularis, VLo = nucleus ventrolateralis, pars oralis, VPLo = nucleus ventralis posterolateralis, pars oralis, VLc = nucleus ventrolateralis, pars caudalis, X = nucleus X (terminology of Olszewski 1952). GPi = globus pallidus, pars interna, SNpr = substantia nigra, pars reticulata, Cereb. nucleu = cerebellar nuclei. The diagram does not show all the projections of the cerebellar nuclei.

(1989) found a projection only from the cerebellar relay, but Darian-Smith *et al.* (1990) claim that there is also a small projection from VLo. The issue would be best resolved by studies in which anterograde tracers are placed in the relevant thalamic nuclei.

Conclusion

Figure 8.18 shows the system as a whole. The hypothesis is that the crucial link is formed by the premotor areas 6 and 8. The premotor areas form part of the loop between frontal cortex and the basal ganglia and also the loop between frontal cortex and cerebellum. The next chapter suggests that the frontal cortex—basal ganglia system learns what action would be appropriate, but that the cerebellum is involved in the process by which the task becomes automatic.

If this were the case, we could then explain how it is that cerebellar lesions can impair the learning of visual–conditional tasks by patients. Damage to the cerebellum would have the same effect as a premotor lesion,

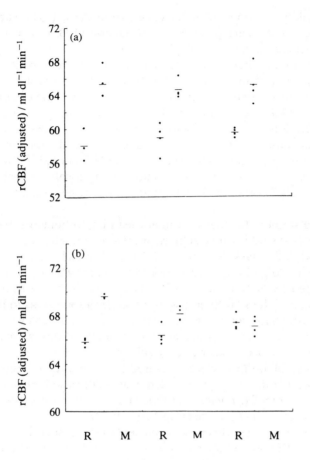

Fig. 8.19 Regional cerebral blood flow (ml/100 ml/minute) (a) sensorimotor cortex, (b) cerebellum. The mean is given by a horizontal line, and each dot gives the value for one subject. R = rest condition, M = condition in which subject practises sequence of finger movements. From Friston *et al.* (1992).

interfering with the retrieval of the appropriate movement.

Motor learning

If this is true, there should be changes in cerebellar activity during learning, just as there are in the premotor cortex. There is indirect evidence that the cerebellum plays a role in learning. Long term depression of activity has been reported in the cerebellar cortex by Ito *et al.* (1982) as the result of stimulation of the climbing fibres and mossy fibres at the same time. Long-term potentiation has also been demonstrated in the cortical and thalamic projections to motor cortex (Iriki *et al.* 1991). Furthermore, both Gilbert and Thach (1977) and Watanabe (1984) have claimed to find modifiable synapses on to the Purkinje cells.

There is more direct evidence that the cerebellum plays a role in the modification of movements (Stein *et al.* 1987). In rabbits, lesions in the interpositus nucleus abolish classical conditional of the eye blink reflex (Thompson 1988; Yeo *et al.* 1985). The cerebellum is also involved in the modification of the vestibulo-ocular reflex (Ito 1984): in monkeys bilateral ablation of the flocculus interferes with the recalibration of this reflex (Lisperger 1988). Miall *et al.* (1987) cooled the interpositus nucleus in one monkey, and injected a local anaesthetic into lateral cerebellar cortex in another, and in both cases visual tracking was impaired.

We have studied the course of motor learning in human subjects using PET. In the first study normal subjects were scanned while they carried out a repetitive skilled task (Friston *et al.* 1992). The task was to oppose the thumb to each digit in turn with brisk movements. The study differs from that reported by Seitz *et al.* (1990) in two respects: the sequence was a simple one, and the movements were paced by a tone so as to control for the rate at which the sequence was performed. The subjects were tested in three sessions, each lasting three and a half minutes. Scans were also taken during three control periods while the subject was at rest.

Changes in blood flow were measured across the three sessions as the subjects became more practised. There was a decrease in activation at the level of the cerebellar nuclei over time (Fig. 8.19*b*, p.199). There was no such change in the motor cortex (Fig. 8.19*a*, p.199).

This preliminary experiment was deficient in two respects. First, only the upper half of the cerebellum was scanned. Second, no record was taken of the finger movements, and there was therefore no demonstration that the performance improved with time.

The second experiment corrected these deficiencies (Jenkins *et al.* 1992*b*). The whole of the cerebellum was scanned, and the task was altered. Rather than simply practising a sequence they had been taught before scanning, the subjects learned which movements to make while they were being scanned. The experiment has been described earlier in the chapter.

We scanned subjects while they learned two new sequences. The cerebral blood flow during learning was compared with the flow when the subjects performed a sequence that they had overlearned prior to scanning. They were trained on this sequence for 75 minutes until they could perform the sequence automatically. The subjects could perform the sequence accurately while repeating five digits numbers spoken to them by the experimenter.

The results were clear cut. There was significantly more blood flow to the cerebellar cortex and cerebellar nuclei when the subjects were learning the sequences as opposed to rehearsing the overlearned sequence

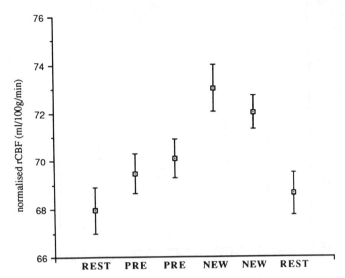

Fig. 8.20 Regional cerebral blood flow (ml/100 g/minute) in left cerebellar nuclei. The bars give the mean and standard error. Rest = rest condition, Pre = prelearned finger sequence, New = learning of a new finger sequence. Data from Jenkins *et al.* (1992*b*).

(Fig. 8.20). This was true both for the lateral cerebellar cortex and the cerebellar nuclei. The changes in blood flow relate to synaptic activity, and this means that a difference in flow to the nuclei may represent a difference in the inhibitory inputs from the Purkinje cells.

The basal ganglia were active in both cases, but there was no significant difference between the activation during learning and performance of the overtrained task (Fig. 8.21). It is the cerebellum that appears to be primarily involved in the process by which motor tasks become automatic.

Summary

The prefrontal cortex can influence the premotor areas by cortico-cortical connections and projections through the basal ganglia. Monkeys are severely impaired at relearning a visual conditional motor task if lesions are placed in the ventral thalamus so as to disrupt the influence of the basal ganglia on frontal cortex.

There are cells in the basal ganglia that fire well before movements when monkeys are repeating a movement from memory or deciding what movement to make.

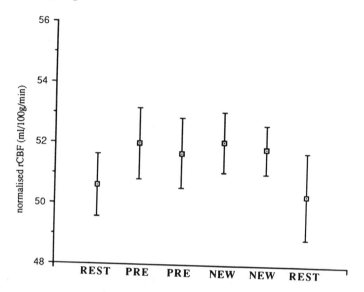

Fig. 8.21   Regional cerebral blood flow (ml/100 g/minute) in left putamen. The bars give the mean and standard error. Rest = rest condition, Pre = prelearned finger sequence, New = learning of a new finger sequence. Data from Jenkins *et al.* (1992*b*).

The premotor areas also interact with the cerebellum via the ventral thalamus. Patients with cerebellar pathology are slow to learn conditional tasks. There is also activation of the lateral cerebellar cortex when subjects habitually produce the same words in response to cue words.

9   The organization of the frontal lobe

The preface promised to describe the functional organization of the frontal lobe. This chapter tries to make sense of the findings of earlier chapters.

When one tries an exercise of the sort attempted here, some of the proposals are bound to be wrong. Hypotheses are informed guesses, and one cannot always guess correctly. The reader should not be deceived by the fact that the statements are written as assertions. It would be tedious to express every sentence in the form 'X may be true'. The hope is that the statements will be clear and thus easy to disprove. The author is well aware that a detailed knowledge of the experiments, whether anatomical or functional, makes one cautious about attempting any

8
6
4

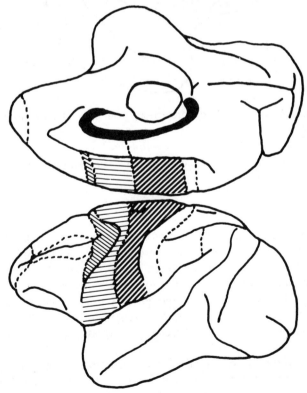

Fig. 9.1   Motor and premotor areas.

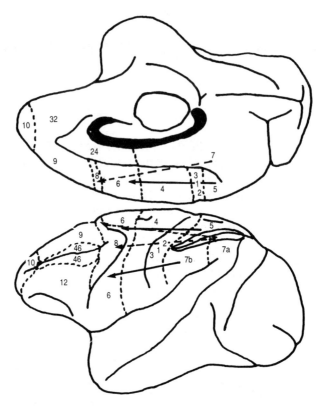

Fig. 9.2   Cortico-cortical projections from parietal cortex to the premotor areas 6 and 8.

synthesis at all; but an attempt may none the less be more helpful than a studied silence.

Parallel motor systems

There are two parallel motor systems (Fig. 9.1). Movements of the limbs, face, and larynx are controlled by the traditional 'motor cortex' (area 4). The map of motor cortex (area 4) does not include a region for movements of the eyes: the eye fields are located more anteriorly. The control of limb and eye movements is necessarily different, since limb movements are directed to targets specified in body coordinates and eye movements must be directed to targets specified in external spatial coordinates.

Each motor area is paired with a premotor area. For area 4 this is area 6, the strip of cortex lying just in front. For the frontal eye field this is the strip of cortex lying anteriorly on the convexity of area 8.

The two premotor areas differ radically in their inputs; the inputs from the parietal lobe are shown in Fig. 9.2. The premotor area 6 receives information about the state of the body from parietal areas 5, 7b, and medial 7. The premotor area 8 receives visuospatial information from parietal area Lip. It also receives visual information from prestriate areas V2 to V5a, the posterior infero-temporal cortex and the lower bank of the superior temporal sulcus; auditory information comes from superior temporal cortex and the upper bank of the superior temporal sulcus (Figs 5.5, p.107). The difference in the inputs is what one would expect given the difference in the targets of the two systems.

The two divisions of the motor system differ in what is selected. One division selects between manipulative movements and the other between orienting movements. In the one case the target is the position of a limb, and in the other an object or location in the world.

Two premotor maps

There are two whole body maps in the premotor areas. Figure 9.3 shows the maps for the macaque brain, based on microstimulation studies (Bruce and Goldberg 1985; Gentilucci *et al.* 1988; Kurata 1989; Godschalk *et al.* 1990; Luppino *et al.* 1991). In the lateral premotor cortex the map is arranged vertically, with the leg at the top and the face at the bottom, with the representation of the eyes lying in front of the representation for the face. In the medial premotor cortex the map is arranged horizontally, with the leg at the back and the face at the front, with the representation of the eyes lying anteriorly and laterally to the representation for the face.

Anterior-posterior premotor divisions

The medial and lateral premotor areas have been treated as unitary areas, but there are anterior and posterior divisions of both areas (Matelli *et al.* 1991; Luppino *et al.* 1991). The posterior part of the lateral premotor cortex (area F2) and of the medial premotor cortex (F3) are interconnected with the motor cortex (area 4). The anterior part of the lateral premotor cortex (area F7) and medial premotor cortex (area F6) are not interconnected with the motor cortex directly, but only indirectly via their connections with the posterior divisions (see Chapter 3).

It is clear that these anatomical divisions reflect functional specializations. First, Luppino *et al.* (1991) found that it is more difficult to elicit movements from the anterior part of the medial premotor cortex (F6) than from the more posterior region F3. Secondly, the activity of cells in area F6 is related to movements of the arm (Rizzolatti *et al.* 1990), whereas there is a full representation of the body in area F3 (Luppino *et al.* 1991). Finally,

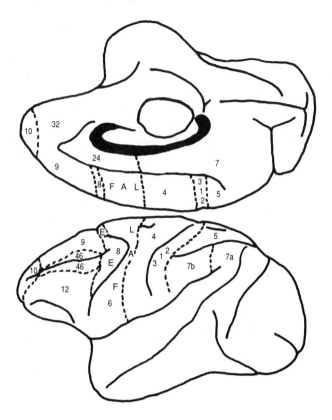

Fig. 9.3 Somatotopic maps revealed by microstimulation in the lateral and medial premotor cortex. E = eyes, F = face, A = arm, L = leg. For references see text.

Matsuzaka *et al.* (1992) found that compared to area F3, a higher proportion of cells in area F6 responded to cues specifying the direction of an arm movement, and a higher proportion were active while monkeys were preparing to move before the trigger stimulus occured.

Deiber *et al.* (1991) also found functional subdivisions using the PET scanner. When subjects performed repetitive movements with their arm, there was activation of the posterior regions of the lateral and medial premotor cortex (Fig. 9.4). There was additional activation of the anterior regions when the subjects had to select between movements (Fig. 9.4). The anterior region of the medial premotor cortex was rostral to the level at which there are gigantopyramidal cells in the cingulate sulcus (Braak 1976).

More work needs to be done before we have a proper idea of the organization of the premotor areas. It would be useful to make anterior or posterior lesions in monkeys trained to perform motor tasks.

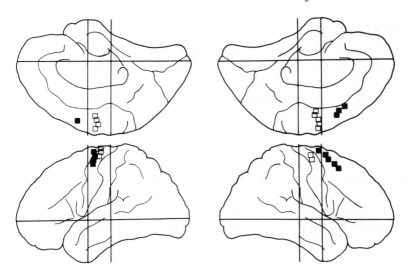

Fig. 9.4 Locations of peaks of maximal significant change of regional cerebral blood flow in lateral premotor cortex and medial premotor cortex. ■ = peaks for four conditions taken together in which subjects had to select between 4 movements (from Deiber *et al.* 1991); ❑ = peaks for four tasks taken together in which subjects made the same movements on each trial of any task (from Colebatch *et al.* 1990*b*). Figure from Deiber *et al.* (1991).

Function of two premotor systems

Chapters 3 and 4 argued that the lateral premotor cortex (area 6) is primarily involved when limb movements are to be selected on the basis of external cues, and that the medial premotor system is primarily involved when limb movements are to selected without prompting from such cues. Chapter 5 argued for a similar distinction between the two premotor areas concerned with the eyes (area 8 and the dorsomedial eye field). The data are less complete, but there are suggestions that area 8 is primarily involved when eye movements are to be selected on the basis of external cues, and the dorsomedial eye field when there are no such cues.

Prefrontal cortex

It has been argued in previous chapters that the premotor areas, prefrontal cortex, and basal ganglia are all involved in the learned selection of responses. It is time to give some account of the different roles that they play.

Prefrontal cortex is divided into two sectors, dorsal (areas 46, lateral and medial 9) and ventral (areas 11, 12, 13, and 14). They differ radically in their connections.

Ventral sector

The ventral sector receives its main input from the temporal lobe, and is directly connected with the amygdala (Chapter 7). Temporal cortex is activated in the PET scanner when subjects are required to make judgements about visual stimuli (Haxby *et al.* in press). Thus, the ventral sector is informed about the external context, that is, about the world.

There is one issue that has not been settled. This is the question of whether the ventral prefrontal cortex is involved in the selection of all responses or is specialized for the selection of responses when there are no external cues. Chapter 7 provided evidence suggesting that lesions in area 12 impair performance on conditional response tasks irrespective of whether the cues are or are not present at the time of response. However, it was argued that the evidence was not yet fully conclusive.

Dorsal sector

The dorsal sector receives its main input from the parietal association cortex and sends outputs to the superior colliculus (Chapter 6). Parietal association cortex is activated in the PET scanner when subjects make voluntary movements of the eyes (Anderson *et al.* 1992; Jenkins *et al.* 1992*a*) or arm (Deiber *et al.* 1991). The dorsal sector is concerned with the animal itself, its eyes and limbs.

Monkeys with lesions in area 46 are very impaired on spatial delayed response tasks; they may never relearn delayed alternation. Yet they are either not impaired or only mildly impaired on spatial conditional tasks on which there is no delay before the animal is allowed to respond (Chapter 6). The dorsal sector is not essential if there is an external cue at the time that the animal responds. Lesions in the dorsal prefrontal cortex in monkeys also impair their ability to produce a sequence of movements (Petrides 1988), and areas 9 and 46 are activated in the PET scanner when subjects generate a series of movements at will (Deiber *et al.* 1991; Frith *et al.* 1991*b*). Dorsal prefrontal cortex is involved *when the subject has to make a decision as to what to do*. This is true whether the subject is learning the appropriate action or making an arbitrary decision.

Dorsal and ventral prefrontal cortex

There are two views that provide a plausible account of the functions of the prefrontal cortex *as a whole*. They provide radically different conceptions.

1. The first is that the prefrontal cortex provides a mechanism by which responses can be selected when there are no external cues at the time of response (Goldman-Rakic 1987). This view assumes that when external cues are present the temporal cortex can influence the premotor area 8

directly. There are visual inputs to area 8 (Chapter five) and lesions in area 8 disrupt the learning of visual conditional tasks (Chapter five). On this view prefrontal cortex need only be addressed when either there have been no external cues or when there were external cues but they are no longer present at the time of response.

2. The second conception is quite different. It assumes that the ventral prefrontal cortex is necessarily involved in the learning of conditional tasks irrespective of whether the cues are present or not when the animal responds. This view points to the fact that the bulk of the projections from the convexity of the temporal lobe pass to the ventral prefrontal cortex and not to ventral area 8 (Barbas 1988; Barbas and Pandya 1991).

On this view the fundamental description of the prefrontal cortex *as a whole* is that it is concerned with the process by which new decisions are taken as to what to do. This is true whether the external context is relevant or not. On some occasions the external context tells the subject what action is appropriate. On other occasions it is the subject that decides; in other words it is the subject that provides the context. Information about the external context is provided by the ventral prefrontal cortex, and responses are generated by the dorsal prefrontal cortex.

It is embarrassing that the data are not yet adequate to force a decision between these two conceptions. On one view prefrontal cortex is engaged on conditional tasks with no external cues, and on the other prefrontal cortex is engaged whenever the task is conditional.

Both conceptions agree in specifying that the task must be conditional. Whether an animal learns a conditional task or a human subject makes arbitrary decisions, they do X on one trial, and Y on another. It is because this is so that prefrontal cortex is involved in attention to action (Shallice 1982). If a fresh decision must be taken on each trial, subjects must attend to what they are doing.

Learning and performance

The word 'voluntary' can be used in a broad sense to mean that the action was learned (Fig. 1.1, level A), but it can also be used to mean that the subjects attended to what they were doing (Fig. 1.1c, level C). When a task has become habitual it becomes 'second nature'. Subjects no longer have to attend to what they are doing, because no new decisions have to be taken.

It has been argued that the prefrontal cortex is necessarily involved when the subjects must make new decisions as to what to do. This formulation leaves open the possibility that prefrontal cortex need not be activated if the subject performs a task that has become habitual. The assumption is that the performance of such a task can come to depend on premotor mechanisms alone.

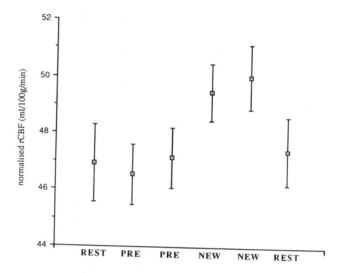

Fig. 9.5   Regional cerebral blood flow (ml/100 g/minute) in right prefrontal cortex (ipsilateral to hand used). The bars give the mean and standard error. Rest = rest condition, Pre = prelearned finger sequence, and New = learning of a new finger sequence. Data from Jenkins *et al.* (1992*b*).

We examined this question with a PET experiment (Jenkins *et al.* 1992*b*). We taught subjects new sequences of finger movements while we scanned them. However, we also scanned them while they performed a sequence that they had learned before scanning and had practised for 75 minutes until they could perform it automatically, without thinking. The evidence that the task had become fairly automatic is that, while they performed the motor task, all the subjects could hold a conversation, and could accurately repeat a series of five digits presented to them by the tester. Prefrontal cortex was extensively activated when subjects were learning new sequences (see frontispiece), but we found no significant activation of the prefrontal cortex when the subjects ran through the automatic sequence (Fig. 9.5).

When the subjects learned new movements, they had to generate movements at will and pay attention to the feedback. When the task was well learned, the sequence was fixed and habitual. Because the sequence was always the same, it could be run off without attending to any external cues.

This result does not imply a general rule that prefrontal cortex is involved early in learning but is dispensable later. It depends whether the task becomes habitual and can be performed automatically.

Monkeys with lesions in area 46 fail to relearn delayed conditional tasks even if they have learned the tasks to criterion before surgery. This is true, for example, of DR and DA. However well they have learned the task, the task never becomes habitual because the monkey must make a new decision on each trial as to what movement to generate. In the PET scanner the dorsal prefrontal cortex is strongly activated when subjects generate movements at will (Deiber *et al.* 1991; Frith *et al.* 1991*b*). It does not matter how long a person performs this task; it always requires them to make a new decision on each trial.

It is a separate issue whether with repetition non-delayed conditional tasks become automatic such that the prefrontal cortex is no longer essential. Once the subject has learned that A means X and B means Y, the subject has only to identify whether A or B is present and then run off the appropriate response. In other words, it is possible that conditional learning of this sort can turn into the retention of paired associates.

In describing work on human subjects, one can rephrase the issue by asking whether conditional learning can turn into 'procedural' learning. The term 'procedural memory' is often contrasted by psychologists with 'semantic memory' (Squire 1987). Human subjects can describe their semantic knowledge but are not able to give a verbal account of how they learn procedural skills such as riding a bicycle.

Consider the experiment by Jenkins *et al.* (1992*b*) in which subjects learned sequences of finger movements by trial and error. Early in learning this task subjects could say that this finger movement follows that one. But if they were asked what the sequence is when the task was overlearned, they responded by trying it with their fingers. Pianists may not be able to tell you the notes of a tune, but they can play it. The task has become a procedural one.

We have not yet scanned subjects *while they learn* non-delayed conditional tasks. However, we have taught auditory conditional tasks to subjects before scanning, and then required them to perform the tasks during scanning (Deiber *et al.* 1991). On the task we called 'conditional', there were four sounds and four responses: the subjects had to pull the joystick given sound A, move it to the right given sound B, and so on. The dorsal prefrontal cortex was not significantly activated during performance of the 'conditional' task that had been learned before scanning.

Now compare this condition with another condition that we called 'opposite'. The same subjects were required to reverse their previous responses. Thus they had to push the joystick given sound A (previously meaning 'pull'), move it to the left given sound B (previously meaning 'right'), and so on. We gave the subjects very little practice before scanning. Now the right prefrontal cortex was activated. In other words, the prefrontal cortex was only activated if the subjects had to make new decisions during the scanning session.

When the subjects generate opposites they have, of course, to inhibit the previously learned response. However, it is important not to interpret the result as evidence that the role of the prefrontal cortex is to inhibit responses. The prefrontal cortex is activated when subjects generate joystick movements (Deiber *et al.* 1991); but this is not because the subjects have unlearned tendencies they must suppress or because they must inhibit responses they have learned previously. In that condition there are no such tendencies and no responses that have been learned. The fundamental description is that the prefrontal cortex is involved when new decisions must be made, irrespective of whether those decisions require the suppression of other responses. Prefrontal cortex did not evolve simply to supply a set of brakes.

Premotor cortex (area 6)

Chapter 3 argued that the lateral premotor cortex (area 6) plays a crucial role in the process by which monkeys learn to base their movements on external cues. However, the analysis of the context is not performed by this area.

Visual cues can be considered as a worked example. Area 8 receives visual information from prestriate cortex and the superior temporal sulcus, and the ventral prefrontal convexity receives visual information from the infero-temporal cortex (Barbas 1988; Barbas and Pandya 1991).

However, it is unlikely that sensory cues influence area 6 via connections from area 8. The connections between these two areas are sparse (Arikuni *et al.* 1980). Furthermore, monkeys with lesions in area 8 have been trained to pull or turn a handle on the basis of a colour cue, and they were not impaired at all (Halsband and Passingham 1985) (Fig. 5.8, p.111). It was argued earlier that information about the visual context must influence action via the projections to the ventral prefrontal cortex.

Timing

On visual conditional tasks the lateral premotor cortex operates at a later stage of processing than the ventral prefrontal cortex does. This can be demonstrated by recording from cells. Pellegrino and Wise (1991) set up an experiment which allowed them to compare the activity of cells in the lateral premotor cortex (area 6) and the ventral prefrontal cortex, areas 12 and ventral 46. Recordings were taken from both areas in the same monkeys. The task was visual matching. Consider the cells that changed their activity before movement ('premovement cells'). The average latency for activity in these cells was 274 milliseconds before movement for prefrontal cortex and 123 milliseconds before movement for premotor cortex.

Cues and responses

The premotor cortex is concerned not with the details of the context but with the direction of the correct movement. Weinrich and Wise (1982) recorded while monkeys performed visual conditional motor tasks. They found that the same cells in the lateral premotor cortex (area 6) changed their activity whether the cues were lights or sounds.

Furthermore, it does not matter whether the cues give instructions directly or via some arbitrary code. Godschalk *et al.* (1985) trained monkeys to expect food in one of three locations. In one condition the location was signalled by the sight of the food at that location. In another condition the locations were indicated by three central lights in a row: the location was specified by which of the three lights was on. Only 13 cells were tested while the monkey performed both versions of the task, but ten of them showed a similar pattern of activity for both conditions.

There is one final demonstration that the responses of cells in lateral premotor cortex are not truly 'sensory'. Wise *et al.* (1992) arranged that the same visual stimulus could specify movements of the limb in different directions on different trials. Seventy eight percent of the cells tested in lateral premotor cortex responded differently to the stimulus according to the direction specified, even though the stimulus was the same in both cases.

Pellegrino and Wise (1991) were also able to compare the degree to which the activity of cells was related to the cues in lateral area 6 and ventral prefrontal cortex (areas 12 and ventral 46). During visual matching 30 per cent of the cells in the prefrontal area changed their activity in relation to the coloured stimuli, but only 11 per cent of the cells in premotor cortex.

The evidence suggests that the premotor areas (6) play a critical role in the learning of *movements*. Monkeys with ventral prefrontal lesions are impaired on visual conditional tasks irrespective of the nature of the response (Chapter 7). But monkeys with LPC lesions are only impaired if the response is a limb movement, such as pulling or turning a handle (Chapter 3). Prefrontal cortex specifies the response in abstract terms. The details of the movements are the province of the basal ganglia and premotor areas.

Prefrontal cortex and basal ganglia

Outputs and loops

The literature has proposed two conceptions of the relations between the frontal cortex and basal ganglia. The first stresses the fact that the basal ganglia can influence the premotor and motor areas (Kemp and Powell 1971). According to this view the prefrontal cortex influences the motor system via the basal ganglia, and one function of the basal ganglia is to

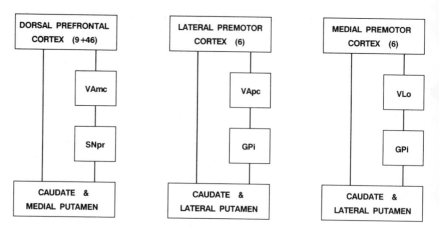

Fig. 9.6 Three possible anatomical loops through the basal ganglia. VApc = nucleus ventralis anterior, pars parvocellularis, VLo = nucleus ventralis lateralis, pars oralis, GPi = globus pallidus, pars interna. For details see text.

allow convergence of the information relevant to action. We can call this the 'funnel hypothesis'

The second conception stresses the fact that each frontal region projects to particular parts of the striatum, and that there are return connections through the GPi/SNpr and ventral thalamus back to each frontal region (Alexander *et al.* 1991). We can call this the 'loop hypothesis'. It states that the areas of the frontal lobe interact with the basal ganglia in a series of parallel loops. Figure 9.6 illustrates some possible loops involving the premotor areas (6 and 8) and prefrontal cortex.

There are four questions that we need to ask in evaluating these two conceptions.

1. Why is the globus pallidus much smaller than the striatum? There must be convergence of some form in the projections from the striatum to the globus pallidus.

2. Is there overlap between the basal ganglia territories of the prefrontal and premotor areas? Alexander *et al.* (1991) have charted the projections through the basal ganglia from the arm area of motor cortex, lateral premotor cortex and medial premotor cortex. They suggest that there is little overlap between these loops.

   But this does not rule out the possibility that there is significant overlap between the prefrontal and premotor loops. Chapter 8 argued that there appears to be overlap between the projections from the lateral premotor cortex and dorsal prefrontal cortex in the caudate, and that there may be further scope for interconnections in the projections from the caudate to the dorsal globus pallidus.

3. Why are there projections from the ventral thalamus back to the prefrontal cortex? It could be argued that these projections cannot be explained on the 'funnel hypothesis'. However, the hypothesis can be reformulated so that it claims only that the basal ganglia project to frontal areas with outputs to the motor system. The dorsal prefrontal cortex has direct outputs to the superior colliculus (Chapter 5).

4. What is the function of the loops that connect areas of frontal cortex to the basal ganglia? One possibility is that these feedback loops play some role in motor learning.

The next two sections discuss the fundamental reason why the frontal cortex and basal ganglia are interconnected and provide evidence that the basal ganglia may be involved in motor learning.

Cortical–subcortical connections

The key is held by comparative anatomy. In amphibians such as frogs there is no neocortex: the basal ganglia receive sensory information via the thalamus and send outputs to the midbrain and lower brain stem (Parent 1986). In reptiles and birds the basal ganglia receive an input from areas thought to be homologous with the mammalian neocortex, but they still send their major output to the tectum (Parent 1986; Reiner *et al.* 1984).

In mammals the basal ganglia both receive an input from the neocortex and send their major output back to the frontal cortex via the thalamus. This indirect route means that the prefrontal cortex can address the premotor areas in parallel with the cerebellar relay which also influences the premotor areas through the ventral thalamus.

The basal ganglia evolved as the telencephalic structure that determines responses. Though the striatum is not a cortical structure, it is unusual for a nucleus in that, just as in cortex, there is considerable scope for lateral interaction between cells (Smith and Bolam 1990). There are local axon collaterals from the medium spiny neurones, and it is thought that many of these synapse onto neighbouring medium spiny neurones. The local GABergic aspiny interneurones have an extensive axonal field, and there are also substance P containing neurones that are probably interneurones, and large aspiny neurones that make contact with the dendritic shafts and spines of medium spiny neurones.

In mammals, unlike in amphibians, sensory information is routed not only to the colliculi but also through the neocortex. We may say that there is a 'long circuit' through the neocortex. Sensory information is analysed in posterior association areas, and responses are determined by prefrontal cortex. But the neocortex still influences the motor system through the basal ganglia, the original system for determining responses. This means that there must be close interconnections between the cortical and subcortical systems involved in determining responses.

Response learning

Are the basal ganglia involved in the *learning* of responses? Traditionally neurologists and neurophysiologists have regarded the basal ganglia as having some executive function. However, some role in learning has been proposed more recently by Oberg and Divac (1979), Robbins *et al.* (1989), Mishkin (1991) and Rolls and Johnstone (1992). There is evidence from anatomy, cell recording, PET studies, and lesion studies.

Anatomy

First, like the hippocampus, the striatum is rich in NMDA receptors (Clark and Goldman-Rakic 1991). Tetanic stimulation of the cortico-striatal fibers produces long term synaptic depression of the excitatory post-synaptic potentials (Calbresi *et al.* 1992). This effect is blocked by an antagonist of NMDA receptors. It can also be blocked by depleting dopamine, and can be restored by applying exogenous dopamine.

Cell recording

No one has yet recorded the activity of cells in the striatum while monkeys learn new tasks. Chapter 3 described the experiment by Mitz *et al.* (1991) in which it was shown that cells in premotor cortex (area 6) change their activity during visual conditional motor learning. This experiment could be repeated while recordings are taken from the striatum or globus pallidus, and this has yet to be done.

However, Llungberg *et al.* (1992) have recorded from dopamine neurones in the substantia nigra, pars compacta (A9) and the neighbouring cell groups of the mesolimbic and mesocortical system (A8 and A10). They taught monkeys a simple instrumental task; the monkey pressed a lever when a light appeared, and was rewarded with juice. Before learning, seven per cent of the cells changed their activity when the light appeared, and 13 per cent when the monkey was given free juice. During learning the figures were 51 per cent and 26 per cent. When the monkey was overtrained there was a moderate decrease in the number of active cells: 40 percent changed their activity to the light, and 11 per cent to the juice.

PET studies

If cells in the basal ganglia change their activity during learning the PET scanner should detect an increase in activation during learning by human subjects. In the experiment by Jenkins *et al.* (1992*b*), we compared activation in the putamen while subjects learned new sequences of finger movements and while they were lying still at rest. We found activation in the putamen during learning (Fig. 8.21, p.202).

However, the activation was as great when the subjects performed a sequence on which they had been overtrained (Fig. 8.21). In the earlier study by Friston *et al.* (1992) we also found that motor cortex showed no change in activation with repeated practice of a simply sequence of movements. It could be argued that these results imply that, like motor cortex, the putamen has an executive role in the control of movement. However the findings do not rule out an role in learning, since it is possible that that role is still necessary even when the task is overlearned. For example, the basal ganglia might be essential for the process of reinforcement or for the retrieval of motor memories. In the study by Llungberg (1992) cells in the substantia nigra were still more responsive when the instrumental task was overlearned than they had been before learning was started.

Lesions
If the basal ganglia play an essential role in learning, lesions in the basal ganglia should disrupt learning. Monkeys with large lesions in the caudate can fail to learn delayed alternation in 2000 trials (Goldman and Rosvold 1972). Monkeys with putamen lesions are impaired on retention of the arm raise task (Nixon *et al.* 1992), and if the outputs of the globus pallidus are cut by lesions in the ventral thalamus monkeys can fail to relearn a visual conditional motor task in 3000 trials (Canavan *et al.* 1989).

Pathology in the basal ganglia can also lead to cognitive impairments in patients. In Parkinson's disease there is a loss of dopamine in the putamen (Brooks *et al.* 1990), and in Huntington's chorea there is a loss of cells which starts in the caudate and progresses through the putamen with time (VonSattel *et al.* 1985). Many experiments have now shown that patients with these diseases tend to perform poorly on the same tasks on which impairments have been demonstrated in patients with prefrontal lesions (Taylor *et al.* 1986; Sagar and Sullivan 1988; Brown and Marsden 1989; Owen *et al.* 1992).

In an important experiment Heindel *et al.* (1989) tested patients with Huntington's chorea on a visual tracking task. The subjects had to learn to keep a stylus on a target on a rotating turntable. The patients with Huntington's chorea showed only slight improvement with practice. It cannot be argued that this resulted from an executive defect because the turntable was first set for each subject at a speed that allowed the subject to keep the stylus on target for 25% of the time; nonetheless control subjects of the same age improved much faster than the patients with Huntington's chorea. Nor can it be argued that these patients learned slowly because they were demented; patients with Alzheimer's disease also improved much faster than the patients with Huntington'schorea.

It could, of course, be argued that in mammals lesions in the basal ganglia will disrupt the activity of the prefrontal and premotor areas with which they are interconnected. The implication of the argument is that lesions in the basal ganglia will not demonstrate the role of the basal ganglia alone.

It is true that immediately after a lesion in the basal ganglia there are effects on cortical function. Piero *et al.* (1990) studied a patient with a small haemorrhage in the left globus pallidus. Ten days after the stroke PET scans revealed hypometabolism in the cortex. Baron *et al.* (1986) scanned patients with unilateral vascular lesions in the thalamus, and found cortical hypometabolism in the ipsilateral hemisphere. However, these effects are not permanent. Baron *et al.* (1986) found that the asymmetry in blood flow between the two hemispheres was decreased some months later.

Furthermore, the objection is one that can be raised whenever we study the effects of lesions in one structure that is reciprocally connected with another. For example, the temporal lobe is reciprocally connected with the amygdala (Mishkin and Aggleton 1981). Lesions in either the infero-temporal cortex (Mishkin 1972) or the amygdala (Jones and Mishkin 1972; Aggleton and Passingham 1981) disrupt visual learning. But no one argues that lesions in the amygdala disrupt learning simply because they disrupt the normal functioning of the temporal lobe.

It would, in any case, be possible to counter the objection by carrying out experiments on amphibians. In amphibians such as frogs there is no neocortical input to the striatum. If the striatum plays a role in the learning of responses, then lesions in the striatum in frogs should disrupt the selection of responses on the basis of learning. This experiment has not been done, but we do know that amphibians are capable of instrumental learning (Macphail 1982). It is therefore plausible that the striatum plays a role in the selection of learned responses, since it is the telencephalic structure which sends descending motor outputs.

Reward and reinforcement

If the basal ganglia do play a role in learning, it has to be admitted that we know little about exactly what that role is. One possibility is that they contribute to the process by which rewards influence the probability of a response.

Compare stimulus learning and response learning. The amygdala and hippocampus are crucially involved in the process by which animals learn to recognize and recall stimuli. In monkeys disconnection of the amygdala from the visual association cortex impairs the learning of associations between stimuli and reward (Gaffan and Harrison 1988); and the learning of associations between stimuli and locations is disrupted by lesions in the hippocampus (Parkinson *et al.* 1988).

There are projections to the basal forebrain from both the amygdala and hippocampus (Aggleton *et al.* 1987). Mishkin (1991) suggests that the modification of the relevant cortical synapses occurs as the result of the cholinergic projections from the basal forebrain to the hippocampus and cortex.

This system for stimulus learning appears not to be critically involved in response learning. There are three results that support this claim. First, removal of the amygdala and hippocampus does not prevent monkeys from learning simple motor tasks (Zola-Morgan and Squire 1984). Second, a patient with the bilateral removal of the amygdala and hippocampus can still improve his performance on a visual tracking task (Corkin 1968). Finally, when subjects learn new motor sequences in the PET scanner the activity of the hippocampus is depressed compared with its activity at rest (Jenkins *et al.* 1992*b*). This strongly suggests that when subjects are attending to a new motor task, the hippocampus is not crucially involved.

It is a reasonable hypothesis that it is the basal ganglia and not the medial limbic system that form the critical subcortical structures for response learning. The dopaminergic system may be involved in the process by which responses are reinforced by learning. If this is so, then depleting the levels of dopamine in the basal ganglia should influence the probability of a response as the result of learning. Dopamine receptor antagonists impair simple response learning (Bradshaw and Szabadi 1989); for example pimozide retards continuously reinforced lever pressing on a free operant schedule (Wise and Schwartz 1981). Furthermore, free operant performance is also disturbed in rats if dopamine is depleted in the ventral striatum by injecting 6-hydroxydopamine (Robbins *et al.* 1983). Finally, infusion of the indirect dopamine agonist D-amphetamine into the ventral striatum enhances responding to a light that serves as a conditioned reinforcer; and the effect of amphetamine is selectively blocked by 6-hydroxydopamine lesions in the ventral but not dorsal striatum (Robbins *et al.* 1989).

There is also suggestive evidence from studies of self-stimulation. Monkeys will learn an instrumental response to stimulate the ventral striatum (Rolls *et al.* 1980), and rats will press a lever to obtain an injection of a rewarding drug (Koob and Goeders 1989; Wise and Rompre 1989). It is also possible to demonstrate self-stimulation in animals at sites in which dopamine is known to be one of the transmitters, although it has not yet proved possible to abolish self-stimulation completely by placing lesions in the dopaminergic system (Wise and Rompre 1989).

There are cell recording studies that are consistent with the hypothesis. There are cells in the substantia nigra pars compacta that change their activity when reward is delivered (Schultz 1986; Llungberg *et al.* 1992), and there are similar cells in the striatum, particularly the ventral striatum (Apicella *et al.* 1991). Llungberg *et al.* (1992) found that cells in the substantia nigra, pars compacta, became more responsive to primary rewards (liquid) or conditioned incentive stimuli (light) when monkeys learned an instrumental response. It would be worth repeating this experiment while recording from the ventral striatum.

However, we should be cautious in our speculations, and for two reasons. First, we have to distinguish the roles played by the ventral striatum and orbital prefrontal cortex in the mechanisms of rewarding responses; and as yet our knowledge is too slight to allow us to do so. Second, many of the studies quoted above concern the ventral striatum, and studies are needed to clarify the role of the dorsal striatum in learning.

Conclusion

The basic hypothesis is that the frontal–basal ganglia system as a whole is involved in the process by which the animal decides what to do, that is what response is *appropriate*. Lesions in this system affect the probability of a particular response.

We do not know where the motor memories are stored. The most likely candidates are the premotor cortex and the cerebellum. The cerebellum appears to be involved in the process by which motor tasks become automatic (Chapter 8).

The premotor areas 6 and 8 form the crucial link between the two systems. They receive an input from both basal ganglia and cerebellum (Chapter 8). They may interact with the prefrontal cortex and basal ganglia in original learning, and with cerebellum in the performance of skills that have become automatic.

It is difficult to imagine the system at work. The cerebellum does not directly receive information about the identity of objects or the nature of the rewards. But it interacts with the premotor areas, and these areas are influenced by the relevant information through their connections with prefrontal cortex and the basal ganglia. The two systems form loops which meet in the premotor areas, and this means that we cannot easily follow the flow of information.

What is needed is a formal model that will run on a computer. However, the aim of this book is just humble anatomy.

Summary

There are parallel cortical motor systems for movements of the limbs and eyes. There are also two premotor systems, both with a map of the whole body. These play a role in the selection of movements, and differ in their reliance on information about the external context.

The prefrontal cortex as a whole selects actions when the subject must make a new decision as to what to do. It is not yet clear whether prefrontal cortex is only engaged when there is no external cue at the time of the response.

If new decisions are required when a task is learned, prefrontal cortex is activated. But if the task can later be run off automatically, prefrontal cortex need no longer be engaged.

The exact role played by the basal ganglia is not clear. In animals without neocortex, such as amphibians, the basal ganglia form the telencephalic mechanism for determining responses. In mammals the frontal cortical and basal ganglia mechanisms are closely interrelated via a system of loops. There are suggestions that the ventral striatum may play a role in the process by which the probability of a response is altered as a result of positive or negative outcomes.

10　Thought and voluntary action

It is time to forget monkeys and their search for peanuts. There are other goals in life. This chapter takes us from the selection of pictures in the laboratory to the choice of shops and restaurants in everyday life.

Responses

In many laboratory tests, patients are required to choose between items. Like the monkeys, the subjects search for the correct item in an external array. It may be a picture or word, as on the subject-ordered task (Petrides and Milner 1982), or a card in a particular location, as on the spatial associative task (Petrides 1985*a*). It does not matter whether the items are objects covering food-wells, pictorial representations of objects, or words that refer to objects.

A distinction should be drawn between those tasks which require the subjects to learn or generate responses and those that do not. Suppose that the tester requires the subject to recognize items. The ability to recognize can be tested by asking the subject to compare two items, either when both are present or when one of them is in memory.

1. Haxby *et al.* (in press) required subjects to recognize a series of faces by comparing each with two others that were presented at the same time. The subjects did this in the PET scanner. The experiment was mentioned in Chapter 7.

   Before the scan the subjects were told how to indicate which face matched the sample face. The subjects did this by pressing a button with either the right or left thumb. During the scan itself the subjects made decisions and responded, but they did not have to *learn* new responses during the scan. Prefrontal cortex was not activated when the subjects made their perceptual judgements.

2. Milner *et al.* (1991) tested recognition memory. The subjects were presented with a series of items on cards, either pictorial or verbal. At intervals they were presented with two cards together. One of the cards had been seen before and the other had not. Patients with prefrontal lobectomies were able to recognize the ones they had seen as well as the control subjects could.

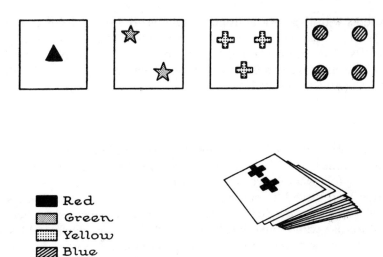

Red
Green
Yellow
Blue

Fig. 10.1 Cards for the Wisconsin Card Sorting task. For details see text. From Milner (1963).

Conditional learning

Compare the tasks above with a series of tasks which require the subjects to learn or generate responses. One such task is conditional or associative learning. Petrides (1985*a*) has devised several versions, differing in the cues used and the responses required. In one the subject chooses between six identical cards laid out in a spatial array; the object is to learn an association between each card and one of six coloured cues. In another version the subject chooses between different patterns. Patients with prefrontal lesions are very slow to learn these tasks (Petrides 1985*a*, 1990; Canavan *et al.* 1989*b*). χ

The tasks are formally similar to the conditional learning tasks used with monkeys. The subjects must learn what responses to make. Area 8 is activated in the PET scanner when subjects choose patterns in the basis of colour cues (Petrides *et al.* 1993*a*).

Wisconsin Card Sorting task

This task requires subjects to learn the correct way to sort cards. On each trial the subject must generate an attempt, sorting the cards according to the shape, colour, or number of the symbols on it (Fig. 10.1). The subject learns by trial and error on the basis of feedback provided by the tester.

On this task the subject does not learn a specific response, but rather a rule that governs their responses. Once they have learned to sort by one rule (such as sorting by shape), the rule is changed and the subject must sort by another rule (such as sorting by colour). When the subject has learned that rule, the rule is again changed, and so on until the subject has sorted all the cards.

Patients with large dorsal frontal excisions are slow to learn a different rule (such as sorting by number) (Milner 1963). This is true even if the subject is given prior warning that the rule is about to change (Nelson 1976). The effect is less reliable with patients with smaller lesions (Grafman *et al.* 1990; Anderson *et al.* 1991).

Subject-ordered task

On the subject-ordered task there are no specified responses which the subject must learn. Instead the subjects generate their own responses. They must follow a rule which states that a particular picture is correct if it has not been picked before, but incorrect if already picked. The task is formally similar to the self-generated sequence task devised by Petrides (1988) for use with monkeys (Chapter 6). Patients with prefrontal lesions also make many errors on the subject-ordered task (Petrides and Milner 1982).

The subject-ordered task is similar to the search task (Chapter 6) in that both require the subject to choose between items, with the restriction that they must not respond more than once to any particular item. Patients with prefrontal excisions make more errors than control subjects when they must search for a target by opening boxes on the screen (Owen *et al.* 1990).

Recency and frequency judgements

However, patients with prefrontal lesions also make errors on tasks devised to test the judgement of recency (Milner *et al.* 1991) or frequency (Smith and Milner 1988). One's first thought is to argue that on such tasks the subject does not have to learn or generate new responses.

The subject is shown a series of pictures or words on cards, and is presented at intervals with two of the items on one card. On the 'recency task' the subject must decide which of these was shown more recently (Milner *et al.* 1991). On the 'frequency task' the subject must decide which of these items has been presented more frequently (Smith and Milner 1988).

Why should patients with prefrontal lesions be impaired on these memory tasks when their recognition memory is unimpaired? To judge recency or frequency, more is required than the comparison of one item with another in memory. The tasks are associative tasks in the sense that when shown one item the subjects must recall the context in which they were presented. In one case the item is associated with a temporal tag, and in the other with the context of other presentations. In neither case can the response be determined by recognition of the items alone. The subjects must follow a response rule.

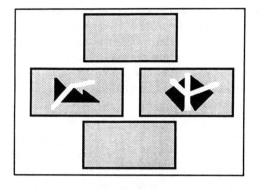

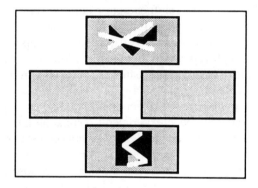

Fig. 10.2 Examples of stimuli used for intradimensional and extradimensional shift problems. From Owen *et al.* (1991).

Attention

Patients with frontal lobe pathology are also poor on tasks requiring selective attention. Attention can be regarded as covert orientation; subjects can attend to a stimulus in the periphery without actually moving their eyes to it.

The impairment of patients with frontal pathology occurs when they are required to shift attention and thus change between responses. Owen *et al.* (1991) gave subjects a series of discrimination problems in which the subject had to learn which of two stimuli was designated correct. The stimuli consisted of white patterns on irregular purple shapes (Fig. 10.2). One dimension was pattern and the other shape.

Two shifts are possible, and these have been termed intradimensional (ID) and extradimensional (ED) shifts. Example problems are presented in Fig. 10.2. For an ID shift, a new problem is given which is solved by making a discrimination on the same dimension: if one of the two white patterns is correct on the first problem, one of two new white patterns is correct on the second problem. For an ED shift, the new problem is solved by making a discrimination on the other dimension: if one of the two white patterns is correct on the first problem, one of two new irregular purple shapes is correct on the second problem. For the ID shift the subject continues to attend to the same dimension, but for the ED shift the subject must shift attention to the other dimension.

Owen *et al.* (1991) tested patients with frontal lobe and temporal lobe excisions on these ID and ED shifts. Many of the patients with frontal lesions were slow to shift attention from one dimension to the other (ED shift) although they were unimpaired at learning new problems on the same dimension (ID shift). As on the Wisconsin Card Sorting Task the subject must attend now to one attribute and now to another.

Patients with Parkinson's disease are also slow to make ED shifts (Downes *et al.* 1989) and to shift categories on the Wisconsin Card Sorting task (Brown and Marsden 1988*a*; Canavan *et al.* 1989). Brown and Marsden (1988*b*) also gave these patients a version of the Stroop test on which they were required to shift repeatedly between reading the word and reporting the colour of the lettering. The patients were impaired at shifting, and particularly so on the first trial after a shift.

The ability to perform such attentional shifts is not a uniquely human characteristic. There have been experiments comparing ID and ED shifts with rats (Slamecka 1968). However, this design has not yet been used with monkeys with prefrontal lesions. A related, but inferior, design requires 'non-reversal shifts'. To give an example, we taught monkeys to choose the larger of two blocks, then required them to choose the block that was blue, and then whichever block was on the left (Passingham 1972*a*). Two pairs of objects were used; in one pair the large block was blue and the small one red, and in the other pair the small block was blue and the large one red. The same stimuli were used throughout, with one set appearing on some trials and the other set on the other.

After removal of the ventral and orbital prefrontal cortex monkeys were retarded in making such shifts (Passingham 1972*a*). This could point to a problem in shifting attention. However, as pointed out by Slamecka (1968), this design has the fault that if the animal distinguishes between the two sets of stimuli, it can reverse simply by continuing to make the same choice with one pair and changing its choice with the other pair. This would not demand a shift in central attention. Thus the experiment with monkeys must be dubbed inconclusive.

Thinking

In all the tasks discussed so far, the subjects choose between items in the outside world. But people can also make choices in their head; they can make a *mental* response.

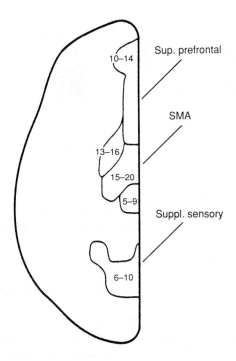

Fig. 10.3 Percentage increase in regional blood flow measured in dorsal cortex using the ^{133}Xenon technique and two-dimensional imaging. The values are those obtained when subjects think of performing a sequence of finger movements but do not actually perform them. Sup. prefrontal = superior prefrontal, SMA = medial premotor cortex, Suppl. sensory = supplementary sensory area in medial parietal cortex. Figure from Roland (1985).

Selection of limb movements

Consider first the selection of limb movements. In pioneering studies Roland and colleagues asked subjects to mentally rehearse a sequence of finger movements (Orgogozo and Larsen 1979; Roland *et al.* 1980). Cerebral blood flow was measured using ^{133}Xenon as a label and two dimensional charting of the activity. Figure 10.3 shows that there was a marked increase in the activity of the medial premotor cortex; but there was no corresponding change in the activity of the motor area itself. There was also activation of the superior prefrontal cortex.

Selection of items

Spatial locations

Roland and Friberg (1985) followed up the success of the earlier studies by asking subjects to perform other mental operations. One task was to

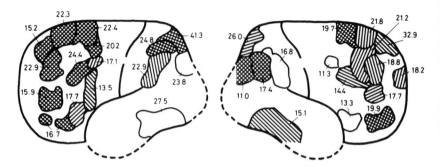

Fig. 10.4 Percentage increase in regional blood flow measured by use of the
[133]Xenon technique and two-dimensional imaging. The values are obtained when
subjects think through a route in their heads. Figure from Roland and Friberg
(1985).

imagine oneself walking along a familiar route, taking first a left turn, then a
right, and so on taking alternate turns along the path. The task is equivalent
to the delayed alternation task, except that there are landmarks along the
way.

The data for six subjects are presented in Fig. 10.4. Unfortunately the
technology available at the time of this experiment did not allow a map of
blood flow to be presented on a standard brain diagram in stereotactic
space. This means that it is only possible to make tentative identifications of
the areas in which there is significant activation. However, it is clear that
there is a significant increase in the dorsal prefrontal cortex, and this
probably includes area 46.

Words and numbers
Roland and Friberg (1985) also gave two other tasks. One was mental
arithmetic, to count backwards in threes, starting from the number 50. The
other was to mentally rehearse a well known nursery rhyme, and to identify
alternate words. Both mental operations require the subject to find the
correct answer, but the subject selects between items in the head, not
between words or numbers that are externally presented.

Again, there was a significant increase in blood flow in specific regions of
the prefrontal cortex. The data for words are illustrated in Fig. 10.5, and the
data for numbers in Fig. 10.6. The areas of significant change included the
more dorsal aspect of the prefrontal cortex.

All three tasks have in common that they are performed without any
input from the external world. Though the task is assigned, the subject
generates the material—whether locations, words, or numbers—and then
performs the operations without further prompting.

It was argued in Chapter 6 that in monkeys the dorsal prefrontal cortex
plays a critical role in selecting responses when there are no external cues
to prompt. This point has also been made by Goldman-Rakic (1987).

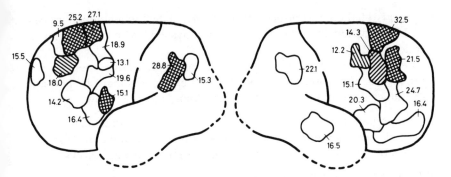

Fig. 10.5 Percentage increase in regional blood flow measured by use of the
133Xenon technique and two-dimensional imaging. The values are obtained when
subjects think through a jingle. Figure from Roland and Friberg (1985).

The difference in the human case is that the responses can be mental.
The same system is used, but it is hijacked for new purposes. A system that
selects objects or locations becomes a system that selects the correct
answer. This can be formulated in two ways. It could be specified in mental
imagery, as with the layout of a route, or it could be formulated in words.
Both images and words can refer to objects and events, even when those
objects or events are not present.

Planning

The mental tasks described above all have a conditional logic. For example,
consider the route: if the last turn was left the next one is right, but if the last
turn was right the next one is left. Similarly for the mental arithmetic, if the
current number is 47, then the correct response is 44; whereas if the current

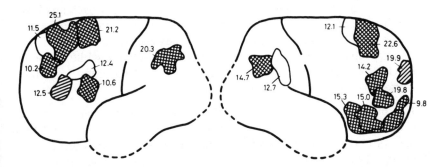

Fig. 10.6 Percentage increase in regional blood flow measured by use of the
133Xenon technique and two-dimensional imaging. The values are obtained when
subjects do mental subtraction of numbers. Figure from Roland and Friberg (1985).

number is 44, then the correct response is 41. Many higher mental processes can be modelled in terms of production systems with conditional logic (Anderson 1983).

We use the word 'plan' when the aim of the cognitive operations is to specify the appropriate actions. It will help to distinguish 'preparing', 'planning,' and following a 'strategy'. The logic is set out below.

1. We prepare to act when the context specifies the correct action but the time is not yet appropriate for performing it. Thus the correct response must be held in working memory. This can be set out as follows:

If P, retrieve (X); when T, perform X
Where:
P = context
(X) = response in working memory
T = trigger stimulus.

2. A plan differs in that both the context and response are imagined or hypothetical. This can be designated by using square brackets. To put it in words, if situation A occurs it would be appropriate to do X.

If $[A]$, retrieve $[X]$
Where:
$[A]$ = imagined or hypothetical situation
$[X]$ = imagined or hypothetical action, held in working memory

3. A strategy involves not a single response but a series. There are two possible situations:

a) If $[A]$, retrieve $[X]$, if $[B]$, retrieve $[Y]$, ...
b) If $[A]$, retrieve $[X]$, $[Y]$, ...

Preparing

Animals can prepare for action. There are many occasions when they know what to do before they have a chance to do it. As they approach an object, the sight of it tells them how to react. Information from the distance receptors gives advance warning of the necessary action.

There are many cells in the frontal cortex that discharge while a monkey waits (Evarts *et al.* 1974). Such 'set cells' or 'set-related cells' have been described in earlier chapters. There are two situations.

1. The monkey is given an external cue that tells it what to do, but is waiting for a trigger stimulus. Set activity has been described in lateral premotor cortex (Wise 1985*a*,*b*), the medial premotor cortex (Tanji *et al.* 1980), prefrontal area 46 (Funahashi *et al.* 1989), the caudate (Hikosaka *et al.* 1989), the putamen (Alexander and Crutcher 1990*b*), and the substantia nigra, pars reticulata (Hikosaka and Wurtz 1985).

2. The monkey prepares to perform an action it has previously learned. Activity in the seconds before movement has been described in the lateral and medial premotor cortex (Romo and Schultz 1987).

Compare this with the increase in blood flow to the medial premotor cortex reported when human subjects mentally rehearse an action (Roland *et al.* 1980). The way in which the activity codes for the action may be the same in monkey and man, but there is a crucial difference in the task. The monkeys are preparing a response that is instructed by cues and that will issue in action; but people can set up the same activity at any time they wish, and can then countermand the action.

We admit that we do not know for certain that animals are unable to do this. It is a challenge to design an experiment that would settle the issue.

Planning and following a strategy

There are two ways of investigating planning. The first is to study the way in which the activities of ordinary life are organized. The second is to devise laboratory tasks which test the ability to formulate a plan.

Real life errands

Shallice and Burgess (1991) set a series of errands for three patients with frontal lobe damage. The patients carried a card with eight tasks written on it. Six were simple, for example to buy a brown loaf; a seventh was to be at a certain place fifteen minutes after starting; and the eighth was to find out and write down four items of information, such as the price of a pound of tomatoes. The card also set out some rules: for example, no shop should be entered other than to buy something. Checks were made that these rules were both understood and remembered.

Thus the patients had to devise a strategy for achieving the various goals, and follow it as they went on their errands. Compared with control subjects the patients tended to break the rules, for example by entering a shop and not buying anything there. Milner (1964) had previously reported that patients with frontal damage broke the rules on a maze task in the laboratory, and this has been confirmed by Canavan (1983). In Milner's task the aim is to learn a route through a maze made up of an array of metal knobs; the subject taps a knob with a stylus and is then informed by clicks whether or not it is on the path. There are simple rules, that the subject must not move diagonally or retrace the correct path, and that when an error is recorded the subject must go back to the previous location. Patients with frontal excisions often disobey these rules, even though when asked, they can say what they were supposed to do (Milner 1964; Canavan 1983).

These errors are reminiscent of the 'slips of action' (Reason 1979) or 'cognitive failures' (Broadbent *et al.* 1982) that are reported by normal subjects in everyday life. It is characteristic that the person knows the

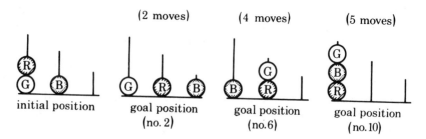

Fig. 10.7   Apparatus for the Tower of London task. The figure illustrates the initial position, and the goal positions for two-move, three-move, and five-move problems. From Shallice (1982).

appropriate action, in the sense that he or she could give an accurate account of it if asked; yet, when it comes to the actual situation the person acts without thinking. Reason (1979) calls one such error 'side-tracking'. He gives an example: the person meant to go from the kitchen to the larder to get some vegetables, but veered off into the living room and talked to her husband instead. She should have suppressed the temptation to enter the living room, as it was inconsistent with her plan. In the same way the patient should have resisted the temptation to leave a shop, given that nothing had been bought there.

Shallice and Burgess (1991) envisage the keeping of rules in terms of a supervisory process. Markers are set up in memory to govern future behaviour. These ensure that routine responses are inhibited if they are inconsistent with the plan.

Laboratory tasks
In the laboratory, subjects can be required to plan how they will make a series of moves. A suitable task is the Tower of Hanoi, on which subjects must move five discs of different sizes from one peg to another, making use of a third peg, so as to keep the discs in the same order. Several versions of this task have been developed for use with patients: the 'Tower of London' uses three pegs, and three coloured balls (Shallice 1982) (Fig. 10.7); a computerized version of this task uses three coloured balls on a screen (Morris *et al.* 1988); and the 'Tower of Toronto' uses three or four discs of different colours (Saint-Cyr *et al.* 1988).

It is possible to solve these tasks in one's head. Consider the five-move version of the Tower of London shown in Fig. 10.7. Number the pegs 1, 2, and 3 from left to right. The moves are red (R) to 2, G3, R1, B1, G1. These can be imagined without touching the balls. To solve the problem it is necessary to think ahead and consider the consequences of the different moves.

Shallice and McCarthy gave patients problems that could be solved in between two and five moves (Shallice 1982). The patients were divided into those with anterior lesions and those with posterior lesions; the method of division meant that some of the patients with anterior lesions had fronto-temporal or fronto-parietal lesions (Shallice 1988). The patients in the left anterior group were less successful at solving the problems within 60 seconds at the first attempt.

The mechanism for making hypothetical moves evolved from a mechanism for making real moves. Monkeys do not place things in order, but they can order their responses. Thus, they can be taught to order their choice of boxes on the basis of colour; and the order is disrupted by removal of dorsal prefrontal cortex (Petrides 1988).

Patients with frontal lobe lesions
That the human prefrontal cortex plays a role in making decisions about actions and planning is now a common view. It was promulgated by Luria (1966), and has been promoted more recently by Shallice (1982), Baddeley (1986), Duncan (1986), and Damasio *et al.* (1991). Baddeley (1986) has coined the term the 'dysexecutive syndrome' to refer to the disorganization of behaviour that can follow damage to the frontal lobes.

However, the evidence cited has not always been adequate to support the conclusions. Luria's (1966) patients tended to have very large tumours, and these would often have interfered with premotor as well as prefrontal areas. For example, in the much quoted paper by Luria *et al.* (1964), the patient had a left frontal meningioma which extended back to the lateral and medial premotor cortex and the motor cortex; and in the related paper by Konow and Pribram (1970) it was not possible to excise all of the tumour because it extended beyond the range of the craniotomy.

That the effects of large tumours may be misleading was argued by Canavan *et al.* (1985). They studied a patient who displayed the disinhibited and impulsive behaviour that Luria *et al.* (1964) characterized as the 'frontal-lobe syndrome'. To quote from the paper by Canavan *et al.* (1985, p.1050): 'when asked to copy a continuous but castellated line she would produce several lines of completed squares. This motor perseveration occurred relatively independently of verbal control. If asked to stop during the course of tapping or drawing, she would say "yes" but continue regardless. If she herself said "I will stop now" the behaviour also continued unchecked'.

The patient had a very large meningioma at the midline, in the posterior part of the frontal lobe. This was removed by the surgeon in its entirety. The description of the patient's behaviour came from observations made 13 days after the operation. At this time she was still confused, but by the eighteenth day the syndrome as described by Luria had completely disappeared. Presumably the symptoms resulted from widespread and bilateral oedema affecting prefrontal, cingulate, supplementary motor, and premotor cortex.

That pathology in the frontal lobe can lead to disorganized action is not in doubt. However, it is necessary to distinguish between the effects of damage to the premotor strip or to the prefrontal cortex that lies in front of it. It is dangerous to base theories of prefrontal cortex on data from patients with widespread disruption of the frontal lobes.

Comparing plans

When solving a problem such as the Tower of Hanoi the subject selects between hypothetical actions in the head. This can be written as:

If [A], then [X] gets [G]
If [A], then [Y] fails to get [G]
Where:
[A] = imagined or hypothetical context
[X] and [Y] are imagined or hypothetical responses
[G] = imagined goal

An example can be given for the fourth move of the five-move version of the Tower of London (Fig. 10.7). 1) If red is on 1, blue is on 2, and green is on 3, placing blue on 1 means that the goal can be achieved. 2) If red is on 1, blue is on 2, and green is on 3, placing green on 1 means that the goal will not be achieved.

A person can compare moves without actually seeing the layout of the three balls, or actually moving them. In other words, a person can engage in mental trial and error. Owen *et al.* (1990) measured the time it took patients with frontal lobe lesions to decide on their next move on the Tower of London. The results were that after the first move the patients spent longer thinking about the next move.

A dramatic case study of slowness in making decisions is provided by Eslinger and Damasio (1985). The patient, EVR, had a very large meningioma affecting both hemispheres. This was removed at operation. CT scans then showed that orbital (areas 11) and medial cortex (including areas 32 and 24) had been removed from both hemispheres (Fig. 10.8). There was some damage to the dorsal prefrontal cortex (areas 9 and 46), but only on one side. The damage included only the most anterior part of area 6 on the right, but there was an interruption of the white matter under the premotor areas on the left.

In his everyday life EVR faced very severe problems. To quote from the report by Eslinger and Damasio (1985, p.1732): 'Deciding where to dine might take hours, as he discussed each restaurant's seating plan, particulars of menu, atmosphere, and management. He would drive to each restaurant to see how busy it was, but even then he could not finally decide which to choose. Purchasing small items required in-depth consideration of brands, prices, and the best method of purchase'.

Thus, EVR had difficulty in making comparisons between possible actions, and in deciding on the course of action that would be best. Eslinger and Damasio (1985) also comment that when there was no external

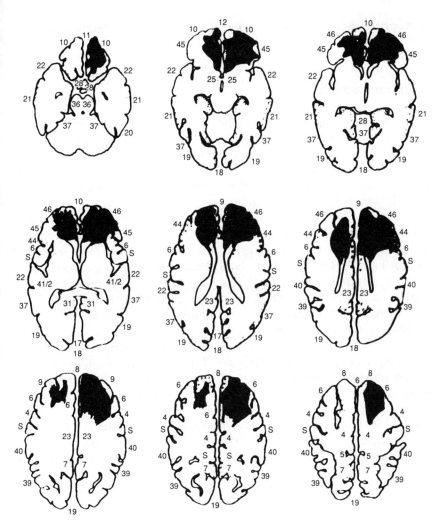

Fig. 10.8 Transverse sections through the lesion in the brain of the patient EVR. The most ventral section is at the top left, and the most dorsal section at the bottom right. From Eslinger and Damasio (1985).

guidance he often conceived inappropriate plans of action. As they put it, 'it was as if he "forgot to remember short- and intermediate-term goals' (Eslinger and Damasio 1985, p. 1738). Saver and Damasio (1991) have demonstrated that EVR has the relevant social knowledge in long-term memory. It is when he is required to act that he has problems.

To make sensible plans one must be able to conceive appropriate plans, make comparisons between them, and evaluate which one will best achieve the current goal. The mechanism that allows animals to learn the appropriate choice by trial and error has been upgraded. People can try out a course of action in the head.

Voluntary action

The consequences of this development are far-reaching. In Chapter 1 a distinction was made between various uses of the word 'voluntary' (Fig. 1.1). The most restrictive usage was to apply the word when different courses of action could be compared and a free choice made (Fig. 1.1, level D). In this sense people are capable of voluntary action, but it is reasonable to doubt whether this is true of animals.

All animals have the capacity to adapt to new or changed circumstances. But the dominance of the human race on earth is owed, more than anything, to our capacity to engage in mental trial and error. Instead of trying out particular actions we can evaluate them beforehand, safely and at a distance.

The point can be put in a different way. Animals are sometimes said to engage in 'strategies'. Maynard Smith (1982) has coined the term 'evolutionarily stable strategy' (ESS). To quote Maynard Smith (1982, p.10): 'an ESS is a strategy such that, if all the members of the population adopt it, then no mutant strategy can invade it under the influence of natural selection'. Examples of strategies are 'hawk' (to fight to injure and kill opponents) and 'dove' (to display and never engage in serious fights). The word 'strategy' is used here without any implication that the animals formulate a strategy or compare different strategies.

For a bird the word 'strategy' is a metaphor, but for a person it is not. But what of a chimpanzee? De Waal (1982) discusses the 'strategic intelligence' of chimpanzees in a captive colony as they compete for dominance. He makes a convincing case that a chimpanzee can pursue a long-term goal, and can form the alliances that will make it possible to achieve that goal. But what is in question is whether the animal can plot its moves away from the relevant situation.

The capacity for mental trial and error brings with it a further consequence. Not only can the strategies be evaluated, but also the goals themselves (Dawkins 1989). Some people choose a life of celibacy in a nunnery; some are prepared to risk their lives for others by putting out in a lifeboat. Human beings can set themselves goals other than simply promoting their genes in the next generation.

Summary

As in monkeys, the prefrontal cortex is also critically involved in the process by which the human brain generates and selects actions. Human beings can select between ideas, and the prefrontal cortex has been elaborated to allow the selection of mental responses.

Human beings can also plan future actions and select between them by mental trial and error. The consequences of this development are far reaching, because it means that human beings can set themselves goals other than simply promoting their genes in the next generation. Human beings are capable of 'voluntary' action in the most restrictive sense.

11 Speech

Speech is the most impressive example of human voluntary action. We spend much of our time freely generating words, and we talk for long periods without repeating a sentence. And nobody tells us what to say or when to say it.

None the less, speech is an activity that is acquired by learning. If the word 'response' is used loosely to include any motor output, then speech is a response. Of course, it sounds demeaning to say so; Skinner (1957) was mocked for using the phrase 'verbal behavior', and for suggesting that speech was only another example of operant learning. By this Skinner did not mean that each utterance was determined by external stimuli. He implied only that utterances were generated in the context of stimuli.

This chapter pursues this simple notion. If the frontal lobe is a mechanism for selecting responses, one can ask what modifications were needed for it to be able to select verbal ones. Evolution works by modifying existing systems so that they can serve new purposes. The speech system was developed by hijacking the mechanisms for directing non-verbal responses.

Naming

Logic

To continue this naïve train of thought, the learning of names obeys conditional logic:

If A, respond {A}
 If B, respond {B}
Where:
A and B are objects or events
{A} and {B} are the names of those objects or events
 The response is a spoken or written word

To put this more simply, the name you give depends on the item presented. When you are learning to speak, you must produce the word 'book' and not 'bread' when shown a picture of a book. The item can be present at the time, as in naming pictures, or stored in memory, as in describing things you have seen.

There is a traditional objection to describing naming in this way. It is said that one must distinguish between mere associative learning and genuine naming. A name is not simply a word that goes with an item; it refers to it.

This distinction can be illustrated by taking an experiment carried out on chimpanzees by Farrer (1967). He presented a list of 24 sequences, each consisting of four designs. For each sequence the chimpanzees had to make an arbitrary response, pressing one of four levers. The chimpanzees could learn the correct answer in each case by rote; or to put it another way they could learn the response associated with each array of cues. But nobody would claim that the animals were naming. The responses on the levers did not refer to the cues; they did not carry meaning.

There have, of course, been attempts to teach chimpanzees to name. For example, Gardner and Gardner (1985) educated four chimpanzees in a gestural language, American Sign Language. The ability to name was tested by showing pictures on a screen, and requiring the animal to produce the appropriate gesture. Three of the four chimpanzees produced the correct name on roughly 80 per cent of trials.

However, critics might object that the fact that the animal produces the correct gesture does not prove that the animal realizes that the gesture refers to the item in the picture. The animal might simply be producing an associate, without realizing that it carries meaning.

In reply to this objection an experiment was carried out with two chimpanzees that had been taught to name items by typing on keys (Savage-Rumbaugh *et al.* 1980; Savage-Rumbaugh 1986). On each key a different symbol was displayed, and each symbol was arbitrarily designated as referring to a particular item. The task was to categorize items into foods or tools. The chimpanzees were able to do this even when they were shown the symbols for the items rather than the items themselves. In other words, when shown the symbol for banana or sponge, the animals could decide whether the symbol referred to a food or a tool. The symbol served to retrieve a mental representation of the item.

Associative mechanisms

If this achievement is accepted, the biologist has a problem. How could evolution generate the ability to name if that ability is not used by the animals in the wild? Problems of this sort have been elegantly discussed by Humphrey (1976). In this case there is a simple, if heretical, solution.

A distinction should be drawn between the *mechanism* for naming and the *social use* to which naming is put. The heretical proposal is that the mechanism for naming is a simple associative mechanism, but that we only call an associate a 'name' when it is used to communicate ideas.

Consider first the mechanism for associative learning. Gaffan and Bolton (1983) did an elegant experiment. Two monkeys were given the opportunity to learn that under one object (A) there was a white penny, and under another object (B) a black penny. The same procedure was repeated with other pairs of objects, C and D, and so on. The pennies were not visible when covered. Single trials were then given on which the animal was cued to search for one or the other penny. The animals could choose the object that was associated with it on roughly 75 per cent of these trials. Thus, the sight of the object served to retrieve a mental representation of the specific penny.

Of course, in this experiment the objects were only associates of the pennies. To use the traditional terms, they were 'signs', not 'symbols'. But now suppose that we invent a language in which we arbitrarily assign A as the name for white penny. Why suppose that there is any difference in the mental procedure by which the symbol retrieves the representation of the referent?

The suggestion is that the distinction between a sign and a symbol does not lie in the mechanism, but in the purpose for which it is used. If I want to retrieve a mental representation of white penny in *your* mind I can show you the words 'white penny'. In the language invented above I could show you object A. In other words, we call an item a symbol when we use it for purposes of communication.

To summarize the argument: chimpanzees can learn a symbolic language because they already have the necessary associative mechanisms (Passingham 1982). These same mechanisms are of value to them in acquiring other knowledge in their natural habitat. Like all animals they must learn to make predictions about future events: the roar of the lion serves to retrieve a mental representation of the lion before the lion arrives.

Whether you are persuaded that apes can name depends on whether you are persuaded that they use gestures or symbols to communicate. Of the experiments that have been performed, those of Savage-Rumbaugh (1986) are the most persuasive. Chimpanzee Austin will type on the keyboard to inform chimpanzee Sherman what tool is needed to unlock the cupboard holding their food. Sherman must hand Austin the appropriate tool. The roles can, of course, be reversed. If the chimpanzees fail to communicate, they will fail to win their share.

Retrieval by object or word

Naming and repeating

There are two situations in which the external context serves as a cue for the retrieval of a word. One is naming, and the other is repeating words, whether seen or heard.

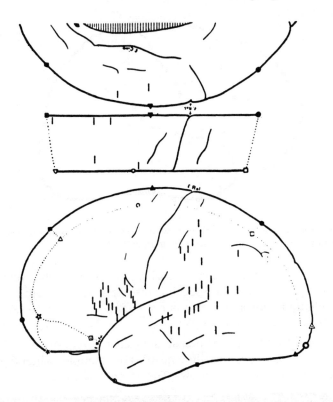

Fig. 11.1 Sites in the human brain at which electrical stimulation produced an inability to name with retained ability to speak. From Penfield and Roberts (1959).

The ability to name or repeat is disturbed by lesions of the superior temporal association cortex or ventrolateral premotor cortex of the left hemisphere (Benson and Geschwind 1985). These areas have, of course, become associated with the names of Wernicke and Broca; but it is more helpful here to identify them by their anatomical location.

Strokes are rarely confined to a cytoarchitectonic area. One might hope to localize the crucial areas more accurately by experiment. There are two methods, electrical stimulation and PET scanning.

1. Penfield and Roberts (1959) stimulated at many sites in the frontal lobe while patients were required to produce concrete names. Figure 11.1 shows the sites at which naming was disturbed even though the patients could still speak. Ojemann (1983) later repeated this procedure, and Fig. 11.2 is adapted from his map to show the sites at which there was interference with naming or reading.

It is unfortunate that neither of these maps is presented in stereotaxic coordinates. This means that the exact location of the sites is not easy to establish. Some of the sites are clearly within ventrolateral premotor

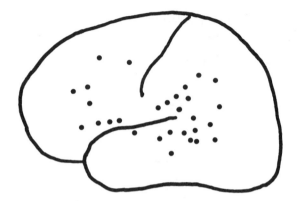

Fig. 11.2 Sites in the human brain at which electrical stimulation disrupted the ability to name or read. Redrawn from Ojemann (1983).

cortex, area 44; but others probably extend into the ventrolateral prefrontal cortex, area 45. Speech is disrupted more severely and more permanently by an infarct that is not confined to area 44 (Mohr *et al.* 1978; Damasio and Damasio 1989).

2. Wise *et al.* (1991) required human subjects to think of verbs that were appropriate for nouns that they heard. For example, when they heard 'flower' they might think 'grow'. They were not to say the words out

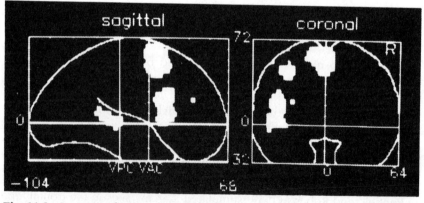

Fig. 11.3 Location of areas of significant increase in regional cerebral blood flow when subjects generate words for actions that are associated with nouns that were presented. The illustrations are drawn as if the brain was transparent; that is, the sagittal view shows all the activity in both hemispheres, and the coronal view shows all the activity from the front to the back of the brain. A comparison of the coronal and sagittal views shows that there is activation in ventral premotor cortex (Broca's area) on the left, superior temporal cortex (Wernicke's area) on the left, the supplementary speech area on the left, and prefrontal cortex on the left. From Wise *et al.* (1991).

(a)

(b)

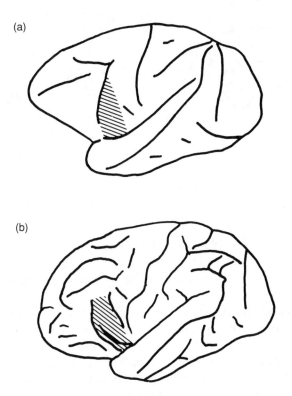

Fig. 11.4   Cytoarchitectonic area FCBm in (a) the macaque monkey brain and (b) the chimpanzee brain. Redrawn from von Bonin and Bailey (1947) and Bailey et al. (1950).

loud, but simply to note them in their head. As will be seen from Fig. 11.3 there was activation of area 44 in the left hemisphere. There was no such activation in the right hemisphere.

Ventral premotor cortex in non-human primates

Cytoarchitecture
It can be countered that it is implausible that speech uses the same mechanisms as those available to animals. It has usually been assumed that Broca's area is unique to the human brain. This view has been challenged by two independent groups of workers.

1. Von Bonin and Bailey examined the premotor cortex in the human brain and also in the brains of the macaque monkey and chimpanzee (von Bonin and Bailey 1947; Bailey *et al.* 1950). They adopted the lettering system devised by von Economo (1929). In this system Broca's area is designated FCBm. In their earlier publications von Bonin and Bailey claimed to identify a region that was similar in architecture both in monkey

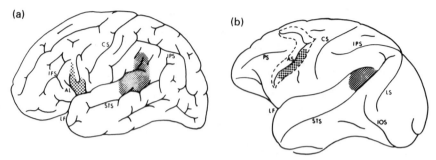

Fig. 11.5   Area 44 in ventral premotor cortex in (a) human brain and (b) macaque monkey brain. The figure also shows area Tpt in posterior temporo-parietal cortex. From Galaburda and Pandya (1982).

(von Bonin and Bailey 1947) and chimpanzee (Bailey *et al.* 1950). These areas are illustrated in Fig. 11.4. However, in their later review von Bonin and Bailey (1961) were less confident that they could distinguish a special subregion of area FC.

2. More recently Galaburda and Pandya (1982) re-examined the brain of the rhesus monkey. They pointed to a more restricted area within FCBm. They claim that the posterior bank of the ventral arcuate sulcus has similarities to area 44 in the human brain (Fig. 11.5). In particular, layer IIIc contains large pyramidal cells, and layer IV is narrow but distinct.

But similarities in architecture do not prove similarities in function. We need to examine the anatomy and physiology of this area.

Anatomical inputs

A cornerstone of the neurology of language has been the belief that there is a direct connection, the arcuate fasciculus, between Wernicke's area and Broca's area. It has been assumed that this connection can only be demonstrated in the human brain.

The standard view of the arcuate fasciculus is shown in an illustration (Fig. 11.6). The basis for this view is an account written by Meynert in 1865: he claimed that the arcuate fasciculus connects these two areas (Meynert 1865). Yet dissections of the white matter could never prove such a point, as the exact termination of the fibres can not be identified. Indeed, it is because this is true that modern tracing methods have been developed, using transport of materials along the axons.

The outputs of the superior temporal cortex have been examined in monkeys. Galaburda and Pandya (1982) briefly report that they placed a radioactive tracer in area Tpt, in the caudal part of the superior temporal cortex; and they say that they found labelling in the area they identify as 44—although no illustration is given. Petrides and Pandya (1988) also placed an anterograde tracers in Tpt. They failed to report a connection to

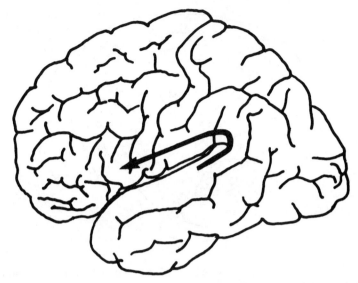

Fig. 11.6   Connections of the arcuate fasciculus as suggested by Geschwind (1972).

the posterior bank of the arcuate sulcus, but they do report a small projection to the ventral tip of the arcuate sulcus. This comes from area Ts3, in the more anterior part of the superior temporal region (Petrides and Pandya 1988, case 4).

In monkeys the superior temporal cortex sends a much more extensive projection to the ventral limb of the *anterior* bank of the arcuate sulcus (Petrides and Pandya 1988). This region was classified as area 8 by Brodmann (1925), and as area 45 by Walker (1940) (Fig. 5.4, p.106). Mesulam (1990) also states that there is a projection from the region surrounding the back of the Sylvian fissure to the region below the arcuate sulcus, including area 45 (Fig. 11.7). In parallel the infero-temporal cortex projects to this region (Barbas 1988).

One possibility must be that at least some of the fibres in the arcuate fasciculus terminate in area 45, and not in area 44 as has usually been supposed. This would be in keeping with the situation in monkeys in which the ventral premotor cortex appears to receive no significant input from the temporal lobe (Chapter 3). It is premature to conclude that the pattern of connections from temporal to ventral frontal cortex differs between the human and monkey brain.

The literature has emphasized connections from superior temporal cortex to frontal cortex. But we know that in monkeys there is a heavy connection from parietal area 7b to the ventral premotor cortex (Petrides and Pandya 1984; Godschalk *et al.* 1984; Cavada and Goldman-Rakic 1989). In the human brain area 40 is probably equivalent to area 7b in the brain of a

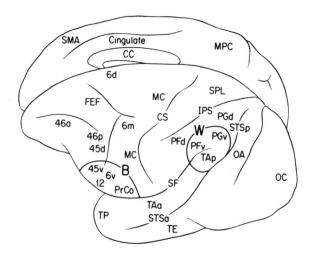

Fig. 11.7 Mesulam's proposal for the location of Wernicke's area (W) and Broca's area (B) in the macaque brain. From Mesulam (1990).

macaque monkey Eidelberg and Pandya, 1984). When human subjects mentally rehearse lists of letters in the PET scanner, there is activation of the ventral part of the left area 40 and of the ventral premotor cortex (Broca's area) (Paulesu *et al.* 1993). The fibres connecting these two areas presumably run in the arcuate fasciculus.

It must also be said that we still have no direct proof that damage to the arcuate fasciculus impairs the production of speech. It is true that conduction aphasics are poor at repeating words they hear, and it is widely believed that the lesion is one that interrupts the arcuate fasciculus. But a lesion in the white matter at the temporo-parietal junction may well also interrupt fibres passing subcortically to the basal ganglia.

Chapter 8 stressed the fact that temporal cortex projects directly to the basal ganglia, and the basal ganglia influence premotor cortex via the ventral thalamus. Non-haemorrhagic infarction of the basal ganglia can cause problems in naming and repetition as well as in reading (Damasio *et al.* 1982, 1984). Electrical stimulation of this part of the thalamus can also disrupt naming (Ojemann 1983).

The truth is that we know little about the way in which visual or auditory material influences speech. This is not surprising. After all the discussion in Chapters 3 and 8, we still lack an account that is universally agreed of how sights and sounds influence actions in monkeys. We cannot rule out the possibility that in the human brain there is a special pathway from superior temporal cortex to Broca's area, and that it is involved in the repetition of words that are heard. But there is, as yet, no proof that this is so.

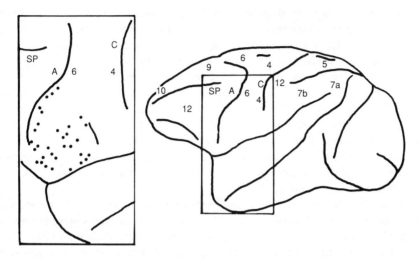

Fig. 11.8   Sites in the brain of the macaque monkey at which electrical stimulation evokes movements of the intrinsic muscles of the larynx. SP = sulcus principalis, A = arcuate sulcus, C = central sulcus. The figure on the right shows the location for the inset shown on the left. Redrawn from Hast *et al.* (1974).

Physiology
We turn from anatomy to physiology. Does the area identified on anatomical grounds as area 44 in monkeys play a role in vocalization? There is a map of the body surface in premotor cortex (Chapters 3 and 9). As is the case for motor cortex, microstimulation of the more ventral regions tend to evoke movements of the face, mouth, and lips (Gentilucci *et al.* 1988). Recordings of the activity of single cells shows much the same distribution (Gentilucci *et al.* 1988).

Using macroelectrodes, Hast *et al.* (1974) were able to evoke movements of the intrinsic laryngeal muscles, the cricothyroid and thyroarytenoid. They identify the critical region as the most ventral part of the convexity of the ventrolateral premotor cortex, adjacent to the Sylvian fissure (Fig. 11.8). This is posterior to the sulcal region identified as area 44 by Galaburda and Pandya (1982). In squirrel monkeys, Jurgens (1982) also identifies a larynx area, and distinguishes it from a more anterior Broca's area from which it receives a projection.

Recordings have also been taken from the cricothyroid and thyro-arytenoid muscles in patients while transcranial magnetic stimulation is applied (Pascual-Leone *et al.* 1991). Stimulation that provokes arrest of speech tends to occur more anteriorly than stimulation that causes activity in the laryngeal muscles.

Behavioural test with monkeys
There should be no need for further conjecture. There is an experiment which would decide the issue. If there is a ventral premotor area in

monkeys that is homologous with Broca's area, we have a confident prediction. By analogy with other regions of premotor cortex (Chapter 3), this area should play a role in the selection of learned vocalizations. This claim can be tested by behavioural experiments, but unfortunately the experiments conducted so far fail to serve as adequate tests.

Sutton taught monkeys to produce a call when given a signal (Sutton *et al.* 1974; Sutton 1979). They could still do this after incomplete removals of the larynx area, but this experiment does not serve as a test of the hypothesis stated above, for two reasons. First, the area removed did not include the sulcal region identified by Galaburda and Pandya (1982) as the homologue of Broca's area. Second, the behavioural test did not require the learned selection of different calls.

A suitable behavioural task has been devised. Chapter 1 described an elegant experiment by Sutton et al. (1978) in which monkeys were taught to coo when one colour was presented and to bark when shown another. This task forms the basis for the critical experiment. Removal of the supposed homologue of Broca's area should impair the ability of monkeys to coo or bark on the basis of external cues such as colours. The analogy is with the experiments described in Chapter 3, in which premotor lesions impair the ability of monkeys to pull or turn a handle on the basis of external cues (Passingham 1985c).

Since the experiment has not been done, it would not be sensible to wax lyrical about the implications. Suffice it to say that if the monkeys were impaired on the vocal task there would be two implications.

1. Broca's area is part of the premotor cortex because it is concerned with directing discriminatory movements of the body. The term 'manipulative' is strictly not applicable to facial or laryngeal movements; but it has proved convenient in previous chapters, and can be used loosely so as to cover them.
2. Broca's area plays a role in the retrieval of spoken words on the basis of visual or auditory cues. The term 'retrieval' is used loosely; it implies only that lesions affect the production of words—there is no implication as to how they do it.

Retrieval by meaning or letter

Meaning

When a subject names or repeats, the cue is an external one, whether object, picture, or spoken word. But it is also possible to generate words on the basis of the meaning of a word. Here the subject must search a mental dictionary, and generate words from that.

Fig. 11.9   Peaks of activation in left prefrontal cortex when subjects produce verbs that are associated with nouns, compared with the condition in which the subjects repeat the nouns. Drawn from plate by Raichle with permission.

Generation of words
Frith *et al.* (1991*a*) describe this as the 'intrinsic generation' of words. They asked their subjects to name as many jobs as they could in two minutes. In the PET scanner the left dorsal prefrontal cortex was significantly activated.

In this experiment the subjects generated words without any external prompt at the time. Petersen *et al.* (1988) gave subjects nouns, and asked them to generate verbs that were appropriate. For example, given the word 'cake' it would be appropriate to respond with 'eat'. Again the subject must search for the right words, but cues were presented at the time. Again the PET scanner demonstrated significant activation in the left prefrontal cortex (Fig 11.9).

Wise *et al.* (1991) also asked subjects to generate verbs that were appropriate to nouns that they heard, but in this experiment the subjects were asked to think of the appropriate verb rather than to say it aloud. Again there was activation of the dorsal prefrontal cortex.

It would be wrong to conceive of the left dorsal prefrontal cortex as a 'semantic area'. Frith *et al.* (1991*a*) gave subjects a task in which the subjects were presented with a series of phonemes; the subjects had to decide whether they formed words or not. There was no significant activation in the dorsal prefrontal cortex when the subjects made these semantic judgements.

It would also be wrong to conceive of this cortex as a 'verbal area'. Frith *et al.* (1991*b*) scanned subjects while they performed a non-verbal task in which they had to generate movements of the fingers. When touched on the fingers, the subjects had to choose whether to move either their forefinger or their second finger. On a control task they were given no choice; they simply moved the finger that was touched. When these two tasks were compared there was significant activation in the dorsal prefrontal

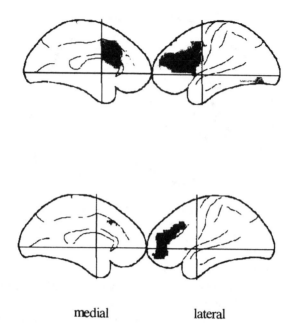

medial   lateral

Fig. 11.10   Areas in which there was a significant increase in blood flow when subjects generated verbal responses (above) or responded by moving their fingers (below). From Frith *et al.* (1991*a*).

cortex in the both hemispheres: on the left the activation was at much the same site as for the verbal task (Fig. 11.10).

Overlearned associates

If subjects are asked to generate a verb given a noun, they must actively search among the appropriate words. An alternative task is to find the opposites for words that are presented, 'woman' for 'man', 'cold' for 'hot'. These associates are overlearned. Frith *et al.* (1991*b*) found no significant activation of the left prefrontal cortex when subjects produced opposites. It can be argued that prefrontal cortex is only taxed when new associates are to be formed.

There is evidence that this may be true. Raichle (1991) reports an experiment in which subjects were asked to generate verbs given nouns, and were given repeated presentation of the same list of nouns. With practice the subjects repeat the same associate for each noun, for example 'eat' when presented with 'cake'. When the subjects had become practised there was a decrease in the activation of the left prefrontal cortex.

These results support the claim made in Chapter 9 that the prefrontal cortex is not essential for performing all associative tasks. Once a new fixed association is set up, it can be retrieved without the operation of prefrontal mechanisms.

4

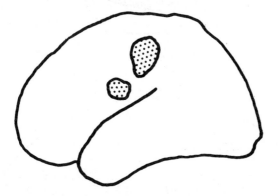

Fig. 11.11   Peaks of activation in left motor cortex and ventral premotor cortex when subjects repeated words, compared with the condition in which the subjects simply listened to the words. Drawn from plate by Raichle with permission.

Naming is an important case. It was stated earlier that the learning of names involves conditional logic, but once the appropriate association is set up, the same name is always correct given a particular object. It is not the case that sometimes one name is correct and sometimes another. Similarly, when repeating a word it is not the case that sometimes it is correct to say one thing and sometimes another. Prefrontal mechanisms are not taxed when subjects repeat words (Fig. 11.11) (Petersen *et al.* 1988), and the same may well be true for producing names once they have been learned. It would be of great interest to find out whether prefrontal mechanisms are involved when subjects learn new names or learn to read.

The process by which associations become overlearned appears to involve the cerebellum. If subjects are required to produce verbs when presented with nouns, there is activation of the lateral cerebellar cortex (Raichle 1991). The task is a simple skill at which one improves. The patient described by Fiez *et al.* (1992) had a lesion in the inferior cerebellar cortex, and he failed to master the skill, often producing words that were not verbs.

The cerebellum interacts with the premotor areas. Both Broca's area and the supplementary speech area lie within premotor cortex. On the basis of cortical stimulation, Penfield and Roberts (1959) described a 'supplementary speech area' as lying in dorsomedial frontal cortex (Fig. 11.12). This region can be visualized in the PET scanner. Wise *et al.* (1991) required subjects to think of verbs that were appropriate for nouns with which they were presented and they report activation of the dorsomedial cortex (Fig 11.3). In the human brain speech mechanisms are represented in both the lateral and medial premotor systems. Broca's area lies near the face area in the

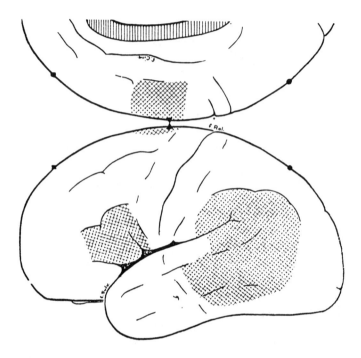

Fig. 11.12 Speech areas as charted by stimulation of the human brain. Supplementary speech area is shown on dorsomedial surface. From Penfield and Roberts (1959).

ventrolateral premotor cortex, and the supplementary speech area in front of the face area of the medial premotor area (SMA).

Letter

It is more difficult to retrieve words by their initial letter. Words are not arranged in alphabetical order in the mental lexicon as they are in a dictionary. Frith *et al.* (1991*b*) asked subjects to produce as many words beginning with 's' as they could find in three minutes. As with the semantic task, there was activation in the left dorsal prefrontal cortex (Fig. 11.10).

This is consistent with the earlier observations of Milner (1964). She found that patients with left prefrontal lobectomies tended to produce few words on a verbal fluency test in which they had to find words beginning with particular letters. Milner (1964) supposed that this impairment could not be due to damage to Broca's area, because the surgeon attempted to spare it.

Conclusion

The ability to generate words by association with their meaning or initial letter makes use of the same prefrontal mechanisms that allow animals to solve problems on the basis of associations—or to put it in a more guarded form, the generation of the correct word on the basis of semantic associations taxes dorsal prefrontal cortex, and the dorsal prefrontal cortex is specialized for the generation of responses.

Retrieval by memory or idea

The previous sections considered the retrieval of single words. But, in everyday life people produce a continuous series of words. This section consider continuous speech, and the next section the grammatical rules that govern it.

We are indebted to the pioneering work of Roland and colleagues. The experiments were performed with the [133]Xenon method, and before tomographic methods were available for the reconstruction of images. This means that the maps produced were in two dimensions. The spatial resolution of the method was also poor, and statements about localization were not as reliable as those made with the more recent PET or SPECT methods.

There is information on two conditions. In the first, the subjects say the months of the year. In the second, they describe the furniture in their living room. In both cases the information is retrieved from long-term memory. But the conditions differ in that in the first the order is fixed, whereas in the second the people mention the items in whatever order they wish.

1. When subjects recall the months of the year, there is activation of the dorsomedial premotor cortex (Roland 1985). This activation is presumably in the dorsomedial or supplementary speech area.

2. When subjects describe from memory the furniture in their own living rooms there is also activation in the dorsomedial speech area, but the activation extends into the middle and posterior parts of the prefrontal cortex (Roland 1985; Roland *et al.* 1985).

In these studies the human subjects were assigned a task: the speech was not fully spontaneous. No activation study has yet examined spontaneous speech in the sense that no subject matter was prescribed. But there are clinical descriptions of patients with medial frontal lesions who fail to produce spontaneous speech. The lesions can be infarctions of the left anterior cerebral artery (Masdeu *et al.* 1978; Damasio and van Hoesen 1983), tumours (Jonas 1987), or cortical removals (Laplane *et al.* 1977b); and they typically involve the medial prefrontal, cingulate, and medial premotor cortex. The mutism recovers in a few weeks, presumably because the lesions are unilateral.

It is remarkable that these patients may be able to answer questions at times when they fail to speak without prompting (Jonas 1987). We could make sense of this if we assume that the dorsomedial speech area is specialized for the spontaneous production of speech, and that Broca's area is specialized for the production of speech on the basis of visual or auditory cues. Studies using ¹³³Xenon and two dimensional imaging suggest that Broca's area is not activated when subjects run through the days of the month (Ingvaar and Schwartz 1984), but that it is activated when subjects read (Lassen *et al.* 1978). Using the PET scanner Wise *et al.* (1991) have shown that the dorsomedial speech area is activated when subjects generate associates of words that they hear. In further PET studies Wise *et al.* (pers.comm.) have found that the dorsomedial speech area, but not Broca's area, is activated when subjects count silently; and that the dorsomedial speech area is not activated when subjects repeat words. To put it crudely, when the patients answer questions it is Broca's area speaking.

Grammar

Grammatical rules cover both the order of words and their inflexions. The use of these rules can be disturbed by lesions in the frontal lobe. Broca's aphasics often produce very short phrases, omitting the connecting words, auxiliaries, and inflexions (Benson and Geschwind 1985). Goodglass and Geschwind (1976) called this 'agrammatism', and so set off a controversy. Others have denied that there is an unvarying syndrome. The arguments are summarized by Caplan (1987) and Ellis and Young (1988). Fortunately, there is no need to take sides here, because everyone agrees that some or other aspect of grammatical construction can be disturbed in Broca's aphasics, and that this can affect the comprehension as well as the production of speech.

The lesions in Broca's aphasics are not usually restricted to Broca's area (Mohr *et al.* 1978; Damasio and Damasio 1989). The reading of grammatical sentences can be disturbed by electrical stimulation of either the prefrontal cortex or Broca's area (Ojemann 1983). It is true that electrical stimulation also evokes syntactic errors when applied to the temporal lobe (Ojemann 1983); but patients with temporal lobe lesions are usually less impaired in their grammatical production than patients with frontal lobe lesions (Benson and Geschwind 1985).

Grammar and the human species

It has been widely accepted that the ability to handle grammar is unique to the human species. It could be assumed that it follows that the mechanism is unique. Both claims can be challenged.

Genetics

In considering the first claim, we should not be overawed by the evidence on the genetics of language. Take, for example, the family described by Hurst *et al.* (1990). Of the 29 members, in three generations, 15 have a severe speech impairment in the absence of dysarthria, hearing loss, or mental retardation. The major features are a dramatic impairment in repeating single words and naming (Vargha-Khadem and Passingham 1990) and in the production and comprehension of word order and morphological markers (Gopnik 1990). The speech disorder is a non-fluent aphasia, and it appears to be caused by a dominant gene.

It is tempting to think that this shows that there is a special mechanism that is peculiar to the human species, and that it is specified by the genes. But in reality the data show no more than we could have concluded from studying adult patients with Broca's aphasia. We know that damage to the brain can interfere with language, and we know that brain mechanisms are specified by the genes; but none of this proves that the mechanism is peculiar to the human species.

Chimpanzee language

This could only be proved by showing that other animals can not be taught to understand or produce grammatical sentences. Terrace *et al.* (1979) taught American Sign Language to a chimpanzee, called Nim. They reported that Nim did not appreciate that word order carried meaning. But this is not the same as demonstrating that the animal cannot be *taught* that word order carries meaning.

Muncer and Ettlinger (1981) taught a chimpanzee, called Jane, to sign in particular orders. For example, she was taught to describe displays such as 'apple in bag', and to obey commands such as 'push apple behind bag'. She was then tested for her understanding of the rules, by being required to produce or understand novel strings. For example, she was asked to describe the display 'bag behind box' or to obey the command to put the 'box behind apple'. She performed above chance on the first trials with new strings. But the experiment is not fully convincing because the same items reappeared in the transfer tests, though in different positions in the strings. The experiment should be performed with chimpanzees which possess a large vocabulary, so that totally new nouns, prepositions, and verbs could be used for the transfer series.

There is an alternative way of carrying out the experiment. This is to take a chimpanzee like Kanzi, who understands many words of spoken English (Savage-Rumbaugh 1986), and to test the comprehension of sentences such as 'cat bites dog'. This can be done by asking the animal to pick between pictures, for example of a cat biting a dog and a dog biting a cat. The experiment would be to train the chimpanzee on a series of sentences, and then to test for comprehension of the rule by giving a new series of sentences, but for one trial each.

Until such critical experiments have been carried out, we must remain agnostic about the chimpanzee's capacity for grammar. It does not follow that, because these animals use no grammar in the wild, they are unable to be taught the rudiments in the laboratory. It only follows that, if they can be taught simple grammatical rules, the mechanism for learning these rules must be a mechanism for learning other, non-linguistic, rules (Passingham 1982).

Conditional rules

In monkeys lesions in the premotor areas (6 or 8) impair the retrieval of responses on the basis of conditional rules (Chapters 3 and 5). In the human brain, area 44 is a specialized region of the lateral premotor area 6. Infarcts of the ventrolateral premotor and prefrontal cortex of the human brain disrupt the use of grammatical rules (Goodglass and Geschwind 1976).

The PET scanner offers the possibility of localizing the relevant mechanisms more accurately. Human subjects could be scanned while they describe the action shown in simple pictures—for example a picture of a cat biting a dog. Alternatively the subjects could be required to use morphological markers, for example producing the past tenses of a series of words. Until such a study has been done we should be cautious in drawing conclusions about the extent to which premotor or prefrontal regions contribute.

Anderson (1983) has modelled the production of grammatical rules by the ACT system, which uses conditional logic. Consider the production of morphological markers such as prepositions and tenses. The rules for generating 'a' or 'the', and 'is' or 'was', depend on conditional logic. In one context (the listener knows of the topic) 'the' is correct; and in another context (the listener does not know of the topic) 'a' is correct. In one context (the action is currently happening) 'is' is correct; and in another context (the action is completed) 'was' is correct.

The evolution of the speech mechanism

The comparison between the monkey tasks and the generation of grammar is naïve. But there are degrees of naïvety. Consider the following claims:

1. The mechanisms of the premotor and associated prefrontal areas are the same in man and monkey, and the inputs and outputs are the same.
2. The mechanisms for handling grammar developed out of the type of mechanism that we can study in a monkey; but the inputs and outputs may differ.
3. The mechanism for handling grammar developed out of the type of mechanism that we can study in the right hemisphere of the human brain.

4. The left hemisphere of the human brain evolved a unique mechanism *de novo* for generating grammar.

Development of the speech mechanisms

The first claim is implausible. The second should be set out with greater precision. It proposes that, in the common ancestor of man and modern apes, the premotor and prefrontal areas played a role in the learning of conditional rules. Grammatical rules have a conditional logic, and may be handled by a mechanism of that sort. However, in the brain of modern man that region is much expanded, and it is possible that the inputs and outputs to that region differ from those that are found in other primates.

The third claim supposes that the premotor and associated prefrontal areas of the non-dominant hemisphere developed out of the type of mechanism that we can study in the premotor and prefrontal areas of monkeys and apes. But it also supposes that the left hemisphere has become specialized for handling grammar. Evidence for this specialization comes from studies of the development of language in patients in whom the left hemisphere has been removed early in life (Vargha-Khadem *et al.* 1991). These patients are able to handle simple grammatical rules, but are none the less markedly impaired in the production and comprehension of morphological markers.

The fourth claim takes it to be certain that the human species is unique in being able to handle grammatical rules. It therefore assumes that there are areas such as Broca's area that evolved for this specific task, and that these areas did not differentiate out of areas with related functions.

The naïvety of the present account is such as to suppose that either the second or third of these claims could be true. Both claims suppose that the development of the specialized mechanism can be understood better when one considers the less specialized mechanisms from which it evolved. We are unable to inspect the brains of our ancestors, and must perforce study modern brains.

An analogy will help. Preuss and Goldman-Rakic (1991) have compared the frontal cortex of macaques (*Macaca*) and bushbabies (*Galago*). These authors can distinguish areas 8A, 8B, and 45 in the bushbaby, but are unable to detect a separate area 46. Yet area 46 presumably differentiated out of areas 8 and 45; it is similar in being involved in the selection of eye movements. In macaques it is similar to area 8 in having inputs from visual areas, though it differs in that these come from later stages of visual processing (Barbas and Pandya 1991).

Several processes could be involved in the development of specialized mechanisms. First, the inputs and outputs to an area could be altered. Second, the area could be expanded. Finally, the area could be differentiated into more specialized subareas. Any or all of these processes

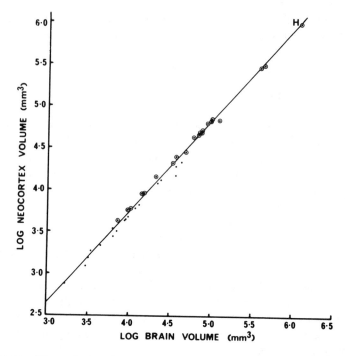

Fig. 11.13 The relation between the volume of the neocortex and the volume of the brain as a whole in primates. H = human brain. From Passingham (1975*a*).

could be involved in the evolution of the specialized mechanisms of the left frontal cortex of the human brain.

The human brain

There is a general suspicion of any attempt to 'reduce' some human capacity, such as handling grammar, to some simpler achievement of which monkeys are capable. There is also a suspicion of the notion that new achievements can be made possible simply by expanding a mechanism. It is essential to distinguish two issues. The first is how to account for the evolutionary development of some capacity. The second is how to account for the *effect* of that development.

Allometric changes in the brain

The effects of differences in size
The distinction can be illustrated by considering studies of the size of brain areas in man and other primates. For any particular area, the size can be

compared with the size of the brain or cortex as a whole. Regression lines can be fitted to the values for the non-human primates, and a prediction made as to the value expected for the human brain. A comparison of the actual and predicted values gives the number of times that the area is larger or smaller than expected for the human brain (Passingham 1982).

Suppose that the values for area X in the human brain are as predicted by the size of the human brain. This tells us that, for area X, the same developmental processes may be at work in the human brain as in the brains of other primates. But the same fact tells us nothing about the *consequences* of expressing this area at a different size.

Consider a worked example: Fig. 11.13 plots the size of the neocortex relative to the size of the whole brain. The value for neocortex of the human brain is as predicted from data on other primates (Passingham 1975*a*). But this does not mean that the functional efficiency is the same in all primates.

Consider the relative size of the neocortex in other primates (Stephan *et al.* 1970). The neocortex forms 76 per cent of the brain in a chimpanzee (*Pan troglodytes*), 72 per cent in a macaque monkey (*Macaca mulatta*), 60 per cent in a marmoset (*Callithrix jacchus*), and 46 percent in a mouse lemur (*Microcebus murinus*). It cannot be that these differences in proportion are without major consequence. The argument is pursued in more detail elsewhere (Passingham *et al.* 1986; Passingham 1989).

The 'same' mechanisms

It is one thing to claim that area 44 and related prefrontal areas are built by the development of mechanisms that are also to be found in monkeys or chimpanzees. It is quite another to claim that these areas are 'the same' in these species. A desktop computer works on the same principles as a mainframe computer; but there are many tasks which can only be carried out by the larger machine. Suppose that areas 44 and related prefrontal areas have evolved from a simple mechanism for handling conditional rules. This does not mean that they are the same in capacity, that the simple mechanism can handle the rules for morphological markers.

It helps us to understand the evolution of Broca's area if we recognize that it may have evolved from an area which played a role in the generation of vocal outputs given particular contexts. This is not to say that the homologous mechanism in monkeys or chimpanzees can deal with the complexity of the contexts that can be distinguished by the human brain or that the repertoire of responses is the same.

Prefrontal cortex

This point can also be made in relation to the prefrontal cortex as well. Uylings and van Eden (1990) have measured the size of the prefrontal cortex (including areas 24 and 25) in man, orang-utan, macaque, marmoset, and rat. When compared with the volume of the brain, the value for the human brain is as

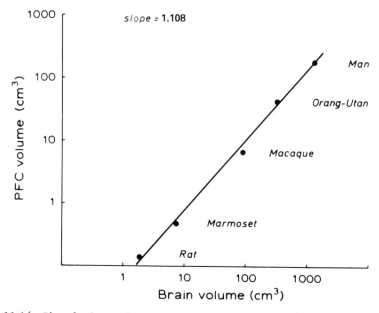

Fig. 11.14 Plot of volume of prefrontal cortex (including anterior cingulate cortex) and volume of whole brain in cm³. Regression line with slope of 1.108 is shown fitted through the data points. Figure from Uylings and van Eden (1990).

predicted from a line fitted to the values for the other animals (Fig. 11.14). There is a lawful relation between the development of the prefrontal cortex and the rest of the brain.

This does not mean that the human prefrontal cortex is 'the same as' the prefrontal cortex in macaque monkeys. An orang-utan is either of a similar weight to man or larger; yet the frontal lobe is roughly five times larger in the human brain. The capacities described in Chapters 10 and 11 may well be available only to a primate brain of the human size. One consequence of expanding the brain to that size may be to allow what we believe to be 'true' voluntary action (Fig. 1.1, level D).

This book has been written on the assumption that it will be a useful strategy to work out the functional anatomy of the frontal lobe in the macaque monkey. It has been assumed that this will give some clues as to the basic functional organization of the frontal lobe in the human brain. But it does not follow that if people have big monkey brains, they are just big monkeys.

Summary

The frontal lobe selects between verbal responses. There are two premotor areas. Broca's area is part of the lateral premotor cortex and the dorsomedial speech area part of the medial premotor cortex.

It is suggested that Broca's area is critically involved when a word must be retrieved on the basis of an object, word, letter or meaning, and that the dorsomedial speech area is critically involved when words must be retrieved without external cues.

Strokes involving Broca's area and the ventral prefrontal cortex impair the ability to use function words and morphological markers. It is claimed that the specialized mechanisms of the left hemisphere may have developed from areas in our primate ancestors that had related functions.

Several processes could be involved in the evolution of specialized mechanisms of the left frontal cortex of the human brain. The inputs and outputs could be altered, areas could be expanded, or areas could be differentiated into more specialized subareas.

Bibliography

Aggleton, J.P. and Passingham, R.E. (1981). Syndrome produced by lesions of the amygdala in monkeys (*Macaca mulatta*). J. Comp. Physiol. Psychol. 95, 961–977.

Aggleton, J.P., Burton, M.J. and Passingham, R.E. (1980). Cortical and subcortical afferents to the amygdala of the rhesus monkey (*Macaca mulatta*). Brain Res. 190, 347–368.

Aggleton, J., Friedman, D.P. and Mishkin, M. (1987). A comparison between the connections of the amygdala and hippocampus with the basal forebrain in the macaque. Exper. Brain Res. 67, 556-568.

Aldridge, J.W., Anderson, R.J. and Murphy, J.T. (1980). The role of the basal ganglia in controlling a movement initiated by a visually presented cue. Brain Res. 192, 3–16.

Alexander, G.E. and Crutcher, M.D. (1990*a*). Functional architecture of basal ganglia circuits: neural substrates of parallel processing. TINS 13, 266–271.

Alexander, G.E. and Crutcher, M.D. (1990*b*). Preparation for movement: neural representations of intending direction in three motor areas of the monkey. J. Neurophysiol. 64, 133–149.

Alexander, G. and Crutcher, M.D. (1991). Parallel processing in the basal ganglia: up to a point. TINS 14, 56–58.

Alexander, G.E., Crutcher, M.D. and DeLong, M.R. (1991). Basal ganglia-thalamocortical circuits: parallel substrates for motor, oculomotor, 'prefrontal' and 'limbic' functions. Progr. Brain Res. 85, 119–146.

Amaral, D.G. and Price, J.L. (1984). Amygdalo-cortical projections in the monkey (*Macaca fascicularis*). J. Comp. Neurol. 230, 465–496.

Andersen, R.A. (1987). The role of the inferior parietal lobule in spatial perception and visual-motor integration. In: The Handbook of Physiology, Vol. IV. (Eds. F. Plum, V.B. Mountcastle and S.R. Geiger) American Physiological Society, Bethesda, Maryland, pp. 483–518.

Andersen, R.A. and Mountcastle, W.B. (1983). The influence of the angle of gaze upon the excitability of the light-sensitive neurons of the posterior parietal cortex. J. Neurosci. 3, 532–548.

Andersen, R.A., Asanuma, C. and Siegel, R.M. (1990). Corticocortical connections of anatomically and physiologically defined subdivisions within the inferior parietal lobule. J. Comp. Neurol. 296, 65–113.

Anderson, J.R. (1983). The Architecture of Cognition. Harvard, Cambridge.

Anderson, M.E. and Horak, F.B. (1985). Influence of the globus pallidus on arm movements in monkeys. III Timing of movement-related information. J. Neurophysiol. 54, 433–448.

Anderson, T.J., Jenkins, I.H., Hawken, M., Frackowiak, R.S.J., Kennard, C. and Brooks, D.J. (1992). Cortical control of saccades and fixation in man: a PET study. Neurol. 42, 373.

Anderson, S.W., Damasio,H., Jones,R.D. and Tranel,D. (1991). Wisconsin card sorting performance as a measure of frontal lobe damage. J. Clinic. Exper. Neuropsychol. 13, 909–922

Apicella, P., Ljündberg, T., Scarnati, E. and Schultz, W. (1991). Responses to reward in monkey dorsal and ventral striatum. Exper. Brain Res. 85, 491–500.

Arikuni, T., Sakai, M., Hamada, I. and Kubota, K. (1980). Topographical projections from the prefrontal cortex to the posterior arcuate area in the rhesus monkey studied by retrograde axonal transport of horseradish peroxidase. Neurosci. Lett. 19, 155–160.

Asanuma, C., Thach, W.T. and Jones, E.G. (1983). Distribution of cerebellar terminations and their relation to other afferent terminations in the ventral lateral thalamic region of the monkey. Brain Res. Rev. 5, 237–265.

Baddeley, A. (1986). Working Memory. Oxford University Press, Oxford.

Baddeley, A.D. and Hitch, G. (1974). Working memory. In: The Psychology of Learning and Motivation, Vol. 8. (Ed. G.H. Bower) Academic Press, New York, pp. 47–90.

Bailey, P., von Bonin, G. and McCullogh, W.S. (1950). The Isocortex of the Chimpanzee. University of Illinois Press, Urbana.

Baleydier, C. and Maugière, F. (1980). The duality of the cingulate gyrus in monkey. Brain 103, 525–554.

Barbas, H. (1988). Anatomical organization of basoventral and mediodorsal visual recipient prefrontal region in the rhesus monkey. J. Comp. Neurol. 276, 313–342.

Barbas, H. and De Olmos, J. (1990). Projections from the amygdala to basoventral and mediodorsal prefrontal regions in the rhesus monkey. J. Comp. Neurol. 300, 549–571.

Barbas, H. and Mesulam, M.-M. (1981). Organization of afferent input to subdivisions of area 8 in the rhesus monkey. J. Comp. Neurol. 200, 407–431.

Barbas, H. and Mesulam, M.-M. (1985). Cortical afferent input to the principalis region of the rhesus monkey. Neurosci. 15, 619–637.

Barbas, H. and Pandya, D.N. (1987). Architecture and frontal cortical connections of the premotor cortex (area 6) in the rhesus monkey. J. Comp. Neurol. 256, 211–228.

Barbas, H. and Pandya, D.N. (1989). Architecture and intrinsic connections of the prefrontal cortex in the rhesus monkey. J. Comp. Neurol. 286, 353–375.

Barbas, H. and Pandya, D.N. (1991). Pattern of connections of the prefrontal cortex in the rhesus monkey associated with cortical architecture. In: Frontal Lobe Function and Dysfunction (Eds. H.S. Levin, H.M. Eisenberg and A.L. Benton) Oxford University Press, New York, pp. 35–58.

Barbas,H., Haswell Henion, T.H. and Dermon, C.R. (1991). Diverse thalamic projections to the prefrontal cortex in the rhesus monkey. J. Comp. Neurol. 313, 65–94.

Baron, J.C., D'Antona, R., Pantano, P., Serdaru, M., Samson, Y. and Bousser, M.G. (1986). Effects of thalamic stroke on energy metabolism of the cerebral cortex. Brain 109, 1243–1259.

Barone, P. and Joseph, J.-P. (1989). Prefrontal cortex and spatial sequencing in macaque monkey. Exper. Brain Res. 78, 447–464.

Barron, D.H. (1934). The results of unilateral pyramidal section in the rat. J. Comp. Neurol. 60, 45–56.

Basso, A., Capitani, E., Sala, S.D., Laiacona, M. and Spinnler, H. (1987). Recovery from ideomotor apraxia: a study on acute stroke patients. Brain 110, 747–760.

Basso, A., Faglioni, P. and Luzzatti, C. (1985). Methods in neuroanatomical research and an experimental study of limb apraxia. In: Neuropsychological Studies of Apraxia (Ed. E.A. Roy) Elsevier, Amsterdam, pp. 179–202.

Bauer, R.H. and Fuster, J.M. (1976). Delayed-matching and delayed-response deficit from cooling dorsolateral prefrontal cortex in monkeys. J. Comp. Physiol. Psychol. 90, 293–302.

Baylis, L.L. and Gaffan, D. (1991). Amygdalectomy and ventromedial prefrontal ablation produce similar defecits on food choice and in simple object discrimination learning for an unseen reward. Exper. Brain Res. 86, 617–622.

Bench, C.J., Friston, K.J., Brown, R.G., Frackowiak, R.S., and Dolan, R.J. (1993). Regional cerebral blood flow in depression measured by positron emission tomography: the relationship with clinical dimensions. *Psychol Med.* **23**.

Benecke, R. (1989). The pathophysiology of Parkinson's disease. In: Disorders of Movement (Eds. N.P. Quinn and P.G. Jenner) Academic Press, New York, pp. 59–72.

Benecke, R., Rothwell, J., Day, B.J., Dick, J.P.R. and Marsden, C.D. (1986). Motor strategies involved in the performance of sequential movements. Exper. Brain Res. 63, 585–595.

Benson, D.F. and Geschwind, N. (1985). Aphasia and related disorders: a clinical approach. In: Principles of Behavioral Neurology (Ed. M.-M. Mesulam) Davis, Philadelphia, pp. 193–238.

Bernston, G.G. and Micco, D.J. (1976). Organization of brainstem behavioral systems. Brain Res. Bull. 1, 471–483.

Bizzi, E. (1968). Discharge of frontal eye field neurons during saccadic and following eye-movements in unanesthetized monkeys. Exper. Brain Res. 6, 69–80.

Bizzi, E. and Schiller, P.H. (1970). Single unit activity in the frontal eye fields of unanesthetized monkeys during eye and head movements. Exper. Brain Res. 10, 151–158.

Black, P., Markowitz, R.S. and Cianci, S.N. (1975). Recovery of motor function after lesions in motor cortex in monkeys. In Outcome of Severe Damage to the Central Nervous System, CIBA symposium, vol. 34. Elsevier, Amsterdam, pp. 65–70.

Blinkov, S.M. and Gleser, I.I. (1968). The Human Brain in Figures and Tables: a Quantitative Handbook. Plenum, New York.

Bolles, R.C. (1978). The role of stimulus learning in defensive behavior. In: Cognitive Processes in Animal Behavior (Eds. S.H. Hulse, H. Fowler and W.K. Honig) Erlbaum, New Jersey, pp. 89–107.

von Bonin, G. (1944). Architecture of the precentral motor cortex and some adjacent areas. In: The Precentral Motor Cortex (Ed. P. Bucy) University of Illinois Press, Urbana, pp. 7–82.

von Bonin, G. and Bailey,P. (1947). The Neocortex of *Macaca mulatta.* University of Illinois Press, Urbana.

von Bonin, G. and Bailey, P. (1961). Pattern of the cerebral isocortex. Primatol. 2, 1–42.

Boschert, J., Hink, R.F. and Deecke, L. (1983). Finger movement versus toe movement related potentials: further evidence for supplementary motor (SMA) participation prior to voluntary action. Exper. Brain Res. 52, 73–80.

Boussaoud, D., Ungerleider, L.G. and Desimone, R. (1990). Pathways of motion analysis: cortical connections of the medial superior temporal and fundus visual areas in the macaque. J. Comp. Neurol. 296, 462–495.

Bowker, R.M. and Coulter, J.D. (1981). Intracortical connections of somatic sensory and motor areas: multiple pathways in monkeys. In: Multiple Visual Areas, Vol. 1. (Ed. C.N. Woolsey) Clifton, New Jersey, pp. 205–242.

Braak, H. (1976). A primitive gigantopyramidal field buried in the depth of the cingulate sulcus of the human brain. Brain Res. 109, 219–233.

Bracke-Tolkmitt, R., Linden, A., Canavan, A.G.M., Rockstroh, B., Scholz, E., Wessel, K. *et al.* (1989). The cerebellum contributes to mental skills. Beh. Neurosci. 103, 442–446.

Bradshaw, C.M. and Szabadi, E. (1989). Central neurotransmitter systems and the control of operant behavior by 'natural' positive reinforcers. In: The Neuropharmacological Basis of Reward (Eds. J.M. Liebman and S.J. Cooper) Oxford University Press, Oxford, pp. 320–378.

Brinkman, C. (1984). Supplementary motor area of the monkey's cerebral cortex: short and long term deficits after unilateral ablation and the effects of subsequent callosal section. J. Neurosci. 4, 918–929.

Broadbent, D., Cooper, P.F., FitzGerald, P. and Parkes, K.R. (1982). The cognitive failures questionnaire (CFQ) and its correlates. Brit. J. Clinic. Psychol. 21, 1–16.

Brodal, A. (1981). Neurological Anatomy, 3rd edn. Oxford University Press.

Brodal, P. (1978). The corticopontine projection in the rhesus monkey. Brain 101, 251–283.

Brodmann, K. (1925). Vergleichende Localisationslehre der Grosshirnrinde, 2nd edn. Barth, Leipzig.

Brody, B.A. and Pribram, K.H. (1978). The role of frontal and parietal cortex in cognitive processes: tests of spatial and sequence function. Brain 101, 607–633.

Brooks, D.J., Ibanez, V., Sawle, G.V., Quinn, N., Lees, A.J., Mathias, C.J., *et al.* (1990). Differing patterns of striatal ^{18}F–Dopa uptake in Parkinson's disease, multiple systems atrophy, and progressive supranuclear palsy. Ann. Neurol. 28, 549–555.

Brown, P.L. and Jenkins, H.M. (1968). Auto-shaping of the pigeon's key peck. J. Exper. Anal. Beh. 11, 1–8.

Brown, R. and Marsden, C.D. (1988*a*). 'Frontal' cognitive function in patients with Parkinson's disease 'on' and 'of' levodopa. Brain 111, 323–345.

Brown, R. and Marsden, C.D. (1988*b*). An investigation into the phenomenon of 'set' in Parkinson's disease. Mov.Dis. 3, 152–161.

Brown, R.G. and Marsden, C.D. (1989). Neuropsychology and cognitive function in Parkinson's disease: an overview. In: Movement Disorders, Vol. 2. (Eds. C.D. Marsden and S. Fahn) Butterworths, London, pp. 99–123.

Bruce, C.J. (1988). Single neuron activity in the monkey's prefrontal cortex. In: Neurobiology of Neocortex, (Eds. P. Rakic and W. Singer) Wiley, New York, pp. 297–329.

Bruce, C.J. and Goldberg, M.E. (1985). Primate frontal eye fields: I Single neurones discharging before saccades. J. Neurophysiol. 53, 607–635.

Bruce, C.J., Goldberg, M.E., Bushnell, M.C. and Stanton, G.B. (1985). Primate frontal eye fields: II Physiological and anatomical correlates of electrically evoked eye movements. J. Neurophysiol. 54, 714–734.

Bucy, P.C., Keplinger, J.E. and Siqueira, E.B. (1964). Destruction of the 'pyramidal tract' in man. J. Neurosurg. 21, 395–398.

Bushnell, M.C., Goldberg, G. and Robinson, D.L. (1981). Behavioral enhancement of visual responses in monkey cerebral cortex. I. Modulation in posterior parietal cortex relevant to selective visual activation. J. Neurophysiol. 46, 755–772.

Butter, C.M. (1969). Perseveration in extinction and in discrimination reversal tasks following selective frontal ablations in *Macaca mulatta*. Physiol. Beh. 4, 163–171.

Butter, C.M. and Snyder, D.R. (1972). Alterations in aversive and aggressive behaviors following orbital frontal lesions in rhesus monkeys. Acta Neurobiol. Exper. 32, 525–565.

Butterworth, G. (1977). Object disappearance and error in Piaget's stage IV task. J. Exper. Child Psychol. 23, 391–401.

Buys, E.J., Lemon, R.N., Mantel, G.W.H. and Muir, R.B. (1986). Selective facilitation of different hand muscles by single corticospinal neurones in the conscious monkey. J. Physiol. 381, 529–549.

Calabresi, P., Maj, M., Pisani, A., Mercuri, N.B. and Bernadi, G. (1992). Long-term synaptic depression in the striatum: physiological and pharmacological characterization. J. Neurosci. 12, 4224–4233.

Camarda, R., Luppino, G., Matelli, M. and Rizzolatti, G. (1991). Cortical connections of two different eye fields in the dorsomedial frontal cortex of the macaque monkey. Soc. Neurosci. Abstr. 17, 185–214.

Canavan, A.G.M. (1983). Stylus-maze performance in patients with frontal-lobe lesions: effects of signal valency and relationship to verbal and spatial abilities. Neuropsychol. 21, 375–382.

Canavan, A.G.M., Janota, I. and Schurr, P.H. (1985). Luria's frontal lobe syndrome: psychological and anatomical considerations. J. Neurol. Neurosurg. Psychiatr. 48, 1049–1053.

Canavan, A.G.M., Nixon, P.D. and Passingham, R. (1989*a*). Motor learning in monkeys (*Macaca fascicularis*) with lesions in motor thalamus. Exper. Brain Res. 77, 113–126.

Canavan, A.G.M., Passingham, R.E., Marsden, C.D., Quinn, N., Wyke, M. and Polkey, C.E. (1989*b*). The performance on learning tasks of patients in the early stages of Parkinson's disease. Neuropsychol. 27, 141–156.

Caplan, D. (1987). Neurolinguistics and Linguistic Aphasiology. Cambridge University Press, Cambridge.

Catsman-Berrevoets, C.E., Kuypers, H.G.J.M. and Lemon, R.N. (1979). Cells of origin of the frontal projections to magnocellular and parvocellular red nucleus and superior colliculus in cynomolgus monkey: an HRP study. Neurosci. Lett. 12, 41–46.

Cavada, C. and Goldman-Rakic, P.S. (1989). Posterior parietal cortex in rhesus monkeys: II Evidence for segregated corticocortical networks linking sensory and limbic areas with the frontal lobe. J. Comp. Neurol. 28, 422–445.

Chapman, C.E. and Wiesendanger, M. (1982). Recovery of function following unilateral lesion of the bulbar pyramid in the monkey. EEG Clinical Neurophysiology 53, 374–387.

Chavis, D.A. and Pandya, D.N. (1976). Further observations on cortico-frontal connections in the rhesus monkey. Brain Res. 117, 369–386.

Clark, A.S. and Goldman-Rakic, P.S. (1991) Quantitative in vitro autoradiography of excitatory amino acid binding in the primate basal ganglia. Soc. Neurosci. Abstr., 17, 334.12.

Cianci, S.N. (1962). The effects of intracranial electrical stimulation on the delayed response task. Unpublished Ph.D. thesis, University of Michigan.

Colebatch, J.G. and Gandevia, S.C. (1989). The distribution of weakness in upper motor neuron lesions affecting the arm. Brain 112, 749–763.

Colebatch, J.G., Adams, L., Murphy, K., Martin, A.J., Lammertsma, A.A., Tochon-Danguy, H.J., (1991*a*). Regional cerebral blood flow during voluntary breathing in man. J. Physiol. 443, 91–103.

Colebatch, J.G., Deiber, M.-B., Passingham, R.E., Friston, K.J. and Frackowiak, R.S.J. (1991*b*). Regional cerebral blood flow during voluntary arm and hand movements in human subjects. J. Neurophysiol. 65, 1392–1401.

Collin, N.G., Cowey, A., Latto, R. and Marzi, C. (1982). The role of frontal eye-fields and superior colliculus in visual search and non-visual search in rhesus monkeys. Beh. Brain Res. 4, 177–193.

Corkin, S. (1968). Acquisition of motor skill after bilateral medial temporal-lobe excision. Neuropsychol. 6, 255–265.

Cowey, A. (1982). Sensory and non-sensory visual disorders in man and monkey. Philosophical Transactions of the Royal Society of London, series B 298, 3–13.

Crammond, D.J. and Kalaska, J.F. (1989). Neuronal activity in primate parietal cortex area 5 varies with intended movement direction during an instructed-delay period. Exper. Brain Res. 76, 458–462.

Crutcher, M.D. and Alexander, G.E. (1990). Movement-related neuronal activity selectively coding either direction or muscle pattern in three motor areas of the monkey. J. Neurophysiol. 64, 151–163.

Crutcher, M.D. and DeLong, M.R. (1984). Single cell studies of the primate putamen: I Functional organization. Exper. Brain Res. 53, 233–243.

Damasio, H. and Damasio, A.R. (1989). Lesion Analysis in Neuropsychology. Oxford University Press, New York.

Damasio, A.R. and van Hoesen, G.W. (1983). Emotional disturbances associated with focal lesions of the limbic frontal lobe. In: Neuropsychology of Human Emotion (Eds. K. Heilman and P. Satz) Guildford Press, New York, pp. 85–110.

Damasio, A.R., Damasio, H., Rizzo, M., Varney, N. and Gersh, F. (1982). Aphasia with nonhemorrhagic lesions in the basal ganglia and internal capsule. Archiv. Neurol. 39, 15–20.

Damasio, H., Eslinger, P. and Adams, H.P. (1984). Aphasia following basal ganglia lesions: new evidence. Semin. in Neurol. 4, 151–161.

Damasio, A.R., Trunel, D. and Damasio, H.C. (1991). Somatic markers and the guidance of behavior: theory and preliminary testing. In: Frontal Lobe Function and Dysfunction (Eds. H.S. Levin, H.M. Eisenberg and A.L. Benton) Oxford University Press, New York, pp. 217–229.

Darian-Smith, C., Darian-Smith, I. and Cheema, S.S. (1990). Thalamic projections to sensorimotor cortex in the macaque monkey: use of multiple retrograde fluorescent tracers. J. Comp. Neurol. 299, 17–46.

Dawkins, R. (1989). Darwinism and human purpose. In: Human Origins, (Ed. J.R. Durant) Oxford University Press, pp. 137–143.

Dean, P. (1982). Visual behavior in monkeys with inferotemporal lesions. In: Analysis of Visual Behavior, (Eds. D.J. Ingle, M.A. Goodale and R.J. Mansfield) MIT Press, Cambridge, Mass, pp. 587–628.

Deecke, L. (1987). Bereitschaftspotential as an indicator of movement preparation in supplementary motor area and motor cortex. In: Motor Areas of the Cerebral Cortex (Ed. R. Porter) Wiley, New York, pp. 231–245.

Deiber, M.-P., Passingham, R.E., Colebatch, J.G., Friston, K.J., Nixon, P.D. and Frackowiak, R.S.J. (1991). Cortical areas and the selection of movement: a study with positron emission tomography. Exper. Brain Res. 84, 393–402.

DeLong, M.R., Crutcher, M.D. and Georgopoulos, A.P. (1983). Relation between movement and single cell discharge in the substantia nigra of the behaving monkey. J. Neurosci. 3, 1599–1606.

DeLong, M.R., Crutcher,M.D. and Georgopoulos,A.P. (1985). Primate globus pallidus and subthalamic nucleus: functional organization. J. Neurophysiol. 53, 530–543.

Deng, S.Y., Goldberg, M.E., Segraves, M.A., Ungerleider, L.G. and Mishkin, M. (1986). The effect of unilateral ablation of the frontal eye fields on saccadic performance in the monkey. In: Adaptive Processes in Visual and Oculomotor Systems (Eds. E.L. Keller and D.S. Zee) Pergamon, Oxford, pp. 201–208.

De Renzi, E. (1985). Methods of limb apraxia examination and their bearing on the interpretation of the disorder. In: Neuropsychological Studies of Apraxia and Related Disorders (Ed. E.A. Roy) Elsevier, Amsterdam, pp. 45–64.

De Renzi, E. and Lucchelli, F. (1988). Ideational apraxia. Brain 111, 1173–1185.

De Renzi, E., Faglioni, P., Lodesani, M. and Vecchi, A. (1983). Performance of left brain-damaged patients on imitation of single movements and motor sequences: frontal and parietal-injured patients compared. Cortex 19, 333–343.

De Renzi, E., Faglioni, P. and Sergato, P. (1982). Modality-specific and supramodal mechanisms of apraxia. Brain 105, 301–312.

Desimone, R. and Ungerleider, L. (1989). Neural mechanisms of visual processing in monkeys. In: Handbook of Neuropsychology, Vol. 2. (Eds. F. Boller and J. Graffman) Elsevier, New York, pp. 267–299.

Desimone, R., Schein, S.J., Moran, J. and Ungerleider, L.G. (1985). Contour, colour and shape analysis beyond the striate cortex. Vis. Res. 25, 441–452.

Deuel, R.K. (1977). Loss of motor habits after cortical lesions. Neuropsychol. 15, 205–215.

Deuel, R.K. and Dunlop, N.L. (1979). Role of frontal polysensory cortex in guidance of limb movements. Brain Res. 169, 183–188.

DeVito, J.L. and Anderson, M.E. (1982). An autoradiographic study of efferent connections of the globus pallidus in *Macaca mulatta*. Exper. Brain Res. 46, 107–117.

DeVito, J.L., Anderson, M.E. and Walsh, X.E. (1980). A horseradish peroxidase study of afferent connections of the globus pallidus in *Macaca mulatta*. Exper.Brain Res. 38, 65–75.

Diamond, A. (1985). The development of the ability to use recall to guide action, as indicated by infant's performance on $\overline{AB}$. *Child Dev.* 56, 868–883.

Diamond, A. (1988). Differences between adult and infant cognition. Is the crucial variable presence or absence of language? In: Thought Without Language (Ed. L. Weiskrantz) Oxford University Press, pp. 337–370.

Diamond, A. and Goldman-Rakic, P.S. (1989). Comparison of human infants and rhesus monkeys on Piaget's $\overline{AB}$ task: evidence for dependence on dorsolateral prefrontal cortex. Exper. Brain Res. 74, 24–40.

DiCara, L.V. and Miller, N.E. (1968). Instrumental learning of systolic blood pressure by curarized rats. Psychosom. Med. 30, 489–494.

Dick, J.P.R., Benecke, R., Rothwell, J.C., Day, B.L. and Marsden, C.D. (1986). Simple and complex movements in a patient with infarction of the right supplementary motor cortex. Mov. Dis. 1, 255–266.

Divac, I. and Mogenson, J. (1985). The prefrontal 'cortex' in the pigeon: catecholamine histofluoresence. Neurosci. 15, 677–682.

Divac, I., Björklund, A., Lindvall, O. and Passingham, R.E. (1978). Converging projections from the mediodorsal thalamic nucleus and mesencephalic dopaminergic neurons to the neocortex in three species. J. Comp. Neurol. 180, 59–72.

Divac, I., Holst, M.-C., Nelson, J. and McKenzie, J.S. (1987). Afferents of the frontal cortex in the echidna (*tachyglossus aculeatus*): indications of an outstandingly large prefrontal area. Brain Beh. Evol. 30, 303–320.

Downes, J.J., Roberts, A.C., Sahakian, B.J., Evenden, J.L., Morris, R.G. and Robbins, T.W. (1989). Impaired extra–dimensional shift performance in medicated and unmedicated Parkinson's disease: evidence for a specific attentional dysfunction. Neuropsychol. 27, 1329–1343.

Dum, R.P. and Strick, P.L. (1991). The origin of corticospinal projections from the premotor areas in the frontal lobe. J. Neurosci. 11, 667–689.

Duncan, J. (1986). Disorganization of behaviour after frontal lobe damage. Cogn. Neuropsychol. 3, 271–290.

Dworkin, B.R. and Miller, N.E. (1986). Failure to replicate visceral learning in the acute curarized rat preparation. Beh. Neurosci. 100, 299–314.

Eacott, M.J. and Gaffan, D. (1989). Reaching to a rewarded visual stimulus: interhemispheric conflict and hand use in monkeys with forebrain commissurotomy. Brain 112, 1215–1230.

Eacott, M.J. and Gaffan, D. (1992). Inferotemporal-frontal disconnection: the role of the uncinate fascicle in associative learning in monkeys. Europ. J. Neurosci. 4, 1320–1332.

Eccles, J.C. (1982). The initiation of voluntary movements by the supplementary motor cortex. Archiv. Psychiat. Nervenkr. 231, 423–441.

von Economo, C. (1929). The Cytoarchitectonics of the Human Cerebral Cortex. Oxford University Press, London.

Eidelberg, D. and Galaburda, A.M. (1984). Inferior parietal lobule: divergent architectonic asymmetries of the human brain. Archiv. Neurol. 41, 843–852.

Ellis, A.W. and Young, A.W. (1988). Human Cognitive Neuropsychology. Erlbaum, Hove.

Eslinger, P.J. and Damasio, A.R. (1985). Severe disturbance of higher cognition after bilateral frontal lobe ablation: patient EVR. Neurol. 35, 1731–1741.

Evarts, E., Shinoda, Y. and Wise, S.P. (1984). Neurophysiological Approaches to Higher Brain Functions. Wiley, New York.

Faglioni, P. and Basso, A. (1985). Historical perspectives on neuroanatomical correlates of limb apraxia. In: Neuropsychological Studies of Apraxia and Related Disorders (Ed. E.A. Roy) North Holland, Amsterdam, pp. 3–44.

Farrer, D.N. (1967). Picture memory in the chimpanzee. Perc. Mot. Skills 25, 305–315.

Fetz, E.E. and Cheney, P.D. (1987). Functional relations between primate motor cortex cells and muscles: fixed and flexible. In: Motor areas of the cerebral cortex, Vol. 132. (Ed. R. Porter) Wiley, New York, pp. 98–112.

Fetz, E.E. and Finocchio, D.V. (1975). Correlations between activity of motor cortex cells and arm muscles during operantly conditioned response patterns. Exper. Brain Res. 23, 217–240.

Fiez, J.A., Petersen, S.E., Cheney, M.K. and Raichle, M.E. (1992). Impaired non-motor learning and error detection associated with cerebellar damage. Brain 115, 155–178.

Fox, P.T., Fox, J.M., Raichle, M.E. and Burde, R.M. (1985). The role of cerebral cortex in the generation of voluntary saccades: a positron tomographic study. J. Neurophysiol. 54, 348–369.

Freund, H.-J. and Hummelsheim, H. (1985). Lesions of premotor cortex in man. Brain 108, 697–734.

Friedman, H.R., Bhalla, S. and Goldman-Rakic, P.S. (1991). Metabolic activation of dorsolateral prefrontal and inferior parietal cortex by cognitive processing: a 2-DG study in rhesus monkeys performing mnemonic tasks. Soc. Neurosci. Abstr. 54, 15.

Friedman, H.R. and Goldman-Rakic, P.S. (1988). Activation of the hippocampus and dentate gyrus by working memory: a 2-deoxyglucose study of behaving rhesus monkeys. J. Neurosci. 8, 4693–4706.

Fries, W. (1984). Cortical projections to the superior colliculus in the macaque monkey: a retrograde study using horseradish peroxidase. J. Comp. Neurol. 230, 55–76.

Fries, W., Danek, A., Scheidtmann, K. and Hamburger, C. (1993). Motor recovery following capsular stroke: role of descending pathways from multiple motor areas. Brain, 116, 369–382.

Friston, K.J., Frith, C.D., Passingham, R.E., Liddle, P.F. and Frackowiak, R.S.J. (1992). Motor practice and neurophysiological adaptation in the cerebellum: a positron tomographic study. Proc. Roy. Soc. Lond. B 248, 223–228.

Frith, C.D. (1991). Positron emission tomography studies of frontal lobe function: relevance to psychiatric disease. In: Exploring Brain Functional Anatomy with Positron Tomography (Eds. D.J. Chadwick and J. Whelan) Wiley, Chichester, pp. 181–191.

Frith, C., Friston, K.J., Liddle, P.F. and Frackowiak, R.S.J. (1991a). A PET study of word finding. Neuropsychol. 29, 1137–1148.

Frith, C.D., Friston, K., Liddle, P.F. and Frackowiak, R.S.J. (1991b). Willed action and the prefrontal cortex in man: a study with PET. Proc. Roy. Soc. Lond. B 244, 241–246.

Fuchs, A.F., Kaneko, C.R.S. and Scudder, C.A. (1985). Brainstem control of saccadic eye movements. Ann.Rev.Neurosci. 8, 307–337.

Funahashi, S. (1983). Responses of monkey prefrontal neurons during a visual tracking task reinforced by substantia innominata self-stimulation. Brain Res. 276, 267–276.

Funahashi, S., Bruce, C.J. and Goldman-Rakic, P.S. (1986). Perimetry of spatial representation in primate prefrontal cortex: evidence for a mnemonic hemianopia. Soc. Neurosci. Abstr. 12, 149.3.

Funahashi, S., Bruce, C.J. and Goldman-Rakic, P.S. (1989). Mnemonic coding of visual space in monkey dorsolateral prefrontal cortex. J. Neurophysiol. 61, 331–349.

Fuster, J.M. (1973). Unit activity in prefrontal cortex during delayed-response performance: neuronal correlates of transient memory. J. Neurophysiol. 36, 61–78.

Fuster, J.M. (1989). The Prefrontal Cortex. Raven Press, New York.

Fuster, J.M. and Alexander, G.E. (1971). Neuron activity related to short term memory. Science 173, 652–654.

Gaffan, D. and Harrison, S. (1988). Disconnection of the amygdala from visual association cortex impairs visual reward-association learning in monkeys. J. Neurosci. 8, 3144–3150.

Gaffan, D. and Bolton, J. (1983). Learning of object-object associations by monkeys. Quart. J. Exper. Psychol. 35B, 149–155.

Gaffan, D. and Harrison, S. (1989). A comparison of the effects of fornix transection and sulcus principalis ablation upon spatial learning by monkeys. Beh. Brain Res. 31, 207–220.

Gaffan, D. and Harrison, S. (1991). Auditory-visual associations, hemispheric specialization and temporal-frontal interaction in the rhesus monkey. Brain 114, 2133–2144.

Gaffan, D. and Murray, E.A. (1990). Amygdalar interaction with the mediodorsal nucleus of the thalamus and the ventromedial prefrontal cortex in stimulus-reward associative learning in the monkey. J. Neurosci. 10, 3479–3493.

Galaburda, A.M. and Pandya, D.N. (1982). Role of architectonics and connections in the study of primate brain evolution. In: Primate Brain Evolution (Eds. E. Armstrong and D. Falk) Plenum, New York, pp. 203–216.

Gandevia, S.C. and Rothwell, J.C. (1987). Knowledge of motor commands and the recruitment of human motorneurons. Brain 110, 1117–1130.

Garcia-Rill, A. (1986). The basal ganglia and the locomotor regions. Brain Res. 11, 47–63.

Gardner, B.T. and Gardner, R.A. (1985). Signs of intelligence in cross-fostered chimpanzees. Phil. Trans. Roy. Soc. Lond.B 308, 159–176.

Gentilucci, M., Fogassi, L., Luppino, G., Matelli, M., Camarda,R. and Rizzolatti, G. (1988). Functional organization of inferior area 6 in the macaque monkey. Exper. Brain Res. 71, 475–490.

Georgopoulos, A.P., DeLong, M.R. and Crutcher, M.D. (1983). Relation between parameters of step-tracking movements and single cell discharge in the globus pallidus and subthalamic nucleus of the behaving monkey. J. Neurosci. 3, 1586–1598.

Georgopoulos, A.P., Caminitti, R. and Kalaska, J.F. (1984). Static spatial effects in motor cortex and area 5: quantitative relations in two dimensional space. Exper. Brain Res. 54, 446–454.

Geschwind, N. (1972). Language and the brain. Scient. Amer. 226, 76–83.

Ghosh, S., Brinkman, C. and Porter, R. (1987). A quantitative study of the distribution of neurons projecting to the precentral motor cortex in the monkey (*Macaca fascicularis*). J. Comp. Neurol. 259, 424–444.

Giguere, M. and Goldman-Rakic, P.S. (1988). Mediodorsal nucleus: areal, laminar and tangential distribution of afferents and efferents in the frontal lobe of the rhesus monkey. J. Comp. Neurol. 277, 195–213.

Gilbert, P.F.C. and Thach, W.T. (1977). Purkinje cell activity during motor learning. Brain Res. 128, 309–328.

Gilman, S., Lieberman, T.S. and Marco, L.A. (1974). Spinal mechanisms underlying the effects of unilateral ablation of area 4 and 6 in monkeys. Brain 97, 49–64.

Glickstein, M., Cohen, J.L., Dixon, B., Gibson, A., Hollins, M., Labossiere, E. *et al.* (1980). Corticopontine visual projections in macaque monkeys. J. Comp. Neurol. 190, 209–229.

Glickstein, M., May, J.G. and Mercier, R.E. (1985). Corticopontine projections in the macaque: the distribution of labelled cortical cells after large injections of horseradish peroxidase in the pontine nuclei. J. Comp. Neurol. 235, 343–359.

Glicktein, M. and May, J.G. (1982). Visual control of movement: the circuits which link visual to motor areas of the brain with special reference to the visual input to the pons and cerebellum. In: Contributions to Sensory Physiology, Vol. 7. (Ed. W.D. Neff) Academic Press, New York, pp. 103–145.

Godschalk, M. and Lemon, R.N. (1989). Preparation of visually cued arm movements in monkey. Brain Beh. Evol. 33, 122–126.

Godschalk, M., Lemon, R., Kuypers, H.G.J.M. and Ronday, H.K. (1984). Cortical afferents and efferents of monkey postarcuate cortex: an anatomical and electrophysiological study. Exper. Brain Res. 56, 410–424.

Godschalk, M., Lemon, R.N., Kuypers, H.G.J.M. and van der Steen, J. (1985). The involvement of monkey premotor cortex neurones in preparation of visually cued arm movements. Beh. Brain Res. 18, 143–157.

Godschalk, M., Mitz, A.R., van der Burg, J. and van Duin, B. (1990). Microstimulation map of the monkey premotor cortex. Soc. Neurosci. Abstr. 16, 1133.

Goldberg, G. (1985). Supplementary motor area structure and function: review and hypotheses. Beh. Brain Res. 8, 567–588.

Goldberg, M.E. and Bushnell, M.C. (1981). Behavioral enhancement of visual responses in monkey cerebral cortex. II. Modulation in frontal eye fields specifically related to saccades. J. Neurophysiol. 46, 773–787.

Goldman, P.S. (1971). Functional development of the prefrontal cortex in early life and the problem of neuronal plasticity. Exper. Neurol. 32, 366–387.

Goldman, P.S. (1972). Developmental determinants of cortical plasticity. Acta Neurobiol. Exper. 32, 495–511.

Goldman, P.S. and Nauta, W.J.H. (1976). Autoradiographic demonstration of a projection from prefrontal association cortex to the superior colliculus in the rhesus monkey. Brain Res. 116, 145–149.

Goldman, P.S. and Rosvold, H.E. (1970). Localization of function within the dorsolateral prefrontal cortex of the rhesus monkey. Exper. Neurol. 27, 291–304.

Goldman, P.S. and Rosvold, H.E. (1972). The effects of selective caudate lesions in infant and juvenile rhesus monkeys. Brain Res. 43, 53–66.

Goldman, P.S., Rosvold, H.E. and Mishkin, M. (1970). Selective sparing of function following prefrontal lobectomy in infant monkey. Exper. Neurol. 29, 221–226.

Goldman, P.S., Rosvold, H.E., Vest, B. and Galkin, T.W. (1971). Analysis of the delayed-alternation deficit produced by dorsolateral prefrontal lesions in the rhesus monkey. J. Comp. Physiol. Psychol. 77, 212–220.

Goldman-Rakic, P.S. (1987). Circuitry of primate prefrontal cortex and regulation of behaviour by representational memory. In: Handbook of Physiology: the Nervous System, Vol. 5. (Eds. F. Plum and V. Mountcastle) American Physiological Society, Bethesda, pp. 373–417.

Goldman-Rakic, P.S. (1990). Cellular and circuit basis of working memory in prefrontal areas of non-human primates. Progr. Brain Res. 85, 325–336.

Goldman-Rakic, P.S., Selemon, L.D. and Schwartz, M.R. (1984). Dual pathway connecting the dorsolateral prefrontal cortex with the hippocampal formation and the perihippocampal cortex in the rhesus monkey. Neurosci. 12, 719–749.

Goodglass, H. and Geschwind, N. (1976). Language disturbance (aphasia). In: Handbook of Perception, Vol. 7. (Eds. E.C. Carterette and M.P. Friedman) Academic Press, New York, pp. 389–428.

Gopnik, M. (1990). Feature-blind grammar and dysphasia. Nature 344, 715.

Grafman, J., Jonas, B. and Salazar, A. (1990). Wisconsin card sorting test performance based on location and size of neuroanatomical lesion in Vietnam veterans with penetrating head injury. Perc. Mot. Skills 71, 1120–1122.

Grueninger, W.E., Kimble, D.P., Grueninger, J. and Levine, S. (1965). GSR and corticosteroid response in monkeys with frontal ablations. Neuropsychol. 3, 205–216.

Guitton, D., Buchtel, A.A. and Douglas, R.M. (1985). Frontal lobe lesions in man cause difficulties in suppressing reflexive glances and in generating goal-directed saccades. Exper. Brain Res. 58, 455–472.

Haaxma, R. and Kuypers, H.G.J.M. (1975). Intracortical connexions and visual guidance of hand and finger movements in the rhesus monkey. Brain 98, 239–260.

Halsband, U. (1982). Higher Movement Disorders in Monkeys. Unpublished D.Phil. thesis, University of Oxford.

Halsband,U. (1987). Higher disturbances of movement in monkeys (*Macaca mulatta*). In: Motor Control (Eds. G.N. Gantchev, B. Dimitev and P.C. Gatev) Plenum, New York, pp. 79–85.

Halsband, U. and Freund, H.-J. (1990). Premotor cortex and conditional motor learning in man. Brain 113, 207–222.

Halsband, U. and Passingham, R.E. (1982). The role of premotor and parietal cortex in the direction of action. Brain Res. 240, 368–372.

Halsband, U. and Passingham, R.E. (1985). Premotor cortex and the conditions for movement in monkeys (*Macaca mulatta*). Beh. Brain Res. 18, 269–276.

Harris, P.L. (1989). Object permanence in infancy. In: Infant Development (Eds. A. Slater and E. Bremner) Erlbaum, London, pp. 103–121.

Hast, M.H., Fischer, J.M., Wetzela, B. and Thompson, V.E. (1974). Cortical motor representation of the laryngeal muscles in *Macaca mulatta*. Brain Res. 73, 229–240.

Haxby, J.V., Grady, C.L., Horwitz, B., Salerno, J.A., Ungerleider, L.G., Mishkin, M. *et al.* (in press). Dissociation of object and spatial visual processing pathways in human extrastriate cortex. In: The Functional Organization of Human Visual Cortex (Eds. P.E. Roland and B. Gulyas) .

Hayes, K.J. and Hayes, C. (1952). Imitation in a home-raised chimpanzee. J. Comp. Physiol. Psychol. 45, 450–459.

Hedreen, J.C. and DeLong, M.R. (1991). Organization of striatopallidal, striatonigral and nigrostriatal projections in the macaque. J. Comp. Neurol. 304, 569–595.

Hedreen, J.C., Martin, L.J., Koliatsos, V.E., Hamada, L., Alexander, G.E. and DeLong, M.R. (1988). Organization of primate basal ganglia 'motor circuit': 4. Ventrolateral thalamus links internal pallidum (GPi) and supplementary motor area (SMA). Soc. Neurosci. Abstr. 14, 287–320.

Heindel, W.C., Salmon, D.P., Shults, C.W., Walicke,P.A. and Butters,N. (1989). Neuropsychological evidence for multiple implicit memory systems: a comparison of Alzheimer's, Huntington's and Parkinson's disease patients. J. Neurosci. 9, 583–587.

Hepp-Raymond, M.C. and Wiesendanger, M. (1972). Unilateral pyramidotomy in monkeys: effects on force and speed of a conditioned precision grip. Brain Res. 36, 117–131.

Hepp-Raymond, M.C. and Wiesendanger, M. (1974). Effects of unilateral and bilateral pyramidotomy on a conditioned rapid precision grip in monkeys (*Macaca fascicularis*). Exper. Brain Res. 21, 519–527.

Hikosaka, O. and Wurtz, R.H. (1983). Visual and oculomotor function of monkey substantia nigra pars reticulata: I Relation of visual and auditory responses to saccades. J. Neurophysiol. 49, 1230–1253.

Hikosaka, O. and Wurtz, R.H. (1985). Modification of saccadic eye movements by GABA-related substances: I Effect of muscimol and bicuculline on monkey superior colliculus. J. Neurophysiol. 53, 266–291.

Hikosaka, O., Sakamoto, M. and Usui, S. (1989). Functional properties of monkey caudate neurons: I Activities related to saccadic eye movements. J. Neurophysiol. 61, 780–798.

van Hoesen, G.W. (1982). The parahippocampal gyrus. TINS 5, 345–350.

van Hoesen, G., Yeterian, E.H. and Lavizzo-Mourey, R. (1981). Widespread corticostriate projection from temporal cortex of the rhesus monkey. J. Comp. Neurol. 199, 205–219.

Hoffman, D.S. and Luschei, E.S. (1980). Response of monkey precentral cortical cells during a controlled jaw bite task. J. Neurophysiol. 44, 333–348.

Holsapple, J.W., Preston, J.B. and Strick, P.L. (1991). The origin of thalamic inputs to the 'hand' representation in the primary motor cortex. J. Neurosci. 11, 2644–2654.

Honig, W.K. (1978). Studies of working memory in the pigeon. In: Cognitive Processes in Animal Behavior (Eds. S.H. Hulse, H. Fowler and W.K. Honig) Erlbaum, Hillsdale, pp. 211–248.

Hopkins, D.A., McLean, J.H. and Takeuchi, Y. (1981). Amygdalotegmental projections: light and electron microscopic studies utilizing anterograde degeneration and the anterograde and retrograde transport of horseradish peroxidase (HRP). In: The Amygdaloid Complex (Ed. Y. Ben-Ari) Elsevier, Amsterdam, pp. 133–147.

Huerta, M.F. and Kaas, J.H. (1990). Supplementary eye field as defined by intracortical microstimulation: connections in macaques. J. Comp. Neurol. 330, 299–330.

Hummelsheim, H., Bianchetti, M., Wiesendanger, M. and Wiesendanger, R. (1988). Sensory inputs to the agranular motor fields: a comparison between precentral, supplementary-motor and premotor areas in the monkey. Exper. Brain Res. 69, 289–298.

Humphrey, N.K. (1976). The social function of intellect. In Growing Points in Ethology (Eds. P.P.G. Bateson and R.A. Hinde) Cambridge University Press pp.303–317.

Hurst, J.A., Baraitser, M., Auger, E., Graham, F. and Norell, S. (1990). An extended family with dominant inherited speech disorder. Dev. Med. Child Neurol. 32, 347–355.

Hutchins, K.D., Martino, A.M. and Strick, P.L. (1988). Corticospinal projections from the medial wall of the hemisphere. Exper. Brain Res. 71, 667–672.

Hyvärinen, J. (1981). Regional distribution of functions in parietal association area 7 of the monkey. Brain Res. 206, 287–303.

Ikeda, A., Luders, H.O., Burgess, R.C. and Shibasaki, H. (1992). Movement-related potentials recorded from supplementary motor area and primary motor area. Brain 115, 1017–1043.

Ilinsky, I.A. and Kultas-Ilinsky, K. (1987). Sagittal cytoarchitectonic maps of the *Macaca mulatta* thalamus with a revised nomenclature of the motor-related nuclei validated by observation of their connectivity. J. Comp. Neurol. 262, 331–364.

Ilinsky, I.A., Jouandet, M.L. and Goldman-Rakic, P.S. (1985). Organization of the nigrothalamocortical system in the rhesus monkey. J. Comp. Neurol. 236, 315–330.

Ingvaar, D.H. and Schwartz, M.S. (1974). Blood flow patterns induced in the dominant hemisphere by speech and reading. Brain 97, 273–288.

Insausti, R., Amaral, D.G. and Cowan, W.M. (1987). The entorhinal cortex of the monkey. II Cortical afferents. J. Comp. Neurol. 264, 356–395.

Iriki, A., Pavlides, C., Keller, A. and Asanuma, H. (1991). Long-term potentiation of thalamic input to the motor cortex induced by coactivation of thalamocortical and corticocortical afferents. J. Neurophysiol. 65, 1435–1441.

Ito, M. (1984). The Cerebellum and Neuronal Control. Raven Press, New York.

Ito, M., Sakurai, M. and Tongroach, P. (1982). Climbing fibre induced depression of both mossy fibre responsiveness and glutamate sensitiviy of cerebellar Purkinje cells. J. Physiol. 324, 113–134.

Iversen, S.D. and Mishkin, M. (1970). Perseverative interference in monkeys following selective lesions of the inferior prefrontal convexity. Exper. Brain Res. 11, 376–386.

Jackson, J.H. (1931). Selected Writings of John Hughlings Jackson. Hodder and Stoughton, London.

Jacobsen, C.F. (1935). Functions of frontal association area in primates. Archiv. Neurol. Psychiatr. 33, 558–569.

Jacobsen, S. and Trojanowski, J.Q. (1977). Prefrontal granular cortex of the rhesus monkey. I. Intrahemispheric cortical afferents. Brain Res. 132, 209–233.

Jason, G.W. (1985). Manual sequence learning after focal cortical lesions. Neuropsychol. 23, 483–496.

Jenkins, H.M. (1977). Sensitivity of different response systems to stimulus-reinforcer and response-reinforcer relations. In: Operant-Pavlovian Interactions (Eds. H. Davis and H.M.B. Hurwitz) Erlbaum, Hillsdale, pp. 47–62.

Jenkins, H.M. and Moore, B.R. (1973). The form of the auto-shpaed response with food or water reinforcers. J. Exper. Anal. Beh. 20, 163–181.

Jenkins, I.H., Fernandez, W., Playford, E.D., Lees, A.J., Frackowiak, R.S.J., Passingham, R.E. *et al* (1992*a*). Akinesia and Parkinson's disease: impaired activation of the supplementary motor area reversed by apomorphine. Annals Neurol. 32, 749–757.

Jenkins, I.H., Passingham, R.E., Nixon, P.D., Frackowiak, R.S.J. and Brooks, D.J. (1992*b*). The learning of motor sequences: a PET study. Europ. J. Neurosci., suppl. 5, 3215.

Jenkins, I.H., Anderson, T.J., Hawken, M., Kennard, C. and Brooks, D.J. (1992*c*). Control of saccades and fixation in man: a PET study. Mov.Dis. 7, P489.

Johnson, T.N., Rosvold, H.E. and Mishkin, M. (1968). Projections from behaviorally defined sectors of the prefrontal cortex to the basal ganglia, septum and diencephalon of the monkey. Exper. Neurol. 21, 20–34.

Jonas, S. (1987). The supplementary motor region and speech. In: The Frontal Lobes Revisited (Ed. E. Perecman) IRBN Press, New York, pp 241–250.

Jones, B. and Mishkin, M. (1972). Limbic lesions and the problem of stimulus-reinforcement associations. Exper. Neurol. 36, 362–377.

Jones, E.G. (1985). The Thalamus. Plenum, New York.

Jones, E.G., Coulter, J.D. and Hendry, S.H.C. (1978). Intracortical connectivity of architectonic fields in the somatic sensory, motor and parietal cortex of monkeys. J. Comp. Neurol. 181, 291–348.

Jürgens, U. (1982). Afferents to the cortical larynx area in the monkey. Brain Res. 239, 377–389.

Jürgens, U. and Ploog, D. (1970). Cerebral representation of vocalization in the squirrel monkey. Exper. Brain Res. 10, 532–554.

Kaada, B.R. (1960). Cingulate, posterior orbital, anterior insular and temporal pole cortex. In: Handbook of Physiology, Vol. 1. (Ed. J. Field) American Physiological Society, Bethesda, pp. 1345–1372.

Kasser, R.J. and Cheney, P.D. (1985). Characteristics of corticomotorneuronal postspike facilitation and reciprocal suppression of EMG activity in the monkey. J. Neurophysiol. 53, 959–978.

Kemp, J.M. and Powell, T.P.S. (1971). The connexions of the striatum and globus pallidus: synthesis and speculations. Phil.Trans.Roy.Soc. Lond.B. 262, 441–457.

Kennard, M.A. (1942). Cortical reorganization of motor function: studies on series of monkeys of various ages from infant to maturity. Archiv. Neurol. Psychiatr. 48, 227–240.

Kertesz, A. and Ferro, J.M. (1984). Lesion size and location in ideomotor apraxia. Brain 107, 921–933.

Kertesz, A., Ferro, J.M. and Shewan, C.M. (1984). Apraxia and aphasia: the functional anatomical basis of their dissociation. Neurol. 34, 40–47.

Kertzman, C., Currie, J.N., Ramsden, B.M., Jackson, C.L., Hallett, M. and Fitzgibbon, E.J. (1992). PET scan study of reflexive, memory guided and antisaccades. Assoc. Res. Vision Opthalmol. 33, 2315–101.

Kievit, J. and Kuypers, H.G.J.M. (1975). Subcortical afferents to the frontal lobe in the rhesus monkey studied by means of retrograde horseradish peroxidase transport. Brain Res. 85, 261–266.

Kim, R., Nakano, A., Jayaraman, A. and Carpenter, M.B. (1976). Projections of the globus pallidus and adjacent structures: an autoradiographic study in the monkey. J. Comp. Neurol. 169, 263–290.

Kimble, D.P., Bagshaw, M.H. and Pribram, K.H. (1965). The GSR of monkeys during orienting and habituation after selective partial ablations of the cingulate and frontal cortex. Neuropsychol. 3, 121–128.

Kimura, D. (1982). Left-hemisphere control of oral and brachial movements and their relation to communication. Phil. Trans. Roy. Soc. Lond. B 298, 135–149.

Kojima, S. and Goldman-Rakic, P.S. (1982). Delay-related activity of prefrontal neurones in rhesus monkeys performing delayed response. Brain Res. 248, 43–49.

Kojima, S.C. and Goldman-Rakic, P.S. (1984). Functional analysis of spatially discriminating neurones in prefrontal cortex of rhesus monkey. Brain Res. 291, 229–240.

Kolb, B. and Milner, B. (1981). Performance of complex arm and facial movements after focal brain lesions. Neuropsychol. 19, 491–504.

Kolb, B. and Whishaw, I.O. (1981). Neonatal frontal lesions in the rat: sparing of learned but not species-typical behavior in the presence of reduced brain weight and cortical thickness. J. Comp. Physiol. Psychol. 95, 863–879.

Konorski, J. (1967). Integrative Activity of the Brain. University of Chicago Press.

Konow, A. and Pribram, K.H. (1970). Error recognition and utilization produced by injury to the frontal cortex in man. Neuropsychol. 8, 489–491.

Koob, G.F. and Goeders, N.E. (1989). Neuroanatomical substrates of drug self-administration. In The Neuropharmacological Basis of Reward, (Eds. J.M. Liebman and S.J. Cooper) Oxford University Press, Oxford, 214–263.

Kornhuber, H.H. and Deecke, L. (1965). Hirnpotentialanderungen bei willkurbewegungen und passiven bewegungen des Menschen: Bereitshcaftspotential und reafferente Potentiale. Pflugers Arch.Physiol. 284, 1–17.

Kowalska, D.M., Bachevalier, J. and Mishkin, M. (1991). The role of the inferior prefrontal convexity in performance of delayed nonmatching-to-sample. Neuropsychol. 29, 583–600.

Kubota, K. and Funahashi, I.S. (1982). Direction specific activation of dorsolateral prefrontal and motor cortex pyramidal tract neurons during visual tracking. J. Neurophysiol. 47, 362–376.

Kunzle, H. (1975). Bilateral projections from precentral motor cortex to the putamen and other parts of the basal ganglia: an autoradiographic study in *Macaca fascicularis*. Brain Res. 88, 195–209.

Kunzle, H. (1977). Projections from the primary somatosensory cortex to basal ganglia and thalamus in the monkey. Exper. Brain Res. 30, 481–492.

Kunzle, H. (1978). An autoradiographic analysis of the efferent connections from premotor and adjacent prefrontal regions (areas 6 and 9) in *Macaca fascicularis*. Brain Beh. Evol. 19, 185–234.

Kurata, K. (1989). Distribution of neurons with set- and movement-related activity before hand and foot movements in the premotor cortex of rhesus monkeys. Exper. Brain Res. 77, 245–256.

Kurata, K. and Wise, S.P. (1988). Premotor cortex of rhesus monkeys: set-related activity during two conditional motor tasks. Exper. Brain Res. 69, 327–344.

Kuypers, H.G.J.M. (1962). Corticospinal connections in postnatal development in the monkey. Science 138, 678–680.

Kuypers, H.G.J.M. (1981). Anatomy of the descending pathways. In Handbook of Physiology, Vol. 2. (Ed. V. Brooks) American Physiological Society, Bethesda, pp. 597–666.

Kuypers, H.G.J.M. and Brinkman, J. (1970). Precentral projections to different parts of the spinal intermediate zone in the rhesus monkey. Brain Res. 24, 29–48.

Kwan, H.C., MacKay, W.A. and Murphy, J.L. (1978). Spatial organization of precentral cortex in awake primates: II motor outputs. J. Neurophysiol. 41, 1120–1131.

Lang, W., Lang, M., Uhl, F., Koska, C., Kornhuber, H.H. and Deecke, L. (1988). Negative cortical DC shifts preceding and accompanying simultaneous and sequential finger movements. Exper. Brain Res. 71, 579–587.

Lang, W., Zilch, O., Koska, C., Lindinger, G. and Deecke, L. (1989). Negative cortical DC shifts preceding and accompanying simple and complex sequential movements. Exper. Brain Res. 74, 99–104.

Laplane, D., Tailarach, J., Meininger, V., Bancaud, J. and Bouchareine, A. (1977a). Motor consequences of motor area ablation in man. J. Neurol. Sci. 31, 29–49.

Laplane, D., Tailarach, J., Meininger, V., Bancaud, J. and Orgogozo, J.M. (1977b). Clinical consequences of corticectomies involving the supplementary motor area in man. J. Neurol. Sci 34, 301–314.

Lassen, N.A., Ingvaar, D. and Skinhøj, E. (1978). Brain function and blood flow. Scient.Amer. 239, 50–59.

Latto, R. (1978). The effects of bilateral frontal eye field, posterior parietal or superior colliculus lesions on visual search in the monkey. Brain Res. 146, 35–50.

Latto, R. (1986). The role of inferior parietal cortex and the frontal eye-fields in visuospatial discrimination in the macaque monkey. Beh. Brain Res. 22, 41–52.

Latto, R. and Cowey, A. (1971). Visual field defects after frontal eye-field lesions in monkeys. Brain Res. 30, 1–21.

Lawicka, W., Mishkin, M. and Rosvold, H.E. (1975). Dissociation of deficits on conditioning tasks following partial prefrontal lesions in monkeys. Acta Neurobiol. Exper. 35, 581–607.

Lawler, K.A. and Cowey, A. (1987). On the role of posterior parietal and prefrontal cortex in visuo-spatial perception and attention. Exper. Brain Res. 65, 695–698.

Lawrence, D.G. and Hopkins, D.A. (1976). The development of motor control in the rhesus monkey: evidence concerning the role of corticomotorneuronal connections. Brain 99, 235–254.

Lawrence, D.G. and Kuypers, H.G.J.M. (1968a). The functional organization of the motor system in the monkey. I. The effects of bilateral pyramidal lesions. Brain 91, 1–14.

Lawrence, D.G. and Kuypers, H.G.J.M. (1968b). The functional organization of the motor system in the monkey. II. The effects of lesions of the descending brainstem pathways. Brain 91, 15–36.

Lees, A.J. (1987). The Steele-Richardson-Olszewski syndrome (progressive supranuclear palsy). In: Movement Disorders, Vol. 2. (Eds. C.D. Marsden and S. Fahn) Butterworths, London, pp. 272–287.

Leichnetz, G.R. (1986). Afferent and efferent connections of the dorsolateral precentral gyrus (area 4, hand/arm region) in the macaque monkey, with comparisons to area 8. J. Comp. Neurol. 254, 460–492.

Leichnetz, G.R., Smith, D.J. and Spencer, R.F. (1984*a*). Cortical projections to the paramedian tegmental and basilar pons in the monkey. J. Comp. Neurol. 228, 388–408.

Leichnetz, G.R., Spencer, R.F. and Smith, D.J. (1984*b*). Cortical projections to nuclei adjacent to the oculomotor complex in the medial dien-mesencephalon tegmentum in the monkey. J. Comp.Neurol. 228, 359–387.

Leiner. HC, Leiner, A.L. and Dow, R.S. (1991). The human cerebro-cerebllar system: its computing, cognitive and language skills. Beh.Brain Res. 44, 113–128.

Lemon, R.N. (1988). The output map of the primate motor cortex. TINS 11, 501–505.

Leonard, G. and Milner, B. (1991). Contribution of the right frontal lobe to the encoding and recall of kinesthetic distance information. Neuropsychol. 29, 47–58.

Levine, M. (1965). Hypothesis behavior. In: Behavior of Nonhuman Primates, Vol. 1. (Eds. A.M. Schrier, H.F. Harlow and F. Stollnitz) Academic Press, New York, pp. 97–127.

Liddell, E.G.T. and Philips, C.G. (1944). Pyramidal section in the cat. Brain 67, 1–.

Liddle, P.F., Friston, K.J., Hirch, S.R. and Frackowiak, R.S.J. (1990). Regional cerebral metabolism activity in chronic schizophrenia. Schiz.Res. 3, 23–24.

Lisberger, S.G. (1988). The neuronal basis for motor learning in the vestibulo-ocular reflex in monkeys. TINS 11, 147–152.

Llüngberg, T., Apicella, P. and Schultz, W. (1992). Responses of monkey dopamine neurons during learning of behavioral reactions. J.Neurophysiol. 67, 145–163.

Luppino, G., Matelli, M., Camarda, R.M., Gallese, V. and Rizzolatti, G. (1991). Multiple representations of body movements in mesial area 6 and the adjacent cingulate cortex: an intracortical microstimulation study in the macaque monkey. J. Comp. Neurol. 311, 463–482.

Luppino, G., Matelli, M. and Rizzolatti, G. (1990). Cortico-cortical connections of two electrophysiologically identified arm representations in the mesial agranular frontal cortex. Exper. Brain Res. 82, 214–218.

Luria, A.R. (1966). Higher Cortical Functions in Man. Basic Books, New York.

Luria, A.R., Pribram, K.H. and Homskaya, E.D. (1964). An experimental analysis of the behavioral disturbance produced by a left frontal arachnoidal endothelioma. Neuropsychol. 2, 257–280.

Lynch, J.C., Graybiel, A.M. and Lobeck, L.J. (1985). The differential projection of two cytoarchitectonic subregions of the inferior parietal lobule of macaque upon the deep layers of the superior colliculus. J. Comp. Neurol. 235, 241–254.

McGonigle, B.O. and Flook, J. (1978). The learning of hand preferences by squirrel monkey. Psychol. Res. 40, 93–98.

MacKintosh, N.J. (1983). Conditioning and Associative Learning. Oxford University Press.

Macphail, E.M. (1982). Brain and Intelligence in Vertebrates. Oxford University Press.

Manning. FJ (1978). Dorsolateral prefrontal lesions and discrimination of movement-produced cues by rhesus monkeys. Brain Res. 149, 77–88.

Martin, J.P. (1967). The Basal Ganglia and Posture. Pitman, London.

Martino, A.M. and Strick, P.L. (1987). Corticospinal projections originate from the arcuate premotor area. Brain Res. 404, 307–312.

Masdeu, J.C., Schoene, W.C. and Funkenstein, A. (1978). Aphasia following infarction of the left supplementary motor area. Neurol. 28, 1220–1223.

Matelli, W., Luppino, G. and Rizzolatti, G. (1985). Pattern of cytochrome oxidase activity in frontal agranular cortex of the macaque monkey. Beh. Brain Res. 18, 125–136.

Matelli, M., Camarda, M., Glickstein, M. and Rizzolatti, G. (1986). Afferent and efferent projections of the inferior area 6 in the macaque monkey. J. Comp. Neurol. 251, 281–298.

Matelli, M., Luppino, G., Fogassi, L. and Rizzolatti, G. (1989). Thalamic input to inferior area 6 and area 4 in the macaque monkey. J .Comp. Neurol. 280, 448–458.

Matelli, M., Luppino, G. and Rizzolatti, G. (1991). Architecture of superior and mesial area 6 and the adjacent cingulate cortex in the macaque monkey. J. Comp. Neurol. 311, 445–462.

Matelli, W., Luppino, G. and Rizzolatti, G. (1985). Pattern of cytochrome oxidase activity in frontal agranular cortex of the macaque monkey. Beh.Brain Res. 18, 125–136.

Matsuzaka, Y, Aisawa, H. and Tanji, J. (1992). Motor area rostral to the supplementary motor area (presupplementary motor area) in the monkey: neuronal activity during a learned motor task. J.Neurophysiol. 68, 653–662.

Matthews, P.B.C. (1991). The human stretch reflex and the motor cortex. TINS 14, 87–91.

Maynard Smith, J. (1982). Evolution and the Theory of Games. Cambridge University Press, Cambridge.

Mesulam, M.-M. (1990). Large-scale neurocognitive networks and distributed processing for attention, language, and memory. Ann.Neurol. 28, 597–613.

Mesulam, M.-M. and Mufson, E.J. (1985). The insula of Reil in man and monkey: architectonics, connectivity, and function. In: Association and Auditory Cortices, (ed. A.Peters and E.G.Jones) Plenum, New York, pp. 179–226.

Meynert, T. (1865). Anatomie der Hirnrinde und ihre Verbindungsbahnen mit den Empfindenden Oberflachen und den bewegenden Massen.. M. Leidesdorf's Lehrbuch der psychiat. Krankheiten, Erlangen.

Miall, R.C., Weir, D.J. and Stein, J.F. (1987). Visuo-motor tracking during reversible inactivation of the cerebellum. Exper. Brain Res. 65, 455–464.

Miller, W.C. and DeLong, M.R. (1988). Altered tonic activity of neurons in the globus pallidus and subthalamic nucleus in the primate MPTP model of Parkinsonism. Ann. N.Y. Acad. Sci. 515, 287–302.

Milner, A.D., Foreman, N.P. and Goodale, M.A. (1978). Go-left go-right discrimination performance and distractibility following lesions of prefrontal cortex or superior colliculus in stumptail macaques. Neuropsychol. 16, 381–391.

Milner, B. (1963). Effects of different brain lesions on card sorting. Archiv. Neurol. 9, 90–100.

Milner, B. (1964). Some effects of frontal lobectomy in man. In The Frontal Granular Cortex and Behavior, (Eds. J.M. Warren and K. Akert) McGraw-Hill, New York, pp. 313–334.

Milner, B., Corsi, P. and Leonard, G. (1991). Frontal cortex contribution to recency judgements. Neuropsychol. 29, 601–618.

Mink, J.W. and Thach, W.T. (1991*a*). Basal ganglia and motor control: I. Nonexclusive relation of pallidal discharge to five movement modes. J. Neurophysiol. 65, 273–300.

Mink, J.W. and Thach, W.T. (1991*b*). Basal ganglia and motor control: II Late pallidal tuning relative to movement onset and inconsistent pallidal coding of movement parameters. J. Neurophysiol. 65, 301–329.

Mishkin, M. (1957). Effects of small frontal lesions on delayed alternation in monkeys. J. Neurophysiol. 20, 615–622.

Mishkin, M. (1964). Perseveration of central sets after frontal lesions in monkeys. In: The Frontal Granular Cortex (Eds. J.M. Warren and K. Akert) McGraw-Hill, New York, pp. 219–241.

Mishkin, M. (1972). Cortical visual areas and their interactions. In The Brain and Human Behavior (Ed. A.G. Karczmar) Springer-Verlag, Berlin, pp. 187–208.

Mishkin, M. (1979). Analogous neural models for tactual and visual learning. Neuropsychol. 17, 139–151.

Mishkin, M. (1982). A memory system in the monkey. Phil. Trans. Roy. Soc. series B 298, 85–95.

Mishkin, M. (1991). Cerebral memory circuits. In Perception, Cognition and Brain, Yakult Honsha, , 7–15.

Mishkin, M. and Aggleton, J. (1981). Multiple functional contributions of the amygdala in the monkey. In: The Amygdaloid Complex, (Ed. Y. Ben-Ari) Elsevier, Amsterdam, pp. 409–420.

Mishkin, M. and Manning, F.J. (1978). Nonspatial memory after selective prefrontal lesions in monkeys. Brain Res. 143, 313–323.

Mishkin, M. and Weiskrantz, L. (1958). Effects of delaying reward on visual-discrimination performance of monkeys with frontal lesions. J. Comp. Physiol. Psychol. 51, 276–281.

Mishkin, M., Vest, B., Waxler, M. and Rosvold, H.E. (1969). A re-examination of the effects of frontal lesions on object alternation. Neuropsychol. 7, 357–364.

Mishkin, M., Pohl, W. and Rosenkilde, C.E. (1977). Kinesthetic discrimination after prefrontal lesions in monkeys. Brain Res. 130, 163–168.

Mishkin, M., Ungerleider, L.G. and Macko, K.A. (1983). Object vision and spatial vision: two cortical pathways. TINS 6, 414–417.

Mitchell, S.J., Richardson, R.T., Baker, F.H. and DeLong, M.R. (1987). The primate globus pallidus: neuronal activity related to direction of movement. Exper. Brain Res. 68, 491–505.

Mitz, A.R., Godschalk, M. and Wise, S.P. (1991). Learning-dependent neuronal activity in the premotor cortex: activity during acquisition of conditional motor associations. J. Neurosci. II, 1855–1872.

Miyata, M. and Sasaki, K. (1983). HRP studies on thalamocortical neurons related to the cerebellocerebral projection in the monkey. Brain Res. 274, 213–224.

Mohr, J.P., Pessin, M.S., Finkelstein, S. and Funkenstein, H.H. (1978). Broca's aphasia: pathology and clinical. Neurol. 28, 311–324.

Moll, L. and Kuypers, H.G.J.M. (1977). Premotor cortex ablation in monkeys: contralateral changes in visually guided reaching behavior. Science 198, 317–319.

Mora, F. and Cobo, M. (1990). The neurobiological basis of prefrontal cortex self-stimulation: a review and integrative hypothesis. Progr.Brain Res. 85, 419–432.

Mora, F., Avrith, D.B., Philips, A.G. and Rolls, E.T. (1979). Effects of satiety on self-stimulation of the orbitofrontal cortex in the rhesus monkey. Neurosci. Lett. 13, 141–145.

Mora, F., Avrith, D.B. and Rolls, E.T. (1980). An electrophysiological and behavioural study of self-stimulation in the orbitofrontal cortex of the rhesus monkey. Brain Res. Bull. 5, 111–115.

Morris, R.G., Downes, J.J., Evenden, J.L., Sahakian, B.J., Heald, B.J. and Robbins, T.W. (1988). Planning and spatial working memory in Parkinson's disease. J.Neurol. Neurosurg.Psychiatr. 51, 757–766.

Mountcastle, V.B., Lynch, J.C., Georgopoulos, A., Sakata, H. and Acuna, C. (1975). Posterior parietal association cortex of the monkey: command functions for operations within extrapersonal space. J. Neurophysiol. 38, 871–908.

Mountcastle, V.B. and Powell, T.P.S. (1959). Central nervous mechanisms subserving position sense and kinesthesis. Bull.J.Hopkins Hosp. 105, 173–200.

Muakkassa, K.F. and Strick, P.L. (1979). Frontal lobe inputs to primate motor cortex: evidence for four somatotopically organized 'premotor areas'. Brain Res. 177, 176–182.

Mufson, E.J. and Pandya, D.N. (1984). Some observations on the course and composition of the cingulate bundle in the rhesus monkey. J .Comp. Neurol. 225, 31–43.

Muncer, S.J. and Ettlinger, G. (1981). Communication by a chimpanzee: first-trial mastery of word order that is crticial for meaning. Neuropsychol. 19, 73–78.

Murphy, M.R., MacLean, P.D. and Hamilton, S.C. (1981). Species-typical behavior of hamsters deprived from birth of the neocortex. Science 213, 459–461.

Murray, E.A. and Coulter, J.D. (1981). Supplementary sensory areas: the medial parietal cortex in the monkey. In: Cortical Sensory Organization: Multiple Somatic Areas, Vol. 1. (Ed. C.N. Woolsey) Humana Press, Clifton, NJ., pp. 167–195.

Mushiake, H., Inase, M. and Tanji, J. (1990). Selective coding of motor sequence in the supplementary motor area of the monkey cerebral cortex. Exper. Brain Res. 82, 208–210.

Mushiake, H., Inase, M. and Tanji, J. (1991). Neuronal activity in the primate premotor, supplementary, and precentral motor cortex during visually guided and internally determined sequential movements. J. Neurophysiol. 66, 705–718.

Napier, J.R. (1961). Prehensility and opposability in the hands of primates. Symp. Zool. Soc. Lond. 5, 115–132.

Neal, J.W., Pearson, R.C.A. and Powell, T.P.S. (1987). The cortic-cortical connections of area 7b, PF, in the parietal lobe of the monkey. Brain Res. 419, 341–346.

Neal, J.W., Pearson, R.C.A. and Powell, T.P.S. (1990). The ipsilateral cortico-cortical connection of area 7 with the frontal lobe in the monkey. Brain Res. 509, 31–40.

Nelson, H.E. (1976). A modified card sorting test sensitive to frontal lobe defecits. Cortex 12, 313–324.

Neshige, R., Luders, H. and Shibasaki, H. (1988). Recording of movement-related potentials from scalp and cortex in man. Brain 111, 719–736.

Niki, H. (1974). Differential activity of prefrontal units during right and left delayed response trials. Brain Res. 70, 346–349.

Niki, H. and Watanabe, M. (1976). Prefrontal unit activity and delayed response: relation to cue location and direction of response. Brain Res. 105, 79–88.

Nixon, P.D., Chen, Y-C., Thaler, D.E. and Passingham, R.E. (1992). Self-generated movements and the frontal lobes. Europ. J. Neurosci. suppl. 5, 3215.

Oberg, R.G.E. and Divac, I (1979). 'Cognitive' functions of the neostriatum. In The Neostriatum (I.Divac and R.G.E. Oberg), Pergamon Press, Oxford, 291–314.

Ojemann, G.A. (1983). Brain organization for language from the perspective of electrical stimulation mapping. Beh. Brain Sci. 2, 189–230.

Okano, K. and Tanji, J. (1987). Neuronal activity in the primate motor fields of the agranular frontal cortex preceding visually triggered and self-paced movements. Exper. Brain Res. 66, 155–166.

Olszewski, J. (1952). The Thalamus of the Macaca Mulatta. Karger, Basel.

Ono, T., Nishino, H., Fukuda, M., Sasaki, K. and Nishijo, H. (1984). Single neuron activity in dorsolateral prefrontal cortex of monkey during operant behavior sustained by food reward. Brain Res. 311, 323–332.

Orgogozo, J.M. and Larsen, B. (1979). Activation of the supplementary motor area during voluntary movement in man suggests that it works as a supramotor area. Science 206, 847–850.

Owen, A.M., Downes, J.J., Sahakian, B.J., Polkey, C.E. and Robbins, T.W. (1990). Planning and spatial working memory following frontal lobe lesions in man. Neuropsychol. 28, 1021–1034.

Owen, A.M., Roberts, A.C., Polkey, C.E., Sahakian, B. and Robbins, T.W. (in press *b*). Extra-dimensional verus intra-dimensionsal set shifting performance following frontal lobe excisions, temporal lobe excisions or amygdalo-hippocampectomy in man. Neuropsychol. 29, 993–1006.

Owen, A.M., James, M., Leigh, P.N., Summers, B., Marsden, C.D., Quinn, N. *et al*. 1992. Fronto-striatal cognitive deficits at different stages of Parkinson's disease. Brain 115, 1727–1751.

Pandya, D.N. and Barnes, C. (1987). Architecture and connections of the frontal lobe. In The Frontal Lobes Revisited, (Ed. E. Perecman) IBRN Press, New York, 41–72.

Pandya, D.N. and Seltzer, B. (1982). Intrinsic connections and architectonics of posterior parietal cortex in the rhesus monkey. J. Comp. Physiol. Psychol. 20, 204.

Pandya, D.N. and Yeterian, E.H. (1985). Architecture and connections of cortical association areas. In Association and Auditory Cortices, (ed. A. Peters and E.G. Jones) Plenum, New York, pp. 3–61.

Pandya, D.N. and Yeterian, E.H. (1990). Prefrontal cortex in relation to other cortical areas in rhesus monkey: architecture and connections. Progr. Brain Res. 85, 63–93.

Pardo, J.V., Fox, P.T. and Raichle, M.E. (1991). Localizaton of a human system for sustained attention by positron emission tomography. Nature 349, 61–64.

Parent, A. (1986). Comparative Neurobiology of the Basal Ganglia. Wiley, New York.

Parent, A. (1990). Extrinsic connections of the basal ganglia. TINS 13, 254–258.

Parkinson, J.K., Murray, E.A. and Mishkin, M. (1988). A selective mnemonic role of the hippocampus in monkeys: memory for the location of objects. J. Neurosci. 8, 4159–4167.

Parthasarathy, H.B., Schall, J.D. and Graybiel, A.M. (1992). Distributed but convergent ordering of corticostriatal projections: analysis of the frontal eye field and the supplementary eye field in the macaque monkey. J. Neurosci. 12, 4468–4488.

Pascual-Leone, A., Dhuna, A. and Gates, J.R. (1991). Identification of presumed Broca's area with rapid transcranial magnetic stimulation. J. Clin. Neurophysiol. 8, 344.

Passingham, R.E. (1971). Behavioural Changes after Lesions of Frontal Granular Cortex in Monkeys (*Macaca mulatta*). Unpublished Ph.D thesis, University of London.

Passingham, R.E. (1972*a*). Non-reversal shifts after selective prefrontal ablations in monkeys (*Macaca mulatta*). Neuropsychol. 10, 17–26.

Passingham, R.E. (1972*b*). Visual discrimination learning after selective prefrontal ablations in monkeys (*Macaca mulatta*). Neuropsychol. 10, 27–39.

Passingham, R.E. (1975*a*). Changes in the size and organization of the brain in man and his ancestors. Brain Beh. Evol. 11, 73–90.

Passingham, R.E. (1975*b*). Delayed matching after selective prefrontal lesions in monkeys. Brain Res. 92, 89–102.

Passingham, R.E. (1978). Information about movements in monkeys (*Macaca mulatta*) with lesions of dorsal prefrontal cortex. Brain Res. 152, 313–328.

Passingham, R.E. (1981). Primate specialization in brain and intelligence. Symp. Zool. Soc. Lond. 46, 361–368.

Passingham, R.E. (1982). The Human Primate. Freeman, Oxford.

Passingham, R.E. (1985*a*). Cortical mechanisms and cues for action. Phil. Trans. Roy. Soc. Lond.B 308, 101–111.

Passingham, R.E. (1985*b*). Memory of monkeys (*Macaca mulatta*) with lesions in prefrontal cortex. Beh. Neurosci. 99, 3–21.

Passingham, R.E. (1985*c*). Premotor cortex: sensory cues and movement. Beh. Brain Res. 18, 175–186.

Passingham, R.E. (1985d). Prefrontal cortex and the sequencing of movement in monkeys (Macaca mulatta). Neuropsychol. 23, 453–462.

Passingham, R.E. (1986). Cues for movement in monkeys (*Macaca mulatta*) with lesions in premotor cortex. Beh. Neurosci. 100, 695–703.

Passingham, R.E. (1987*a*). From where does motor cortex get its instructions? In Neural and Behavioral Approaches to Higher Brain Function, (Ed. S. Wise) Wiley, New York, pp. 67–97.

Passingham, R.E. (1987*b*). Two cortical systems for directing movements. In: Motor Areas of the Cerebral Cortex (Ed. R. Porter) Wiley, Chichester, pp. 151–164.

Passingham, R.E. (1988). Premotor cortex and preparation for movement. Exper. Brain Res. 70, 590–596.

Passingham, R.E. (1989). The origins of human intelligence. In: Human Origins, (Ed. J.R. Durant) Oxford University Press pp. 123–136.

Passingham, R.E. and Ettlinger, G. (1972). Tactile discrimination learning after selective prefrontal ablations in monkeys (*Macaca mulatta*). Neuropsychol. 10, 17–26.

Passingham, R.E., Perry, H. and Wilkinson, F. (1983). The long-term effects of removal of sensorimotor cortex in infant and adult rhesus monkeys. Brain 106, 675–705.

Passingham, R.E., Heywood, C.A. and Nixon, P.D. (1986). Reorganization in the human brain as illustrated by the thalamus. Brain Beh. Evol. 29, 68–76.

Passingham, R.E., Myers, C., Rawlins, N., Lightfoot, V. and Fearn, S. (1988). Premotor cortex in the rat. Beh. Neurosci. 102, 101–109.

Passingham, R.E., Thaler, D.E. and Chen, Y. (1989). Supplementary motor cortex and self-initiated movement. In: Neural Programming (Ed. M. Ito) Karger, Basel, pp. 13–24.

Paulesu, E., Frith, C.D. and Frackowiack, R.S.J. (1993). The neural correlates of the verbal component of working memory. Nature 362, 342–345.

Pearson, R.C.A. and Powell, T.P.S. (1985). The projection of the primary sensory cortex upon area 5 in the monkey. Brain Res. 9, 89–103.

Pearce, J.M., Colwill, R.M. and Hall, G. (1978). Instrumental conditioning of scratching in the laboratory rat. Learn. Motiv. 9, 255–271.

Pellegrino, G.di and Wise, S.P. (1991). A neurophysiological comparison of three distinct regions of the primate frontal lobe. Brain 114, 951–978.

Penfield, W. and Roberts, L. (1959). Speech and Brain Mechanisms. Princeton University Press, Princeton.

Pepperberg, I.M. (1981). Functional vocalization by an African Grey Parrot. Zeit. Tierpsychol. 55, 139–160.

Pepperberg, I.M. (1987). Evidence for conceptual quantitative abilities in the African Grey Parrot: labelling of cardinal sets. Ethol. 75, 37–61.

Percheron, G. and Filion, M. (1991). Parallel processing in the basal ganglia: up to a point. TINS 14, 55–56.

Percheron, G., Yelnik, J. and Francois, C. (1984). A Golgi analysis of the primate globus pallidus: III Spatial organization of the striato-pallidal complex. J. Comp. Neurol. 227, 214–227.

Petersen, S.E., Fox, P.T., Posner, M.I., Mintun, M. and Raichle, M.E. (1988). Positron emission tomographic studies of the cortical anatomy of single-word processing. Nature 331, 585–589.

Petrides, M. (1982). Motor conditional associative-learning after selective prefrontal lesions in the monkey. Beh. Brain Res. 5, 407–413.

Petrides, M. (1985*a*). Deficits on conditional associative-learning tasks after frontal and temporal lobe lesions in man. Neuropsychol. 23, 601–614.

Petrides, M. (1985*b*). Deficits in nonspatial conditional associative learning after periarcuate lesions in the monkey. Beh. Brain Res. 16, 95–101.

Petrides, M. (1986). The effect of periarcuate lesions in the monkey on the performance of symmetrically and asymmetrically reinforced visual and auditory go, no-go tasks. J. Neurosci. 6, 2054–2063.

Petrides, M. (1987). Conditional learning and primate frontal lobes. In: The Frontal Lobes Revisited, (Ed. E. Perecman) IBRN press, New York, pp. 91–108.

Petrides, M. (1988). Performance on a nonspatial self-ordered task after selective lesions of the primate frontal cortex. Soc. Neurosci. Abstr. 14, 4–8.

Petrides, M. (1989). Frontal lobes and memory. In Handbook of Neuropsychology (Ed. F.Boller and J.Grafman), Elsevier, Amsterdam, 75–90.

Petrides, M. (1990). Nonspatial conditional learning impaired in patients with unilateral frontal but not unilateral temporal lobe excisions. Neuropsychol. 28, 137–149.

Petrides, M. (1991*a*). Monitoring of selections of visual stimuli and the primate frontal cortex. Proc. Roy. Soc. Lond. B 246, 293–298.

Petrides, M. (1991*b*). Functional specialization within the dorsolateral frontal cortex for serial order memory. Proc. Roy. Soc. Lond. B 246, 299–306.

Petrides, M. and Milner, B. (1982). Deficits on subject-ordered tasks after frontal- and temporal- lobe lesions in man. Neuropsychol. 20, 249–262.

Petrides, M. and Pandya, D.N. (1984). Projections to the frontal lobe from the posterior-parietal region in the rhesus monkey. J. Comp. Neurol. 228, 105–116.

Petrides, M. and Pandya, D.N. (1988). Associative fiber pathways to the frontal cortex from the superior temporal region in the rhesus monkey.J.Comp.Neurol. 273, 52–66.

Petrides, M. Alivisatos, B., Evans, A.C. and Meyer, E. (1993*a*). Dissociation of human mid-dorsolateral from posterior dorsolateral frontal cortex in memory processing. Proc. Natl Acad. Sci. 90, 873–877.

Petrides, M., Alivisatos, B., Meyer, E. and Evans, A.C. (1993*b*). Functional activation of the human frontal cortex during performance of verbal working memory tasks. Proc. Natl. Acad. Sci. 90, 878–882.

Philips, A.G., Mora, F. and Rolls, E.T. (1981). Intracerebral self-administration of amphetamine by rhesus monkeys. Neurosci. Lett. 24, 81–86.

Philips, C.G. (1971). Evolution of the corticospinal tract in primates with special reference to the hand. In: Proceedings of the Third International Congress of Primatology, Vol. 2. Karger, Basel, pp. 2–23.

Philips, C.G. and Porter, R. (1977). Corticospinal neurones. Academic Press, London.

Piaget, J. (1954). The Construction of Reality in the Child. Basic Books, New York.

Piero, V.D., Chollet, F., Dolan, R.J., Thomas, D.J. and Frackowiak, R. (1990). The functional nature of cerebellar diaschisis. Stroke 21, 1365–1369.

Pierrot-Deselligny, C., Rivaud, S., Gaymard, B. and Agid, Y. (1991*a*). Cortical control of memory-guided saccades in man. Exper. Brain Res. 83, 607–617.

Pierrot-Deselligny, C., Rivaud, S., Gaymard, B. and Agid, Y. (1991*b*). Cortical control of reflexive visually-guided saccades. Brain 114, 1475–1485.

Pinto-Hamuy, T. and Linck, P. (1965). Effects of frontal lesions on performance of sequential tasks by monkeys. Exper. Neurol. 12, 96–107.

Playford, E.D., Jenkins, I.H., Passingham, R.E., Nutt, J., Frackowiak, R.S.J. and Brooks, D.J. (1992). Impaired mesial frontal and putamen activation in Parkinson's disease: a PET study. Ann. Neurol., 32, 151–161.

Pohl, W. (1973). Dissociation of spatial discrimination defects following frontal and parietal lesions in monkeys. J. Comp. Physiol. Psychol. 82, 227–239.

Porrino, L.J., Crane, A.M. and Goldman-Rakic, P.S. (1981). Direct and indirect pathways from the amygdala to the frontal lobe in rhesus monkeys. J. Comp. Neurol. 198, 121–136.

Posner, M.I. (1990). The attention system of the human brain. Ann. Rev. Neurosci. 13, 25–42.

Posner, M.I., Petersen, S.E., Fox, P.T. and Raichle, M.E. (1988). Localization of cognitive operations in the human brain. Science 240, 1627–1631.

Potter, H. and Nauta, W.J.H. (1979). A note on the problem of olfactory associations of the orbitofrontal cortex in the monkey. Neurosci. 4, 341–367.

Preuss, T.M. and Goldman-Rakic, P.S. (1991). Myelo- and cytoarchitecture of the granular frontal cortex and surrounding regions in the strepsirhine primate *Galago* and the anthropoid primate *Macaca*. J. Comp. Neurol. 310, 429–474.

Pribram, K.H., Kruger, C., Robinson, F. and Berman, A.J. (1955). The effects of precentral lesions on the behavior of monkeys. Yale J. Biol. Med. 28, 428–443.

Quintana, J., Yajeva, J. and Fuster, J.M. (1988). Prefrontal representation of stimulus attributes during delay tasks. I Unit activity in cross-temporal integration of sensory and sensory-motor information. Brain Res. 474, 211–221.

Raichle, M.E. (1987). Circulatory and metabolic correlates of brain function in normal humans. In: The Nervous System (Ed. V.B. Mountcastle) American Physiological Society, Bethesda, pp. 643–674.

Raichle, M.E. (1991). Memory mechanisms in the processing of words and word-like symbols. In: Exploring Functional Anatomy with Positron Tomography (Eds. D.J. Chadwick and J. Whelan) Wiley, Chichester, pp. 198–217.

Rea, G.L., Ebner, T.J. and Bloedel, J.R. (1987). Evaluations of combined premotor and supplementary motor cortex lesions on a visually guided arm movement. Brain Res. 418, 58–67.

Reason, J. (1979). Actions not as planned: the price of automatization. In: Aspects of Consciousness (Eds. G. Underwood and R. Stevens) Academic Press, New York, pp. 67–90.

Reep, R. (1984). Relationship between prefrontal and limbic cortex: a comparative anatomical review. Brain Beh. Evol. 25, 5–80.

Reiner, A., Brauth, S.E. and Karten, H.J. (1984). Evolution of the amniote basal ganglia. TINS 7, 220–225.

Rizzolatti, G., Scandalora, C., Matelli, M. and Gentilucci, M. (1981). Afferent. properties of periarcuate neurones in macaque monkeys. I Somato-sensory responses. Beh. Brain Res. 2, 125–146.

Rizzolatti, G., Matelli, M. and Pavesi, G. (1983). Defecits in attention and movement following the removal of postarcuate (area 6) and prearcuate (area 8) cortex in macaque monkeys. Brain 106, 655–673.

Rizzolatti, G., Camarda, R., Fogassi, L., Gentilucci, M., Luppino, G. and Matelli, M. (1988). Functional organization of inferior area 6 in the macaque monkey. II. Area F5 and the control of distal movements. Exper. Brain Res. 71, 491–507.

Rizzolatti, G., Gentilucci, M., Camada, R., Gallese, V., Luppino, G. and Matelli, M. (1990). Neurones related to reaching–grasping arm movements in the rostral part of area 6. Exper. Brain Res. 82, 337–350.

Robbins, T.W., Roberts, D.C.S. and Koob, G.F. (1983). Effects of d-amphetamine and apomorphine upon operant behavior and schedule-induced licking in rats with 6–hydroxydopamine-induced lesions of the nucleus accumbens. J. Pharmacol. Exper. Therap. 224, 662–673.

Robbins, T.W., Cador, M., Taylor, J.R. and Everitt, B.J. (1989). Limbic-striatal interactions in reward-related processes. Neurosci. Biobeh. Rev. 13, 155–162.

Robinson, B.W. (1967). Vocalization evoked from forebrain in *Macaca mulatta*. Physiol. Beh. 2, 345–354.

Robinson, C.J. and Burton, H. (1980). Organization of somatosensory receptive fields in cortical area 7b, retroinsular, postauditory and granular insula of *Macaca fascicularis.* J. Comp. Neurol. 192, 69–92.

Roland, P. (1985). Cortical organization of voluntary behavior in man. Hum. Neurobiol. 4, 155–167.

Roland, P., Friberg, L., Lassen, N.A. and Olsen, T.S. (1985). Regional cortical blood flow changes during production of fluent speech and during conversation. J. Cer. Blood Flow, 5, suppl. 1, S205

Roland, P.F. and Friberg, L. (1985). Localization of cortical areas activated by thinking. J.Neurophysiol. 53, 1219–1243.

Roland, P.E., Gulyás, B. and Seitz, R.J. (1991). Structures in the human brain participating in visual learning, tactile learning, and motor learning. In: Memory, Organization and Locus of Change, (Eds. L.R. Squire, N.M. Wienberger, G. Lynch and J.L. McGaugh) Oxford University Press, pp. 95–113.

Roland, P.E., Larsen, B., Lassen, N.A. and Skinhøj, E. (1980). Supplementary motor area and other cortical areas in organization of voluntary movements in man. J. Neurophysiol. 43, 118–136.

Roland, P.E., Meyer, E., Shibasaki, T. and Yamamoto, Y.L. (1982). Regional blood flow changes in cortex and basal ganglia during voluntary movements in normal human volunteers. J. Neurophysiol. 48, 467–480.

Rolls, E.T. and Wiggins, L.L. (1989). Convergence of taste, olfactory and visual inputs in the orbitofrontal cortex of primates. Chemical Senses, 14, 741.

Rolls, E.T., Burton, M.J. and Mora, F. (1980). Neurophsyiological analysis of brain-stimulation reward in the monkey. Brain Res. 194, 339–357.

Rolls, E.T. and Johnstone, S. (1992). Neurophysiological analysis of striatal function. In Neuropsychological Disorders Associated with Subcortical Lesions (G.Vallar, S.F.Cappa and C.W.Wallesch). Oxford University Press, Oxford, 61–97.

Rolls, E.T., Sienkiewicz, Z.J. and Yaxley, S. (1989). Hunger modulates the response to gustatory stimuli of single neurons in the caudolateral orbitofrontal cortex of the macaque monkey. Europ.J. Neurosci. 1, 53–60.

Rolls, E.T., Yaxley, S. and Sienkiewicz, Z.J. (1990). Gustatory responses of single neurons in the caudolateral orbitofrontal cortex of the macaque monkey. J. Neurophysiol. 64, 1055–1066.

Romo, R. and Schultz, W. (1987). Neuronal activity preceding self-initiated or externally timed arm movements in area 6 of monkey cortex. Exper. Brain Res. 67, 656–662.

Ropper, A.H., Fisher, C.M. and Kleinman, M.D. (1979). Pyramidal infarction in the medulla: a cause of pure motor hemiplegia sparing the face. Neurol. 29, 91–95.

Ruch, T.C. (1965). Transection of the human spinal cord: the nature of higher control. In: Neurophysiology (Eds. T.C. Ruch, H.D. Patton, J.W. Woodbury and A.L. Towe) Saunders, Philadelphia, pp. 207–214.

Russchen, F.T., Amaral, D.G. and Price, J.L. (1987). The afferent input to the magnocellular division of the mediodorsal thalamic nucleus in the monkey, *Macaca fascicularis.* J. Comp. Neurol. 256, 175–210.

Sagar, H.J. and Sullivan, E.V. (1988). Patterns of cognitive impairment in dementia. In: Recent Advances in Clinical Neurology, Vol. 5. (Ed. C. Kennard) Churchill Livingstone, Edinburgh, pp. 47–86.

Sahakian, B.J., Morris, R.G., Evenden, J.L., Heald, A., Levy, R., Philpot, M. *et al.* (1988). A comparative study of visuo-spatial memory and learning in Alzheimer-type dementia and Parkinson's disease. Brain 111, 695–719.

Saint-Cyr, J.A., Taylor, A.E. and Lang, A.E. (1988). Procedural learning and neostriatal dysfunction in man. Brain 111, 941–959.

Saint-Cyr, J., Ungerleider, L.G. and Desimone, R. (1990). Organization of visual cortical inputs to the striatum and subsequent outputs to the pallido-nigral complex in the monkey. J. Comp. Neurol. 298, 129–156.

Sakata, H. and Iwamura, Y. (1978). Cortical processing of tactile information in the first somatosensory and parietal association areas in the monkey. In: Active Touch (Ed. G. Gordon) Pergamon, Oxford, pp. 55–72.

Saper, C.B., Loewy, A.D., Swanson, L.W. and Cowan, W.M. (1976). Direct hypothalamo-autonomic connections. Brain Res. 117, 305–312.

Sasaki, K. and Gemba, H. (1982). Development and change of cortical field potentials during learning processes of visually initiated hand movements in the monkey. Exper. Brain Res. 48, 429–437.

Sasaki, K., Jinnai, H., Gemba, H., Hashimoto, S. and Mizuno, N. (1979). Projections of the cerebellar dentate nucleus onto the frontal association cortex in monkeys. Exper. Brain Res. 37, 193–198.

Savage-Rumbaugh, E.S. (1986). Ape Language. Oxford University Press.

Savage-Rumbaugh, E.S., Rumbaugh, D.M., Smith, S.T. and Lawson, J. (1980). Reference: the linguistic essential. Science 210, 922–925.

Saver, J.L. and Damasio, A.R. (1991). Preserved access and processing of social knowledge in a patient with acquired sociopathy due to ventromedial frontal damage. Neuropsychol. 29, 1241–1249.

Sawaguchi, T. (1987). Properties of neuronal activity related to a visual reaction time task in the monkey prefrontal cortex. J.Neurophysiol. 58, 1080–1099.

Schall, J.D. (1991). Neuronal activity related to visually guided saccades in the frontal eye fields of rhesus monkeys: comparison with supplementary eye fields. J. Neurophysiol. 66, 559–579.

Schell, G.R. and Strick, P.L. (1984). The origin of thalamic inputs to the arcuate premotor and supplementary motor areas. J. Neurosci. 4, 539–560.

Schiller, P.H., True, S.D. and Conway, J.L. (1979). Effects of frontal eye field and superior colliculus ablation on eye movements. Science 206, 590–592.

Schiller, P.H., Sandell, J.H. and Maunsell, J.H.R. (1987). The effect of frontal eye field and superior colliculus lesions on saccadic latencies in the rhesus monkey. J. Neurophysiol. 57, 1033–1049.

Schlag, J. and Schlag-Rey, M. (1985). Unit activity related to spontaneous saccades in frontal dorsomedial cortex of monkey. Exper. Brain Res. 58, 208–211.

Schlag, J. and Schlag-Rey, M. (1987). Evidence for a supplementary eye field. J. Neurophysiol. 57, 179–200.

Schmahmann, J.D. and Pandya, D.N. (1991). Projections to the basis pontis from the superior temporal sulcus and superior temporal region in the rhesus monkey. J. Comp. Neurol. 308, 224–248.

Schultz, W. (1986). Responses of midbrain dopamine neurons to behavioral trigger stimuli in the monkey. J. Neurophysiol. 56, 1439–1461.

Schultz, W. and Romo, R. (1988). Neuronal activity in the monkey striatum during the initiation of movements. Exper. Brain Res. 71, 431–436.

Schwartz, B. and Williams, D.R. (1972). The role of the response-reinforcer contingency in negative automaintenance. Journal of Experimental Analysis of Behaviour 17, 351–357.

Seal, J., Cross, C. and Bioulac, B. (1983). Different neuronal populations within area 5 of the monkey. Exper. Brain Res. Suppl. 7, 157–163.

Seitz, R.J., Roland, P.E., Bohm, C., Greitz, T. and Stone-Elanders, S. (1990). Motor learning in man: a positron emission tomographic study. Neurorep. 1, 17–20.

Selemon, L.D. (1990). Connections of the basal ganglia in primates. TINS 13, C1-C4.

Selemon, L.D. and Goldman-Rakic, P.S. (1985). Longitudinal topography and interdigitation of corticostriatal projections in the rhesus monkey. J. Neurosci. 5, 776–794.

Selemon, L.D. and Goldman-Rakic, P.S. (1988). Common cortical and subcortical targets of the dorsolateral prefrontal and parietal cortices in the rhesus monkey: evidence for a distributed neural network subserving spatially guided behavior. J. Neurosci. 8, 4049–4068.

Selemon, L.D. and Goldman-Rakic, P.S. (1990). Topographic intermingling of striatonigral and striatopallidal neurons in the rhesus monkey. J. Comp. Neurol. 297, 359–376.

Selemon, L.D. and Goldman-Rakic, P.S. (1991). Parallel processing in the basal ganglia: up to a point. TINS 14, 58–59.

Seltzer, B. and Pandya, D.N. (1984). Further observations on parieto-temporal connections in the rhesus monkey. Exper. Brain Res. 55, 301–312.

Seltzer, B. and Pandya, D.N. (1989). Frontal lobe connections of the superior temporal sulcus in the rhesus monkey. J. Comp. Neurol. 281, 97–113.

Shallice, T. (1982). Specific impairments of planning. Phil. Trans. Roy. Soc. Lond. B 298, 199–209.

Shallice, T. (1988). From Neuropsychology to Mental Structure. Cambridge University Press.

Shallice, T. and Burgess, P. (1991). Specific impairments of planning. Brain 114, 727–741.

Shima, K., Aya, K., Mushiake, H., Inase, M., Aizawa, H. and Tanji, J. (1991). Two movement-related foci in the primate cingulate cortex observed in signal-triggered and self-paced forelimb movements. J. Neurophysiol. 65, 188–202.

Shook, B.L., Schlag-Rey, M. and Schlag, J. (1990). The primate supplementary eye field. I. Comparative aspects of mesencephalic and pontine connections. J. Comp. Neurol. 301, 618–642.

Shook, B.L., Schlag-Rey, M. and Schlag, J. (1991). Primate supplementary eye field. II Comparative aspects of connections with the thalamus, corpus striatum, and related forebrain nuclei. J. Comp. Neurol. 307, 562–583.

Skinner, F. (1957). Verbal Behavior. Methuen, London.

Slamecka, N.J.A. (1968). A methodological analysis of shift paradigms in human discrimination learning. Psychol. Bull. 69, 423–438.

Smith, A.D. and Bolam, P. (1990). The neural network of the basal ganglia as revealed by the study of synaptic connections of identified neurones. TINS 13, 259–265.

Smith, A.M., Bourbonnais, D. and Banchette, G. (1981). Interaction between forced grasping and a learned precision grip after ablation of the supplementary motor area. Brain Res. 222, 395–400.

Smith, M.L. and Milner, B. (1988). Estimation of frequency of occurrence of abstract designs after frontal or temporal lobectomy. Neuropsychol. 26, 297–306.

Smith, Y. and Parent, A. (1986). Differential connections of caudate nucleus and putamen in the squirrel monkey. Neurosci. 18, 347–371.

Soper, H.V. (1979). Principal sulcus and posterior parieto-occipital cortex lesions in the monkey. Cortex 15, 83–96.

Sparks, D.L. (1989). Neural commands for the control of saccadic eye movement: required transformations of signals observed in the superior colliculus. In: Neural Programming (Ed. M. Ito) Karger, Basel, pp. 125–136.

Sperry, R.W. (1955). On the neural basis of the conditioned response. Brit. J. Anim. Beh. 3, 41–44.

Squire, L.R. (1987). Memory and the Brain. Oxford University Press, New York.

Stamm, J.S. (1973). Functional dissociation between the inferior and arcuate segments of dorsolateral prefrontal cortex in the monkey. Neuropsychol. 11, 181–190.

Stamm, J.S. and Rosen, S.C. (1972). Cortical steady potential shifts and anodal polarization during delayed response performance. Acta Neurobiol. Exper. 32, 193–209.

Stanton, G.B., Goldberg, M.E. and Bruce, C.J. (1988). Frontal eye field efferents in the macaque monkey: II Topography of terminal fields in midbrain and pons. J. Comp. Neurol. 271, 493–506.

van der Steen, J., Russel, I.S. and James, G.O. (1986). Effect of unilateral frontal eye-field lesions in eye-head coordination in monkey. J. Neurophysiol. 55, 696–714.

Stein, J.F., Miall, R.C. and Weir, D. (1987). The role of the cerebellum in the visual guidance of movement. In Cerebellum and Neuronal Plasticity (Eds. M. Glickstein, C. Yeo and J. Stein) Plenum, New York, pp. 175–191.

Stephan, H., Bauchot, R. and Andy, A.J. (1970). Data on size of the brain and of various brain parts in insectivores and primates. In The Primate Brain (Eds. C.R. Noback and W. Montagna) Appleton-Century-Crofts, New York, pp. 289–297.

Stern, C. (1987). Functions of the Ventral Striatum. Unpublished D.Phil. thesis, University of Oxford.

Straub, A. and Siegel, K. (1988). Parkinsonian syndrome caused by a tumour of the left supplementary motor area. J. Neurol. Neurosurg. Psychiatr. 51, 730–731.

Strick, P.L. (1985). How do the basal ganglia and cerebellum gain access to the cortical motor areas? Beh. Brain Res. 18, 107–124.

Sutton, D. (1979). Mechanisms underlying vocal control in nonhuman primates. In:

Neurobiology of Social Communication in Primates (Eds. H.D. Steklis and M.J. Raleigh) Academic Press, New York, pp. 45–67.

Sutton, D., Larson, C.R., Taylor, E.M. and Lindeman, R.C. (1973). Vocalization in rhesus monkeys: conditionability. Brain Res. 52, 225–231.

Sutton, D., Larson, C. and Lindeman, R.C. (1974). Neocortical and limbic lesion effects on primate phonation. Brain Res. 71, 61–75.

Sutton, D., Herman, H. and Larson, C.R. (1978). Brain mechanisms in learned phonation of *Macaca mulatta*. In: Recent Advances in Primatology, Vol. 1. (Eds. D.J. Chivers and J. Herbert) Academic Press, New York, pp. 769–784.

Sutton, D., Trachy, R.E. and Lindeman, R.C. (1981). Vocal and nonvocal discrimination performance in monkeys. Brain Lang. 14, 95–105.

Talairach, J., Szikla, G. and Tournoux, P. (1967). Atlas d'Anatomie Stereotaxic du Telencephale.1st edn. Masson, Paris.

Tamas, L.H. and Shibasaki, H. (1985). Cortical potentials associated with movement: a review. J.Clin. Neurophysiol. 2, 157–171.

Tanabe, T., Iino, M., Ooshima, Y. and Takagi, S.F. (1974). An olfactory area in the prefrontal lobe. Brain Res. 80, 127–130.

Tanji, J., Taniguchi, K. and Saga, T. (1980). The supplementary motor area: neuronal responses to motor instructions. J. Neurophysiol. 43, 60–68.

Taylor, A.E., Saint-Cyr, J.A. and Lang, A.E. (1986). Frontal lobe dysfunction in Parkinson's disease. The cortical focus of neostriatal outflow. Brain 109, 845–883.

Terrace, H.S., Petitto, L.A., Sanders, R.J. and Bever, T.G. (1979). Can an ape create a sentence? Science 206, 891–902.

Thaler, D.E. (1988). Supplementary motor cortex and the control of action. Unpublished D.Phil. thesis, University of Oxford.

Thaler, D.E., Rolls, E.T. and Passingham, R.E. (1988). Neuronal activity of the supplementary motor area (SMA) during internally- and externally- triggered wrist movement. Neurosci.Lett. 93, 264–269.

Thaler, D.E. and Passingham, R.E. (1989). The supplementary motor cortex and internally directed movement. In: Neural Mechanisms in Disorders of Movement (Ed. A.R. Crossman) Libbey, London, pp. 175–181.

Thompson, R.F. (1988). The neural basis of basic associative learning of discrete behavioral responses. TINS 11, 152–155.

Thorpe, S.J., Rolls, E.T. and Maddison, S. (1983). The orbitofrontal cortex: neuronal activity in the behaving monkey. Exper. Brain Res. 49, 93–115.

Tobias, T.J. (1975). Afferents to prefrontal cortex from the thalamic mediodorsal nucleus in the rhesus monkey. Brain Res. 83, 191–212.

Tognala, G. and Vignolo, L. (1980). Brain lesions associated with oral apraxia in stroke patients: a clinico-radiological investigation with the CT scan. Neuropsychol. 18, 257–271.

Tower, S.S. (1940). Pyramidal lesions in the monkey. Brain, 63, 36–90.

Traverse, J. and Latto, R. (1986). Impairments in route negotiation through a maze after dorsolateral frontal, inferior parietal or premotor lesions in cynomolgous monkeys. Beh. Brain Res. 20, 203–215.

Travis, A.M. (1955). Neurological deficiencies after ablation of the precentral motor area in *Macaca mulatta*. Brain 78, 155–173.

Trouche, E., Beaubaton, D., Amato, G. and Grangetto, A. (1979). Impairments and recovery of the spatial and temporal components of a visuo-motor pointing movement after unilateral destruction of the dentate nucleus in the baboon. Appl. Neurophysiol. 42, 248–254.

Turner, B.H., Mishkin, M. and Knapp, M. (1980). Organization of the amygdalopetal projections from modality-specific cortical association areas in the monkey. J. Comp. Neurol. 191, 515–643.

Twitchell, T.E. (1951). The restoration of motor function following hemiplegia in man. Brain 74, 443–480.

Ungerleider, L.G., Desimone, R., Galkin, T. and Mishkin, M. (1984). Subcortical projections of area MT in the macaque. J. Comp. Neurol. 223, 368–386.

Ungerleider, L.G., Gaffan, D. and Pelak, V.S. (1989). Projections from infero temporal cortex to prefrontal cortex via the uncinate fascicle in rhesus monkeys. Exper. Brain Res. 76, 473–484.

Uylings, H.B.M. and van Eden, C.G. (1990). Qualitative and quantitative comparison of the prefrontal cortex in rat and in primates, including humans. Progr. Brain Res. 85, 31–63.

Vanderwolf, C.H., Kolb, B. and Cooley, R.K. (1978). Behavior of the rat after removal of the neocortex and hippocampal formation. J. Comp. Physiol. Psychol. 92, 156–175.

Van Sommers, P. (1962). Oxygen-motivated behavior in the goldfish, *Carassius auratus*. Science 137, 678–679.

Vargha-Khadem, F. and Passingham, R.E. (1990). Speech and language defects. Nature 346, 226.

Varga-Khadem, F., Isaacs, E.B., Papaleloudi, H., Polkey, C. and Wilson, J. (1991). Development of language in six hemispherectomized patients. Brain 114, 473–495.

Velayos, J.L. and Reinoso-Suarez, F. (1985). Prosencephalic afferents to the mediodorsal thalamic nucleus. J. Comp. Neurol. 242, 161–181.

Vives, F., Gayoso, M.J., Osorio, C. and Mora, F. (1983). Afferent pathways to points of self-stimulation in the medial prefrontal cortex of the rat as revealed by horseradish peroxidase technique. Beh. Brain Res. 8, 23–32.

Vogt, B.A. and Pandya, D.N. (1978). Cortico-cortical connections of somatic sensory cortex (areas 3, 1 and 2) in the rhesus monkey. J. Comp. Neurol. 177, 179–192.

Vogt, B.A. and Pandya, D.N. (1987). Cingulate cortex of the rhesus monkey: II Cortical afferents. J. Comp. Neurol. 262, 271–289.

VonSattel, J.P., Ferrante, R.J., Stevens, T.J. and Richardson, E.P. (1985). Neuropathological classification of Huntington's disease. J. Neuropath. Exper. Neurol. 44, 559–577.

Voronin, L.G. (1962). Some results of comparative-physiological investigations of higher nervous activity. Psychol. Bull. 59, 161–195.

Voytko, M.L. (1985). Cooling orbital frontal cortex disrupts matching-to-sample and visual discrimination learning in monkeys. Physiol. Psychol. 13, 219–229.

Waal, F. de (1982). Chimpanzee Politics. Cape, London.

Walker, E.A. (1940). A cytoarchitectural study of the prefrontal area of the macaque monkey. J. Comp. Neurol. 73, 59–86.

Walker, E.A. and Fulton, J.F. (1938). Hemidecortication in chimpanzee, baboon, macaque, cat and coati: a study in encephalization. J. Nerv. Ment. Dis. 87, 677–700.

Warabi, T., Inoue, K., Noda, H. and Murakami, S. (1990). Recovery of voluntary movement in hemiplegic patients. Brain 113, 177–189.

Warren, J.M. (1965). Primate learning in comparative perspective. In: Behavior of Nonhuman Primates, Vol. 1. (Eds. A.M. Schrier, H.F. Harlow and F. Stollnitz) Academic Press, New York, pp. 249–281.

Watanabe, E. (1984). Neuronal events correlated with long-term adaptation of the horizontal vestibulo-ocular reflex in the primate flocculus. Brain Res. 297, 169–174.

Watanabe, M. (1990). Prefrontal unit activity during associative learning in the monkey. Exper. Brain Res. 80, 296–309.

Weber, J.T. and Yin, T.C.T. (1984). Subcortical projection of the inferior parietal cortex (area 7) in the stumptailed monkey. J.Comp.Neurol. 224, 206–230.

Weinrich, M. and Wise, S.P. (1982). The premotor cortex of the monkey. J. Neurosci. 2, 1329–1345.

Weinrich, M., Wise, S.P. and Mauritz, K.-H. (1984). A neurophysiological study of the premotor cortex in the rhesus monkey. Brain 107, 385–414.

Whishaw, I.Q. and Kolb, B. (1985). The mating movements of male decorticate rats: evidence for subcortically generated movements by the male but regulation of approaches by the female. Beh. Brain Res. 17, 171–192.

Whitsel, B.L., Petrucelli, L.M. and Werner, G. (1969). Symmetry and connectivity in the map of the body surface in somatosensory cortex area II of primates. J. Neurophysiol. 32, 170–183.

Wiesendanger, M. and Wiesendanger, R. (1984). The supplementary motor cortex in the light of recent investigations. Exper.Brain Res. Suppl. 9, 382–392.

Wiesendanger, R. and Wiesendanger, M. (1985a). The thalamic connections with medial area 6 (supplementary motor cortex) in the monkey (*Macaca fascicularis*). Exper. Brain Res. 59, 91–104.

Wiesendanger, R. and Wiesendanger, M. (1985b). Cerebro-cortical linkage in the monkey as revealed by cerebellar labelling with the lectin wheat germ agglutin conjugated to the marker horseradish peroxidase. Exper. Brain Res. 59, 105–117.

Wiggins, L.L., Rolls, E.T. and Baylis, G.C. (1987). Afferent connections of the caudolateral orbitofrontal cortex taste area of the primate. Soc. Neurosci. Abstr. 13, 1406.

Winter, P., Handley, P., Ploog, D. and Schott, D. (1974). Ontogeny of squirrel monkey calls under normal conditions and under acoustic isolation. Beh. 47, 230–239.

Wise, R.A. and Rompre, P.-P. (1989). Brain dopamine and reward. Ann. Rev. Psychol. 40, 191–225.

Wise, R., Chollet, F., Hadar, U., Friston, K., Hoffner, E. and Frackowiak, R. (1991). Distribution of cortical neural networks involved in word comprehension and word retrieval. Brain 114, 1803–1817.

Wise, R.A. and Schwartz, H.V. (1981). Pimozide attenuates acquisition of lever-pressing for food in rats. Pharmacol. Biochem. Beh. 15, 655–656.

Wise, S.P. (1985a). The primate premotor cortex fifty years after Fulton. Beh. Brain Res. 18, 79–89.

Wise, S.P. (1985b). The primate premotor cortex: past, present and preparatory. Ann. Rev. Neurosci. 8, 1–20.

Wise, S.P. and Mauritz, K.-H. (1985). Set-related neuronal activity in the premotor cortex of rhesus monkeys: effects of change in motor set. Proc. Roy. Soc. Lond. B. 223, 331–354.

Wise, S.P., Pellegrino, G.D. and Boussaoud, D. (1992). Primate premotor cortex: dissociation of visuomotor from sensory signals. J.Neurophysiol. 68, 969–972.

Woods, J.W. (1964). Behavior of chronic decerebrate rats. J. Neurophysiol. 27, 635–644.

Woolsey, C.N., Settlage, P.H., Meyer, D.R., Sencer, W., Pinto-Hamuy, T. and Travis, M. (1952). Pattern of localization in precentral and 'supplementary' motor area and their relation to the concept of a premotor cortex. Assoc. Res. Nerv. Ment. Dis. 30, 238–264.

Yelnik, J., Percheron, G. and Francois, C. (1984). A Golgi analysis of the primate globus pallidus: II Quantitative morphology and spatial orientation of dendritic arborizations. J. Comp. Neurol. 227, 200–213.

Yeo, C.H., Hardiman, M.J. and Glickstein, M. (1985). Classical conditioning of the nictitating membrane response of the rabbit: I Lesions of the cerebellar nuclei. Exper. Brain Res. 60, 87–98.

Yeterian, E.H. and van Hoesen, G.W. (1978). Cortico-striate projections in the rhesus monkey: the organization of certain cortico-candate connections. Brain Res. 139, 43–63.

Yeterian, E.H. and Pandya, D.N. (1991). Prefrontostriatal connections in relation to cortical architectonic organization in rhesus monkeys. J. Comp. Neurol. 312, 43–67.

Zeffiro, T.A., Kertzmann, C., Peilzzari, C. and Hallet, M. (1991). The role of the supplementary motor area in the control of self-paced movements: a PET study. Soc. Neurosci. Abstr. 17, 443.3.

Zola-Morgan, S. and Squire, L.R. (1984). Preserved learning in monkeys with medial temporal lobe lesions. Sparing of motor and cognitive skills. J. Neurosci. 4, 1072–1085.

Index

This book presents an argument rather than a review. It proposes that the frontal lobes as a whole are specialized for the selection of voluntary action. A specific role is proposed for each area within the frontal lobes. Chapters 1–5 discuss the execution and selection of movements in the motor cortex and premotor areas. Chapters 6 and 7 cover decision-making in the prefrontal cortex, and Chapter 8 the role of the basal ganglia in response learning. Chapter 9 summarizes the functional organization of the frontal lobes and Chapters 10–11 extend the argument to the mental trial and error that forms the basis for future responses and to the selection of verbal responses.

The analysis is based on the author's own work, including the use of imaging techniques. Controversial and thought-provoking, it will serve as the basis for future work and debate on the subject.

From a review of the hardback edition

The value of this book will be not only to neuropsychologists, but to students of neuroanatomy, neurophysiology and clinical neurology. It is clearly written and simply illustrated. Its coverage of the relevant anatomical, physiological and behavioural observations which relate to frontal lobe function is broad but well-focused. I feel certain that this will become a standard 'honours' text for courses which include the study of human voluntary movement.

Brain

ALSO PUBLISHED BY OXFORD UNIVERSITY PRESS

Multisensory control of movement
Edited by A. Berthoz *et al.*

Corticospinal function and voluntary movement
R. Porter and R. Lemon

ISBN 0-19-852364-5

9 780198 523642